PENGUIN BOOKS

ENGLISH SOCIETY IN THE LATER MIDDLE AGES

Maurice Keen was educated at Winchester and at Balliol College, Oxford, where he read modern history, graduating in 1957. Since 1961 he has been a Fellow of Balliol and tutor in medieval history there. He is also a Fellow of Winchester College. He has written several books on medieval topics: *The Outlaws of Medieval Legend* (1961), *The Laws of War in the Later Middle Ages* (1965), *The Pelican History of Medieval Europe* (1969, reissued as *The Penguin History of Medieval Europe* in 1991), *England in the Later Middle Ages* (1973), *Chivalry* (1984) and *English Society in the Later Middle Ages 1348–1500* (1990). He is married and has three daughters.

THE PENGUIN SOCIAL HISTORY OF BRITAIN
General Editor: J. H. Plumb

Already published:

Joyce Youings: *Sixteenth-Century England*
Roy Porter: *English Society in the Eighteenth Century*
Jose Harris: *Private Lives, Public Spirit: Britain 1870–1914*
John Stevenson: *British Society 1914–45*
Arthur Marwick: *British Society Since 1945*

Maurice Keen

English Society in the Later Middle Ages 1348–1500

Penguin Books

PENGUIN BOOKS

Published by the Penguin Group
Penguin Books Ltd, 27 Wrights Lane, London W8 5TZ, England
Penguin Books USA Inc., 375 Hudson Street, New York, New York 10014, USA
Penguin Books Australia Ltd, Ringwood, Victoria, Australia
Penguin Books Canada Ltd, 10 Alcorn Avenue, Toronto, Ontario, Canada M4V 3B2
Penguin Books (NZ) Ltd, 182–190 Wairau Road, Auckland 10, New Zealand

Penguin Books Ltd, Registered Offices: Harmondsworth, Middlesex, England

First published 1990
Published simultaneously in hardback by Allen Lane The Penguin Press
10 9 8 7 6 5 4

Printed in England by Clays Ltd, St Ives plc

Contents

Preface vii

Chronological Table of Principal Political Events ix

1. Social Hierarchy and Social Change 1

PART I   *The Third Estate: the Commons*

2. Plague, Depopulation and Labour Shortage 27
3. The Life of the Countryside 48
4. Towns, Trade and Urban Culture 77
5. Westminster and London 108

PART II   *The Second Estate: the 'Chivalry'*

6. The Hundred Years War and its Effects on Society and Government 131
7. The Aristocracy at Home: Household, Estates and Family 160
8. Aristocratic Violence: from Civil Strife to Forcible Entry 187

PART III   *The First Estate: the Clerks*

9. The Spread of Literacy 217
10. The Clerical Estate 240
11. Popular Religion 271

12. Epilogue 298

Bibliography 304

Index 315

Preface

Seventeen years ago I was finishing a book in which I tried to trace the political history of later medieval England. Coming back to the English history of this period has reminded me of its enduring fascination for me. It has also reminded me of how much there is that ought to be included and somehow at the end turns out to have been omitted, whether one is writing a narrative history that elbows out social issues, or a social history that imposes a thematic rather than a chronological approach.

I have not found this book an easy one to write. One reason for this is that there has lately been so much scholarly activity in the area of later medieval English social history. In the last fifteen years or so a very large number of major studies and articles, based on new research and full of exciting new insights, have appeared in print; more are forthcoming. It is not, in consequence, an easy moment at which to attempt an overview, and even interim judgements may date fast. A second reason why I have often felt the going hard is a more personal one. The computer and statistical analysis are among the keenest up-to-date weapons of the social historian; I, from my schooldays on, have always found myself bewildered in the world of numbers. For that reason I have avoided including any graphs or tables in this book, since I know that if I had I should have got them wrong; and I fear that I have often not done justice to the statistical findings in the works of others. As a result there is probably too much of the anecdotal and the 'history of everyday things' in what I have written, but there were enough un-everyday things happening in later medieval England – plagues, famines, foreign and civil wars – to make it impossible to write about that and no more. It is because it was such a tumultuous period that I have felt it necessary to include just one table, not a statistical one but a chronological table of the chief events in political history, so as to enable the reader who feels the need (as I often do) to relate references to dates and events in non-narrative discussion to their rough place in a conventional narrative framework.

I have received much help in writing this book which I must acknowledge with deep gratitude. My principal debts are to four friends and colleagues in Oxford. Miss Barbara Harvey gave me generous guidance and counsel on a number of topics in social history on which I felt rather at sea, and later read what I had written about them and offered invaluable comment and criticism. Dr Jonathan Hughes allowed me to read and to make extensive use of material from his distinguished thesis (since published by the Boydell Press under the title *Pastors and Visionaries*). Dr Simon Payling too allowed me to see and to use material that he was preparing for publication, and read and commented on parts of my book in typescript. Dr Jeremy Catto read what I had written on the church and religion and offered invaluable advice. To these scholars, and to the many scholars whose books and articles have guided me and educated me, I am profoundly grateful. The errors and misconceptions in what I have written remain my own; without the help that I have received there would be many more of them.

I must also very warmly thank Dr Rowena Archer for her help with proof-reading and Norma MacManaway for relieving me of the principal share of the labour of compiling an index. The publishers and the general editor of the series, Sir John Plumb, have been more than helpful with their guidance.

There are two other debts of gratitude that I must acknowledge. One is to the Master and Fellows of Balliol College, who granted me the sabbatical leave that enabled me to complete the writing. The other is to my wife, for her unstinting aid with punctuation, phraseology, proofs and the preservation of my sanity.

MAURICE KEEN

Chronological Table
of Principal Political Events

EDWARD III	1327	Following the deposition of Edward II by Queen Isabella and Roger Mortimer, Edward III succeeds, aged fourteen
	1328	On death of Charles IV of France, Edward's claim to the French throne, *via* his mother Isabella, is passed over in favour of Philip VI
	1330	Edward assumes direct power; Mortimer executed
	1337	Outbreak of the Hundred Years War with France
	1340	Edward assumes the title of King of France; Battle of Sluys (English naval victory)
	1346	Edward defeats Philip VI at the Battle of Crecy; Scots defeated at Neville's Cross
	1347	Capture of Calais from the French
	1348/9	The Black Death
	1351	The Statute of Labourers
	1356	Battle of Poitiers; King John II of France taken prisoner
	1360	Peace of Bretigny between France and England
	1361/2	The 'second pestilence'
	1367	Expedition of the Black Prince to Spain; victory at Najera over Franco-Castilian army of Henry of Trastamare

1369   New outbreak of war with France
            Widespread plague in England

1375   Widespread plague

1376   The 'Good' Parliament (impeachment of
            Alice Perrers, Edward's mistress, and her
            financial associates)
            Death of the Black Prince

1377   First poll tax (granted in spring
            Parliament)
            Death of Edward III (June)

RICHARD II   1377   Richard accedes, aged ten; minority
            council appointed

1378   Outbreak of the Great Schism; rival
            Popes at Rome and Avignon

1379   Graduated poll tax

1380   Third poll tax granted
            Wyclif forced to cease teaching at Oxford
            in consequence of his heretical opinions

1381   The Peasants' Revolt

1384   Death of Wyclif

1386   The 'Wonderful' Parliament; Chancellor
            Michael de la Pole impeached and a
            Council appointed

1387   Confrontation between Richard II and
            the Council appointed in Parliament
            Battle of Radcot Bridge; Richard's
            favourite, Robert de Vere, defeated by
            the 'Appellant Lords', Gloucester,
            Warwick, Arundel, Mowbray of
            Nottingham, Henry Bolingbroke of
            Derby

1388   The 'Merciless' Parliament; Richard's
            close advisers 'appealed' of treason by the
            Appellants; Sir Nicholas Brembre, Sir
            Simon Burley and Chief Justice Tressilian
            executed; Pole and de Vere exiled

	1389	Richard resumes control of government
	1390	Widespread plague
	1394	Death of Richard's Queen, Anne of Bohemia; Richard's first Irish expedition
	1396	Twenty-six-year truce with France agreed; Richard married to Isabella of France
	1397	Gloucester, Warwick and Arundel charged with treason in Parliament; Arundel executed, Warwick imprisoned, Gloucester murdered in Calais gaol
	1398	Parliament at Shrewsbury; Bolingbroke accuses Mowbray of treason; both are subsequently exiled
	1399	On the death of John of Gaunt, Richard seizes the Lancaster inheritance and sails to Ireland Henry Bolingbroke returns to claim his father's inheritance and deposes Richard II
HENRY IV	1399	Henry crowned king, 12 October
	1400	Failure of an attempted coup by Richard's courtiers; death of Richard II
	1401	Statute *De Heretico Comburendo* (burning of heretics)
	1402	Outbreak of Glendower's revolt in Wales (continues actively until *c.*1408)
	1403	First revolt of the Percies; crushed by Henry at the battle of Shrewsbury
	1405	Second revolt of the Percies; Archbishop Richard Scrope of York executed for his involvement
	1407	Widespread plague
	1413	Death of Henry IV

HENRY V	1413	Accession and coronation of Henry V Widespread plague
	1414	Rising of the Lollards under Sir John Oldcastle Church Council assembles at Constance to seek an end to the Great Schism
	1415	Henry V's first expedition to France; battle of Agincourt
	1417	Henry V's second French expedition Martin V elected sole Pope at Constance
	1419	John Duke of Burgundy murdered by adherents of the Dauphin Charles; Philip, the new duke, allies with the English
	1420	Treaty of Troyes with France; Henry marries Catherine of France and is recognized as heir to her father, King Charles VI, 'the Mad'
	1421	Birth to Catherine of an heir, Prince Henry
	1422	Henry V dies in France, 31 Aug.
HENRY VI	1422	Minority Council appointed; Humphrey of Gloucester to be 'Protector' of the Realm On the death of Charles VI (Oct. 21), John Duke of Bedford becomes Regent for Henry in France, but the Dauphin Charles also claims to succeed and war continues
	1424	Battle of Verneuil; English victory
	1429	Joan of Arc relieves Orleans and defeats the English at Jargeau and Patay; Charles VII crowned at Reims
	1430	Henry VI crowned King of France in Paris
	1434	Widespread plague

1435	Congress of Arras; the Duke of Burgundy abandons alliance with England Death of the Regent, John, Duke of Bedford
1437	Henry VI comes of age; end of the minority
1444	Truce of Tours with France; Henry betrothed to Margaret of Anjou
1447	Humphrey of Gloucester arrested at Bury Parliament, and dies in custody. Edmund, Duke of Somerset, replaces Richard, Duke of York, as the King's lieutenant in Normandy
1449	Truce with France broken by England, and war is resumed
1450	Normandy reconquered by the French Suffolk, Henry's chief councillor, is impeached (Feb.–March), and murdered on his way into exile (May) Revolt of Jack Cade (June–July)
1452	York demands trial of Somerset on charges relating to the loss of Normandy; armed confrontation narrowly avoided
1453	Battle of Castillon (July); final loss of English Gascony to France Henry VI loses his sanity for the first time (Aug.); Queen Margaret gives birth to an heir, Prince Edward (Oct.)
1454	York appointed Protector of the Realm; Somerset taken to the Tower
1455	Henry recovers his sanity; York's Protectorate revoked (Feb.) Battle of St Albans between Lancastrians and Yorkists; Somerset, Northumberland and Clifford killed York resumes Protectorate (Nov.)

	1456	Henry relieves York of Protectorate
	1459	The Yorkist lords (York and the Neville earls of Salisbury and Warwick) assemble an army, but are routed at Ludford (Oct.); York escapes to Ireland, the Nevilles to Calais Parliament at Coventry attaints the Yorkists (Nov.)
	1460	Warwick and Salisbury return from Calais, and defeat and capture Henry at the battle of Northampton (July) York returns and claims the throne in Parliament (Oct.); he is recognized as heir to Henry, to the exclusion of Prince Edward Queen Margaret raises an army and defeats the Yorkists at the battle of Wakefield; York and Salisbury killed (Dec.)
	1461	Edward of York is victorious at Mortimer's Cross (Feb.), and with Warwick takes London
EDWARD IV	1461	Edward of York is proclaimed king in London (March); the Lancastrians are defeated at Towton; Henry VI and Margaret escape to Scotland
	1464	Marriage of Edward II to Elizabeth Woodville; relations between the king and Warwick deteriorate Widespread plague
	1469	Rising of Warwick and Clarence against Edward
	1470	Henry VI restored as king; Edward escapes to Flanders
	1471	Edward IV returns, and defeats the Lancastrians at Barnet (Warwick killed) and Tewkesbury (Prince Edward killed) Death of Henry VI in the Tower Widespread plague

	1475	Edward IV invades France, but at Piquigny agrees to withdraw and accepts a pension from Louis XI
	1478	Clarence is attainted in Parliament, and killed in the Tower
	1479	Widespread plague
	1483	Death of Edward IV (April)
EDWARD V	1483	April, Edward V accedes formally as king April 30, Edward, on his way to London, is met at Stony Stratford by his uncle, Richard of Gloucester; his guardian, Lord Rivers, is arrested and executed May, Edward reaches London with Gloucester and is lodged at the Tower; coronation postponed June 24–5, Richard of Gloucester claims the throne and is declared king
RICHARD III	1483	Richard is crowned (July); Edward V and his brother Richard remain in the Tower; the revolt of the Duke of Buckingham is suppressed (Oct.)
	1485	Henry Tudor lands in Wales; Richard III defeated and killed at the battle of Bosworth
HENRY VII	1485	Henry Tudor crowned king
	1486	Henry marries Elizabeth, daughter of Edward IV
	1487	Yorkist rising in favour of the pretender Lambert Simnel is defeated at the battle of Stoke
	1491/2	The pretender Warbeck appears in Ireland
	1497	The Cornish rebellion; Warbeck captured by Henry VII
	1509	Death of Henry VII

1. Social Hierarchy and Social Change

If one looks back into the past, beyond the time when Rousseau sent out his clarion call for liberty, equality and fraternity, one looks back into what we nowadays call a deference society. Deference implies an ordered gradation of society, its hierarchic arrangement by scales which regulate the respect and the kind of services which one man or woman may expect of another, or may expect to pay another. It would not be the case, though, that the further one looks back the more such scales of deference one should expect to find. In the very last days of the Ancien Régime in Europe, the niceties of social rank were probably more refined in their definition than they had ever been before. The processes of refinement which reached their apogee in the rules of precedence of the courts of Versailles and Vienna had their origins in the late middle ages. That is one of the reasons why the later medieval period is an important and formative one in social history: it is also the reason why, if one is to understand the history of that period, even in England where social grades were more flexible and less sharply defined than they were in other European lands, one must know something about the contemporary hierarchy as men then saw it. For in the minds of the men of that age, the relations of deference and service that persisted between the grades were the basis of social order, of its essence: they had not yet come to regard social distinctions as divisive, as forces with the potential to tear society apart, as Rousseau and later Marx were to do.

'You know that there be three estates of men,' said John Gower, Chaucer's fellow poet and contemporary. To him the statement was a truism. In his time it was traditional wisdom that society was composed of three orders, functionally defined in their relation to one another: the clergy whose business was with prayer and spiritual well-being; the warriors who defended the land and people with their arms; and the labourers whose toil supported the other two 'orders' or 'estates'. In England this view of society was first given expression (as far as we know) by King Alfred in an aside in his translation of Orosius. A king needs tools to help him in his work, he says: he must have men who will pray, men who will fight and men who will work the land to support these others. But the idea is certainly older: it has echoes, clearly, of Plato's tripartite division of the inhabitants of his ideal *Republic*, into philosopher rulers, warriors and workers, and is reminiscent too of the Hindu caste system that identifies separate castes of priests (Brahmins), warriors and peasants. Some have argued that the quest for its origins leads back into the remote history of the Indo-European past.

About the medieval version of the idea perhaps the first thing to stress is its specifically Christian framework. 'In the church there be needful these three offices,' says a fourteenth-century homilist, 'priesthood, knighthood, and labourers': to him the church, the community of Christian people, *was* society, and the performance of the tasks of his station a man's Christian duty:

And one thing I dare well say, that he that is not labouring in this world on studying, on prayers, on preaching for help of the people – as it falleth to priests; nor in ruling the people, maintaining them and defending them from enemies, as it falleth to knights; nor labouring on earth in divers crafts, as it falleth to labourers: when the day of reckoning cometh, right as he lived here without labour, so he shall there lack the reward of 'the penny', that is, the endless joy of heaven.

Laborare est orare, to work is to pray, that is the message, and that attention to the duties of one's station discharges simultaneously obligation to God and to one's neighbour. William Langland caught this last point beautifully in the terms of the deal struck by his personified labourer Piers the Plowman with the knight:

> By St Paul quoth Perkin you proffer so freely
> That I'll swink and sweat and sow for us both,
> And other labours do for thy love all my lifetime.
> In covenant that thou keep Holy Church and myself
> From wasters and wicked men that this world destroy,

And go hunt hardily for hares and for foxes,
For boars and for badgers that break down my hedges,
And go train thy falcons wildfowls to kill,
For such come to my croft and crop off my wheat.

The medieval view of the three estates thus had a Christian
framework, and a functional approach to their relationship to
one another. Two other aspects require emphasis also. First it
must be stressed that it was explicitly hierarchic: the priest had
primacy in order of dignity, the knight or warrior came second
and the place of the labourer was in social subjection to these
other two. The functions of the first two estates involved them
in the exercise of authority, each one in its own sphere; the
labourer's did not. 'To the knight it sufficeth not that he be
given the best arms and the best beast,' says the fifteenth-century
translation of Ramon Lull's *Order of Chivalry*, 'but also that he
be given *seignory*', that is, lordship over lesser men. The estates
view of society was thus firmly anti-egalitarian. The second
point that I must stress is connected to this first one; it is that it
was no warmer towards social mobility than it was to social
equality. Principally because hierarchical ordering was seen in
terms of divine intention, the relationship between the three
orders was viewed in a static way. 'When God could have made
all men strong, wise and rich,' wrote Master Ralph Acton, 'he
was unwilling to do so . . . He willed these men to be strong and
healthy, wise or rich, that they might save their own souls by
helping others through love of them: those others he willed to
be weak or foolish or in want, that they might save their souls
by enduring hardship in patience. Hence God says, the poor ye
have always with you.'

The social quietism of the preacher's message here may ring
strangely on the ear of the modern age which has been so
thoroughly attuned to the notion of social progress; but it had
the authority of St Paul behind it: 'Let each man abide in the
same calling wherein he was called.'

The conception of the three estates and their relations to one
another was of course an ideal vision: it never did and never
could have corresponded to reality. No doubt that is part of the
reason why some thinkers sought to explain the relationships of

different degrees or callings in the body politic in more complex, analogical terms. Thus John of Salisbury (d. 1180) used the symbol of the human body in his analogy: the priesthood is the soul (the animating principle without which the body cannot live) of the community; the prince is the head; the senate (or council) the heart; the judges the eyes; the warriors the armed hands; the tax-gatherers the intestines; the labourers and crafts-men the feet. But for a very long period the straight three-estates view held the field as the commonest and most basic mode of expressing a hierarchic, functionally structured social ideal; and it did so, no doubt, because for a long time it could be seen as relating well enough, if rather roughly and approxi-mately, to real social conditions.

That was in the earlier, predominantly rural period of the middle ages, when independent towns were mere islets in the great sea of feudal lordship, when commercial exchange was at its slackest and slightest, and the merchant most often a stranger; when, also, the need for protection that only expensively armed warriors could provide (against marauding Vikings or Welshmen in England; against Vikings, Hungarians and Saracens in other parts of Europe) was at a premium. These times were also the great age of the monasteries, those powerhouses of prayer whose liturgical round of services offered up a steady stream of inter-cession for the *patria* and for all Christian people dead and living, and which were protected and sustained in this vital task by the arms and endowments of nobles and the toil of peas-ants. In these conditions the three-estates view, if somewhat ideal, could and did seem a not inappropriate model of social relations.

Even as late as the early fourteenth century, at the eve of the period that this book seeks to examine, this traditional view had not yet entirely lost all semblance of appropriateness to con-temporary English conditions. Things had changed a great deal, it is true, since the end of what might be called the 'age of invasions' of the eleventh and preceding centuries (the last of them had been, for England, the Norman Conquest of 1066). The Normans had settled down and become anglicized. The pace of trade had quickened: towns had grown in number and in population density. Government had become more stable, and also more complex and bureaucratic. In the religious sphere, the monastic movement had found no fresh impetus since the end of the twelfth century, and by 1300 the vigour even of the new orders of religion of the thirteenth century, the mendicant friars, was beginning to look tarnished. Nevertheless, England was still a predominantly rural society. The wealth and influence of her ecclesiastical aristocracy (the bishops, the greater mon-asteries, and the richer among the beneficed clergy) depended on land and a pre-emptive right to a lion's share of the fruits of the labour of those who tilled and tended it: and the same was true of the secular aristocracy of barons and knights. Though a good many knights (and other substantial freeholders) had lost most of their taste for martial activity and were beginning to look more like country gentlemen than cavaliers, the reckoning of their social obligations, as landholders, in terms of military service (owed either to the king directly or mediately in respect of tenures held of some baronial overlord), stood as a reminder of the traditional relations between martial function and secular privilege. All this was still true, as I say, around 1300, even perhaps for a little longer, and in these conditions the three-estates description of social relations could still enjoy some appearance of relevance to real circumstances.

A hundred and fifty or so years later, at the end of the fifteenth century, this was no longer so. Things had by then changed too much. Traditional views die hard, and as we have seen, at the end of the fourteenth century Gower could still refer to the tripartite division of society as if it were a truism, and some clung to the view much longer, into the sixteenth century and even beyond. But by the late fourteenth century it was already fast losing what had been at least a seeming relation to reality, and by the end of the fifteenth, long before Henry VIII finally laid secular hands on monastic wealth, it had lost it. The changes in the structure of society that took place during the period between around 1350 and around 1500 were vast ones, and are what make the intervening years so important in the social history of England.

As Dr Jonathan Hughes has recently said, 'the period between the Black Death and the Wars of the Roses was a social and cultural watershed in English history'. The forces underlying the great shifts of these times were multiplex and many faceted: pride of place may however be given to three principal factors. First, there were the effects of the great Hundred Years War between England and France, which broke out in 1337 and rumbled on till 1453, when the English lost their last footholds on the soil of France, bar Calais. This war and the strains that it engendered had a profound impact on the relations of government and governed in England, and contributed significantly to the development of a new consciousness of national identity. A second factor was the spread of literacy, especially of vernacular literacy, to a much broader cross-section of society. To quote Hughes again, 'narrative poems were written that offered a broader and more realistic perspective on human nature ... Chaucer's *Canterbury Tales* celebrated the new diversity of English society ... more people than ever before were reading books for instruction and entertainment'. The third factor, the most dramatic and the most wide-ranging in its consequences, was the demographic recession that followed the onset in the mid fourteenth century of the great plagues – in the first outbreak, the Black Death of 1348–9, up to a third of the population of England may, it is thought, have perished.

It is not irrelevant to what has gone before in this chapter that the impact of the third of these factors, of plague and demographic decline, though it affected all and sundry, was particularly significant for the labouring sectors of the population. The effects of the French war were likewise felt at all levels of society, but inevitably most of all by the nobles, knights and gentry who provided the leadership for the hosts that fought in France and were the agents of their recruitment; and whose representatives voted in Parliament the taxes that paid for the fighting. The spread of literacy and the rise of the vernacular affected in a particular way the clerical estate, whose influence and privileged position had been previously so firmly buttressed by the clerks' near monopoly of any sophisticated degree of literacy, especially of literacy in Latin, the traditional language not only of intellectual debate and of Christian liturgy but also of administration. It is thus clear why the forces that in this period were effecting major changes in society were such as inevitably to affect also the relation of the three-estates view to the realities of living.

Hughes describes Chaucer's *Canterbury Tales* as celebrating 'the new diversity of English society'. If one looks carefully at the vivid pen portraits of his pilgrims that Chaucer offers in the 'General Prologue' to the *Tales*, the enduring influence of the three-estates approach is still visible: it can be no accident that the three most clearly idealized figures in his company are the knight, the parson and the ploughman. Nevertheless the new diversity is also very clearly there. Leaving aside for a moment his clerical characters, into which of the three estates, one may ask, is one to fit his man of law, his franklin, his merchant, his shipman, his wife of Bath? If one looks again, and more carefully, something else appears too. Most (though not perhaps all) of his figures are based on stereotypes, often adverse stereotypes of persons untrue to what ought to be the principles of their calling (and so the key to its position in the social whole) – the uncloistered monk, the friar too familiar with women and taverns, the partial judge, the reeve who knows how to cheat his master, the domineering female. Chaucer has concealed the stereotyping by the skill with which he has individualized his description of each, giving the monk a bald head 'that shone as any glass', telling of how the friar's eyes twinkled when he took the harp, of the franklin's sanguine countenance that reflected his prodigal hospitality, of the wife of Bath's red stockings. But the stereotypes are there, and one can find their analogues, shorn of the measure of personality that Chaucer gave them, in more pedestrian works, say in Gower's *Mirour de l'omme* or in the invective of contemporary homilists who seek to review the typical shortcomings of particular sectors of society. My point here is that even if a good many of Chaucer's figures are hard to fit into a three-estates scheme, he is still trying to relate each to a specific place and a specific function in the social hierarchy, following the same principle as that in which the three-estates view was based. Indeed, Chaucer is quite explicit that this is what he is trying to do. He is going, he says at the beginning of the 'Prologue', to tell of each of his pilgrims what was his 'condition' and his 'degree'; and at the end of it he apologizes for not putting them in the right hierarchic order, in 'here

degree ... as thei schulde stonde'. Rather as the far-sighted John
of Salisbury in an earlier age, Chaucer has not reacted to 'new
diversity' by breaking with a functional hierarchic view of the
ordering of society, but by multiplying the number of 'degrees'
or 'estates' that must be fitted into their place in the body
politic. The reaction to overt signs of changing conditions is not
to conclude that the framework needs loosening, but almost the
opposite, to seek to define more narrowly and relate more
carefully functions and 'degrees' within the social whole.

    Fortunately – from an historian's point of view – this was not just
a reaction of poets, but of administrators and legislators also. The
same idea underlay for instance what is called the Statute of
Additions of 1413, which specified that in legal indictments the
party charged should be identified by his 'estate', 'degree' or
'mystery' (that is, his occupation) as well as by name and locality. A
similar approach informed likewise the numerous acts of Parliament that sought to define, commonly in terms of annual
income from land or rent, who might be entitled to discharge
particular functions or offices. Thus we find an act of 1371
laying down a qualification of £20 p.a. from land for sheriffs,
and an act of 1439 establishing the same qualifications for justices
of the peace. An act of 1414 imposed a qualification of 40s.
freehold for jurymen in cases of homicide and in real-estate
disputes, and an act of 1429 confirmed the county franchise to
the same people, setting off the famous 40s. freeholders on their
long career of privilege in parliamentary elections. An act of
1445 inhibited any of 'yeoman' status or below from sitting in
Parliament, and set a £40 p.a. qualification for knights sitting as
shire representatives. It was in a spirit similar to that of these acts
that in the early sixteenth century Garter King of Arms replied
to the charge that he had been upsetting the social order by
making gentlemen of 'bondmen and vile persons' by granting
them arms, that he had not admitted to arms any but such as
had 'lands and possessions' of free tenure to the value of £10
sterling or in moveable goods £300 sterling. The blessing for
the historian here is that from this sort of legislation, from the
records of legal cases and from asides such as Garter's, as well as
from the writing of such as Chaucer and Langland, he can begin
to see something of how men of the time sought to reschematize

the ordering of their changing society, how they tried to come to terms with its shifting conditions and redefine its gradations.

Three further pieces of legislation are particularly revealing from this point of view. They are the regulations for the graduated poll tax of 1379, and the sumptuary laws of Edward III and Edward IV. Let us look at the first of these first. In 1379 the Commons of Parliament granted to King Richard II for war purposes a poll tax, with a graduated descending scale of charges designed to take account of the wealth and degree of those liable. At the top of the scale came the pair who were the only two dukes in England, John of Gaunt and John of Brittany, each charged 10 marks (£6 13s. 4d. – the mark was worth 13s. 4d.). In the next category came the earls, charged £4, followed by barons and knights banneret (greater knights, entitled to raise a banner in the king's hosts) charged 40s. Next, at 20s., came knights bachelor and those liable to be distrained to be knights (i.e. those with at least £40 p.a. from land or rent, all such persons being liable to a financial penalty if they wished to avoid taking up knighthood) and after them esquires charged 6s. 8d. (half a mark). The lowest degree of the secular aristocracy recognized in these regulations were landless esquires, charged 3s. 4d. (for the most part, presumably, cadets of good family, capable of bearing arms).

What is so interesting is the way in which others, whose 'degree' had no place in the framework of the traditional warrior estate, were fitted into the scale. Among lawyers, justices of the bench were charged even more than earls, £5: sergeants of the law (senior barristers), the same as barons, 40s., and junior barristers at the same rate as knights. The mayor of London was charged at the same rate as an earl (£4), London aldermen and mayors of major cities at 40s., greater merchants at 20s. (as knights bachelor) and mayors of lesser towns at the same rate or less according to their borough's capacity. Lesser merchants and well-off artificers, and also franklins (substantial freeholders), were charged at the same rate as esquires, at 6s. 8d. If one omits some small groups (summoners, pardoners, farmers of granges) one then comes down at last to the ordinary working men and women, charged as married couples or individually if single, at a groat each, 4d. a head.

The graduated poll tax thus established a scale of equivalences, that are in themselves interesting, between persons who could be fitted into one of the old three-estates categories (the knightly estate) and other men of different calling, notably lawyers, merchants and townsmen. It is therefore most striking to find Edward III's sumptuary laws of 1363, stated significantly to be aimed against 'the outrageous and excessive apparell of divers people, against their estate and degree', should make a number of similar equivalences. Cloth of gold is here reserved to the highest, the lords and the most elevated. Richer knights may choose what other cloth they wish, and their ladies may wear embroidery of pearls in their headdress. Lesser knights are limited, for vesture and hose, to cloth worth 6 marks the broadcloth, and forbidden to trim mantle or gown with ermine. Richer esquires are permitted cloth worth 5 marks, and lesser esquires cloth worth 4 marks: the former may wear girdles or ribbons 'reasonably garnished of silver' and trim with fur of miniver. Then come the equivalences. Merchants, citizens and artificers of London and elsewhere, with chattels worth £1,000 or above, are to observe the same limitations as the richer esquires, those with chattels worth £500 or above the same as lesser esquires and gentlefolk. We are also told that, in the matter of wearing furs, clerks with stalls in cathedrals and colleges must abide by the statutes of their particular institutions, that clerks with 200 marks of land or rent must abide by the same rules as knights of equivalent wealth, and those with £100 of rent by the same rules as lesser esquires. Below these ranks 'men of handicraft' and yeomen – the aristocracy of the lower deck in the social strata – are limited to cloth worth 40s., and forbidden any fur save that of lamb, cony, cat or fox; and carters, ploughmen, shepherds, and all below the yeoman level are to wear no cloth but blanket or russet wool and girdles of linen.

Edward IV's sumptuary laws of 1463 do little more than add a few refinements for a dressier age. Some are rather quaint. It is nice to hear of yeomen being forbidden to 'stuff out' their doublets for ostentation with 'wool, cadas or cotton', and knights and other lesser men being forbidden to wear jackets 'but of such a length as may cover his buttocks and privy parts'. The parliamentary peers, with cloth of gold reserved to them and their children, are set apart a little more clearly than in the previous legislation; and sensible exceptions from the rules are made for clerical vestments, the robes of judges sitting at the bench, for academic dress in schools and universities, and for the uniforms of heralds, civic officers, messengers and minstrels. But otherwise the gradations or degrees for which it is seen fit to legislate reappear and so do the old kind of equivalences, with the Mayor of London on a par with a knight, the aldermen of London, the Barons of the Cinque Ports and mayors of boroughs corporate on a par with esquires, and so on. The new mould of a hundred years previous seems by this time to be beginning to set.

The outlines of a picture of how men perceived a more diverse ordering of society and its hierarchical structure thus begin to emerge. Where we have to focus our attention most closely, it is clear, is on landowning wealth and rank, for that is what provides the key to the gradations, and in doing so testifies to the continuing dominance of the landed interest in a still predominantly rural population. At the top of the social scale come the lords, by the fifteenth century standing apart a little more sharply in their dignity as a parliamentary peerage from the greater knights than they formerly did (barons and greater knights are lumped together below the earls in the 1379 poll-tax gradations: the sumptuary laws of Edward IV distinguish them quite clearly). After the lords come the knights (those genuinely dubbed as such, through arming to knighthood), and next below them in dignity the esquires. Below the esquires, we see the status of gentleman beginning to define itself as the last rung in the ladder of secular, aristocratic gradation in the fifteenth century, as the Statute of Additions forced a sharper distinction between esquires and other claimants to gentility. It is here worth noting that it was in the later fourteenth century that the heralds began to recognize esquires as armigerous, as entitled to blazon their own arms: earlier rolls of arms record only the blazon of lords and genuine knights. Before the end of the fifteenth century the idea of the 'gentleman of coat armour' had become a familiar one, though there was some doubt as to what precisely it meant ('there are no more gentlemen in Lancashire but my Lord of Derby and Monteagle', Sir Thomas Townley declared to Clarenceux Herald in 1530). Nevertheless the numerous books and tracts on heraldry that survive attest to the widespread interest that the subject commanded, and to the quest for a satisfactory definition. So does the proliferation of armorial sculpture, brass plates and perhaps above all armorial glass in churches. The reason is not hard to seek: we are looking here at testimony that 'gentility' was seen as the common bond linking all the scales of aristocracy, from great lord down to mere gentleman; and that blazon was the outward and visible sign of standing clear of the common herd.

Across that line there was always a good deal of movement to and fro, for the distinction was not sharp. For all the science of the heralds, in England no judicial status of *noblesse* ever developed, like that which across the Channel distinguished the petty noble from the often richer *roturier* or commoner. It must also be stressed that the gradations that we have been looking at are presented in terms of perceived dignity and rank, not of wealth, and that on that scale (which, as has been seen, was also much used contemporarily) the categories overlap. We are able to know quite a lot about income from land from the returns of two taxes on landed income that were imposed in the fifteenth century, in 1412 and 1436. Working with the 1436 returns, H. L. Gray was able to divide the landowning aristocracy, greater and lesser, into five categories defined in terms of wealth. He found 51 lay barons, heads of their families, with incomes averaging £882 p.a.; 183 'greater knights' with incomes over £100 (average £208); 750 'lesser knights' with incomes of between £40 and £100 (average £60); 1,200 esquires with incomes between £20 and £40 (average just under £25); and two groups of gentry, 1,600 gentlemen with incomes between £10 and £20, and 3,400 with incomes between £5 and £10. Lack of enthusiasm for paying taxes means that the figures are all, probably, too low. The titles of the categories are also somewhat artificial, since many of Gray's 'knights' had never been dubbed, and so would officially be termed esquires: and many of the 3,400 lesser 'gentry' would probably have been described by their neighbours as yeomen rather than gentlemen. The averages too are somewhat misleading. As K. B. McFarlane

showed from a close study of the 1412 returns for two counties,
Dorset and Sussex, one can find a number of greater knights
with incomes not far off Gray's baronial 'average'. Thus one can
find some knights distinctly richer than poorer barons, and also
some who were technically esquires and were a good deal richer
than poor knights. Above all, one will find a handful of greater
barons, dukes and earls, with incomes so far in excess of Gray's
average of £882 as almost to set them apart in a separate
category as a kind of princely supra-nobility. There was a good
general relationship between degree and wealth, but not a
precise one.

There was a good general relation also between wealth and
degree on the one hand and social role or function on the other.
The very word knight had clear martial overtones. Heraldic
arms were, likewise, insignia with military associations, and the
fourteenth-century recognition of esquires as being armigerous
recognized them as being included in the estate whose traditional
function was military. In fourteenth-century contracts for war-
service men-at-arms are indeed often simply termed 'esquires'.
In the administrative sphere the relation between social degree
and wealth and social responsibilities was even clearer, as we
have seen. The £10 qualification to be a juryman in a case of
homicide or a property dispute meant that the jury would be
composed of men who could at least theoretically support the
rank of gentleman. The £20 qualification for sheriffs and justices
of the peace meant that they needed to have an income that
would support at least the rank of esquire. The statute of 1445
which required that representatives of the shires in Parliament
must have an income of £40 limited that role to those who,
whether they were dubbed knights or not, were legally liable to
be distrained to take up knighthood. These property qualifications are illuminating about the esteem in which offices such as
these were held, of the dignity associated with their exercise.
They tell us also of factors that tended, in any given region, to
buttress solidly the social influence of its leading families. Here
one point may be added in parenthesis. Though the overall
number of genteel families in England does not seem to have
altered very much over the period we are looking at, from
around 1350 to around 1500, the richer among them – for a

variety of reasons but especially on account of their greater capacity to arrange advantageous marriages – tended to become even richer. Thus we see among the magnates the dukes and greater earls pulling away further from their fellow lay barons, and it looks as if this was probably true, at a lower level, of the greater knights with respect to their fellows.

As we have seen from the sumptuary laws and the regulations for the graduated poll tax of 1379, the stratifications of genteel, landed society offered a standard by which the 'degrees' of other sectors in society could be measured. It is particularly interesting, in the sumptuary laws of Edward III, to find some effort to make an equation between clerks with income from land and rent and secular knights and esquires. There was, obviously, a kind of analogy between the stratifications of the clerical estate and the genteel secular one. In Parliament the bishops and the heads of greater monasteries sat with the lay barons as their peers (and, in the convocations of the two archdioceses, the representatives of the lower clergy played a role comparable to that of parliamentary representatives). In a local society, the abbots of lesser houses and perhaps some of the officials of the greater ones carried clout comparable with that of knights, lesser or greater. It is no accident that Chaucer's monk was a great man for hunting, the favourite sport of the lay gentry: the hunting field often brought them and their monastic neighbours together, and the Leicester Abbey chronicle tells us that the influence with the lay aristocracy of Abbot Clowne in the mid fourtrenth century was built upon his knowledge of hounds and venery. Among the secular clergy, the canons of cathedrals and collegiate churches formed a kind of lesser clerical aristocracy, with incomes from their endowments which would put them somewhere at least on the scale of gentility, and possibly quite high (the richest prebendal stall in England, Masham Vetus in the chapter of York, was worth 600 marks p.a.). The incomes of clergy from parish benefices, rectories, and vicarages varied so enormously (to say nothing of the effects of pluralism) that it is impossible to generalize about them: but a very high proportion brought their holders at least something near the £5 level that is at the bottom of Gray's scale of genteel or near-genteel incomes. Indeed even unbeneficed priests, chaplains serving temporary chantries and others, might be able to string together something not far off that sum by singing masses for the departed, officiating at funerals, and so on. Any respect attaching to the cloth quite apart, clergy really were in a privileged position in comparison with the common lot of the great majority of the population, at any rate in terms of what they could spend by the year (in contrast with secular men, they could not of course transmit the benefices which were the sources of their income hereditarily). And there were a great many of them, more than there were gentlemen.

The sumptuary laws make a more determined and careful effort to bring merchants, substantial artificers and townsmen into equation with landed people, in terms of dress and degree; and the 1379 poll-tax regulations bring another group, the lawyers, into the scale as well. That merchants and townsmen should be put on a par with gentry witnesses to the increased and increasing importance of commercial activity, and to the esteem in which it was held. An increasing number of leading London merchants, as time went by, came to be dubbed knights: John Pulteney, John Philipot and Nicholas Brembre in the fourteenth century were rather exceptional; Geoffrey Boleyn, Edmond Shaa, John Plomer, John Young and Ralph Asty in the later fifteenth century seem quite typical. A considerably greater number among them used their wealth to buy land and found genteel dynasties. Outside London, the histories of men who used the profits of trading to buy themselves into landed gentility are not so common, unless one takes account of daughters of theirs marrying into genteel families: in the provinces, and perhaps especially in the remoter regions, something more of the traditional separateness of rural and urban society lingered longer than in the home counties.

The lawyers of the central courts were more spectacularly successful in making their way in landed society than even the London merchants. Their profession threw numerous opportunities to buy land advantageously in their way, and they did not neglect them. A substantial number of the most important new dynasties among the gentility of the late middle ages were founded through fortunes made at the law. Names such as those of Scrope, Markham, Fortescue, Lyttleton and Fairfax would have a long history, lasting far beyond our period. In the 1450s we find William Worcester complaining that nowadays in the counties men who have a training in law and 'civil matter' and hold their heads high at court sessions are held of more account than gentlemen who have spent 'thirty or forty years in great jeopardy' in the king's wars in France. It does not take a great deal of digging into the genealogical history of county families to show that there must in his time have been adequate ground for his complaint.

The sumptuary laws and the poll-tax regulations tell us about the gradations of society: another kind of legislation, the statutes of livery and maintenance of Richard II and subsequent kings, offers an insight into a matter equally important, the relations of service and deference among its upper echelons. Richard II's statute of 1390 was prompted by the complaints of the Commons in Parliament that retainers 'who wore the badges of lords were so swollen with pride that no fear would deter them from committing extortions in their shires' and from obstructing the course of justice. The king responded with an ordinance, drawn up by the council, inhibiting men of standing from giving any 'livery of company' to anyone 'unless he is a family servant living in the household'. But he made one exception, significantly phrased in the same terms of degree and condition with which we have been dealing, which was this. Dukes, earls, barons and bannerets were permitted to give liveries to men of the 'estate' of knights and esquires who were not household servants, but to such only as were 'retained with them for the term of their lives in peace and war by indenture'. Litigation under this statute (and subsequent legislation) made some slight modifications to these rules in practice. In the fifteenth century the giving of liveries by lords to gentlemen, on the same terms as knights and esquires, was clearly tolerated. The giving of liveries to officials (such as stewards of manors) and to counsellors learned in the law (functional roles, note), on the same terms as household servants, was besides interpreted as lawful.

There are some terms used here which need explanation. 'Liveries' could take the form of robes in a lord's colours, of a cap or a collar (like John of Gaunt's famous livery collar of

Ss*), or a badge. Some livery badges became very celebrated, the Percy crescent, Neville of Warwick's bear with a ragged staff, Richard II's badge of the white hart (for kings as well as noblemen would and commonly did retain men by fee and the giving of livery). What is meant by an indenture is perhaps best illustrated by quoting an example. Here (suitably abbreviated) is the text of the retaining indenture struck between Henry, Earl of Lancaster, and Sir Edmond Ufford on 21 March 1348:

To all those who may see or hear these letters, Henry Earl of Lancaster, Derby and Leicester gives greeting in God's name. Now, our very dear cousin Sir Edmond Ufford, son of Sir Thomas Ufford, is engaged with us to serve us for the term of his life in war and peace on the terms as follows: That is to say in the time of war himself and three mounted men at arms, well armed and mounted as is proper: and he himself shall be mounted at our livery, and he shall have ten horses for himself and his liveried men ... and nine garcons at wages, and a chamberlain fed in the household ... And in time of peace whenever he is summoned by us he shall come to where we are with one esquire, and he shall have four horses liveried, and a chamberlain fed in the household and three garcons at wages. And at all those times when we make livery of robes to our other knights we shall do toward him as we do toward others of his condition. And for the good service that the said Sir Edmond has done us before this, as also for the good service that he shall do ... we have given and granted to the said Sir Edmond forty marks of rent to draw year by year on our manor of Higham Ferrers ... and we Henry Earl of Lancaster and our heirs will warrant and maintain the said annuity in the manner abovesaid against all and sundry. In witness of which we have set our seal to that part of the indenture that shall remain with the said Sir Edmond, and to the part [i.e. the copy] that shall remain with us the said Sir Edmond has set his seal. These are the witnesses, etc.

By this agreement, as we see, Sir Edmond as the earl's indentured retainer promised him good service, including specifically military service. In return the earl promised him an annual fee,

---

* This was a collar of Ss wrought in metal (gold, silver or brass) either strung together or fixed to a strap, and worn like a chain about the neck by favoured retainers and associates of Gaunt and of his descendants the Lancastrian kings.

livery of robes, that he and his men should be fed in the earl's household when in attendance on him; and generally, by implication, the earl's favour and protection (his 'good lordship') was extended to him.

In framing the ordinance of 1390 concerning livery, King Richard and his councillors clearly had certain specific considerations and purposes in view. The Commons would have liked to see all giving of 'liveries of company' forbidden, because retainers used these emblems of the powerful backing that they enjoyed to overawe and mistreat neighbours and rivals. The king and his advisers however would not go as far as that. To be able to dress his household men in uniform of his choosing was for a man of standing a vital outward sign of his 'degree' and 'worship' and to forbid that would be overreaching. In addition, they saw that, within certain limitations, there were useful ends to be served by permitting lords and magnates to retain, besides household servants, men of standing such as knights and esquires. In these days before the birth of standing armies, if the king wished to mobilize a military force he needed to be able to look to the lords of his kingdom and to their influence to bring together the companies of men that would collectively form the royal host: they in turn needed to be able to call on reliable followers, bound to them against just such emergencies, to help them recruit the rank and file of their kinsmen, neighbours and tenants. Retaining could be, in short, the means towards bringing men of the warrior estate to fulfil their traditional role as such.

It was not, on the other hand, desirable that great lords should have at their beck and call large bands of lesser, more irresponsible persons, embryonic private armies. The danger here was not so much that this would facilitate rebellion (though that consideration may have crossed the minds of King Richard and his councillors), but that such bands could grow into local mafias, through whom a magnate and his intimate associates would be able to direct, manipulate and, when needful, obstruct administration and above all the course of justice in areas where their influence could be made sufficiently powerful. Maintenance, interference with the course of law by means of force, partiality or pressure, was the classic abuse alleged against the practice of retaining and the giving of liveries. So the right to retain men outside and beyond the household had to be limited to lords, the king's hereditary councillors and companions without whose support and cooperation his kingdom could not be governed: and their right to so retain had to be limited to the degrees of men, such as knights, esquires and gentlemen, whose standing gave them a stake in the stability and reasonable governance of the locality in which they lived.

The relation of lord and retainer has often been described as 'bastard feudal', in the same way as 'livery and maintenance' are often described as characteristic abuses of an age of 'bastard feudalism'. These words are neologisms, terms that modern historians have invented. But they are not inappropriate. The kind of relation that, say, the indenture between Henry of Lancaster and Edmond Ufford established, is comparable to (though not the same as) the kind of relation that was established under what is called the feudal system between a lord and his feudal tenant (the word 'feudal' *was* used contemporarily). Under that system a lord might grant to a follower the hereditary freehold of an estate – the right to the profits from it and a measure of jurisdiction over the peasants who lived on it and would till the land for him – in return for homage and stipulated services, usually military (the service of one or more knights, or a fractional contribution thereto, in the lord's company). The lord reserved the right to charge an entry fee (relief) at each succession, and to take the land back into his hand temporarily during the minority of an heir who was under age (wardship), and a say in the marriage of such a ward or an heiress. The tenant in turn might grant away ('enfeoff') part of the land to a subtenant on similar terms (or indeed could give or sell the whole, provided the new tenant would observe the same obligations towards his lord as he had). This system bred a kind of hierarchy of tenures, graded by the value and extent of the conditional holdings and of the obligations that went with them, loosely comparable to the social hierarchy of landed 'degrees', from duke and earl down to 'mere' gentlemen.

The two scales were, nevertheless, quite different. In the fourteenth and fifteenth centuries the feudal system of tenures

(tenures in 'fee simple') continued to provide the basis of the common law concerning real property. But the processes by which one man in one generation found as a wife an heiress to lands held of a lord other than his own, and their son in the next generation, say, purchased land held of yet another, and so on, meant that inevitably, over the course of time and long before the fourteenth century, grades in the hierarchy of tenure lost any meaningful relation to total wealth, and that any one lord's control over a tenant, who might hold parcels of land of several other lords besides himself, had been eroded. Also eroded, as a result of slow inflation, was the value of the entry fine, which had been fixed for military tenures early in the thirteenth century at a relatively inexpensive level. Even the right to wardship had come to be threatened by the device of 'enfeoffment to use' whereby the freeholder of an estate granted his land away to a group of trusted associates (his 'feoffees'), who became the owners at common law and undertook to apply the profits of the estate to the use of the grantor and his heirs. No right to wardship could now arise, because when the owner died the land remained – in legal theory – the property of the trustees that he had enfeoffed in his lifetime. Among the many advantages that feudal lords had once enjoyed and that they lost in these conditions was any meaningful degree of control over the service, and especially the military service, of their tenants.

A lord could, however, by such an agreement as Henry of Lancaster made with Edmond Ufford, buy with an annuity the promise of military service and – perhaps more important – the assurance of political and social support through his retainer's promise of more general peaceful services. Unlike the 'feudal' relation, an agreement of this kind was an individual one, not hereditary but for the retainer's lifetime only; it did not give the retainer any landed freehold, only the assurance of a pension; and it was more flexible than a feudal relationship, since the lord if he was dissatisfied could simply stop the annuity, and the retainer in the same circumstances could simply transfer his services elsewhere. But such an agreement did secure to the lord vital service and support, and to the retainer a vital source of protection and good lordship of the same kind that they had

once often found in feudal tenurial relationships: whence the
name 'bastard feudal'.* For the same reason, agreements of this
kind were very common in our period.

Most peers did not retain very large followings of knights and
esquires indentured for life service in peace and war. The huge
retinue of John of Gaunt, who at one time had one earl, three
barons, eighty-three knights and 112 esquires indentured with
him, was quite exceptional. Much more typical for a high-
ranking peer would be the Duke of Buckingham's retinue of
1448, of ten knights and twenty-seven esquires; and a lesser
baron would probably not have been able to count half that
number. With some exceptions, such as the Percy Earls of
Northumberland who needed to retain numerous followers
against border emergencies, most great men did not wish to tie
up more than perhaps 10 per cent or so of their income in
commitments to retainers, even including followers not indentured. For the indentured knights and esquires of a lord's company were merely the inner core of a wider affinity, stretching
outwards in concentric circles, of annuitants with a yearly fee
but no security in a life agreement, of professional administrators
and legal counsel (who might be serving several masters) and of
substantial local men who came intermittently within the orbit
of the good lordship of its leader. Almost always, in any given
shire or region, there were enough substantial knights or gentlefolk who were not bound preferentially to any peer to ensure
that the local influence of any lord, however high and well
served, was less than a stranglehold (though the Courtenay Earls
of Devon in the late fourteenth century and the Beauchamp
Earls of Warwick in the fifteenth, may in those counties have
not been so far off that position). Besides, few even among
indentured retainers were dependent on their annuities for more
than a fraction of their income. If they had been, they would
indeed have hardly been worth retaining.

* It is not intended here to imply that 'bastard feudal' relationships were a
  later modification of older 'feudal' relationships, as has sometimes been
  argued. Their origin seems rather to be sought in an extension of the
  household relationships of lords with those they called their *familiares*,
  which in early times co-existed with, and interacted with, the feudal
  relation of lord and vassal.

'Bastard feudal' relations were of vital social significance in late medieval England because, on the one hand, they served to uphold the worship and dignity of great men, earls and barons, in what they would have called their 'country', the regions where their landed estates gave them prominence and interest. Men born to distinction in the national community, as earls and barons were, needed to be seen visibly to enjoy the respect, service and loyalty of men who 'stood tall' in regional society. Reciprocally, the good lordship and protection that these great men could offer gave security to the standing of those who could be seen to be their clients and associates, and added to their 'worth'. The liveries and badges that lords distributed and that retainers wore with pride were thus outward signs of networks of mutual support, which helped all parties, patrons and clients alike, to maintain their 'worship' within the established social hierarchy. For the retainer the relationship with his lord also opened the hope of advancement, through the rewards earned by good service, which in this deferential, status-conscious age was the broadest and least demeaning avenue of upward social mobility.

That is probably the most important point about the kind of relationship we have been looking at, its relation to social mobility. In late medieval England the service of the great, or at least of the greater, was the most important channel for ambition and careerism. Upward mobility, it should be stressed, was not just a matter of finding a complaisant patron, of patronage in the corrupt sense: lordly patrons were looking out not just for clients equipped by birth and position to fit into their established networks of influence, but also for talent. Talent could be displayed in many fields, in many forms of service, in arms, in administration, in estate stewardship, in supplying a household or lending to its master, or in the tendering of sound legal advice. Good education could therefore be as important towards advancement as a solid heritage, especially for cadets and for the humbler born. The gradations of landed society remained crucial none the less, since assimilation into them remained, consistently, the ultimate hallmark of successful achievement, whether one started as an adventurer, or in trade, or in the law, or from nothing: they remained too the indices of achievement for those

who started off within their charmed circle. This was an important balancing factor of stability in the dominant sector of a
society exposed to the impact of forces external and internal,
such as the effects of war, of plague and of spreading literacy,
that were steadily altering its texture. It helped to absorb what
might otherwise have been sharp tensions between groups with
different backgrounds, different birthrights and different brands
of service and expertise to offer.

All through this chapter so far, I have talked in terms of men, of
male degrees of worship, masculine qualifications. This has been
deliberate. This was an age when, by and large, most men and
most women, if they survived long enough, married. The
physiological aspects of life apart, what principally dictated the
pattern of living, of leisure preoccupations and work for a
woman was not her sex, but rather the degree and standing of
her male connections, her husband, her father, her brothers.
Whether the wife as well as the husband was or was not
expected actually to labour (as opposed to merely busying
herself in the family interest) probably marked the sharpest of all
dividing lines in society, in countryside and town alike, separating the genteel and those that might be equated with them from
all others. For this reason, in this chapter and succeeding ones, it
has seemed to me better not to treat womankind separately, but
in the context of the class, standing and preoccupations into
which their partnerships with their menfolk drew them.

All the same, there has probably been too little said so far of
women. There were callings, in this age as in all others, that
were purely female, those of the nun, the midwife, the 'wise
woman', the prostitute (there were plenty of these). There were
also avenues of living that were not open to women: they could
not become priests or go to university, hold offices or practise at
law. But they could retain men, employ workers, administer
their own estates and sue at law in their own right; if they were
born into wealthy or genteel condition they could play a powerful role personally. If their chattels were deemed at law to be
their husband's property (while he lived), lands that they brought
him were not by any means in his free disposal, even though the
income from them might be. As heiresses, well-born girls could

often be the victims of arranged marriages (so indeed could rich young men), but they could also be the vital agents in the advancement of their husbands. Perhaps most importantly of all, women as widows, in almost every rank of society, enjoyed a great degree of independence and significant legal rights. They were virtually always assured of a share at least in their dead husbands' goods or property, whether by way of dower, or through a joint settlement of lands, or under the rules of *free bench* (the widow's right to a share of the marital home) or *legitim* (the woman's legitimate share in the chattels of her deceased husband). In widowhood, a woman might have to shoulder significant responsibilities, the raising of her late husband's children, the management of his holding, his business or his estates. But widows also enjoyed a large measure of free choice not only in the discharge of these responsibilities, but as to how they should live and, above all, whether they should remarry. Marriage, by her agreement, to a well-placed widow, could be a very important step in the upward progress of an aspiring man. Though the historical record usually does not leave much evidence of it, she no doubt often made a man of him in more than one other sense as well.

Part I

The Third Estate:
the Commons

Countrymen and townsmen in an age of plague
and demographic decline

2. Plague, Depopulation and Labour Shortage

Of all the forces that were changing the face of English society in the late middle ages, the most wide ranging in its effects was the drop in population following the visitations of the fourteenth-century plagues. The coming of the plagues was unheralded and dramatic; the impact of the disease indiscriminating, striking down high and low alike. It had originated in Asia; ships' rats were what brought it to England, traditionally in two vessels that sailed into the harbour of Melcombe Regis in Dorset in 1348. From then on it spread rapidly in the western and southern counties: by winter it had reached London. It reached its peak in the summer of 1349. Before the epidemic subsided, a third of the population may have perished.

Something clearly needs to be said at the start about the medical aspects of the plague that struck England in 1348–9, which came later to be known as the Black Death. It seems apparent that we are dealing with an epidemic, indeed a pandemic, of bubonic plague. No English writer is very specific about the symptoms, but European sources are: 'In men and women alike,' says Boccaccio, 'it first betrayed itself by the emergence of certain tumours, in the groin or the armpit, some of which grew as large as a common apple – from the said parts of the body the deadly disease soon began to propagate and spread itself in all directions.' Guy de Chauliac, the papal physician at Avignon, likewise speaks of 'apostumes and carbuncles on the external parts, principally the armpits and the groin'. These are the buboes typical of bubonic plague. Bubonic plague is carried by rats and other rodents, and the infection is passed on by rat fleas. The bacillus is endemic in the blood among some rodents: the fleas which infect them become infected, and the effect is to glut the gullets of these parasites. They consequently become fiercely hungry, and in these conditions will leave their host animal and attack others including, notably, men. Rat fleas multiply best in warm weather, especially in humid conditions (the summer of 1348 was very wet). The onset of winter therefore puts a term, normally, to an outbreak of bubonic plague in northern latitudes. Because the disease is transmitted through the blood, usually through the flea-bite, 'pure' bubonic plague spreads, and can only spread really effectively, where there is rodent infestation (though fleas infected with the bacillus can travel long distances in grain, clothing and merchandise). In the crowded and un-hygienic conditions of medieval towns and of many villages this would cause the comparatively rapid and extensive spread of infection, but with a term to it, the onset of winter. 'Pure' bubonic plague, for this reason, is probably incapable, in the countryside at any rate, of having the sort of effects in terms of mortality that are associated with the Black Death. This is why some epidemiologists, notably J. F. D. Shrewsbury, have been sceptical about historians' estimates of the plague's mortality.

There is however a second variety of plague which in more recent pandemics has been associated with bubonic outbreaks, pneumonic plague. This seems to develop when humans with a pneumonic infection contract bubonic plague. This is a much more infectious disease – it can be contracted by inhalation – and is relatively more fatal. Though Shrewsbury dismissed it as a factor in the fourteenth century, Guy de Chauliac describes symptoms which are precisely those of pneumonic plague as observed by, for instance, Dr Wu Lien Teh in Manchuria in 1911–12. Guy speaks of 'continuous fever and spitting of blood, and from this one died in three days', and he distinguishes this brand of plague quite explicitly from that which showed the 'bubonic' symptoms. In twentieth-century experience in Asia pneumonic outbreaks were not halted by the onset of winter. Since bacilli mutate, and may behave differently in different periods, it can be dangerous to argue from their modern be-haviour; but in the light of this it certainly looks significant that the plagues of 1348–9 and 1361–2 were not so halted. It seems reasonably certain, in short, that in England in the fourteenth century we have to deal with the effects of simultaneous pneu-monic and bubonic outbreaks, with the possibility of a third strain, septicaemic plague, which is still more fatal but rather less contagious (though it can be carried by human fleas), playing a part as well. That is how the very high mortality rates that the sources indicate become credible.

So much for the gory medical details: one more point of medical history needs however to be made. That is, that for the remainder of the middle ages and beyond, plague remained endemic in England. A long list of recorded outbreaks can be compiled. To judge simply by the chroniclers' sense of shock and devastation, the first two outbreaks, those of 1348–9 and 1361–2, were the most serious, and both lasted through the winter: those of 1369 and 1375 were also very severe. But setting aside local outbreaks confined to London or some other city, we have records of serious epidemics also in 1390, 1407, 1413, 1434, 1464, 1471, 1479 and 1485: the last in the series was of course the great London plague of 1665. The evidence suggests that, progressively, the impact of these major outbreaks became on the whole less severe, and that they were more and more limited to the towns. It looks therefore as if the specially virulent pneumonic strain was a significant factor only in the earlier stages of the plague pandemic.

There was nothing to herald the first onset of the plague, and the reaction to it of the chronicles is accordingly of a different order to what they have to say of later outbreaks, when they had seen such a thing as a raging epidemic and knew what it could mean. What they recorded of 1348 is therefore appropriately dramatic. 'So great a multitude was not swept away, it was believed, even by the flood in the days of Noah,' wrote the chronicler of Louth Park Abbey in Lincolnshire. John of Clyn wrote in Anglo-Irish Kilkenny, 'I leave the parchment for the work to be continued, in case in future any of the race of Adam should be able to escape this plague and continue what I have begun.' 'This dreadful pestilence penetrated through the coastal regions and came from Southampton to Bristol,' wrote Henry Knighton of Leicester

and almost the whole strength of the town perished, as if overcome by sudden death, for few there were who kept their beds more than two

or three days . . . at Leicester in the little parish of St Leonard's more
than 380 people perished, in the parish of the Holy Cross 400, in the
parish of St Margaret 700, and so in every parish a great multitude . . .
the cruel death spread everywhere, following the course of the sun.

And, in the winter following, he wrote,

There was such a dearth of servants for all kinds of work that men
believed there had never been such a shortage before, for beasts and
cattle strayed everywhere, for none were left to tend them.

These are vivid, horrid descriptions. Troubles begin for the
historian the moment that he tries to translate their dramatized
statements into terms of numbers, and to judge just how sharp
the demographic impact really was. Here straightaway the poor
and uncertain quality of medieval quantitative evidence creates a
problem. As the demographic historian Russell has pointed out,
the only death rates which we can calculate with any degree of
accuracy are those of men who held land directly of the Crown
(from the inquisitions *post mortem* held to establish what lands
they had so held 'in chief'), that is to say of a group of better-off
people who had a better than average chance of survival, because
they were likely to be well nourished and healthy and had the
chance to move away from infected areas. Here, among the
most prosperous of all, those summoned to attend Parliament as
lords, a mere 4½ per cent died in 1348, and 13 per cent in 1349;
among tenants 'in chief' of the Crown generally the figure for
1348–9 was much higher, 27 per cent. When one finds that for
the plague of 1361–2 the corresponding death rates turn out to
be 24 per cent and 22 per cent respectively, the significance of
even these relatively firm figures begins to look problematic.
Much lower down the social scale one can of course try analysing
manorial evidence concerning peasant tenants, principally from
court rolls, and some very startling figures for mortality emerge
if one does. Miss Page, looking at a series of Crowland Abbey
manors, found that, in 1348–9, 35 out of 50 tenants had died at
Oakington, 33 out of 58 at Cottenham, 20 out of 42 at Dry
Drayton (Ravensdale has corrected her figures for Cottenham,
to 22 out of 45: the other figures no doubt need adjusting too

but the scale remains uncomfortably around 50 per cent). On the Bishop of Winchester's manor of Bishop's Waltham 264 tenants died – nearly 66 per cent – and the level was comparable at Downton, Witney and Cuxham. But on the bishop's manor of Brightwell only about a third died in 1348. In 1361–2 the death rate generally seems to be very much lower than that, where it can be traced, though children are noted to have been especially badly hit. The fact is that manorial records are too scattered and their survival too haphazard to establish a reliable overall picture.

That is why so much attention has been concentrated on another class of sources, whose survival is much more regular, the records in bishops' registers of new institutions to church benefices. Registers of course often do not give the reason for the vacation of a benefice (by no means necessarily death), and their evidence relates only to a single sector of society, one arguably especially exposed to contagion, but at least the class is broad and the records reasonably systematic. Hamilton Thompson was the pioneer here in his 1911 survey of the northern archdiocese; Lunn in a 1937 thesis made a general survey. The picture that emerges is dramatically dismal in terms of sheer mortality; but at the same time it reveals some interesting variations. The Lichfield registers are particularly useful because they specify when a benefice was vacated by death (though not necessarily by a plague death): here the mortality rate was 40 per cent. In the Lincoln diocese the overall figure is similar, but varying from 28 per cent in the deanery of Groscote to just over 60 per cent in the deanery of Louth. In Ely the disparities are even sharper, 33 per cent in Barton and 75 per cent in Wisbech. The figures that Hamilton Thompson finally extracted from the York register, which is badly entered up and hard to interpret, are specially interesting in their variation, as the figures for the three deaneries of the Cleveland archdeaconry illustrate. In Bulmer deanery, a good arable district with populous village settlements, the death rate seems to be about 50 per cent. In Ryedale deanery, a hill-farming area, the figure drops to 28 per cent: in Cleveland itself, among the high moors, it drops still further, to 22 per cent. This pattern chimes well with the interesting remark of Archbishop FitzRalph of Armagh about the incidence of the plague in Ireland: 'the pestilence is believed to have destroyed two thirds of the English nation, but not, I am assured, to have done much harm to the nation of the Irish or Scots'. The Anglo-Irish settlers lived for the most part in nucleated villages and in towns: the Gaels, driven into the high ground, lived largely by herding beasts, and outside nuclear settlements. The Yorkshire evidence has to be handled with care, because of the widespread practice of non-residence among beneficed clergy; the incumbent of a parish in any given diocese may have died not there but somewhere far away. Even so, together with the Irish evidence it does seem to suggest that the impact of plague was sharper, often notably so, in areas of prosperous nuclear village settlement and in towns. There is other evidence which hints that, in the post-plague period, the remoter, highland areas of England may have had importance as reserves of manpower, and the reason seems likely to be that they were less severely hit by the plagues.

If it is hard to be dogmatic about the mortality of the plague of 1348–9, it is harder still to generalize about the cumulative demographic effect of the great pneumonic outbreaks of the fourteenth century, the plagues of 1348–9, 1361–2 and 1369. The trouble is again with the sources, and now it is still more acute. Only two sources provide figures on which a serious attempt to calculate the total medieval population of England can be based, the poll-tax returns of 1377 (which are post-plague), and the Domesday Book, from way back in 1086. Neither of course has a census quality: Domesday Book gives figures for households, and so an estimated average for the numbers in a household has to be used as a multiplier, and allowance has also to be made for areas omitted from the survey (much of northern England, and some important towns, including London and Winchester). The poll-tax returns omit clergy and children under fourteen, and allowance has in this case also to be made for substantial evasion. Worst of all, there is no comparable nationwide evidence on which to base any calculation of the growth of the population between 1086 and the first outbreak of plague. The indications are that it was very substantial, not to say spectacular: the evidence concerning the growth of towns, the taking into cultivation of marginal lands, of the splitting of manorial holdings into smaller and smaller units, all suggests that down to 1300 the increase in population was steady and very considerable. After that it may have been halted, even dented, by the serious famines of 1315–17. J. C. Russell, who used a 3.5 multiplier for the size of the household, calculated the Domesday population of England to be some 1.1 million, and suggested 2.25 million for 1377, on the basis of the poll-tax returns: he believed that the figure in 1348 stood at about 3.7 million. Postan and others, who believe his figures are too low throughout (and there is widespread agreement that 3.5 is too low a figure for the average household number), think in terms of over one and a half million in 1086, of perhaps around six million in 1300, and of about three million in 1377. The argument for the very high level attributed to *c.* 1300 does not depend on the Domesday and poll-tax aggregates, but on extrapolating a figure from the evidence of very dense population (which is certainly impressive for some regions, for example the Fens) around the turn of the thirteenth and fourteenth centuries. Thus according to one view, Postan's, there was a reduction of population by some 50 per cent or even more between *c.* 1300 and the late 1370s, not all the result of the plague though, since he believed that between 1300 and 1348 famine, soil exhaustion and Malthusian pressures in an overcrowded population were bringing the figures 'tumbling down'. According to the other, Russell's, there was a contraction of some 40 per cent or thereabout between 1348 and 1377. Most in the end come out with speculative suggestions for an enduring fall of something between a third and 40 per cent in the population overall, between the beginning and the end of the fourteenth century. Any attempt at greater precision rapidly degenerates into guess-work: but whatever way one looks at it, the figure for the drop in population level remains dismally high.

Given this, in some ways the most surprising thing about the Black Death of 1348–9 is not its impact, but, in the short term at least, how little seems to have changed because of it. Here is the most dramatic single event, arguably, of the fourteenth century, but the effects that catch the eye seem immediate and evanescent to a striking degree. There was no marked change after 1348 in

the pattern of government. The Christian church and the hold
of religion on men's minds remained unshaken and unaltered. In
1350 and in 1400 in the countryside we still move in the same
old world of lords and serfs that people knew before the plague.
There was indeed one major, overt governmental reaction to
the plague, the famous Statute of Labourers of 1351, which
sought to pin back wages and prices to pre-plague levels. Of this
more must be said presently: meantime it has to be pointed out
that, as Bridbury has shown, in the years between 1349 and
1375, agricultural prices remained high, and the ratio of prices to
wages was not altered much, if at all, from their pre-plague
correlation. The social and governmental structure and indeed
the economy of fourteenth-century England were, it seems,
strong enough to withstand the shock even of the dramatic
swathe cut through the population by the Black Death. There is
no sharp break at 1348–9 in institutional or religious or economic
history. In the longer term, the drastic reduction in the population level, if it was maintained (as in fact it was), was bound
to have profound effects, but there is surprisingly little that
is immediately apparent.

In a parallel way, English history offers no direct analogies to
the more hysterical reactions to the plague that are recorded
from the Continent. There is nothing to compare with the
excesses of the Rhineland flagellants or the hideous persecutions
of the Jews there and elsewhere. (There were, of course, no Jews
to persecute in England: they had been expelled by Edward I.)
Men explained the plague in the same terms as they did abroad,
of divine retribution brought down by men's wrong-doing on a
proud and sinful generation: the preacher in William Langland's
Piers Plowman 'proved these pestilences were for pure sin'. But
there is nothing like the frantic reactions that Villani and Boccaccio describe, when they tell of men with their moral restraints
unhinged fleeing to the country to take, while health was left,
what they still could of wine and sexual delights. We do hear in
1348 of how the king and court moved away from London, and
later, in correspondence such as that of the Pastons in the
fifteenth century, of prosperous people who had the means to
do so making for the country during the recurrent outbreaks of
plague in London; but that was just common sense. In England

all seems to be in rather a minor key when it comes to reaction. Some of the morbidities of late medieval English culture, the popularity of the concept of the *danse macabre* and of illustrations of it, or the cadaver tombs that portray beneath the effigy of the departed a second effigy of the rotting carrion degenerating into a skeleton, may be related to the mental impact of the recurrent plagues. Here, however, we are moving into a realm where all is a matter of suggestion, and nothing can be proved.

More directly telling, in terms of mental impact, is the evidence of the popularity of treatises on the plague and how to avoid it. The most important of these – the *ur*-text – is the *De pestilencia* of John of Burgundy, who proves to be (or to claim to be) the same as the famous Sir John Mandeville, the account of whose fictional travels in the Orient and Africa was popular and circulated widely. John of Burgundy's work was translated into English, as was also an abbreviated version of it attributed to one John of Bordeaux. There are twenty-two manuscripts of this work in the British Library alone, of which seventeen are the English version, and there are eleven more copies in Oxford and Cambridge libraries. Another abbreviation of John of Bordeaux, this one in Latin, was made by an English author: the fullest texts have this introduction:

this letter was made in Oxford in the time of the pestilence by the masters and doctors of King Henry IV in the 8th year of his reign [1407, a plague year], and was sent by him to the Mayor of London where it was greatly praised by many physicians, apothecaries and others.

Another plague tract that circulated in England and was translated into English was that by the fifteenth-century Scandinavian cleric, Bergt Knutsson: two printed editions appeared in 1480 and a third in 1485. This was a distinctly substantial output on the subject, for the time, and the number of English versions of the continental works shows how much men's minds were occupied by it.

The means of prophylaxis recommended in these treatises were not, of course, medically sound ones. The author of the Latin tract that was purportedly sent to Henry IV made it clear that clean living, 'that shall be pleasing to God', was the only

true safeguard, echoing the view that retribution for sin was at
the root of pestilence. 'Beloved brother,' he opens,

I hear thou goest in great fear of the plague . . . but surely a little faith
would reassure thee . . . by contrition of the heart, and true confession
to God, give thyself to better things, for assuredly from a healthy mind
comes health of body . . . and when thy soul is washed clean from sin,
thus mayest thou preserve thy body from this pestilential malady.

John of Burgundy was more directly scientific, in aspiration at
least. He believed that the plague was carried on 'pestilential air',
and that a healthy, temperate life was therefore the best defence.
He recommended exercise, a light diet, aromatic wines – and the
avoidance of baths, since hot water opens the pores in the skin
and so facilitates the penetration of 'pestilential air'. In cold or
misty weather it was wise to keep windows shut and to purify
the air indoors by burning juniper branches or sprinkling a
patent powder on the fire (obtainable from a Low Countries
apothecary of his recommendation). It could be useful to carry
in the hand a *pomum arbre*, a kind of block of expensive drugs,
mostly resinous. Bergt Knutsson had a more plebeian and readily
available version of this. On his travels, he wrote, he always
carried

a sponge, or else bread put in vinegar, and bear it with me, putting it
to my nose and to my mouth. For why? All manner of sharp liquors
such as vinegar, and such others, they stop the ways of the humours
and cause that venomous things shall not enter. And by this means I
scaped pestilence.

There was clearly no lack of demand for patent medicines and
recipes. For actual sufferers bleeding was recommended, and
here care should be taken, it was said, to identify the diseased
side of the body and to bleed from that: otherwise good blood
from the healthy side would be let out and infected blood from
the other would flow in to restore the balance, rather as water
finds its own level. Perhaps Thomas fforestier, another plague
author, who dedicated his work to Henry VII, had a point when
he remarked, among other and woollier counsels, that on the

whole it was probably a good idea, as far as possible, to avoid doctors.

The plague tracts and their popularity attest the concern that pestilence naturally aroused, and a thoroughly understandable anxiety for prophylaxis. Their tone, though, is decidedly un-hysterical, indeed pretty rational, even if the medicine is un-scientific. If we wish to see where plague really did leave a profound and clearly identifiable mark we must look not to mental reactions, nor (as we have seen) to the realm of govern-ment, but to the world of work, to that 'dearth of servants for all kinds of labour' that Knighton remarked on. He was writing of the effects of the first pestilence, of 1348, but the phenomenon was not a passing one. Over the decades following the first outbreaks of plague, the losses in population were not replaced: the downturn in the population level proved to be a lasting one, and the consequence, scarcity of labour, was enduring. This brings us up against yet another of the great problems of plague history in late medieval England, why the replacement rate after the mortality remained, apparently, so low.

The opposite is what we should have expected. Relatively rapid replacement of lost population has characterized more recent pandemics, for instance in Asia at the beginning of this century. Besides, in post-plague England there were fewer mouths to feed, and scarcity of labour was putting upward pressure on wage rates in real terms. There was more per capita wealth in the population, the poor were better nourished and new opportunities for raising their standard of living were opening to them. This ought to have encouraged earlier mar-riage, greater fertility and a consequently rising birth rate. But it did not. All sorts of reasons have been advanced for this, including modification of marriage customs (and as will be seen in due course there may be something in this, even though it does fly in the face of rational expectation). The most convincing general explanation, however, is that which looks to the cum-ulative effect of recurrent plague, combined with the effects of famine, and of other diseases besides plague that were rife in the society.

In particular, the fact that in later outbreaks children seem to

have been especially at risk appears significant. The point was
well noted. The Meaux chronicle describes the outbreak of
1361-2 as 'the second pestilence, which is called the plague of
infants': Walsingham describes that of 1390 as 'a great plague,
especially of youths and young children, who died everywhere
in towns and villages, in incredible and excessive numbers'. The
phenomenon was indeed sufficiently marked for some to give it
a special place in the explanation of plague in terms of divine
wrath: as did the preacher who surmised that

it may be for vengeance of this sin of unworshipping and despising of
fathers and mothers that God slayeth children by pestilence, as ye see
everyday; for in the old law children that were rebel and unbuxom to
their fathers and mothers were i-punished with death, as the fifth book
of Holy Writ witnesseth.

If children, because they had no chance to develop immunity,
were particularly prone to the later plagues, then that would
mean that after each successive major epidemic, 'the fertility
schedule would be lowered for a decade or more, as depleted
cohorts reached marriageable and child-bearing age' (Hatcher).
Child mortality, reducing the ability of the population to re-
produce itself because too few children grew up to the age
where they could do their bit in reproduction, seems the best
explanation of the enduring drop in the level of the population
of England in the late middle ages. In the absence of parish
registers it is impossible to give its significance any sharp statistical definition; but its importance is not easy to doubt.

What we can, however, be quite sure about is the effect of the
drop in the population on the labour market. The one really
striking reaction of the government to the first onset of the
plague was the Ordinance of Labourers of 1349. This was
enlarged and amended into a statute in 1351 because, as its
preamble states,

servants, having no regard to the ordinance, but to their own ease and
covetousness, do withdraw themselves from serving great men and
others, unless they have living [in food] and wages double or treble of

what they were wont to take in the 20th year [of the king's reign: i.e.
in 1346–7] and earlier, to the great damage of all the community.

The ordinance and the statute that followed it up were the first
attempts ever of an English government to legislate generally on
the subject of wages and prices. The most important clauses of
the statute established maximum wage levels (the levels of 1346–7
serving as a guide); confirmed to their personal lords (or to
their contracted masters in the case of journeymen) their prior
claim on their labourers' services; and enjoined that absconding
labourers should be brought before commissions of justices of
labourers appointed in each county, to be first punished and
then returned to their masters. Prices of manufactured goods
were fixed at their pre-plague level; those of foodstuffs were to
be 'reasonable'. The object of the act was clear and straightforward, to hold up the economic weather by protecting the
interests of lords and employers (the great men) against any and
all attempts on the part of the rest of the population to exploit
the favourable opportunities which the new shortage of labour
opened for them, and so to preserve the existing – and threatened
– social hierarchy.

For something like a quarter of a century the Statute of
Labourers was not ineffective in achieving its objects. It bound
all able-bodied men, whether bond or free, and was rigorously
enforced. Some extraneous factors also helped to cushion lords
and employers against the effects of the plague for a time.
Before the plague, land had been in such sharp demand that
most lords had little difficulty in filling vacant holdings after
1349: and a succession of poor harvests in the 1350s and 1360s
kept the prices of agricultural products at a high level. Besides,
the vigorous enforcement of the repressive statute was only part
of a general 'seigneurial reaction' to changed circumstances:
landlords found other legal means as well of protecting their
interests.

Manorial lords in particular could achieve much by more
rigorous exploitation of their rights at law over their unfree
tenants – their bondmen; by insisting on their preferential right
to their labour, by making the most out of manorial dues such
as *merchet* (the fine leviable on a bondwoman's marriage) and

leyrwite (the fine leviable for a bondwoman's fornication), and
of seigneurial monopolies (of milling, for instance, or of baking
and brewing). Post-plague conditions had besides added to the
significance of bond tenures from a landlord's point of view.
Though common law favoured the lord, manorial custom had
always given a protection to bond tenants that was not ineffective, and in practice it was hard for a lord to alter its time-
honoured usages. Before the plagues, the fact that the customary
dues and services that bond tenants owed – and the rates at
which these were commuted into money payments – were in
consequence relatively inflexible had often been an advantage to
them, pinning the value of their dues and services at a low level
in monetary terms. That is why some landlords preferred,
when opportunity arose, to offer leases to tenants who were not
their bondmen and were not so protected by the custom of the
manor, and who in those land-hungry times were prepared to
pay something more like a 'going rate'. When, after the plagues,
demand for land slackened and its value collapsed, this situation
was reversed, and the initial reaction of landlords was therefore
to assert their rights over their bond tenants with renewed
vigour, because the worth of their dues and services at customary
rates was now greater than the 'free market' value. So effective
was the general 'seigneurial reaction' that, Professor Holmes
finds, income from landed properties in the 1370s was 'generally
not 10 per cent lower than it had been in the 1340s': indeed it is
arguable, he suggests, that between 1349 and 1380 the great
man, the magnate, 'far from suffering from the effects of the
Black Death, was consuming a rather higher proportion of
the national income than before, and this may still have been the
case even if the national income had declined less than the
population'.

The overall effect of this on the way in which things developed
over the twenty to thirty years following the 'first pestilence'
was to generate a greater cohesion between the groups standing
on either side of the great dividing line in society between those
who worked for themselves and for others, and those who
depended on the work of others to maintain them, and to
exacerbate the natural tensions between them. The greater lords
and the classes that sent representatives to Parliament, that is to

say those who belonged to the latter group, were drawn closer together by a sharpened identity in their interests as employers of labour. So in 1376 we find Parliament issuing a warning to master craftsmen not to apprentice men from townships where there was a scarcity of labour, and in 1377 a Commons petition seeking redress generally against 'villeins and those who hold in villeinage' who are 'refusing the customs and services due to their lords ... for by colour of certain exemplifications out of Domesday Book they claim they are quit and utterly discharged of all serfdom'. On the other side we hear not only of 'great rumours' and of banding together to claim freedom, but also of attacks on the sessions of justices of labourers, of rescues of offenders from their custody and of seditious popular preaching that posed the disconcerting question

> When Adam delved and Eve span
> Who was then the gentleman?

The pent-up anger broke in the Peasants' Revolt of 1381. This movement, which saw the commons of Kent and Essex converging on London in June of that year and large-scale rebellion throughout East Anglia, together with scattered risings elsewhere, was the most general, the most alarming and the most concerted popular revolt of English medieval history. For a few days from 12 to 15 June, when the rebels held control of the capital, royal government appeared to be paralysed and at its mercy. The rebellion cannot of course be explained simply as the inevitable reaction to three decades of widespread seigneurial oppression following the first onset of the plague. The spark that ignited the flame of revolt was the effort to collect in full the poll tax of 1380, levied at the unprecedented rate of three groats (12d.) a head, a fiscal burden imposed by the imperious demands of war (but which represented also, it must be added, a typical effort on the part of the prosperous to shift more of that burden on to the shoulders of those whom they regarded as the newly and unreasonably advantaged labouring classes). A sharper political consciousness at the humbler social level also had something to do with the rising. There was a clear sense among the rebels that the ruling élite had recently been mismanaging things,

notably in that inadequate defence measures had laid the Channel
coast open to French attack. They knew, and by name, whom
they wished to hold responsible for misgovernment: John of
Gaunt, eldest of the young King Richard's uncles ('we will have
no king called John' was one of their passwords); the Chancellor,
Archbishop Simon Sudbury; the Treasurer, Sir Robert Hales,
Prior of the Hospital of St John; the sergeant-at-law John Legge,
who was blamed for the rigorous inquiries into evasions of the
poll tax. The last three of these were dragged from the Tower
and executed by the peasants during the brief days in which the
rebels were in control in London.

There was also a rudimentary ideological level to the revolt.
It is perhaps most marked in the demands of the rebels for
'freedom', for the abolition of serfdom and equality of status
before the law, which are a feature of all accounts of the reforms
that they demanded. Langland says that revolutionary friars
were preaching a kind of primitive communism:

> They preach men by Plato and proven it by Seneca
> That all things under heaven ought to be in common.

The little letters which, according to the continuator of
Knighton's chronicle, circulated among the rebels, certainly show
ideas and phrases culled from sermons and literary social satire percolating down to an unexpected social level. 'Jack Trewman doth
you to understand that falseness and guile have reigned too
long,' begins one: and here is another:

Jack Carter prays you all that ye make a good end of that ye have
begun, and do well and aye better and better ... Let Piers the
Plowman my brother dwell at home and dight us corn, and I will go
with you and help that I may to dight your meat and your drink, that
ye none fail: look that Hobbe the Robber be well chastised for losing
of your grace, for ye have great need to take God with you in all your
deeds.

Here we can see the effect of the growth of literacy in a wider
social cross-section at work in the revolt, alongside the economic
effects, primary and secondary, of the plagues. We also see at the
same time signs that, in the Home Counties at least, people at a

distinctly humble level were sharply aware of contemporary political issues, personalities and problems, and capable of reacting sharply to them.

There is no doubt, however, about the underlying importance of matters that were consequent upon the plagues, or about the sharp and discernible mark that they left on the story of the revolt. They show clearly in the widespread resentment of serfdom, which had been so harshly exploited in the decades following 1348; witness the charters of manumission demanded and obtained from King Richard at Blackheath; the burning of court rolls that recorded servitude at St Benet's Holme, at Canterbury, at the Abbey of the Holy Cross at Waltham; and the accounts of John Ball in his sermons calling on men to 'lay aside the yoke of serfdom'. The demand of Wat Tyler, the Kentish leader, at Smithfield that 'no one should work for any man but at his own will, and on terms of regular covenant' aimed a clear and direct blow at the clause in the Statute of Labourers that gave a lord a preferential hold over his men's labour and demanded the freedom to negotiate on wages that it inhibited. The rebels of 1381 openly sought the advantages that the new post-plague conditions ought to have given them, and which they had been denied; and it was the systematic denial of those advantages that brought a popular movement on the scale of that of 1381 into the range of possibilities.

It is usually said that the Peasants' Revolt had small consequences, and it is true that the end of June 1381 saw the rebels everywhere dispersed, and their charters of manumission were quashed within little over a month from the height of the rebellion. I believe that this approach underestimates the terrible shock to the governing classes of the events of the 'hurling time'. Gower's description of the peasant 'rabble' under the guise of animals at the beginning of his poem *Vox clamantis* reveals the alarmed anger of one eyewitness and tells of his fears for a society in which this sort of thing could happen, fears shared by many other ordinary landowners, and which took a long time to die down. The nervousness that they generated undermined the seigneurial reaction that had characterized the period between 1348 and 1381. Though the Statute of Labourers was re-enacted (and some of its clauses stiffened) in 1388, the vigour went out of its enforcement. Wages, which had been moving up since the mid-1370s, stabilized at a comparatively high level in real terms. Perhaps most important of all, no Parliament after 1381 dared again to impose a poll tax. The idea behind that tax had been to transfer a greater share of the burden of war taxation from the genteel to the labouring classes: it was of a piece, that is to say, with the sort of development that overseas, in France for instance, made the 'commons' responsible almost totally for direct taxation, and entrenched the *noblesse*, greater and lesser, in fiscal immunity. The fears generated by the Peasants' Revolt made sure that in England things would not go that way, and this had much to do with the fact that a juridical, privileged noble class on the continental model did not develop in England – which was one of the most individual and striking features distinguishing her social system from that of other West European lands at the end of the middle ages. The opportunities for social mobility, both vertically and in lateral, geographic terms, that the impact of the plagues had opened up were instead allowed remarkably free play; and that in turn was why English society emerged from the medieval period less rigidly stratified than was the case with most of her continental neighbours, with numerous gradations, indeed, but without sharp juridical barriers between them.

One further aspect of the evidence relating to the social impact of demographic decline in the post-plague period demands mention. It is abundantly clear that the times saw new opportunities opening up for working men, especially when, after 1381, the vigour began to go out of seigneurial efforts to maintain the pre-plague status quo. As recent work by Dr J. Goldberg has revealingly stressed, they also saw new opportunities for women in work. This, in its turn, may have something to do with the markedly slow replacement rate of the lost population.

Of course there was nothing novel, in the late fourteenth century, about women in work. Whether their womenfolk worked or not was one of the traditional dividing lines between the humble and the more well-to-do. Among the former, women had always taken their part, notably in the labour of agricultural communities, and heavy work it could be too:

gleaning, stacking the sheaves at harvest, walking beside the plough, as well as tending the dairy, spinning and brewing. What seems different in the post-plague period is a new degree of independence for women in work in consequence of the changed situation in the labour market. In the records of the hustings court in the City of London we begin to hear, and quite frequently, of women, not necessarily unmarried, trading as *femme sole*, who in that capacity could sue and be sued, and could make valid business contracts. The guild regulations reveal that women could obtain the freedom of the city, and so become burgage tenants in their own right (though they could not vote in elections for city offices as free men could). We hear also of girls being apprenticed in the London guilds (apprenticeship was indeed one of the ways of obtaining the freedom of the city). Dr Jenny Kermode has observed the same kind of developments in northern towns: women discharging works that one would expect to be male preserves (there were two women smiths in Sheffield in 1379): women entering on apprenticeships: and single women appearing in the poll-tax returns as heads of households. Above all, in these returns, the significance of women in 'service' stands out, and not in domestic but in trade service, as wool carders, spinners and weavers, or at piece-work making pins or nails.

Service in this sense was in high demand. The household in this time was commonly also the workshop; in northern towns studied by Goldberg and Kermode about one household in three included servants. The names given in the poll-tax returns show that though some of the girls listed as 'servants' were members of the family, a good many were not, and it looks as if there was some migration into the towns, often perhaps temporary, of young women from rural areas. In service to the craft sector of the towns, these women could play an economically active role, acquiring real skills. This put them in a position to save money, perhaps to provide a dowry when they returned home to their village, and so helped to offer a new freedom of choice in marriage.

The last point is a particularly significant one (and there are signs of it, we should note, in the countryside as well as the towns; for instance in the increasing frequency in court rolls of records of women paying their own fees for merchet, the fine leviable to the lord when a bondwoman married, and traditionally paid by her father). We get a hint of what begins to look like a shift in the pattern of the life-cycle of a working woman, one that takes her more frequently into work, and remunerated work, especially in the years before marriage. The evidence of church court records, for instance the depositions of the York consistory court, seem to confirm this. Testamentary evidence of wills proved there reveals a good number of unmarried women disposing of chattels which one can only presume that they had put together out of the fruit of earnings. Matrimonial litigation suggests individual feelings behind the arrangements – or disarrangements – that gave rise to suits, hinting at relations based in affection between partners who had chosen each other independently of family pressures. The general picture emerging is of conditions in which there were more opportunities for unmarried women to maintain themselves singly through work, and opportunities in work that could lead women to postpone marriage. Later marriages mean fewer children: fewer children the slowing down of the rate of population replacement. Because hard evidence regarding age at marriage is virtually unobtainable, one can only be very tentative here, but it does look as if that encouragement to early marriage which the rise in per capita wealth among the male population after the plagues would lead us to expect may have been offset, in part at least, by new chances for women of putting together some little competence for themselves by postponing it.

It is noticeable that when, in the later fifteenth century, signs appear that the population level was starting very slowly to pick up again, signs also appear of 'male domination' reasserting itself. We hear of women, in a number of northern towns, being excluded from the weaving guilds in the 1450s. The records of female apprenticeships in London begin to fade out with the end of the century. In a more competitive labour market, the position of women, it seems, once again began to be marginalized. But in a way that only makes the atypical conditions of the intervening period the more striking. That the demographic decline of the post-plague generations should for a time have altered markedly the work opportunities not just for one sex but for both is in its way more telling testimony to the impact of this decline than any number of bishops' registers with their tallies of benefices vacated by death during the pestilences.*

<hr />

* I must acknowledge the strong influence on the last section of this chapter of the writing and ideas of Dr J. Goldberg, which have opened up the subject of women in work in the late medieval period in important new ways.

3. The Life of the Countryside

Over time, every sector of English society was affected profoundly in one way or another by the fall in population level subsequent to the great plagues of the fourteenth century. In a kingdom in which nine out of ten people lived on and by the land, it was natural that the effect should leave a very deep mark on the life of the countryside. In the immediate aftermath of the first pestilence, it is true, things did not change much. The pressure of population on the available land had been such before the plague that most landlords did not experience very much difficulty in finding tenants who would take up vacant holdings on the same sort of terms as their dead predecessors. Here and there landlords even managed to increase the level of the dues that they expected from their new tenants to above their pre-plague level. But the 'seigneurial reaction' of the decades following 1348 could not hold up the weather indefinitely, as we have already seen. The whole balance of social relations and economic pressures in the countryside had been thrown out by the mortality, and time made the consequences apparent: a collapse in the demand for tenant land, acute shortage of labour and falling prices for arable produce as demand slackened.

If one is to understand how these factors made themselves felt and how they impinged on the lives of country dwellers, one must know something of the structure of rural society before it was struck by the Black Death. In the first part of this chapter, therefore, we must consider what, up to then, had given it its cohesion; how the land was tilled, what bound the villager to his lord and to his neighbours, what the pattern of his life and living were. Then, in the second part of the chapter we can look at how the structures were modified and even, in some respects, radically altered by the changed economic and demographic conditions.

★

Before 1300 the contours of land settlement in England had already reached a point where they would not change very much until well into the modern period. Earlier centuries had witnessed a long, arduous and cumulatively mighty process of reclamation of land through the clearing of wood, the drainage of marshland and the ploughing of waste. Some of this work of reclamation had been directed by enterprising landlords: some was the fruit of the individual labour of single peasant families who with axe and spade had slowly wrested a plot of land from the moor or forest around an isolated homestead that in due course became a little farm. But far and away the greatest contribution was made by settled village communities which gradually extended by collective efforts the land available to them for cultivation and grazing, expanding steadily over a very long period into the waste land around their settlements and infilling unreclaimed ground. That still left a good deal of land that the sources describe as 'waste', for 'waste' was necessary to survival: there had to be woodland in which to gather firewood and to pannage pigs, and uncultivated commons for the pasturing of villagers' beasts. Parish boundaries were mainly settled by *c.* 1100, and well before 1300 continuous reclamation and the land-hunger generated by population pressure had generally carried village boundaries to their limits, so that the fields of one village marched with those of another. Whence the custom of 'beating the bounds' annually, in order to warn neighbouring communities against encroachment. Very nearly all the villages of present-day England are on sites that were long settled in 1300 and the same is true even of a good many isolated farmsteads. Indeed more villages have disappeared than have grown up, for a good many were deserted, as we shall see, in the generations following the great plagues.

England is a country of thoroughly varied landscape and soils; naturally, in the past as now, these imposed differences of land use and field systems in different regions. The economy of what has come to be known as the Highland Zone (Northumberland, the north-west, the West Riding of Yorkshire; Hereford, Shropshire and Cheshire in the Welsh marches; Devon, Cornwall and parts of Somerset) was mainly pastoral. Of course there was everywhere some arable land: in an age of poor communications

and high transportation costs it was universally necessary to
grow some cereals, if only for subsistence. In this zone isolated
farmsteads abounded, with their small enclosed fields often
abutting on the moory waste of the higher ground. There were
many hamlets and what is called the 'infield–outfield' system of
cultivation was common. The 'infield', the better land close to
the settlement, was heavily manured and ploughed yearly: in
addition an 'outfield', a tract of the extensive common or waste,
was ploughed and sown for a few years, until its fertility was
exhausted, when it would revert to pasture while another tract
of waste was cultivated. In virtually every county, however,
there were some settlements that followed the system known as
the 'open-field' system of cultivation (which was by no means
incompatible with infield–outfield cultivation: in some villages
both schemes were followed simultaneously, on different parts
of the village land). In the Lowland Zone, the midlands and
southern and eastern England, the open-field system predominated. Arable cultivation was its focus, and was the preoccupation
that shaped the lives and the social relations of the inhabitants of
the substantial, nucleated villages characteristic of this 'champion'
country.

As has been said, the reclamation of the land that by 1300 had
come under the plough was, for the most part, the communal
achievement of villagers, and the open-field system of farming
was communal likewise. Almost everyone must be familiar with
its outline, have seen at some time an ideal picture of a medieval
village, with its cottages clustering around the church and the
manor house, surrounded by two or more probably three great
unfenced fields, perhaps of several hundred acres, divided into
strips and cultivated on a rotation of crops: winter cereals, spring
cereals and fallow (with legumes, peas, beans and vetch sometimes added into the spring leg of the rotation). The strip maps
of the sixteenth and later centuries give accurate detail to this
ideal picture. They show the strips (or 'selions', reckoned as one
day's ploughing) laid out in blocks (furlongs) running this way
and that in the field with the lie of the land for ease of
ploughing and drainage, and the green balks or common ways
that gave access to them. They show how the strips of individual
tenants (and in the middle ages probably those of the lord's

demesne too) were scattered over the whole field, making a
patchwork of proprietorship and ensuring a roughly equitable
distribution of poor and better land (and so of heavier and
lighter labour) to each holding. This made perfectly good sense
agriculturally as well as socially; the long strips cut the time lost
turning the plough at the end of the furrow, and each tenant
could get on with the cultivation of his own plot in manageable
sections and in rough pace with his fellows (very desirable when
two or three might, for instance, have to pool their oxen to
make a plough team, and when the tenants, as a condition of
tenure, could have to contribute their labour and perhaps their
beasts to cultivate the lord's shares in the field). Above all,
though, this system imposed the necessity of a measure of
communal control and organization of the processes of agriculture, which is why, in its developed form, it is often known as
the 'common-field' system.

Some control of cooperation in ploughing was clearly necessary, if only to define who was to help whom and when: 'it is
found by an inquisition of neighbours that Richard de Tuthill
was the companion of Roger de Bosco to plough jointly,' runs
an entry in the Wakefield court rolls, 'but at the time of
ploughing Roger cast him off so that his land lies untilled'.
Cooperative control of sowing was still more obviously vital.
Wheat and rye were the chief bread crops and sown in autumn:
the spring sowing was of oats, barley, peas and beans, sown so as
to ripen about the same time as the autumn crops, so that the
whole harvest could be cleared over one period at the end of the
summer and the fields then turned over to pasture. Harvest
itself, precariously dependent on the weather, above all
demanded cooperation. It was heavily labour-intensive. Barley
and oats were cut with the scythe, wheat with the sickle, back-
breaking work: binders must follow the reapers to gather and tie
the corn into sheaves and stack them into shocks to dry (one
binder to four reapers, usually). Inevitably a good many ears of
corn were lost in the process of gathering and binding: gleaners
must follow to save this share of the harvest. It was imperative
that while good weather lasted all hands should be available,
men and women alike. 'No woman at harvest time who is able
to work and willing to receive a penny a day for wages and

food for her refreshment in the field shall be allowed to glean,' runs an ordinance of the manor of Basingstoke, Hants. (gleaning was to be left to children and the elderly till the heavy work was finished). 'All manner labourers that dwell in the township and have commons among us shall work harvest work . . . for their hire reasonable as custom is, and not go to other towns but if they have no other work . . . if they do, they shall be chastized as the law wills,' declared an ordinance of Wymeswold in Leicestershire. The Statute of Labourers made much the same point, with the overt object of protecting the lord's rights to tenant labour, especially at harvest. But it was not just to the lord's interest but to that of the whole community that at harvest all able-bodied hands should be available and at work in the fields, for on the harvest the whole community depended to keep famine from the door over the coming year.

So far we have been concentrating on human labour and the arable crop; but animals were just as crucial as workmen to this system of farming, and their needs likewise imposed a measure of communal control. Sheep, with their fleeces, were probably more valuable as a cash crop than were cereals to the peasant farmer, and the richer customary tenants might sometimes have quite substantial flocks to graze. Dairy produce, whey, cheese and buttermilk were important elements in peasant diet. Besides and above all, animals provided the vital source of motive power for agriculture, oxen to draw the plough, harrow and farm cart, and horses for larger waggons. The great problem on the animal side of open-field husbandry was the provision of feed through the year, and every acre brought under the plough made it more formidable. Though there might be a considerable slaughter of beasts in the autumn, enough had to be maintained, for stock, for draught, for milking, and in the case of sheep to maintain a worthwhile flock. This was why a portion of the village land, perhaps near a stream, was always reserved as meadow (for hay): this was shared out in lots like the strips in the open fields, and because hay was so vital, shares in the meadow, acre for acre, were usually valued more highly (sometimes much more highly) than arable strips. This was also what made the right of the customary tenant to pasture beasts upon the common so important (and imposed a need, too, to limit the

number of beasts he might so pasture). The only other sources
of pasture were the fallows, and the stubble left after harvest, on
which, as soon as the crops were in, the beasts of the villagers
were driven out to graze until the next ploughing. Because
pasture was so precious there had to be communal regulation of
when the beasts were to be allowed on to the stubble and when
they were to be off it: there could be no question of waiting
because one man was lazy with his reaping, or of incommoding
it by letting the first to get their corn gathered put their beasts in
the field while harvest work was still in progress. 'No one shall
pasture or consume any stubble with any beasts during autumn
before the feast of the nativity of the Blessed Virgin [8 Septem-
ber],' according to an ordinance of Burwell, Cambridgeshire.
On the Huntingdonshire manors of Ramsey Abbey the corresponding date was Michaelmas. At Aylsham in Norfolk a 'shack
bell' was rung to give the signal that the harvest was deemed
to be over and that beasts could be driven on to the stubble to
pasture.

The need for cooperation in the tilling and harvesting of their
fields generated a strong sense of identity and of social cohesion
in the village community. We can see this in the way in which
people from outside the village were described as 'strangers' or
'foreigners' in manor-court rolls, and in the strict regulations
laid down about harbouring them. The tendency for holdings to
be handed down in the same family, generation after generation
(until the aftermath of the Black Death opened up new opportunities for mobility), no doubt strengthened the sense of
identity. The cohesion of the village community is also reflected,
and strikingly, in village by-laws that we encounter from time
to time in the court rolls. These were the products of meetings,
held with the lord's approval, of the villagers themselves. 'It is
ordered that all tenants shall be ready to come to the plebiscite
(*sic*) when summoned and to obey the by-laws established and
ordered by them,' runs a note in a Fountains Abbey manor-
court roll. By-laws dealt with all sorts of details of agricultural
relations – harvest labour, the right to glean, the tethering of
beasts on stubble when the harvest was not yet fully gathered –
and with other aspects of life too. 'All the tenants of the lord,

free and bond, are agreed that if any of them takes his neighbours to a tavern outside the village, he shall incur a penalty of 12d.,' declares one by-law of Newington Longueville, Bucks.; another orders that 'no pauper shall gather beans among the strips but only at the head and along the edges'. 'No one shall admit any stranger to gleaning,' says a by-law of Great Horwood. The village was indeed a tight community; it was one thing to allow one's own paupers to gather peas or beans between the strips (a very common custom), quite another to admit a foreigner to gleaning, unless someone would stand surety for him.

We know about village by-laws chiefly from manor-court rolls. Village and manor might coincide, but they did not necessarily do so. The manor of Halesowen in Worcestershire encompassed no less than twelve villages. In contrast, in the village of Wymeswold in Leicestershire there were three manors: so when in 1425 the villagers wished to establish some by-laws, a gathering had to be held of the whole township together with the representatives of the three manorial lords (Sir John Neville, Sir Hugh Willoughby, and the Abbot of Beauchief). In the former case, Halesowen, each village had its own fields but all were subject to the same lord and the same court; in the latter case, strips belonging to the different manors were mingled in the same fields, but the services and dues owed by those who tilled them were owing to different lords, to whichever of the three the farmer of an individual strip or strips was bound. The village was the vital social and agricultural community, the manor an administrative unit. Where, as at Wymeswold, the village and its fields included more than one manor, meetings of the villagers were probably more important than elsewhere, virtually a necessity in order to coordinate the agricultural efforts of farmers who in law were responsible to different manor courts.

The manor court is most often principally considered as the institution through which the lord exploited his seigneurial rights. It was indeed a vital instrument to this end, for it was through this court and its judgements that the lord enforced his right to the labour of his customary tenants (or to payments in lieu), to *heriots* (the best beast of a dead tenant, a kind of death duty), to entry fines from incoming tenants, to merchet when a bondman's daughter married, and his monopolies, as of milling, perhaps of baking too. The custom of the manor which its court enforced ensured that the lord's land was cultivated and that his dues were paid in full; and the fines imposed for breaches of the rules went to add to his profits. In Marxist terms, it ensured that the best part of any profitable surplus from the labour of the lord's tenants was creamed off to his advantage.

This side of the activity of the manor court can, however, be overstressed. Significantly, the reeve, the manorial official on whose organizing competence its efficient operation largely depended, was not normally the lord's nominee, but was chosen by the customary tenants from among themselves; he was quite as much their representative as the lord's. Under the open-field system, the court was in fact almost as vital to the tenants as it was to the lord. For them it was the means of ensuring their reciprocal rights and obligations towards one another, of imposing sanctions on those who let their beasts stray on to the cultivated lands, or who let their strips grow unruly so that weeds and thistles spread into their neighbours' crops, or who would not help in maintaining roads and common ways. It was in the manor court that they sued each other for trespass and for debt, and enforced an elementary degree of policing in their own society. Above all, the manor court was for them the medium for regularizing their mutual transactions, especially sales and exchanges of land, for there was a brisk land market among the peasantry. The plots involved were usually very small, an acre or so here or there of which one tenant wished to dispose, perhaps because he was getting elderly, or in order to raise cash for some commitment (perhaps he had borrowed to buy beasts or some equipment, and was pressed for repayment), or in hard times so as to buy food for himself and his family. There was no lack of buyers among tenants who wished to build up a holding for a second or third son, or to put together a little dowry for a daughter – at least until plague mortality put a period to land hunger. The record of the transaction in the court roll furnished the evidence that it had the lord's approval (he charged a fine for making the record), for in common law, as opposed to the customary law of the manor, the land was his; and so the court-roll entry provided a kind of title deed for the purchaser. In effect, the manor was what institutionalized the community of the village, and that is why manorial records are our principal evidence for the structure of its social life.

Among villagers there would normally be considerable variations of wealth, as the operation of the peasant land market would lead us to expect. At the top of the scale stood those (usually a small minority) whose holdings in the fields totalled more than one virgate (a variable measure, but say about thirty acres). These men and their families formed the village aristocracy, and these richer villagers, if there were enough of them, could more or less monopolize as reeves, jurors, messors and ale tasters the coveted manorial offices. Those with rather less, say half a virgate or a quarter, were the most numerous; such holdings were just about sufficient to maintain them and their families in subsistence, but with precious little left over (and in hard seasons nothing). The poorest group, the cottagers, with perhaps a garden or at most an acre or two in the fields, were dependent on what they could earn, in money or kind, by labouring for others: in thin times they were likely to be the first to go to the wall. The labour services which the bond tenants owed to their lord (but which could be and very often were commuted for a money rent) were assessed upon their holdings in the fields; in this sense the cottager was freer than his wealthier neighbour, but the economic distinctions between the groups to which families belonged, rich, middling or poorer, were more important, probably, to the villagers than the legal measure of their freedom. Bond status did indeed impose severe limitations. Without the lord's leave the servile tenant could not sell his land, or marry his daughter, or put his children to school, and there were always a host of dues to which he was subject, boon work (extra services at ploughing and harvest), tallages (arbitrary levies), wood-silver (a payment for access to the lord's wood for timber and firewood) and heriot (the tender to the lord of the best beast of a dead tenant). His tenure of his plot was unprotected at common law: the lord was the legal owner. There was also a measure of social stigma commonly associated with servile condition. Nevertheless, within the village community what really mattered was whether a man was well or ill off in comparative terms, how many strips he had in the fields and how many beasts, and into which neighbouring families his children were likely to be accepted in marriage. In the year's hard round of agricultural labour these were what decided how he and his would fare, and also whether they had any chance of prospering beyond their original lot.

Though agriculture was the principal occupation of most villagers, it was by no means the sole occupation of all. Every village would have some craftsmen, as smiths, carpenters, tailors and bakers (most peasants did not make their own clothes, and most cooked over open fires and so could not bake). Brewing was an occupation in which a good many tenants engaged, and in which women were often prominent. To sell ale one had only to put up a sign, to show it was for sale, so that taverns were for the most part private houses too; but in some villages there was a regular tavern (that was where the villagers of Crowcombe in Somerset, for instance, held celebrations to raise money for their church). The miller was of course an important village figure: Chaucer's miller is one of the most prosperous of his rustic types – 'he had a thumb of gold, pardee'. The miller's skill was vital, for corn must be ground into flour before it could make the bread that was the ultimate bedrock of subsistence.

A good deal of medieval industry, moreover, was rurally based. The later middle ages saw a very substantial movement of the profitable cloth industry away from urban centres and into the countryside, which brought a new prosperity to areas such as the Cotswolds and the West Riding, good sheep-rearing districts where water power could easily be harnessed to drive fulling mills. Some other industries were traditionally rural. The lead mines of Chewton and other places in the Mendips were worked by men who had holdings in the common fields of their villages (perhaps half a virgate or less), like the ordinary agricultural tenants who were their neighbours. In the summer, before the harvest, these miners might be away for long periods, camping out close to their workings in the hills: meanwhile other members of the family tended their holdings, perhaps with the aid of hired labour. Coal-mining on the Bishop of Durham's northern estates was organized similarly, on the basis

of the manor. Mining was very arduous labour, but it was not a
road to riches. The miners of the Mendips held their place in
village society through hard times with what they won from
their workings, but they did not on the whole prosper beyond
it. The miners of the Weald of Kent and the Cornish tinners
(who did not usually have agricultural holdings) were among
the poorer, not the richer, sectors of the rural populations of
their regions. Farming was by no means the only occupation of
villagers, but in the end it was the one through which, at their
humble level, the fortunate had the best chance to prosper and
better themselves.

Apart from the common involvement in the rhythms of the
agricultural year, the other bonds that were of supreme importance in the peasant world were those of household and family,
of hearth and home. Though in legal relations, for instance in
finding pledges to stand surety in the manor court, people relied
usually on their neighbours rather than kin, wife and children
were the relations that mattered most of all to the householders
of the peasant world. If they lived long enough, most youths
and girls married. The nuclear family was thus the basic unit of
village life, and the raising of the family and providing for it the
principal preoccupation of the conjugal partnership at its centre.

   Court roll evidence, once again, offers the best insights into
the familial thinking and the economic strategies that it encouraged in the countryman's world. Peasants thought of their
holdings as family land, and were much concerned with maintaining their unity. There were various factors that could militate
against this and which they had to take into account. One was
local inheritance custom. Though primogeniture and 'borough
English' (ultimogeniture) were the commonest rules of inheritance for peasant holdings, in some regions (in Kent, for example) partible inheritance was the rule, and imposed division.
Inconvenient customary regulations of this sort could be circum-
vented by forward planning, and the multiplicity of entries on
court rolls recording transactions aimed to achieve this are prime
evidence of the anxiety of peasants to preserve the integrity of
their holdings. A very common practice was for man and wife
to come into court and surrender their holding into the lord's

hands, and then to take it up again as a joint tenancy: this ensured that the whole would pass to the survivor and so in due course to the heir. Peasants were also concerned about children other than the heir: the anxiety to provide for them by the purchase of small bits and pieces of land as opportunity arose seems to have been a significant stimulus to the peasant land market. Family circumstances – better or worse fortune as a cultivator, fecundity or childlessness – determined whether one was a buyer or seller, and when one bought or sold.

If possible, children would be provided for in their parents' lifetime. There was a variety of ways in which this could be achieved. Advantageous marriage was a principal one, and in the land-hungry days widows were often at a premium in the village marriage market. Or elderly parents might put their lands into their heir's hands in their lifetime, stipulating as a condition of his entry that he would maintain them in old age. Such agreements could be quite complicated: Professor Hanawalt quotes the case of one Ralph Beaumond who, when he allowed his kinsmen to take over his tenement, stipulated that he, Ralph, should have a cottage, a pair of linen hose and a woollen pair annually, and a pair of shoes, four bushels of wheat and four bushels of barley. A son, if there was one, would have the land, but daughters had a right if one was lacking; and every effort was made in any case to ensure them, if at all possible, a dowry, either in lands or in chattels. Court rolls are not a good source for the history of sentiment, but every now and again we do get a glimpse of strong feelings of family solidarity from them, as in this testamentary direction of a Yorkshire father, 'that my wife show a faithful love and favour in bringing up her children and mine, as she will answer to God and me'. It is no accident that when, at the very end of the medieval period, peasant wills begin to survive more commonly than before, the wife is the person most usually named as executor by her husband. Among the humble, the conjugal partnership was a real and meaningful one, by necessity, and clearly often an affectionate and trustful one as well.

As has been said, it was a nuclear, not an extended family that gathered about the peasant hearth. Peasant housing was too cramped to permit the sort of gathering of working man and wife, siblings too poor to marry and maintained on the holding, together with ageing parents and an army of children, that misapprehensions about the 'world we have lost' sometimes encourage us to imagine. The average household size was quite small, four or five persons (a great many children, it must be remembered, died in infancy). Of the houses that they once lived in, virtually nothing now remains, and for what we know of them we are mostly dependent on archaeology. Here and there a medieval tithe barn still stands, but the cottages of an English village, old though they may be, are constructions of a later age. Those of the middle ages were too flimsily built to last more than a generation, in most cases. Even in areas such as the Cotswolds, where good stone was available, the commonest kind of peasant housing was the cottage built on a frame of timber 'crucks'. A cruck is a substantial beam, curved or angular, sawn from the trunk of a large tree. Set up ('reared') in pairs at regular intervals, so as to form as it were a series of arches, these crucks supported the ridge pole of the roof; and the space between each pair was known as a 'bay'. The walls of the bays were most commonly of wattle and daub, and might be strengthened with a wooden frame: the roof was usually of thatch, steep pitched to throw off the rain. The interior of the house was open to the roof, and in a two-bay cottage (a very common size, requiring three pairs of crucks) would be divided by a wooden screen into a living-room (or 'hall') and a bedroom (or 'bower'). There was no chimney, and an aperture in the roof let out the smoke from a hearth fire in the middle of the floor of the living-room. No wonder that Chaucer wrote of the 'narrow cottage' of the poor widow in the 'Nun's Priest's Tale' that 'Ful sooty was her bower and eke her hall.'

By using more crucks, this house design could be extended: a rich peasant would very likely have a three-bay house, and some houses had four or five bays. The further bays might provide, beyond more partitions, storage space and shelter for beasts as well as men. Most three-bay houses provided accommodation in this way for men and animals under a single roof. Cruck houses were easy and relatively inexpensive to build, and could even be dismantled and re-erected on a new site. Inside, conditions were cramped and crowded and surely malodorous, but every village house would have a yard or a patch of garden to the rear, which might sometimes be quite substantial. Weather permitting, it was no doubt preferable to spend as much time as one might in this yard, or at the door facing on to the street.

Such was the sort of dwelling in which a peasant child grew up. From an early age, children began to contribute to the economic life of the family. A boy of seven would be old enough to tend a flock of geese on the common, and perhaps to walk beside the plough, goading the oxen: soon he would be old enough to take beasts to water, to go gathering firewood or to fetch and carry straw or rushes. Girls could help mind younger children, fetch water, and help with cooking, or in season go gathering fruits and 'worts'. As they grew older, of course, boys and girls would begin to hope to work for wages for other villagers. Children were anything but an encumbrance in a peasant world where for subsistence so much depended on supplemental economic activities, over and above tilling of the fields. A mother who was, say, a brewstress on any scale needed all the help she could get from her family. Supplementary activities generally fell heavily to the wife's and mother's lot, spinning, milking, making butter and cheese, collecting the eggs of her chickens, looking to all sorts of items that might eke out diet or be carried to a local market to be sold. In her multifarious tasks there was a great deal of help that her children could give her, and from an early age.

In the household, there was a sharp and continuous need for money as well as for produce, because the economy of the family could not be self-supporting for subsistence. There were too many goods that had to be bought as well as the many dues that had to be paid with coin. Even if the family produced enough seed corn for the coming year and the stock of beasts could be maintained and fed through the winter (neither of these would by any means always be the case) there were items in the way of clothing, pots and pans, tools and equipment that had to be purchased, not to mention services that cost money, in building or at the smithy. In a village economy that was substantially monetized but in which subsistence was often precarious, the family needed to work as a unit, and there was work for all hands except infant ones.

Peasant life was harsh, often very harsh in the land-hungry times before the mid fourteenth century, and pitiably at the mercy of the weather. All the same, one must be careful not to overdraw the picture of human misery. Statistics based on cereal yields which suggest that nearly half the population were living at or below subsistence give a good indication of just how desperate the consequences of a run of two or three bad harvests in succession might be (this was the cause of the 'great famine' of 1315–17), but take too little note of the reserves a country dweller could often fall back on. Of course there were those cottagers whose children's first lesson was in how to go out to beg bread, and who must have rejoiced exceedingly when the year brought round the time when it was the paupers' privilege to go out to glean peas between the strips in the field. Peasant diet no doubt was dull even for the better off: wheaten bread was a luxury for their betters, and brown bread (of 'maslin', a mixture of wheat and rye, or of heavy 'drege', mixed barley and oats), peas porridge and ale were its most stable elements. But most had a pig or two, and some scrawny chickens, perhaps geese; and gathering and hunting could contribute to the table too. People did go and eat in one another's houses, and weddings and baptisms were occasions for celebration. When a lord demanded boon works, extra services at harvest time, he might also have to provide a harvest supper. At Bishopstone in Sussex in the thirteenth century the boon-work dinner consisted of soup, wheaten bread, beef and cheese on the first day, and of soup, fish, cheese and plenty of ale on the second. There was enough ale in the village to make drunkenness a recurrent problem, both at work and in the home.

There was too some leisure as well as much labour. Children were set to work early, but they also spent time at play (as Barbara Hanawalt's melancholy tally of stories of accidents at play, taken from the coroners' rolls, makes clear). Village feasts and games gave opportunities for dance and courting in these 'bad old days' just as they did in later, often not very much better ones. There were a good many church feasts to celebrate one way or another. Spicy nut-brown ale, and stories told of the man-in-the-moon, Puck and Reynard the Fox really were part of the history of country people's life in the middle ages, though only part. 'Merry England' and its festivals, and the piteous picture in the 'Song of the Husbandman' of the ploughman, with his wife walking beside the oxen with her bleeding feet wrapped in rags and their infant lying in a bowl at the end of the strip, are genuine ingredients in the story of one and the same world, not of different ones.

We now have some picture of the social and economic organization of the rural population which experienced in 1348 the first shock of the plague, which was to become recurrent. Because control of the system, as it has so far been described, rested ultimately in the hands of the manorial landlord as the legal proprietor, it will be best to begin looking at the effects of the shock, and of the subsequent fall in population level, from his point of view.

The period before the onset of the plague had on the whole been a good time for the landlord, especially for the great landlord who could organize the farming of his demesnes for profit on a large scale. The twelfth and thirteenth centuries had seen a great increase in the number of towns and expansion of their population, and demand for agricultural produce was strong. In the heavily populated countryside land was in demand; rents and entry fines were high, labour plentiful and inexpensive. These were very advantageous circumstances for the landlord. On those estates where he farmed the demesne himself (whether through the extraction of *corvées* or with wage labour) he could expect a good price for his corn on the market. On those estates where the demesne was leased and the labour services of customary tenants commuted for a cash payment, he would expect a substantial return from rents. Manorial dues from his customary tenants and the profits of manorial courts swelled his income further. He might of course also be involved in pastoral farming on a large scale: sheep could be very profitable, and some great landlords had flocks that were very large indeed, running into thousands.

The prosperity and profitability of high farming on a large scale encouraged the development of estate management into a bureaucratic art, with a strong emphasis on accounting. The village reeve handed over his monies to the lord's steward, after

a careful account before the lord's receiver; the accounts both of
the reeves and the local receivers were checked by the lord's
auditors. When, annually at Michaelmas, they went over the
reeve's activities to put together the manor's account on a roll,
they checked the ratio of grain to seed sown, the average weight
of fleeces and the dairy yield per cow milked, to make sure these
were up to expectation: if they thought sale prices too low they
surcharged the reeve's account, and if disbursements seemed to
them unjustified they disallowed them. The reeve and the villagers would have to make up any consequent shortfall. At the
end there was a clear statement of what was still owing to the
lord over and above what had actually been paid over. The
system was not very just and did not encourage honesty among
reeves, but it made sure that, blow fair wind or foul, the lord
got his profit from the farming of his manors.

The first response of the landowning classes to the consequences of plague was, as we have seen, reactionary. Labour was
now in short supply; the demand for land and for the produce
of its tillage had slumped. Accordingly, landowners sought to
freeze wages and prices at their pre-plague levels, to assert more
aggressively their legal rights over labourers, and especially over
their bond tenants, and to maximize the profitability of their
manorial rights and dues. But this could only palliate temporarily
the effects of the reduction of population both in the countryside
and in towns (the centres of demand). In the longer run it
became inevitably apparent that it was no longer worthwhile
putting more energy into the effort to maintain the profits of
direct farming. So, gradually and piecemeal, landlords found
themselves forced to change tack, and by the end of the fourteenth century the principal direction in which things were
altering began to emerge clearly.

John Smith, the seventeenth-century historian of the Berkeley
family, noted in his history of the management of their estates a
great change that began in the time of Thomas IV, Lord of
Berkeley, in the reign of Richard II:

Then began the times to change, and he with them, and then instead of
manuring his demesnes in each manor with his own servants, oxen,
kine, and sheep . . . under the oversight of the reeves of the manors . . .

this lord began to joist and tack in other men's cattle into his pasture grounds by the week, month and quarter, and to sell his meadow grounds by the acre: and so between wind and water as it were continued part in tillage and part let out . . . and after in the time of Henry the Fourth let out by the year still more and more as he found chapmen and price to his liking . . . But in the next age that succeeded his nephew and heir male James who succeeded in these manors . . . let out the manor-houses and demesne lands, sometimes at racked improved rents according to the estimate of the time and sometimes at smaller rents . . . which is the general course and husbandry for the most part to this day [1618].

The development that John Smith so eloquently describes on the Berkeley estates was a general one. Everywhere in the late fourteenth and fifteenth centuries, we find lords leasing out their demesnes, and the leases, as time went by, tended to become longer. Between 1391 and 1411 Prior Chillenden of Canterbury leased virtually all the demesnes of Christ Church, taking food rents on some of the Kentish manors to supply the monastery. Crowland Abbey had leased most of its demesnes by 1430, Leicester Abbey did the same over the period 1408–77. The process was not always fast, but it was sure: every decade, as Miss Harvey writes of the Westminster Abbey estates, saw more leasing of the demesne. Lesser secular landlords, substantial gentry, were on the whole slower in following the trend than the greater estate owners, and probably continued to farm directly a higher proportion of their less extensive estates. They lived closer to the soil than their superiors, and needed in most cases to maintain at least some home farm; sometimes, indeed, we find gentlemen taking up leases of the demesne or of parcels of the demesne of greater landowners. Overall, however, a quiet revolution took place, the result of which was a complete change of the predominant role of the landlord in agriculture, from entrepreneurial farmer to *rentier*.

The changes consequent on this were as profound for the tenant as for the landlord. Wage labour, always important, became the pivot of all cultivation on any scale larger than a single peasant's family holding. The market in wage labour became at the same time much freer, because the man for whom the labourer now worked was so much less often a lord with a pre-emptive right to his labour service. The pattern of distribution of tenant holdings was also sharply affected. Among those who took leases of demesnes or of parts of demesnes prospering peasants (especially well-placed reeves) were prominent; and of course parcels of demesne were not the only lands now thrown on the market, for in the period after the plagues there were a good many vacant peasant tenements going begging too. The results show if one compares the pattern of holding on an individual manor in the mid thirteenth and the early fifteenth centuries. At Wistow (Bucks.) in 1252 there were no customary tenants holding more than a virgate; 13 per cent were virgaters: 44 per cent held between half and one virgate; 43 per cent held a quarter of a virgate or less, a substantial proportion of these being mere cottagers. In 1414 on this same manor 19 per cent of the tenants held between one and three virgates, 19 per cent were virgaters; 34 per cent held between a half and one virgate and 28 per cent less than that. If one bears in mind the calculation that in arable country, a quarter of a virgate has been suggested as just about the minimum adequate to support a family at or near subsistence level, the increase in the percentage who by 1414 held comfortably more than that becomes decidedly significant. There were fewer people living on the land, and their holdings of land were larger, in some cases appreciably so. Those who had little and who were principally dependent on working for others were, moreover, in a position to command more in wages, owing to the greater scarcity of labour and the greater freedom of the labour market. All were better off than they had been.

Percentage figures such as those quoted above do not do full justice to the change of situation from a peasant point of view. In the fifteenth century, as before the plagues, it is possible to divide the agricultural population broadly into three groups, the richer, the middling, and the poorer, but for each the conditions and prospects had changed substantially. New names identifying the groups begin to become common in the sources, and hint at more important social changes behind the percentage figures; 'yeoman', 'husbandman' or 'ploughman', and 'hind', replacing words with stronger manorial overtones, as villein, bondman, or cottar.

The most elevated and the richest of these new groupings, the yeomen, was also naturally the smallest. These were men for the most part who had succeeded in taking up leases of good land, probably including some demesne, and perhaps with parcels scattered over more than one parish. The holdings of such a man would together be likely to amount to at least 60 acres, probably more: he had become what we would call a farmer rather than a smallholder, producing for the market and employing a number of men on his own account. The classic description of a yeoman at the end of the fifteenth century is Bishop Latimer's picture of his father, who was

a yeoman, and held no land of his own: but he had a farm of three or four pounds by the year [probably of about 150 acres, that would imply] and hereupon he tilled as much as kept half a dozen men. He had a walk for a hundred sheep, and my mother milked thirty kine . . . he kept me to school . . . he married my sisters with five pounds apiece or twenty nobles: he kept hospitality for his poor neighbours and some alms he gave to the poor.

Chief Justice Fortescue's testimony, a little older, is similar:

there is scarce a small village [in England] in which you may not find a knight, esquire, or some substantial householder called a franklin . . . there are others who are called freeholders and many yeomen, of estate sufficient to make a substantial jury. There are several of these yeomen who are able to spend by the year a hundred pounds.

As both accounts imply, the prosperous yeoman's status was beginning to pull him away from the community of the village towards that of the county. Fortescue thought of yeomen as the kind of men who might serve on county juries, and Latimer told of how his father had found his own horse when he went to serve the king against the Cornish rebels in 1497: 'I remember that I buckled his harness,' he says. The line between yeoman and gentleman was becoming a fine one, and we can see some yeoman families thriving into gentility. On the Battle Abbey manor of Marley in the early fifteenth century two families, the Gunnes and the Hammonds, were drawing away from their peers, extending their holdings into farms: when Simon Hammond in 1450 brought the two inheritances together by marriage it was the foundation of the genteel fortune of his descendants.

The home of a substantial yeoman would be something a good deal more than the cruck house of three bays described earlier; a fair house with halls and chambers and 'the gladdest garden that gome* ever had' is what the author of *Mumme and the Soothsayer* (1400) pictured for him. The chattels its master might dispose of might also be quite impressive. When Robert Nottingham, son of John Nottingham, yeoman, died in 1498 he directed as follows:

my great pan, best spit, with all the apparel of the hall, to remain and abide to my tenement. To my son Vincent, a feather bed, bolster, pair of blankets, a horse, a cow, cart, plough, harrow and all the bacon hanging in the roof and all the wheat growing at Colwood, and as much corn as will sow his lands . . . to the wife of my brother William, a pair of coral beads, and to William a piece of silver, and to each son two silver spoons and to each daughter a silver spoon. To the wife of my brother Thomas, a furred gown. To Richard my brother, my russet gown.

Richard Nottingham was perhaps richer than many yeomen, but the picture of his possessions gives a good impression of how substantial one could be who was a member of that class of farmers that was now growing up between the gentility and the peasant world. They were almost coming to constitute an estate of their own, the 'estate of yeomanry' with which the makers of the Robin Hood ballads proudly identified their hero.

Of the more middling peasant and his fortune in the new dispensation Chaucer and Langland have both left us epic descriptions. Chaucer pictured him as a 'true swinker and a good' who would help his neighbour with his threshing 'without hire' if he was able. Langland's Piers had a plot of land and 'a cow and a calf, a cart mare also'; he hungered in the weeks before harvest, but was sworn to 'swink and sweat and sow' for others as well as for himself. Men of this standing, smallholders rather than farmers, perhaps employing labour now and then but still much

* *gome*, a Middle English word meaning a man or a fellow.

dependent on their own family and on reciprocal services between neighbours for the tilling of their plots, were probably the most numerous group in many villages. Their lot was also a good deal better than that of their forebears had been: they held more strips in the village field and with rather more security, and (as we shall see presently) the burden of seigneurial dues now sat a good deal more lightly upon them.

But such new-found prosperity as the ploughman or husband enjoyed was a great deal more flimsily based than that of the yeoman: and in a sense that the yeoman did not, he remained identifiably a peasant figure. John Palmer, of South Coxton, who died in 1515, was a very prosperous smallholder: his house had four rooms and he left 16 acres sown with peas and 20 sown with wheat and barley, and held some 18 acres more in the fallows. He had 80 sheep and 13 kine. No doubt he had some good pots and pans and a straw mattress: but there are no feather beds or silver spoons in the inventory of his goods and no doubt his capital was pretty well entirely tied up in his stock and equipment. And he was a well-off man of his kind. At about the same time William Tanner, of Long Whatton in the same county of Leicestershire, left 20 acres, 6 of them sown with peas and 4½ with barley and wheat, plus an ox, three kine, a heifer, two calves and nine pigs. Looking at the two men, at opposite ends of a single spectrum, it seems clear that John Palmer, with his 80 sheep and 36 acres sown, was farming for the market; William Tanner, with his 10½ acres sown and his handful of beasts, was presumably concerned principally with his own subsistence and that of his family. Out of all the countryside population of the late medieval period, the lesser smallholders strike one as those who, if better off than of yore, had moved the least from their old position. The poem 'God Speed the Plough' speaks of the 'husbandmen' as those who 'maintain this world'; almost the same function as the traditional one of the labouring estate, even if now discharged more often by the payment of rent to superiors than by service to them. Family life and its cycle, and the focus on the village community, likewise remained for these people much the same as before. Their lot had eased without in any sense becoming easy.

*

For the countryman dependent on what he could win by working for others, the 'hind' or labourer, the post-plague era opened new but precarious prospects of increased prosperity. Labour was in demand, and after the mid-1370s the level of wages, in real terms, could no longer be held down. As landlords progressively withdrew from direct farming, the freedom of the labourer that Wat Tyler demanded in 1381 'to take work at his own will' (and that the Statute of Labourers had endeavoured to restrict) was greatly enhanced. The literary sources are explicit about the higher wages and better standard of living that labourers expected in these conditions, and critical of their intransigence. Gower reviles them as brutish and godless, and complains that they will no longer take hire by the year or month, but want to be paid by the day and ask for excessive rations. Langland says much the same, though with less class spite:

> May no penny ale them pay, nor a piece of bacon
> But it be fresh flesh or fish fried or y-baked,
> And that *chaud* and *pluschaud* for chilling of their mouths;
> But he be highly y-hired, else will he chide.

Significantly, in Langland it is no lord but Piers the Plowman who complains of the greed and laziness of labourers. Farmers and peasants with larger plots than before had more need now of labour beyond what their own family could muster: there was no lack of work for the hind in the village.

Even more to the point, there was no lack of work elsewhere. In consequence, the late middle ages became a period of great mobility in the rural world. It was not just the wage labourer that was involved here, for in many communities there was plenty of land that was looking for cultivators. From the late fourteenth until well into the fifteenth century evidence abounds in manorial records that lords were experiencing difficulties in finding takers for vacant tenements, especially of course on poor ground. An inquisition *post mortem* of 1427 for the Beaumont estates in Leicestershire gives a good picture of what the scale of the problem could be in what was probably one of the worst decades: at Whitwick, an important manor, twelve houses were vacant out of thirty-one, and 289 acres had gone to waste; at Markfield twelve out of twenty-nine houses were in decay; at

Hugglescote ten messuages were in the lord's hand for want of tenants. Just as a workman who thought he could get better wages elsewhere went to find them, so did the husbandman who thought he could get better land or better terms. The pattern shows in a very general phenomenon, the sharp rise in the percentage of names new to a village or manor in court-roll records of those taking up tenancies (and there seems to be a rise too in the number of women marrying outside their native manor). Migration was not always to any great distance. At Forncett in Norfolk, Miss Davenport was able to trace the movements of 126 bondmen who left the manor between 1400 and 1575. Most (53 per cent) ended up in villages within a ten-mile radius; another 30 per cent settled within twenty miles (a number of these in the city of Norwich); 17 per cent went farther afield. People were on the move, widely, and in many directions.

One very striking evidence of the new freedom of movement of this period is the complete desertion of a quite significant number of village settlements. A few, like Tilgarsley in Oxford-shire, seem to have been deserted as a direct result of plague mortality, which left too few hands to till the soil, but this was rare. More commonly the reason was that the land was poor, or that there was a high proportion of customary tenants with smallholdings (and so, probably, with insufficient capital to take on more land): most of the abandoned settlements were relatively small ones in the first place. The process of desertion was usually a gradual one. Dunsthorpe in Lincolnshire had been slowly ruined, so the rector wrote in 1437, 'by the lack of parishioners, the fewness of the peasants, lack of cultivation, and the pestilences with which the Lord afflicts his people'. At Wyville, not far away, it was the same story: 'the three carucates are worth little, for the land is poor and stony and lies uncultivated for want of tenants'. There are examples of the abandonment of settlements in every county, but the incidence was heaviest in the old corn-growing lands of the Midlands. In that way, desertion of village sites underscores the decline in the late middle ages of the profitability of arable cultivation, on which the landlords of the past age of high farming had once ridden tall.

*

The prevalence of internal migration, and the abandonment of unfruitful holdings, in combination with the break-up and leasing of demesnes and the lower profits of tillage, had two very important repercussions. First, they encouraged a marked shift in the agricultural world towards pasture farming, which in its turn gave rise to enclosure. Pasturing was less labour-intensive than tillage, and in consequence could offer good returns. Sheep farming, always popular, seems to have become even more so, but had its risks, because murrains were common and could literally decimate a flock. Moreover the quantity of wool that was exported from England (whether as raw wool or made up into cloth) was not rising; in the late middle ages it declined. It seems likely however that domestic demand more than made up for the fall, and also that more sheep were being grazed principally for their mutton, of which enormous quantities were consumed in, for instance, monasteries and aristocratic households. Besides, the better-paid workers of the later middle ages expected a better diet, and ate more meat than their forebears. Cattle-farming could also be profitable, for the same reason and on account of the value of hides. John Brome, lord of the manor of Baddesley Clinton (Warwickshire) in the mid fifteenth century, is a good example of one who was making pasture pay this way; he had enclosed 300 acres of his demesne on which he fattened cattle bought in the markets of Coventry and Birmingham and which he then sold to local butchers (and sometimes to London butchers too). In a region where some of those who stuck to renting for tillage were encountering difficulties he seems to have been doing pretty well.

The history of medieval enclosure is not easy to trace, since the evidence that pre-dates the findings of the Enclosure Commissioners of 1517 is very fragmentary. But it was clearly extensive. In the 1490s John Rous was lamenting the destruction of villages in Warwickshire by enclosure, and John Hale in 1549 gave it as his opinion that 'the chief destruction of towns and decay of houses was before the beginning of the reign of King Henry VII'. In fact, down to the end of the fifteenth century, enclosure seems more often to have followed the abandonment of holdings than to have caused it: the Abbot of Leicester's manor of Wantley, for instance, was more or less deserted by the end of the 1370s, but it is not until 1480 that the records make clear that the land had been enclosed with hedges and ditches, and was leased to two Winchcombe men. The process could be decidedly piecemeal: in 1484 John Peyto at Great Chesterton (Leics.) had enclosed much of the arable, but it is clear that part of the manor (including the 'great town field') was still under open-field husbandry. It was not only landlords that enclosed, it must be added. We find tenants laying holding to holding and hedging them into fields, with the lord's agreement. It is hard, in consequence, to plot the progress of enclosure, even on individual manors, but it is clear that by the end of the fifteenth century it had been very extensive. The distress that evictions in order to enclose could cause and the unemployment that it generated were beginning to be a matter of concern, witness the complaint of the preamble to a statute of 1489 that

where in some towns two hundred persons were occupied and lived by their lawful labour, now be there occupied two or three herdsmen, and the residue fallen in idleness: the husbandry . . . is decayed, the service of God withdrawn, the bodies not prayed for.

For all the enclosures, there were still wide areas, especially in southern and central England, where the open-field system of husbandry persisted and predominated. It was in those villages and manors where it did so that the signs of the other great development consequent on the changed circumstances of the post-plague period are most striking. This second consequence was the decline of serfdom. Serfdom was never abolished, as the peasant rebels of 1381 had demanded that it should be, but simply sank, in the course of the fifteenth century, into desuetude. In the new conditions, it ceased to be practicable for lords to press their legal right to customary dues and services, or to seek to enforce customary rents that were higher than the market level: if they tried to, there was a real danger that their tenants would simply leave their holdings and thereby reduce still further their landlord's already diminished revenue from rents. Thus when, for instance, the Bishop of Worcester's estates were in the king's hand in 1433, and a customary sum called a 'recognition' was demanded on his behalf, it was reported that

The customary tenants of the aforesaid manors were . . . in such great poverty that if these recognitions were levied from them they would leave the land, holdings and tenures of the aforesaid lordship vacant, to the great prejudice of the lord King and the final destruction of the aforesaid manors.

The bishop's tenants never paid another recognition, and shook themselves free too of seigneurial tallages and a number of other manorial dues and 'perquisites of court'. We find the same sort of thing happening elsewhere. On the Kimber lordship in Warwick in 1434 the lord agreed, after the tenants had refused certain services, to commute heriots and all services for two shillings p.a. per tenant. A few years earlier we find the Earl of Warwick instructing his steward to negotiate with his tenants over their grievances that their rents were too heavy and that they were tallaged so frequently that it would drive them off the land.

Much commoner and much more general than these dramatic histories of successful collective protests by manorial tenants are the records of individuals being offered tenancies at a fixed rent, with no extra services. Rent as such peasant tenants did not grudge; even Wat Tyler had only asked for fair rents of 4d. per acre. What they did grudge were the extra dues and services that went with bond tenure: boon works, wood-silver, tallages, tributes in kind and seigneurial monopolies. When lords ceased to be able to exact these any longer, for fear that otherwise their tenants would simply decamp, it ceased to be important to them and their stewards to remember who were and who were not bondmen.

It was the development of arrangements for fixed rents such as those outlined above that led ultimately to the copyhold tenures that had become so widespread by the end of the fifteenth century. These developed where, when a tenant in villeinage died, and his holding came into the lord's hands, the heir or new tenant, instead of taking it up on the old customary terms, obtained after paying his entry fine a copy of the manor-court roll entry recording his admission to the land on stipulated terms of tenure (usually a money rent). The tenancy was most often for a term of lives, normally three: the heirs still had to pay an entry fine and remained liable to heriot, and nothing in the copy declared that the new tenant was free. Nevertheless he was in fact free in a way that his bond predecessors had not been. His rent was fixed, there was no room for arbitrary tallage or boon works; and provided that he registered the transfer and that an entry fine was paid, he could sell his copyhold to another without any risk that the landlord might spoil the bargain by intervening to change the terms when the tenancy changed (he could not do that until the copyhold lease had run its course, at the term of three lives or whenever). By the end of the fifteenth century the courts of common law were beginning to protect the tenure of the copyholder (which they had never done for bond tenures), something that Chancery had begun to do rather earlier. No doubt the principal reason was that by now a good many men of substance held copyholds as well as freeholds, for there were enterprising gentlemen as well as yeomen who could see and seized the opportunities opened to them in consequence of so much land being available for lease at attractive rents. But once the common law had come to uphold copy of court roll, serfdom as an institution of social significance was not just dead but buried; what had been the essence of its legal precariousness and of its social stigma was now finally eroded. One will still hear occasionally of bond tenants even in the sixteenth century, it is true, but the status had become an anachronism and was no longer meaningful.

The developments in the countryside in the century and a half that followed the Black Death spelled the end of the 'manorial system' of the preceding age of high farming. A looser web of relationships, in which leases and wages played the key roles, replaced the old structure of lords and bond tenants. Wherever there were copyholds and wherever there were open fields the manor remained significant, especially where the manor coincided with a village whose inhabitants were engaged in common tillage and felt the need of a formal arena in which to regulate their reciprocal relations and cooperative activities. Inevitably, though, the manor became less significant with the decay of what historians have called 'manorialism'. In this, and in the new degree of tenant mobility which was the decisive factor in the erosion of the old system, there was loss as well as gain for peasants and labourers as well as for lords. The manor had helped to give village life a powerful measure of cohesion; that cohesion, in the old days, had been the principal brake on seigneurial oppression. In the new world of leases and wages, the small man would find that he had less protection against the big man, not more, if new circumstances should tip the balance of the agricultural economy back into the big man's favour – as the sixteenth and subsequent centuries would show. But the main point remains that, when times did begin to alter once more, things had changed out of recognition from what they had been at the start of the fourteenth century. The squire, the yeoman and Hodge the farm labourer are clean different figures from the lord, the reeve and the quarter virgater, and by 1500 they were all on the rural scene.

4. Towns, Trade and Urban Culture

The plagues of the late fourteenth century hit town and country-side alike. In crowded and insanitary urban conditions their effect was even more devastating than in the country, and towns were more vulnerable to the recurrent outbreaks of bubonic disease of the fifteenth century. The records of late medieval English towns are in consequence full of the same melancholy stories of deserted tenements and shrunken population that we have heard of from the villages. The repeated laments of city fathers over the lack of men to contribute to traditional dues and taxes, even of the lack of men willing to take up civic office, easily give the impression of a consistent and overall urban decline and decay. The fortunes of towns, however, were also affected by other factors, changes in the pattern of trade and production and in the geographical distribution of prosperity in England, whose effects were very far from unitary, working to civic advantage here and to disadvantage there. So complex does the picture become on close inspection, indeed, that sometimes it seems as if the history of each individual town can only be satisfactorily treated separately. Development was not really quite as diffuse as this, but diverse, complicated and overlapping factors were at work, and there is almost unlimited controversy among historians as to how to draw the balance of emphasis between them.

In dealing with the urban history of this period, there is an initial problem of how precisely one is to define a town, as to what it was that distinguished such a settlement definitively from the kind of substantial village out of which many towns had grown. An older generation of historians tended to answer this question squarely in legal terms. A town was distinguished by burgage tenures which gave the individual burgess the right to hold his house and plot at a customary rent and to give or sell it freely; and by chartered privileges which gave the burgesses a measure of communal self-government; the right to elect their own governing council and to regulate the everyday lives and commercial dealings of the inhabitants through the borough court, and the right to collect tolls and rents in return for an annual payment (the fee-farm), paid to the lord of the borough (usually the king). There remains much to be said for this sort of definition, but it has some drawbacks. Not only are there occasional exceptions, communities clearly urban in some sense but which lacked some or all of these privileges, but it also suggests a greater degree of uniformity than really existed among communities of very heterogeneous character. Besides, the enjoyment of borough privileges did not and could not ensure the capacity of a settlement to maintain itself as a distinctively urban community. The tiny boroughs of the English parts of medieval Ireland are a good reminder of this; in reality no more than villages, their burgage tenures had been created by their lords not in order to found a town but in the hope that this privileged form of tenure would attract agricultural settlers.

What really made a town is probably better seen in terms of what made it a centre of a way of life that was distinct from that of the surrounding countryside. All sorts of factors could be at work here, the presence of a cathedral or a major collegiate church that made it a focus of ecclesiastical administration, or the fact that it was a county town where the sheriff had his headquarters and at which the assizes regularly assembled people from the surrounding area, on legal or other business. But perhaps the most important factors were the occupations of the inhabitants, and the holding of regular markets. Occupation was a much clearer indication of urban living than size. In the 1381 poll-tax returns, as Professor Hilton has pointed out, the Gloucestershire village of Sherborne housed more taxpayers (176) than neighbouring Stow-on-the-Wold (166), which was reckoned to be a town. The difference between the two settlements appears when one looks at the occupational descriptions of the inhabitants that the returns supply. All the taxpayers of Sherborne are described as cultivators. In Stow, contrastingly, only four heads of households are so described, the rest being divided between twenty-eight different specialized crafts or trades. It was the practice of these crafts and trades that made the way of life of Stow's inhabitants distinctively non-rural. Its market gave the craftsmen and tradesmen the opportunity that they needed to buy and sell profitably, at a fixed location and on a regular basis.

Stow was a very small town, with perhaps 250 or 300 inhabitants in all. The size of late medieval towns varied very considerably, but most were, by modern standards, very small indeed, though not quite as small as Stow was. London, with a population of perhaps 40,000 in the fifteenth century, was the only city of England that could compare with the great continental conurbations, with Bruges or Ghent in Flanders or with the great cities of Italy. At the end of the middle ages Norwich was probably the only other English city with more than 10,000 inhabitants. Bristol, York, Salisbury, Canterbury and Coventry were among nine cities with populations of over 6,000; Lincoln, Oxford, Cambridge, Hereford and Worcester among those (a further eleven) with 4,000–5,000 people. The predominance in this list of cities to which a cathedral or a university gave a focal centre is no accident (and most of them are county towns too). Altogether there were some forty towns with a population of over 2,000. They included the principal ports, Southampton, Plymouth, Great Yarmouth, Hull and King's Lynn (as well as Bristol and London, already mentioned). If one bears in mind that in this time there were some 200 boroughs in England that sent representatives to Parliament and that every county boasted a number of market towns that did not, it will be clear that the average English town of the late medieval period was indeed very small, in size and appearance more like an overgrown village than a town to our minds, but distinguished therefrom by the occupations and preoccupations of its people and a rhythm of life different from that of the countryside.

The sort of factors that determined the size, status and prosperity of a town were its position in terms of communications, the patterns of production and demand of the hinterland that it served, its own potential as a centre of production, and any historical traditions that might make it, administratively or religiously, a centre of local significance. Thus Canterbury was important because the city was the centre of an archdiocese and a county town. Bristol flourished because she not only had excellent access to the sea, but because of her relations with a well-off hinterland, the Cotswolds, which were noted for their fine wools, and the smaller towns of neighbouring Gloucestershire and Somerset that were active in textile manufacture. As a port, Bristol was a great centre of the wine trade with Gascony, which in turn provided an outlet for the cloths her merchants exported; this was why Bristol was hard hit, temporarily, by the loss in the 1450s of the English lands in south-western France. York similarly prospered because the city was a textile centre close to a major region of wool and cloth production, and because through Hull there was a good outlet to the sea: York was a major focus of the overseas trade between England and the Hanse towns of Germany. Coventry's prosperity was built on her own textile industry and on her location at a nodal point of inland communications. Skins and salt came to Coventry from Chester *en route* to London; wines came from Bristol; fish and Baltic wares from the ports of the Wash; wood and alum from Southampton. The routes leading to and fro in this variety of directions intersected at Coventry, bringing goods from outside into her markets and carrying away her cloth to markets elsewhere. Southampton, by way of contrast, remained smaller than any of these towns, because although she was a major port she could boast no major labour-intensive industry of her own. Salisbury, not Southampton, was the nodal centre of production of the cloth that passed through this port.

All these were major cities. The fortunes of the smaller 'country' towns depended in part on local industry, especially in areas of textile production, but above all on the weekly market which, as Professor Hilton puts it, was 'the focus of their lives'. Their chief function, as he says, was to provide a range of services and manufactured goods for the people of the surrounding villages. These came to town to purchase cloth, shoes, implements, pots and pans: the richer might bring to market wool, corn and cattle, the poorer butter, cheese, eggs and perhaps the products of some cottage industry. The pattern of life in such small towns is reflected in the occupations of their inhabitants, as listed in the poll-tax returns of 1381. The little Gloucestershire town of Winchcombe then had a population of perhaps 400:

among its taxpayers 42 per cent were in the clothing or victualling trades; 28 per cent were craftsmen in leather, wood and building; 14 per cent were textile craftsmen. A handful were described as merchants or were in transport. In a small town like this a smith or a carpenter could be a prominent man, a cornmonger would expect to be so.

The kind of properties that we hear of in the records of this sort of town are for the most part cottages, shops and barns. The business with which their borough courts were principally concerned (petty crime apart) included keeping the streets clean, control of livestock (especially pigs: there was plenty of room for these in the gardens behind cottages on the street), the regulation of prices and the maintenance of honest measures and quality, in particular of food and drink. When a little town like Pershore (Worcs.) could boast more than sixty brewers and twenty taverns, and had enough butchers for there to be a Butchers' Row, this last kind of business was clearly important. Though the occupations of the inhabitants of small towns marked off their way of living sharply enough from that of the agricultural village, they remained very much part of the countryside world.

How individual towns fared in the late middle ages depended largely on fluctuations and variations in the conditions that, in the preceding period, had been the base of their urban prosperity. The thirteenth century had been generally a period of growth for the towns, of rising urban population (swelled by emigration from the countryside), of the foundation of new towns (Kingston-on-Hull, Liverpool, and Harwich are good examples), and of the rise to urban status of villages which flourished as a result of the very numerous grants of the right to hold a market. In the later period with which we are concerned two kinds of factors in particular affected the way things developed for individual towns and cities: changes in the population level, manner of living and pattern of demand in their rural hinterlands (small towns in particular were affected here), and changes in the pattern of the production of and the demand for the commodities and finished goods in whose marketing they specialized. In the latter area, changes in the shape of England's external trade were important, and to understand what was involved here one must know something about how that trade was developing immediately before our period.

The acceleration of England's international commerce, of the export trade in wool and in the demand for goods that had to be imported, such as wines, spices and fine cloths, had been a significant factor in the urban growth of the twelfth and thirteenth centuries. What had fostered it most strongly of all, however, was the demand (internal on the whole rather than external at this stage) for goods whose production involved specialized skills, and especially skills that were labour intensive. Among these last the most important was the manufacture of cloth. Because of the number of separate processes that were involved, the industry lent itself to large-scale organization. Raw wool, before it could be spun into yarn (a woman's task), had to be washed and combed (or 'carded'). The yarn passed to the weaver, who worked it up into unfinished cloth on a 'bed loom' (a horizontal frame supported by four upright 'bed posts', with a roller at each end): the warp threads were wound around one roller, the weaver passed the shuttle with the weft thread to and fro, and wound the cloth on to the second roller. Then the fuller took over, placing the cloth in troughs filled with water and fuller's earth, in which it was pounded to thicken and felt it (either underfoot, or in a water-powered mill driving wooden hammers). After this it had to be rinsed, dried and sheared. The last process was the dyeing of the cloth, a skilled and heavy labour, and a process which often required imported agents (woad, the basis of blue dyes, did not grow in England; 'grain' for rich scarlet had to come from Spain, and 'vermillion' from the east). The cloth merchant, the man who in the end sold the finished product, was also normally the organizer and controller of the industry, supplying the craftsmen and women who carried out the various skilled processes with their raw material, their wool, their yarn, their agents for fulling and dyeing: he might own the weavers' looms too. These merchants needed to tie up a good deal of working capital in their business, and formed a rich élite in the growing towns. It will be apparent now why textile workers figure so prominently in the occupational statistics of so many medieval English towns.

Leather was another economically important product that involved processes in which capital needed to be invested and which stimulated specialist craftsmanship. Tanning the leather, which had to be soaked in great vats in a solution containing tannin, was a slow and expensive business; making it up, into leather clothing, saddlery, gloves or shoes, was the occupation of a series of individual and specialized skilled craftsmen. In some towns, the various branches of leather work accounted for an even higher occupational proportion of its tax-paying population than did the textile industry.

Building was another labour-intensive business: you cannot have a town, town churches or a cathedral, without masons and carpenters. Really substantial building work, however, was most often local and temporary, so there was a good deal of itinerancy in the trade, and it was not in itself a stimulus to urban growth in the way that textile and leather production for the domestic market were.

Mining and metalwork also required a numerous labour force, and lead and tin were, after raw wool and hides, among England's most important items of export. Mining, as we have seen earlier, was largely rural-based, and so was smelting; it was because of the need for charcoal for this process that iron-mining, in particular, was concentrated in well-wooded areas, such as the Sussex Weald and the Forest of Dean in Gloucestershire. The merchant who dealt in iron bars, block tin or lead, supplying the exporter and the domestic metalworker, was however a townsman; the fortunes of, for instance, the Stannary towns of Devon and Cornwall (among which Tavistock achieved the most sustained prosperity) were founded on their importance as market centres of the trade in tin. Skilled smiths and specialist metalworkers, as pewterers, cutlers and armourers, were townsmen likewise. Every town had its complement of them, and it was often a significant one. In York in the reign of Edward I, no less than 17 per cent of those admitted to the freedom and whose occupation was recorded were metalworkers. Like the weavers in cloth and leather, they needed access to a stable supply of raw material and to an active market, which meant that their industry needed an urban base.

*

The growth of towns and markets was inevitably related to and dependent on the system of communications. The cheapest and most effective way of moving goods in bulk was by water, and this put seaports and towns with good access to the sea or to navigable sections of river at a special advantage. But inland communications were important and decisive too. The distance that a man can walk, from his home in the morning and back again by dusk, was the ultimate limit of the catchment area of the small market town that throve on serving the needs of its surrounding countryside, say a ten-mile radius at the uttermost. A shorter range was more normal in practice: the dictum of the great thirteenth-century lawyer, Henry of Bracton, that (in order to protect vested interests) no new market should be licensed within a radius of $6\frac{2}{3}$ miles of an existing one held on the same day gives a better picture of the usual case. Towns that were major centres of distribution or production needed connections to long-distance lines of communication if they were to flourish. The principal means of transportation inland was by pack-horse or cart: the first method could make the best of bad roads, but was least apt for moving goods in bulk, and carting was more important. Poor the roads may have been, but they were capable of carrying a considerable volume of traffic nevertheless, and the cost of perhaps 3d. per ton per mile by common carrier was not prohibitive. The Gough map of the mid fourteenth century shows a national network of roads, with the towns and cities through which they passed clearly marked on it, together with estimates of the distance between each major centre (seldom strictly accurate, but a reasonable guide in most cases). Whoever drew it knew the main carrier routes of the whole kingdom well, the nodal points of their intersections (such as helped to make the fortune of Coventry), and the way in which they related to the river systems. The shape of the coastline up to the Tweed is presented in the map with some accuracy: it is a remarkable testimony as to how well, by the middle of the fourteenth century, transportation had taught the lessons of geography.

Such, in very broad outline, was the urban and commercial system when the plague first struck in 1348. The initial impact was very severe, and it was sustained. Towns were more vulnerable to the later outbreaks of bubonic plague than were rural areas, and the consequences of mortality were serious. Shortage of labour posed a problem that could be pressing for manufacturing activity. The burden of the fee-farm of the city or borough, and of parliamentary subsidies, fell more heavily on those that survived the plague because they were assessed on the town in round sums and there were fewer to contribute. By the fifteenth century the cry was going up from one after another of England's ancient boroughs that there were too few citizens and they too poor to meet what was demanded of them. 'The city is impoverished by withdrawal of merchants and great pestilence,' the people of Lincoln pleaded in 1446, 'so that scarce 700 citizens stay there, of whom none can support the charge of the said farm.' 'There is not half the number of good men in your said city as there hath been in times past,' the men of York alleged to Henry VII in 1487. Winchester, 'which in ancient times was chosen out for the coronations and burials of kings', so its citizens declared in 1440, 'through pestilence and loss of trade has had 11 streets, 17 parish churches, and 987 messuages in ruins during the last 50 years, and is so impoverished as to be unable to pay the fee-farm'. Leland, in his *Itinerary* (1527), noted again and again open signs and memories of better times long past in the towns he visited. 'The town hath yet great privileges with a mayor and bailiffs,' he wrote of Scarborough, 'but where it had in Edward III's time many good ships and rich merchants, now there be but few boats and no merchants of any estimation.' Boston would never recover 'the old glory and riches it had'. Brougham (Cumberland), he reflected, 'hath been some notable thing', but 'the town . . . is now very bare'.

'Only the existence of prolonged and remorseless demographic attrition in England as a whole . . . seems capable of explaining the ubiquity of the urban malaise,' Professor Barrie Dobson writes of the late medieval English towns. There can be no doubt that decline in population was at the root of the decay that was apparent in so many of them. There was still immigration into the towns from the countryside; but it was not enough to balance the ravages of mortality and emigration away from them. It was not just of dwindling numbers that cities like

Lincoln and Winchester complained, however, but also of loss
of trade. 'Here cometh no repair of lords nor other gentlemen,'
the Lincoln men grumbled in 1486, 'wherethrough the craftsmen
and victuallers are departed out of your city, and inhabit them
in other places in this shire, where more recourse of people is.'
While they were in distress, others were doing all right, they
implied: and when one comes to look at developments in detail
in individual towns, it is clear that other factors were at work
besides demographic attrition, and that a picture of general,
universal and consistent urban decay will not stand up. The fall
in the fortunes of Lincoln and Winchester may have been pretty
steady, but York, for instance, enjoyed a period of high prosperity in the late fourteenth century, and may even have
increased her population after the first plagues. The prosperity
of Coventry held up well too, until after *c.* 1450. The population
of Norwich just about doubled in the course of the fifteenth
century, and its wealth increased notably. Some smaller towns,
moreover, like Lavenham in Suffolk or Totnes in Devon, grew
substantially, both in wealth and population, in the later middle
ages. The variations of changes and developments are very
diverse.

If one compares the list of the forty or so most prosperous towns
in England that can be compiled from the 1377 poll-tax returns
with one compiled from the returns for the subsidy of 1524 (see
table opposite), some interesting aspects of these variations strike
the eye. Boston, Beverley and Scarborough (ninth, tenth and
thirtieth in 1377) have dropped out of the league by the
early sixteenth century. Norwich, with a population of probably
under 6,000 in 1377, was the only town (London apart) with a
population of over 10,000 in 1524; York, in 1377 the only city
in that position, had dropped to third place and had perhaps
7,000 inhabitants a hundred and fifty years later. In both tables
Bristol appears as the second provincial city of England; but
Coventry and Lincoln had by 1524 fallen from third and fifth to
ninth and twelfth places respectively. Most interesting of all,
perhaps, are the towns with no place in the 1377 list, but which
appear on that for 1524, such as Crediton and Tiverton in
Devon, Hadleigh in Essex, Beccles in Suffolk. Moreover, if one

Leading Towns and their Populations in Late Medieval England

In 1377	In the 1520s
Over 10,000	*Over 10,000*
York	Norwich
Bristol	
Over 6,000	*Over 6,000*
Coventry	Bristol
Norwich	York
Lincoln	Salisbury
Salisbury	Exeter
Lynn	Colchester
Colchester	Canterbury
	Newcastle-on-Tyne
	Coventry
4,000–6,000	*4,000–6,000*
Boston	Bury St Edmunds
Beverley	St Albans
Newcastle-on-Tyne	Lincoln
Canterbury	Hereford
Bury St Edmunds	Oxford
Oxford	Reading
Gloucester	Cambridge
Leicester	Worcester
Shrewsbury	Lynn
	Yarmouth
	Ipswich
3,000–4,000	*3,000–4,000*
Yarmouth	Northampton
Hereford	Gloucester
Cambridge	Chester
Ely	Crediton
Plymouth	Newbury
Exeter	Shrewsbury
Hull	Durham
Worcester	
Ipswich	

Leading Towns and their Populations in Late Medieval England (cont.)

In 1377	In the 1520s
Over 2,000	*Over 2,000*
Northampton	Leicester
Nottingham	Lichfield
Winchester	Ely
Scarborough	Southampton
Stamford	Chipping Walden
Newark	Winchester
Ludlow	Hadleigh
Southampton	Plymouth
Pontefract	Beccles
Reading	Chichester
Derby	Nottingham
Lichfield	Tiverton
Newbury	Wymondham
	Bodmin
c. 2,000	Hull
Wells	
Bridgnorth	
Cirencester	

The list in the first column comes from W. G. Hoskins, *Local History* (London, 1955), pp. 174–6, and is based on the poll-tax returns of 1377. My estimates of populations are very rough, and have been obtained by multiplying the number of taxpayers by two to allow for exemptions and evasions; this is, as C. Phythian Adams suggests, a minimum multiplier. Lacunae in the records explain the non-appearance of one or two towns that are in the second list, e.g. Chester, Durham.

The list in the second column comes from C. Phythian Adams, *The Desolation of a City: Coventry and the Urban Crisis of the Later Middle Ages* (Cambridge, 1979), and is based on lists of contributors to the subsidies of the 1520s.

were to continue the list beyond forty odd, there are a number of other smaller towns whose rise would be equally striking; such as Wakefield and Leeds in Yorkshire, or Mere and Castle Combe in Wiltshire. Birmingham too had begun her long, slow climb to prominence: her cattle-market was becoming important, and Leland remarked on the town's new 'beauty' and the great number of smiths 'that use to make knives and all manner of cutting tools . . . so that a great party of town is maintained by the smiths'.

There seems to be some hint of a pattern, or of patterns, behind these variations. Times had been bad, clearly, for a good many towns towards the eastern seaboard: Boston, Hull, Stamford, Scarborough. The Cinque Ports on the south coast had sunk into obscurity and Southampton was in difficulties maintaining her position. A number of towns in the Midlands and especially the western Midlands were experiencing trouble: Warwick, Gloucester, Shrewsbury and Ludlow, for instance, and a good many smaller towns in the central Midlands likewise. Above all, a number of major cities whose fortunes were closely linked with the textile industry came to encounter serious problems, most notably York, Lincoln and Coventry (perhaps Winchester should come into this category too, but her decline had really started earlier). Norwich, however, had flourished and Bristol's population and prosperity were little dented, though both were much involved in the textile trade; and in certain regions a number of small towns that were involved in textile manufacture had made notable advances, as Tiverton and Totnes in the south-west, Lavenham and Beccles in East Anglia, and Wakefield, Leeds and Halifax in Yorkshire.

In some significant respects, these changes reflect the development that Schofield has traced, on a county basis, in the geographical distribution of wealth in England, calculated from the shire assessments for the parliamentary subsidies of 1334 (which provided the base for assessment for the rest of the medieval period) and 1514–15 (when a new method of assessment was introduced). In 1334 the Holland district of Lincolnshire, Oxfordshire and Norfolk were the richest areas assessed; by the sixteenth century they had fallen to eighteenth, thirteenth and sixteenth places respectively. Devon, the second poorest county of 1334, in 1515 ranked fifteenth, and Wiltshire had risen from fifteenth to fifth. In terms of growth over the period, Devon, Middlesex, Cornwall and Somerset were the leaders, and in the north the West Riding of Yorkshire was the most significant growth area (and by 1515 the richest assessed district north of the Trent). In 1334 the wealthiest region of England was the central belt, stretching from the Severn estuary in the west towards London to the south and up to the Wash northward, through the great corn-growing counties. In 1515 English wealth was concentrated in the home counties, East Anglia, Wessex and the south-west, that is to say in the area around the capital and in some principal areas of cloth production. In short, there had been a distinct shift in the pattern of the regional distribution of wealth (and also, it should be added, of population) from the north to the south, a familiar story.

The relationship between this pattern and the pattern of urban development demonstrates sharply the close connection between urban fortunes and the prosperity (or otherwise) of the surrounding countryside. This is most dramatically clear in the case of the smaller towns. There was a marked reduction in the number of active market centres, especially in the old corn-growing areas, which were also the areas where the depopulation of villages was most marked. The shrinkage of population meant that there was too little demand, in many places, to keep the craftsmen who had provided services to the rural district in profitable business: the seeds of the degradation of a good many of the rotten boroughs of the future were sown in this way. But where a local industry produced a commodity in wide demand the effects of demographic decline were not felt so sharply. The prosperity of small ports that fitted out fishing fleets, and of towns in for instance the salt-panning areas of Cheshire, was not much affected, even if their populations were reduced somewhat, for these were staple elements in the country's diet. Again, market centres in mining areas, like the Stannary towns of Tavistock, Plympton and Ashburton, could hold up well. In cloth-producing regions, many small and middling towns preserved a good measure of prosperity, and some flourished as they never had before.

There was another factor beside demographic decline and quite separate from it underlying the developments and changes of fortune that we have been following. This was a shift in the pattern of England's export trade, which was one of the most striking features of her late medieval history. At the beginning of the fourteenth century England's most important item of export, far and away, was raw wool, whose worth, according to the protesting barons in 1297, amounted 'almost to the value of half the whole land'. The export trade was at that time largely in the hands of alien merchants, mostly Italians, who bought either direct from the grower (as, for example, from some of the great northern abbeys) or from an English wool merchant who dealt in bulk, wholesale. The Italians shipped most of the wool to Flanders, where it was woven up into cloth in the great industrial cities of Ghent, Bruges and Ypres. Some of the finer Flemish cloth was then re-imported back to England, which is perhaps why, in the late thirteenth century, some traditional domestic centres of cloth manufacture were experiencing difficulties. But in the early fourteenth century the Flemish industry was violently disrupted, by confrontations between the weavers and the great merchants who controlled and exploited their labour, and by wars between France and Flanders. This gave English manufacturers a golden chance to break into the European market in cloth, which they seized: ultimately, they were to capture the lion's share of it.

From 1347 on (when a tax on exported cloth was first levied, and we begin to get reliable figures), the volume of the trade, mostly carried in English ships, increased remarkably steadily. In 1400, for the first time, the number of fully finished cloths exported topped the 40,000 mark, and in 1439 it reached 60,000. The loss of the English provinces in France (a useful market) and the civil disorders of the Wars of the Roses generated a recession after 1450, but after 1470 exports began to rise again, strongly, and held their own far into the sixteenth century. Correspondingly, the export trade in wool (from the mid fourteenth century also mostly carried in English ships) dwindled. It was adversely affected both by the higher customs duty that was payable on exported wool, and by the growing dependence of the Crown on loans from the native wool merchants to finance the war with France (especially after the wool staple, with a monopoly of export, was established at Calais). At the beginning of the fourteenth century England had been exporting 30,000 sacks of wool in most years, but from 1350 to 1400 the average was only 23,000; in the fifteenth century it sank again, much lower, averaging over the years 1400–1500 somewhere near 10,000 sacks a year. The decline of the wool trade had a direct adverse effect on towns which had once been major ports of export (like Hull and Boston), or (like Lincoln) whose fairs had been famous and had brought trade into the city. It undoubtedly has much to do with the general decline of towns towards the eastern seaboard. Conversely, the rise in the export trade in cloth enhanced the prosperity of such cities as Bristol, Coventry and Norwich. Norwich was hard hit by the first pestilence, and a rent roll of 1357 shows shops, stalls and tenements in ruins, but she was saved by the trade in worsteds. The communities of the surrounding rural area were very active in the manufacture of these, and Norwich was the principal centre of their sale. Norwich's prosperity lasted and her population grew, as we have seen, throughout most of the fifteenth century.

The later experience of York and Coventry – and of a number of other cities heavily involved in textile manufacture – was not the same as that of Norwich, however. In the late fourteenth century their prosperity increased like hers, and so did their populations, outstripping pre-plague levels. But during the fifteenth century a further development began to have visible and, for them, adverse effects. The increasing demand for cloth helped to stimulate the growth of production in other, smaller centres, and the competition began to be serious. The trade 'goeth these days into the country', the York fullers complained in the 1470s: Halifax, Leeds and Wakefield were prospering, but the city that had once been second only to London was beginning to feel hard pressed. By the early six-teenth century even Bristol and Norwich were beginning to suffer depression, complaining of 'households desolate, vacant and decayed' and of 'dwellings that stood unletten and grew to ruin'.

The countryside and country towns enjoyed many advantages in cloth manufacture. The harnessing of water power to drive fulling mills had greatly reduced the labour requirements of one important process: all that was needed to make a success of it was a steady supply of fast-running water and reasonable proxim-ity to supplies of raw wool (the small weaving towns of the Cotswolds and of the West Riding enjoyed these advantages liberally). Rents (and fee-farms) were lower in country towns and boroughs than in the greater cities. Journeymen and aspiring craftsmen might find better terms, consequently, in the country, and as trade throve small merchants found that they could bypass regional centres of distribution and sell direct further afield (it looks as if this may have had much to do with Coventry's difficulties). In face of competition, the restrictive practices of the guilds in larger cities, their efforts to control the level of wages and prices and to limit hours of work, could all too easily prove counterproductive. Thus people as well as prosperity were drawn away from the older cities into the 'country' towns, whence those 'dwellings that stood unletten'.

The story of Castle Combe offers a good example of the way in which the textile industry could bring new prosperity, indeed could virtually create a country town. Good luck brought this manor into the hands of that great soldier, Sir John Fastolf, and throughout his long military career in France in the reigns of Henry V and VI he clothed the soldiers of his company in its cloth 'purchasing yearly more than £100 [worth] of his tenants there'; and throughout his tenure, its population grew. Artisans, who paid 2d. a year to live within the manor boundaries, began to arrive in numbers, and the growing reputation of the town's fine red cloths led clothmakers from elsewhere in the region (like Roger Robin of Cirencester) to send their cloths to be dyed there. By soon after the mid-century, 'Castle Combes' had come to be a trade name in London for fine reds. The widow of one of Fastolf's bond tenants, William Haynes, who had risen to be a substantial producer with chattels valued at 3,000 marks when he died, was able to pay £100 for the lord's leave to remarry: when she died she left a fulling mill, a grain mill, a shop and stall, and two houses that she had had built. No wonder that not only the clothmen but also the local wool merchants of the textile regions who supplied them with their raw materials (as well as engaging in the export trade) flourished so highly, men like William Grevel of Chipping Camden, described as the 'flower of the wool merchants of England' in Richard II's time, or John Thame of Fairford whose brass one may see in Fairford church and who ordered the magnificent glass for its windows.

The rise of Castle Combe was more than usually dramatic, but the story of, say, Wakefield or Tiverton was not, in essence, so very different. For centres of real urban significance, cities with a tradition of regional dominance and an established sense of civic identity, the competition of the new country centres of manufacture, in tandem with demographic decline that was the consequence both of plague mortality and emigration, threatened undoing. To make things worse, those who (probably genuinely) felt most threatened were the rich and dominant, those leading citizens who could aspire to call themselves 'merchants of estimation'. These were the men who had, traditionally, shouldered the major share of their city's fiscal burden, had put money into civic building and into civic festivals and pageantry, and had monopolized civic and guild offices (which could be expensive to hold). One of the most depressing signs of what Professor Dobson so aptly calls the 'urban malaise' that was almost ubiquitous in the greater cities, was the widespread and growing difficulty, in the fifteenth century, of finding citizens willing to take up these offices. Where once they had been eager for the worship as well as the advantage that office conferred, they were now unwilling to shoulder the concomitant expense. 'There is neither craftsman nor sojourner that will come to abide here, for fear of the said offices,' the citizens of Lincoln declared in their long moan of 1486. Men were ready to pay to be excused: William Dale, picked to be sheriff of Bristol in 1518, protested that others 'had passed the danger of the said office by the great substance they had before gotten'. Others quitted town to avoid the threat of onerous responsibility: 'when a man hath gotten any goods to find his living, for fear of office[s] which be so chargeable, he . . . goeth to a farm in the country', they said at Coventry. With their leadership in such disarray, it is not surprising that the cities of England at the end of the middle ages were suffering from 'malaise'. London apart, the centres that were in the fullest sense urban were not acting as the 'accelerators' either of the culture or of the economy of the kingdom, as they were in other parts of Europe and as they would do in England at other times.

Yet if the cities and larger towns of later medieval England were not acting as the accelerators of culture or the economy, they nevertheless did have their own distinctive, specifically urban culture and way of life. Even in decline, a substantial town could not just slip back into rusticity as a smaller town

might, to be 'now but a village like' as Leland wrote of
Reculver in its decay. It is to that way of life and its patterns
that we must now turn attention.

Physically, a city is defined by its buildings and architecture,
and they make a good starting-point. The walls of a city, or if
there were no walls the surrounding town ditch, marked a clear
perimeter. Though a number of important English towns, like
Salisbury and Derby, were unwalled, there were over a hundred
walled towns in England in the late middle ages. As defences
these walls were not of a very effective standard, and they
were often not very well kept (building and repair were a
charge on the citizens, and not a welcome one). But they
were psychologically important, separating the town from the
countryside and from the suburbs – ribbon developments of
cottages and hovels along the ways leading to the city gates and
housing, usually, the poorest among those who sought their
livelihood in it. Walls were also important in another way,
facilitating the city government's meticulous regulation of the
course of its life, of its police, its hygiene, its comings and goings
and curfews, and the hours of work. These were tight, and those
labourers who lived in the suburbs could not make their way to
their workplace in the morning until the hour when the city
gates opened.

Within the perimeter, the streets were laid out on a natural
grid plan, focusing usually on the market (the main street might
itself be broad enough to contain a market). Streets marked the
boundaries of the wards into which the town was divided. What
ward a man lived in depended more often on occupation than
on wealth: common sense dictated separating out noxious or
unhygienic trades (tanners for instance) and dangerous ones (as
smiths, whose business created a risk of fire). The standard of
housing in any one street was therefore likely to be quite
variable, though the wealthier, with better houses, might be
concentrated in those wards or streets where the wealthier trades
or crafts were concentrated. Town houses, sometimes of stone,
more usually timber-framed, crowded and huddled directly on
to the street, built either parallel or, more commonly, at right
angles to it and with the gable end facing on to it. The plots
behind the houses, with their yards and gardens, were long and

narrow and took up much space; from the air, a late medieval town would have given something of the look of a garden city.

There was a great variation of scale in town housing. In a Southampton terrier of 1454, listing properties in the city, about 6 per cent are described as 'capital tenements', 60 per cent as 'tenements' or 'small tenements', just over 30 per cent as 'cottages'. The grander houses were commonly built on a court-yard plan, as that of Strangers' Hall in Norwich, rebuilt by William Bailey in 1450. On the ground floor there was a front range of shops with upper chambers above them; this was pierced by an arched gateway which opened into a court. Across the court, opposite, was the hall block, containing at one end a hall (34 × 19 ft) and at the other a two-storey bay, with the buttery and pantry (wet and dry stores) on the ground floor, and chambers above. John Hall's house in Salisbury offers an example of a more middling but still substantial town house. It was built at right angles to the street, with the gable end facing on to it: a ground-floor shop abutted on the street with a chamber above: to the rear of this was the hall (30 × 18 ft), open to the roof. A two-storey continuation contained a service room or store with a chamber above. The kitchen was probably separate, in the back yard. Where there was no alley between houses, a house like this might have to include a passage running the length of the building at ground-floor level, with a gallery above it serving as a connection through the hall area between the upper rooms at front and rear. A privy, cupboard size, might be squeezed into a corner of the upper chamber at the rear, with a shute to a cesspit in a cellar. A house at 16 Edmund Street, Exeter, shows what a lot could be squashed on to a site much smaller than John Hall's house. The ground floor of this timber-framed building contained a shop and kitchen and is little more than 10 × 14 ft in area. Two further storeys were jetted to the side and out over the street, with a hall on the first floor and two chambers on the second. Smaller and humbler dwellings than this were listed as cottages. A cottage might be a two-roomed building, like those at Spon Street, Coventry, with a hall, open to the roof across one half of the building and with an upper chamber over the other half, floored to the line of the central roof truss. Or it might be a flimsy, single-cell hovel: only occasional archaeological traces remain of such very humble dwellings.

The difference between a house and a cottage was one of the marks of a distinction of considerable social significance in town life, between the wage-earner (or cottager) who left home to work and the householder whose shop was part of his house, and for whom home and workplace were one and the same. A 'household' thus brought together during the day more than just the householder, his family and any living-in apprentice; and his hired man or men from without would expect to take at least one meal a day with these. They would not go home again until the labouring day was over. Although such figures as can be obtained suggest that a substantial proportion of households (perhaps a third) included at least one living-in 'servant' or worker, the average household size seems to have been smaller than in the country. As in the country, a young man did not usually think of setting up house until he married and the conjugal couple (or the single survivor) was the focus of the household group. The small average size of households suggests late marriage, and in many towns it looks as if the population was barely reproducing itself, or even failing to do so. Crowded and unhygienic conditions no doubt made infant mortality even more of a scourge in the town than in the countryside.

The proportional distribution of different standards of housing in the Southampton 1454 terrier gives a good impression of the sort of distribution of wealth to be expected in a substantial, late medieval English town. The élite of the very wealthy at the top of the scale was a very small one. Phythian Adams has calculated that what he calls the 'magisterial élite' in early-sixteenth-century Coventry comprised perhaps forty households, or 2 per cent. Subsidy assessments of the same period give comparable percentages for the richest sector among the citizens in a number of other towns. Those assessed on lands and goods worth more (and usually a great deal more) than £40 come to 2 per cent in Southampton and 3 per cent at Leicester. In the same two towns, the percentage of those assessed at between £10 and £40 were 8 per cent in the one case and 7 per cent in the other. Below this level, Adams's Coventry figures allot 320 households to the better-off freemen ('honest commoners', the top third among them being distinctly better off than the rest), 400 households to the smaller masters of crafts, 600 to journeymen (regularly employed skilled labourers) and 500 to other labourers and out-servants. This is probably a not atypical distribution. The base of the pyramid of wealth was thus by no means a broad one. Given that a wage labourer might earn up to 4d. a day, that the employer would have provided at least one meal most days, and that a cottage rent would probably be somewhere between 4s. and 6s. a year, it looks as if those close to the subsistence line cannot have been a large class, even allowing for under employment and for the many days lost each year as a result of compulsory holidays. But the class of those who depended on their fellow citizens for their livelihood was a large one, for it included not only journeymen, servants and labourers but also a good many among the smaller master craftsmen, who lived largely by piece-work performed for better-off colleagues in their trade. That is why any development that put pressure on the fortunes of the better-off was felt through the whole society.

Townsmen were sharply conscious of the stratifications of wealth in their world, and had their own names for them, 'men of degree', 'honest commoners', 'mere commoners' and so on. In some towns, as at Coventry, the gradations were reinforced by local sumptuary laws. There none save those that were 'noted and known in this city to be of the substance of £300 and above' were to trim their gowns with marten fur or wear velvet doublets; substantial commoners might trim with fox fur or lambs' wool 'but none other furs'; no servant 'man or woman retained for wages' might wear velvet 'in any apparell upon them'. In the light of this sort of regulation it is not surprising that city government was markedly oligarchic in tendency. To have any part at all in this government, to be eligible for office or to vote in mayoral elections, one had to be a 'freeman': this was usually achieved by serving apprenticeship in a recognized craft, though it could be purchased or acquired hereditarily. But although very generally in the late middle ages registers of freemen show admissions to the franchise rising, the sector of town society from which the civic officers (the mayor, alderman, sheriffs or bailiffs) and the governing councils of the city were chosen remained much more restricted, to those near the top of the scales of wealth and dignity.

This was partly the result of the way in which men were elected to city office. Thus at Hull (a fairly typical example) we find in the 1440s that the mayor was formally elected by all the burgesses, but the two candidates between whom they chose were nominated by the aldermen, who also nominated the candidates for the shrievalty. The aldermen, who formed a council of twelve advising the mayor, were chosen from among candidates nominated by themselves when a vacancy occurred, and then served for life. This was the only formal town council at Hull: in many towns there was a second, outer council from among whose members candidates to be aldermen would be chosen. In the later fifteenth century the oligarchic, restrictive tendency inherent in these sorts of arrangements were further strengthened by the establishment of 'closed corporations'. Incorporation (by royal charter, for which the city paid) gave the mayor and his council the right to represent the civic community at law; and to purchase and hold property in its name. A corporation became closed when its governing body became fully self-selecting, as happened for instance at Colchester in 1412. In that year a new council was added to the old town council that the mayor and bailiffs headed; the new council was to be nominated by the old one, and vacancies on the old one by the aldermen and bailiffs. All the powers of the community were thus henceforth vested in a tight group of forty-two persons, chosen by themselves.

For admission to the charmed circle of the civic establishment, wealth was a vital criterion, if an informal one. In order to aspire to office, one needed to be rich, for office could be decidedly expensive. A man of 'worship' was expected to maintain a certain style, to contribute handsomely in alms giving, to guild suppers and to civic junketings at Christmas and on other church feasts. The prominent besides bore, as has been said earlier, a disproportionately heavy share of the city's fiscal burdens. Very generally and very naturally, influence and authority tended in consequence to be concentrated in the hands of men of 'merchant' status, those who dealt in bulk, wholesale, who were substantial employers and landlords and had contacts

in other communities. Prominent men in the richer craft guilds
(those that traded most widely, such as drapers, mercers, grocers)
were the other group that might be well enough off to compete
for office. Thus in 1420 in York the governing councils counted
twenty-two 'merchants' among their membership, but only five
men drawn from the manufacturing guilds. There was often a
kind of *cursus honorum*, linking office in the guilds with the city
government, wardenship of a guild opening the way to the
shrievalty and so later to the mayoralty. Family connections and
influence also often counted for much, but mortality, the fluidity
of commercial fortunes and a fair degree of social mobility
checked the tendency, observable in an earlier period, towards
the establishment of hereditary patriciates. The English towns of
the late middle ages bred no governing clans like the Medici of
Florence.

The actual responsibilities of civic dignity, in terms of official
business and functions, could be heavy. The mayor of Coventry's
day began at 7 a.m., when he and his officers processed to
church; by 9 a.m. he would have inspected victuals that would
be put on sale in the market that day, and he had a mass of
further business on his hands, in court, in council and in super-
vising and enforcing city rules and regulations. City life was
very highly regulated, almost hour by hour. At the ringing of
the day bell in the churches (perhaps as early as 4 a.m.) the gates
(if gates there were) were opened: after the evening curfew bell
had been rung they would be locked again. Hours of work, and
the lengths of dinner breaks, were strictly controlled. It was a
long day, starting very early and ending perhaps at 6 or 7 p.m.,
six days a week; in most crafts in most cities there were strict
rules about what might be undertaken after hours (usually very
little). Other rules and regulations limited opening hours of
taverns, when dogs might be allowed to roam, when and where
waste might be disposed of. There was thus a very great deal for
the mayor, his court and the city officials to have an eye to.

We find this sort of business being added to, moreover, as
time goes by, as city governments began to take on more
responsibilities. By the end of the fifteenth century a quite
substantial body of salaried civic servants, responsible to the
city's officers, was established in many places. The more dignified

among these, the town clerk, the recorder, perhaps a mayor's sergeant administering city properties, might have a legal training, and with a clerk or clerks assisting them formed a nascent city bureaucracy. Others might be specialists, like the municipal paviour whom Nottingham appointed in 1501 at an annual salary of 33s. 4d. and a gown, to 'make and mend all the defaults in all places of the said town in the pavements'. A variety of humbler figures might include a city clock keeper, a town crier, beadles, porters, watchmen, constables and street cleaners, all with carefully assigned duties and all drawing wages from the civic purse that the mayor and his colleagues controlled.

The dominance in the towns of a rich, narrow civic élite naturally generated some class tension from time to time. 'Sirs, hear me,' declared the Coventry radical, Lawrence Sanders, in 1494; 'we shall never have our rights until we have struck off three or four heads of the churls that rule us.' But it is easy to exaggerate the sharpness of the urban class antipathies of this period. In a society where social attitudes were on the whole hierarchic and organic rather than egalitarian, it seemed only natural that authority should be vested in the 'sadder and wiser' or 'the more honest and discreet', and to identify these with the richer citizens; and to applaud the exclusion from influence of 'the multitude of inhabitants of little substance and of no discretion, who ... by their confederations, exclamations and headiness ... [cause] ... great troubles in the elections and the assessing of lawful charges'. The conscious motive for the establishment of closed corporations was not so much the social and economic exclusiveness of the well-off and their desire to entrench themselves in the positions of influence and advantage, as the anxiety to uphold order, which the rivalries of guilds and factions could easily threaten. Their brand of rivalry, rather than class tensions as we now understand the term, were usually at the root of the riots and violence which were a recurrent feature of individual city histories and which flared easily if election to some city office (especially to mayoral office) became tinged with the factional or guild competition. Significantly, tensions usually died down again, once the 'sadder and wiser' got themselves securely back into the saddle.

★

The guilds and their officials, though formally separate from the city or borough government, were closely associated, often intertwined with it, and they played a vital part in city life. Three different kinds of guilds need here to be distinguished. The oldest were the guilds merchant, associations of leading citizens whose chief business was to regulate local trade; over time, and mainly before our period, the guilds merchant tended to become absorbed into or assimilated with the borough or city government. The craft guilds, which became very important in the fourteenth century, were associations of the qualified practitioners of particular trades or crafts ('mysteries'), and their chief purpose was to oversee and regulate the conduct of their particular 'mystery'. The third kind of guilds were the religious guilds, or fraternities, which were very numerous. Some were associated with particular crafts, others drew their members from all walks of life. Some were associated with parishes, others had members from all quarters of their town, and most of them admitted women as well as men. They were rather like friendly societies, with a religious involvement. Entrance fees and subscriptions established a common fund, and some came to hold substantial properties in their native towns. Their income went to maintain lights at a church altar or in a chantry (perhaps the guild's own chantry), to pay for funeral masses for departed members, to assist in their need the 'brothers and sisters' of the society and to meet the cost of guild suppers. The functions of the religious guilds and of the craft guilds often overlapped to some extent and both types were very influential. They are the guilds that must occupy our attention.

The craft guilds have been described by Phythian Adams as the 'basic reference group' in late medieval urban society. Formally associations of master craftsmen, they were at once social as well as economic institutions. Guild members dined together at formal feasts two or three times a year, they attended each others' marriages and funerals, and took their appointed place together in civic processions and civic worship. Altogether their activity was very closely intertwined with city life. Guild office was normally an essential first step on the way to city office (as it usually took anything up to fourteen years to achieve senior office in a guild, this helped to give government a distinctly 'sad', elderly cast). Office was usually monopolized by the wealthier masters, and in this way authority within the craft associations mirrored the oligarchical structure of the city establishment. Guild regulations were subject to the approval of the city authorities, and fines for breaches of them went as often to swell city funds as those of the guild.

In the economic sphere, the most profound effect of guild regulations was to ensure the decentralization of commerce and manufacture, by maintaining the household unit as the essential focus of production and trade. They inhibited the poaching of trade by one master from another by establishing minimum prices, and by regulations such as that 'no man shall take in more work than he is able and may do in his house'. They limited the number of apprentices that a master might take on (usually one or two) as well as the length of apprenticeship (usually seven years). By the regulation of wages, of hours of work and conditions of work they discouraged the poaching of labour. By strict rules aimed to keep control of craft skills in craft hands ('no person of the said craft disclose nor utter nothing that ought of right to be secretly kept among themselves') they made larger-scale industrial organization difficult. In all these respects their influence can be said to have been restrictive, and no doubt their regulations did lay town manufacture open to countryside competition, notably in the textile industry. On the whole, though, they more than made up for this by the way in which they helped to limit industrial dissension (between craft and craft, master and master, and master and servants), and to integrate manufacture into the framework of city life. Perhaps their most important service of all was the responsibility that they took for maintaining standards of quality in the products of their craft, and in this area they showed considerable open-mindedness. The searchers whom they permitted to check their standards were often appointed by the city, not the craft authorities: the city's reputation as well as that of the craft depended on the quality reputation of its goods, and all parties were alive to their common interest in this respect.

The part that religious fraternities played in city life was less obviously vital than the role of the craft guilds, but it could be very important. There was an almost infinite variation in their

size, their significance, and the status of their members. Some
were small and consciously, even self-consciously humble:
'whereas this guild was founded by folks of common and
middling rank, it is ordained that no one of the rank of mayor
or bailiff shall become a member of the guild, unless he is found
of humble, good and honest conversation,' say the rules of the
Corpus Christi Guild of Lincoln. Other fraternities, however,
were in effect clubs of wealthy citizens, and very influential.
Thus at Coventry the Corpus Christi Guild was recruited from
among the sons of the governing city élite and from among the
wealthier masters of the greater crafts (the sort of men who
would go on to craft office). The Trinity Guild of the same city
was still more exalted, with an entrance fee of no less than £5;
Corpus Christi members usually transferred to this senior guild
at about the time that they came into the group (in terms of age
and status) from among whom the city officers would be
chosen. It was usual for one who had been Master of the Corpus
Christi Guild to become mayor within one or two years; and
within one or two years of laying down office to become
Master of the Trinity Guild. At Norwich, more formally, the
outgoing mayor automatically took up the mastership of the
Guild of St George. The ordinances of the Guild of the Holy
Cross at Stratford-upon-Avon are ostensibly concerned with the
lights that the brothers and sisters maintained in the parish
church, and with their annual feast in Easter week: but at the
same time it was the principal property owner in the town and
in effect 'the social and political organization behind the front
provided by the borough court' (Hilton).

The membership of the prestigious Holy Cross Guild of
Stratford was drawn not only from among the burgesses, but
also included prosperous people from the villages and small
towns of the surrounding region. In a similar way, the registers
of the Coventry Corpus Christi Guild associated with the membership merchants and traders from a number of other towns, as
Bristol, Boston, Warwick and even Dublin. In this way a city's
religious guilds could help to establish links with the commercial
élites of other towns, and also, indeed, with gentlemen of the
neighbouring countryside (Norwich's Guild of St George would
not admit any non-citizen 'but if he be a knight or a squire, or

else notably known for a gentleman of birth'). Gentry and visitors from other towns would also be honoured guests of the guild on the occasions when, on the feast day of its dedication, a fraternity took the lead in organizing a civic procession – as on Corpus Christi day in Coventry, when 'all the brethren and sisters [of the guild] shall be clad in their livery, at their own cost, and shall carry viii torches around the body of Christ, when it is borne through the town of Coventry'. A ceremony such as this, and the feast that was likely to follow, at one and the same time displayed religious respect for a church festival, upheld the worship of the guild in the city and oiled the wheels of commerce and sound connections.

The great processions on holy days of the church (especially at the feast of Corpus Christi), and the staging of pageants and 'mystery' plays that were often associated with them, were perhaps the most remarkable and distinctive expression of the urban culture of late medieval England. In those cities where it took place, the Corpus Christi procession was a major civic occasion, a great gathering of all the city's principal associations, lay and ecclesiastical. The procession assembled at one of the city churches, where the consecrated host was taken up, and marshalled in a defined order. The Corpus Christi Guild might very likely head the procession (as it did at York); the craft guilds dressed in their livery followed, the humbler crafts leading and others following in order of dignity; then came the aldermen, councillors and sheriffs, and finally the mayor, with the clergy accompanying the host. In the most ambitious arrangements, as at York, Coventry and Chester, pageants and plays were associated with the procession, which sought to depict or enact the whole Christian scriptural story. A play or pageant, or both, was allotted to each guild or to a group of guilds, often on the ground of some particular association. Thus in the York cycle of plays 'Noah and the Ark' fell to the shipwrights and 'The Last Supper' to the bakers, and at Coventry the lovely shepherds' play went to the shearmen. The texts of such plays as have survived are vivid, human, full of shrewd contemporary perceptions and often crudely humorous (especially when the devil was on stage). They were tremendously appreciated, drawing great

crowds of spectators, giving occasion to much feasting and drinking, and involving for the city and the particular guilds huge
efforts in staging and preparation and very considerable expense.

Civic plays and pageantry had a religious didactic purpose,
but they had something else too to teach that was important.
They have been called 'mirrors of the community', aptly, because
their spectacle reflected at once its hierarchic structure and the
bonds, religious and institutional, that held together the parts of
the corporate civic society. They brought together, on a sacred
occasion, the interrelated groupings of craft, religious fraternity,
city government and city clergy. Of course tensions could arise
out of them, wrangles as to which play should be allotted to
whom, or between crafts over the ordering of precedence in the
procession. On the whole, though, they seem to have been
accepted as an expression of the 'worship' of the city, of its
identity and dignity. An ordinance from Beverley commanded
that the Corpus Christi plays were to be presented in perpetuity
'in order that the honour of God and the repute of the town
may be enhanced'. The Coventry pageants were described as
being staged 'for the wealth and worship of the whole city', and
contributions to maintain them were deemed to be paid so as to
'please God, and continue the good name and fame that this city
hath'. Pageants and processions could also be reminders of the
city's place in the wider community. The mayor's robes and the
mace that was borne before him were ceremonial symbols of the
fact that he held office as the king's representative. Pageants
were an integral element in the civic greeting of visiting royalty,
just as they were of church feasts: when Edward IV's queen,
Elizabeth Woodville, came to Norwich in 1469 she was
welcomed with pageants representing the Annunciation and the
Salutation. And it seems very likely that the citizens of Norwich
who took part in the annual St George's day 'riding' and were
spectators of the play that presented his encounter with the
dragon (a new dragon cost the city 9s. 4d. in 1421) were not
unaware that St George was the patron saint of English arms as
well as of their city's most prestigious guild.

The life of the cities and towns of late medieval England was
closely intertwined with that of the wider community. Many of

them, and all of the most important, sent representatives to Parliament, where they took their seats beside the genteel representatives of the shires. There were, in fact, a good many gentry who had houses in regional towns, and more, probably, who had association with the religious guilds of a local urban centre. The relationship was not just one way; there were gentlemen, so we find, who were keen, if they could not represent the shire, to go to Parliament as representatives of a local borough, and there were merchants — more than a trickle by the late fifteenth century — who, when they had prospered, began to think of purchasing an estate and settling themselves and their family in the country. There were also urban dwellers, substantial people, who if not quite gentry in the ordinary sense, might easily call themselves gentlemen, clothier graziers or butcher graziers, perhaps, who had purchased lands with an eye to pasturing sheep or cattle, but preferred to remain domiciled in town; or lawyers and administrators who had clients in town and country, who found residence in a regional centre convenient for business. The lives of men such as these are reminders of what was said at the beginning of this chapter, that trade and manufacture are not the only things that make a town. They are also a reminder that the life of medieval English towns, perhaps because of their relatively small size, was never quite as sharply separated from that of the surrounding countryside as was the case in some other European lands, and that the identification of their leading people both with regional society and with national interest was the stronger for it.

5. *Westminster and London*

In some respects, London's story in the late middle ages was very like that of most other great English towns. But it was larger, much larger than any other among them, the only city of the kingdom that could compare in the size of its population to the great urban centres of the continent, as those of Flanders and Italy. And there were other ways too in which it was so different from other English towns that it demands a chapter to itself; even a complete chapter cannot do justice to the full range of its varied life.

Crowded and unhygienic conditions meant that the capital, like other cities, was hard hit by the first plagues, and London proved particularly vulnerable to later recurrences of pestilence and to outbreaks of other diseases. Its population in consequence shrank perceptibly from a high point in the early fourteenth century. Through most of the period 1350–1500 it stood, probably, at around 40,000, though towards the end it seems to have been beginning to increase once more. The prosperity and pride of the city were not however dented, and though there was always emigration out of London it was more than balanced by the immigration into the city of people of every social level coming to seek their fortune. Here was no urban decay, no 'malaise' in the sense in which that word was used in the last chapter, though there was plenty of tumult and riot. London's leading citizens remained the richest men of the kingdom: the mayor, taxed in 1379 at the same rate as an earl, was hailed as 'the full honourable the Lord Mayor'. London was a vigorous, crowded capital city.

In terms of physical layout and living conditions, London was much like any other major port situated on a navigable estuary, only larger. Already before the mid fourteenth century the city had sprawled well beyond the ancient walls; the limits of civic jurisdiction were not here, but at the 'bars' (Temple Bar on the road out from Ludgate, the bar at what is now Spital Square beyond Bishopsgate, and so on). Beyond the bars, suburban villages like Kensington and Hammersmith grew and flourished as a result of the part they played in supplying fresh produce for the city; and some others provided different services (Southwark was famous for its brothels). Within the city, shops, cottages and taverns crowded on to the streets, with great houses interspersed here and there among them; there were of course more great houses in London than in any other city. As in other cities, there were plenty of gardens and of open green spaces, but some wards (Farringdon, for example) were already so populous in the later fourteenth century that, gardens apart, there was little open ground left. Rubbish and sewage naturally presented severe problems, though piped water helped the fight against pollution as well as filling the various famous 'conduits' where the poorer inhabitants (those who had no private supply) went to draw water. The worst sewage was washed down into the Thames. There wharves lined the river, which was crowded with ships and also with small boats, for it was a main artery of local communication (the easiest route, for instance, from the city to Westminster was by water). Old London Bridge, with its nine-teen pointed arches, spanned the Thames, lined with buildings (mostly shops): a gateway stood two arches back from the Southwark end, and the seventh arch from the south was spanned by a drawbridge, which could be hauled up against a second gateway. Looking towards London from high ground to the south, the three most prominent features would have been this bridge, the Tower and the great church of old St Paul's with its tall spire rising over the city centre.

In the late middle ages, as so often later, London drew the poets to her, and they have left us some vivid pictures. Chaucer, of course, was a Londoner born, and his writing is full of flashes of his experience and observation of the city. Langland came to London from the country, from the western midlands, and has left us some marvellous vignettes of the crowd about West-minster Hall, of a Parliament, of clerks chasing up the king's debts in the Exchequer. Best of all though, is his epic evocation of low life in his account of how Glutton settled into the alehouse in the morning and drank himself out of his mind, finally throwing up his guts at the door after a day's boozing in the company of Clarice of Cock Lane, Davy the ditcher, the street sweeper of Cheapside, Griffith the Welshman, Rose the dish seller and 'old clothesmen a heap'. A quite different aspect of the capital struck the Scot Dunbar, for whom London was 'the flower of cities all':

> London, thou art of townes *A per se*.
> Sovereign of cities, seemliest in sight,
> Of high renoun, riches, and royaltie;
> Of lordis, barons, and many a goodly knight;
> Of most delectable lusty ladies bright;
> Of famous prelatis, in habits clericall,
> Of marchaunts full of substance and of might.

Somewhere in between comes the London that Thomas Hoccleve recalled, in his poetic memories of what he called 'an ill-ruled' life. Hoccleve was a civil servant, a clerk in the Privy Seal Office at Westminster for more than thirty years, who spent his days crouched over parchment drafting and copying official letters. What in age he liked to remember, with nostalgia and querulous self-pity for his decline in years and fortune, was not his work, but his young days when he had had money in his purse, and could get the boatmen to row him from his lodgings in the Strand to Westminster, and could spend nights drinking with a club of cronies called 'the court of good fellowship'. Or sometimes he would take out girls, for whom he always insisted on paying. Afterwards there would be a bit of kissing, but he was not very good, by his own confession, at getting much further. In youth he dreamt of a rich benefice, but he ended up married to a termagant wife and with an inadequate annuity of £4. His story has a familiar ring: London must have seen countless men go much the same way as he did, before and since, just as it has impressed others in the same ways as it did Dunbar on the one hand and Langland on the other.

There is one point in Hoccleve's memories that is of particular interest, the way in which they illustrate the connection of London (where he lodged and where he went out on the town

at night) and Westminster (where he worked). What really
made London different from other cities, and had already made
it so before the mid fourteenth century, was the symbiosis of
these two originally separate urban communities. London
brought together the greatest concentration of merchants and of
commercial wealth in the kingdom, drawn to the wharves of
the country's leading port. Westminster, from the twelfth century on, had become the headquarters of the kingdom's government, chosen as such by her kings because of its proximity to
London. Formally, the two communities remained distinct. The
borough of Westminster, with a resident population (*c.* 3,000) that
was tiny compared with London's, was the abbot's liberty, and
outside the jurisdiction of the Mayor of London and the city
authorities. But the distance between Westminster and London
was so small that they grew together socially, and their prosperity was interdependent. Many of those who worked in Westminster by day, like Hoccleve, lodged in London. Westminster
drew people to London on legal business of their own or about
the king's affairs, and so drew them as customers to the shops
and warehouses of the city, and to its taverns too, buttressing
and stimulating commercial activity. Conversely, the great throngs
of the poor who crowded the gates of the abbey to receive alms
from the monks came from London, not Westminster.

Two buildings dominated Westminster, the Abbey, with its
famous sanctuary, and the Palace of Westminster, the king's
chief residence in the capital. The sanctuary, defined by the
precinct wall of the Abbey, offered much more than just a
refuge for those accused of crime and for businessmen in difficulties with their creditors. The sole authority recognized there
was that of the abbot and his monk-archdeacon, so that it
offered a freedom from all sorts of commercial regulations in
force elsewhere, and was crowded with the stalls of shopkeepers
trading in a very wide variety of goods. Because they were
outside the city, the tradespeople of Westminster were un-
shackled by the restrictions imposed on their London neighbours
in such matters as guild membership, price control and standards
of quality of their goods; they also enjoyed the privilege of
being on the spot to a well-heeled clientele of visitors on
government business. As Gervase Rosser puts it, Westminster,

and especially the sanctuary, was an 'island of ungoverned commerce', which brought prosperity to the borough, and very considerable wealth from the rents of shops and stalls to the Abbey and to the abbot who was the borough's lord.

The Palace of Westminster adjoined the Abbey precinct. Its great hall was rebuilt in the reign of Richard II; it was then that its splendid hammer-beam roof was constructed. By an irony, Richard himself was never to preside in the new building, but Henry IV, who usurped his crown, was able to hold his coronation banquet there. For such a feast the rudimentary, removable fittings of the central courts, which sat in Westminster Hall, had to be shifted. Ordinarily the King's Bench sat at the dais at the south end of the hall, with Chancery close by and Common Pleas against the west wall, close to the door leading to the Exchequer. This was housed in a building alongside the hall at its north-west end. The chamber where the royal council deliberated was alongside the east wall, in the room that was to become famous in Tudor times as the Star Chamber. The private side of the palace, to the south of the great hall, included a lesser hall, the king's own chambers, his privy wardrobe, apartments for noblemen, knights and esquires of the household, and for officials attendant on him. The king himself was only occasionally in residence at Westminster (or at his other London residence, the Tower), for on the whole the English kings of the later middle ages preferred to spend more time at Windsor, or at such royal manors in the home counties as Sheen, Eltham and King's Langley. Whether the king and his household were there or not, Westminster Hall and the public chambers round it which housed the nucleus of the government's offices were continuously thronged with people there on business, especially during the law terms. It was a very busy place, a hive of activity.

Well before the middle of the fourteenth century, Westminster had become the most usual venue for Parliaments. From time to time, all through the late middle ages, they were held elsewhere, but usually only when political tensions seemed to make it impolitic to call a session to the capital – in 1378, for instance, when Parliament met at Gloucester following a breach of the Westminster sanctuary by royal officials which had roused ill-feeling in London; or in 1459, when after the rout of the Yorkists at Ludford the Lancastrian government felt more secure to proceed against its enemies at Coventry than in the capital. At Westminster, plenary sessions of Parliament were held in the palace; for their separate debates, the Commons were usually allotted the chapter house of the Abbey. Parliaments were frequent, often meeting twice in the year, and brought together far more people than just the lords and representatives who had been summoned by writ. Lords came well attended – as they always were – by servants and retainers, and there were always a good many people who, though not members, had come up to London in Parliament time in the hope of furthering business of their own or that was of interest to their local communities. The crowd that gathered in and around Parliaments was far larger than Westminster on its own could lodge, and brought a great influx of custom to the inns, taverns and lodging-houses of London as well.

Those who came to London most regularly had their regular haunts. John Paston put up so often at the Bull Tavern in Westminster that messages could be left for him there. Great men needed more ample accommodation for themselves and their followers than a tavern could afford, and many of the great lords had their own 'inns', great town houses built about a court or courts after the style of a country manor. The Savoy Palace was the London house of the Dukes of Lancaster, until the peasants burned it down in the revolt of 1381. Coldharbour, one of two great houses (it had forty rooms) built by the rich merchant Sir John Pulteney, was acquired by the Earl of Salisbury; the other, Pountney's Inn, was for a time the Black Prince's London residence. The great inn of the Earls of Warwick was in Old Dean's Lane, that of the Earls of March near Aldgate. The great churchmen, bishops and abbots, also had their own inns, for they had very often to be in London, not only for Parliaments and councils but also for convocations (often held in the church of Blackfriars). The inns of the abbots of Cirencester, Tewkesbury and Faversham were all in Fleet Street, and a number of bishops had inns on the Strand. Westminster business was principally what made it useful or necessary for men such as these and others too, knights and gentlemen of substance as well as lords and bishops, to have their own town houses, but for the most part these were in London proper, not the suburb.

Westminster thus made London a political capital, setting the city at the hub of national affairs as a place where great events were witnessed and great achievements celebrated. As in other towns, ceremony and pageantry played an important part in civic life, but in London these were more politically oriented and less specifically urban in style than elsewhere, and they helped to draw together the king and his nobles with the people of his capital. Westminster was the scene of coronations, Smithfield was a favourite location for richly staged jousts and tournaments; it was there that, in 1359, Edward III, four of his sons and nineteen noblemen jousted dressed as the mayor and aldermen of London (as a compliment to the city) during the celebrations that marked the marriage of John of Gaunt to Blanche of Lancaster; and it was there, at a tournament in 1390, that Richard II first displayed his famous badge of the white hart. Richard's formal reconciliation with London in August 1392 was celebrated by a royal progress through the city; houses were decked with cloth of gold, the conduits flowed with red and white wine, and finally the king and queen with their nobles entertained the leading men of London at a great feast in (the old) Westminster Hall.

The pageants that greeted Henry V returning victorious from Agincourt give a good impression of what the city could do when it put its mind to it. At London Bridge, against the king's approach, had been set up the figure of a giant, with an axe in one hand and the keys of the city in the other. A little further on a wooden tower had been built, and half-way up it, in a canopied niche, 'there stood a most beautiful statue of St George in armour'; in a house beside it were boys dressed as angels singing 'Blessed is he who comes in the name of the Lord'. By the conduit of Cornhill another tower had been built, decorated with the arms of St Edward, St Edmund and the arms of England; before it, under a canopy,

was a company of prophets, with venerable white hair, in tunicles and golden copes, their heads turbaned with gold and crimson, who when

the king came by released a great flock of sparrows and other tiny
birds, as an acceptable sacrifice to God for the victory he had conferred.

At Cheapside Cross a model castle had been erected, with a
bridge from its gatehouse to the ground, over which a choir of
maidens, dressed in virginal white, came out to greet the king,
singing 'Welcome Henry the Fifth, King of England and of
France'. As Henry progressed slowly towards St Paul's, past
further tableaux, to render thanks, the press, says the chronicler,
was so thick that the horsemen could hardly force their way
through. At the end of the day, with a crowd still with him, he
came to the Palace of Westminster, where he spent the night.

London and Westminster were where kings naturally headed
for, when they came home from abroad, or when they felt the
need to seek counsel, or to meet Parliament. Equally naturally,
London and Westminster were the places which news reached
first and from which news radiated, and where people loitered
in the hope of catching it early. News from the capital would be
reliable: 'I pray you send me tidings from beyond the sea,'
Agnes Paston wrote in 1445 to her son Edmund, who was in
London; 'here [in Norfolk] they be afeared to tell what is
reported.' 'Tidings' of great affairs, for good or ill, were what
correspondents from the country constantly sought of their
contacts and kinsfolk in the metropolis. County gentlefolk like
the Pastons knew that what they heard from London would be
the surest guide to the conduct of their affairs in their own
'country'. Through its twinning with Westminster, London in
the later middle ages had penetrated the consciousness of at least
the political classes of provincial England as the single most
significant national and cosmopolitan centre to which they could
look, politically, economically and culturally.

It was the law that first drew the Pastons to London, and the
fortune that William Paston made in the courts there and the
connections that he forged were what enabled him by purchase
to set up as a landowner in his own native Norfolk. His son
John was in consequence able to live as a Norfolk squire, but his
business affairs, especially his lawsuits, took him constantly to
Westminster and to the city. Thus his wife Margaret learned to

look to the capital for quality goods, and her letters to him are full of instructions for purchases:

I pray you will vouchsafe to buy me 1 lb of almonds and 1 lb of sugar, and that ye will buy some frieze to make your children gowns: ye shall have the best cheap and the best choice of Haye's wife, as it is told me. And that ye would buy a yard of broadcloth of black for an hood for me, of 44d. or 4s. the yard, for there is neither good cloth nor good frieze in this town.

In the next generation the family was aiming higher socially. John's son Sir John came to London in the first place, like his father and grandfather, to study law; but he was drawn by the attraction of court life, and came to prefer London to his native Norfolk. He had a 'place' in Fleet Street, learned fashionable manners in wooing, and became engaged to a cousin of Lord Rivers (but never married her), and dabbled (to no great effect) in politics. The story of these three Pastons gives an illuminating insight into how London, largely through Westminster, acted as a magnet to people of status who were quite untouched by the attraction of the commercial opportunities that the city offered. They came there first because Westminster was an administrative and legal centre; that introduced them to cosmopolitan attractions that encouraged them to linger in London longer, to purchase there more and more, and to look to the capital for standards of manners, taste and reading.

The 'passage migrant' throng that Westminster played such a significant part in attracting to the capital helps to explain the importance of service occupations in London's economy, and why a high proportion of the city's population was involved in them. It ensured that victuallers, brewers, taverners and lodging keepers would never lack for custom, not to mention prostitutes and those who ran the stew-houses of Southwark. The very considerable wealth of the London vintners depended substantially on their virtual monopoly of the supply of wine to taverns and to the houses of the great. Large-scale manufacture did not contribute much to London's prosperity, in the way that, for instance, textile manufacture contributed to the prosperity of

Coventry or Norwich. There were of course certain manufacturing trades that did flourish, especially those that specialized in the production of high-class and luxury articles, as the goldsmiths, the armourers, the saddlers and the tailors. But the provision of services, to residents and to temporary sojourners, and wholesale commerce on a large scale in such merchandise as wool, mercery, victuals and spices were the mainstay of the city's prosperity, and the principal preoccupations of the working and trading population.

Among London's resident population, perhaps a third belonged to citizen families, headed by freemen who enjoyed full civic rights and were entitled to take part in elections to ward and city office, and most of whom belonged to one or other of the city's 120-odd guilds. A small governing élite of wealthy merchant capitalists more or less monopolized the higher city offices, that of mayor, the two shrievalties, and the aldermanries of the various wards. Most of the members of this group belonged to what were already known informally as the greater guilds: the vintners, mercers, fishmongers, grocers, goldsmiths, skinners, drapers and a few more. Below this level there was a numerous middling group of citizenry, masters of their crafts; the more substantial among these, those whose trade was wider than the average and who had acquired city property of their own, were the only people who could offer any serious rivalry to the established mercantile aristocracy. Most, though, were small masters, many of them principally occupied with piece-work for richer men. Among the un-enfranchised, apprentices, who would be hoping one day to become freemen, and journeymen regularly employed in craft work formed a substantial group.

London's population also included a significant number of resident aliens: the Steelyard's colony of German merchants of the Hanse towns, groups of Italian merchants (bankers like the Medici had London branches), and a good many foreign artisans. These foreigners were often resented, on the ground that they took trade or work away from natives; there was an ugly massacre of Flemish workers in 1381 and in 1457 the Italians felt so threatened that many of them temporarily quitted London (mostly for Southampton). Naturally the city had in addition a large clerical population, for besides its hundred or so parish churches the city boasted a number of important collegiate churches, such as St Paul's and St Martin le Grand, as well as houses of all the orders of friars, the London Charter-house and the monastery of St Mary Graces, and numerous hospitals and almshouses. Finally, London was home to a large class of the very poor – menial servants, street vendors and casual labourers, 'a mass of destitution, misfortune and rascality' as A. H. Thomas described them. In times of political crisis or class tension they constituted a volatile 'crowd', of excitable and uncertain temper, and capable of presenting a serious threat to order and authority.

There was room for much tension in this society, both between crafts and groups of crafts, and between class and class. Both brands of rivalry were involved in the fourteenth-century movement to democratize in some measure the mode of the city's government, which reached its climax in the mayoralty of John of Northampton (1381–3). Northampton was a draper, well-off but not of the standing in wealth of the merchant élite, and his support was drawn substantially from the small master class in the crafts. This was why his movement strove for annual elections to the aldermanries (traditionally aldermen had served effectively for life), and for elections to the Common Council (London's second governing council, which the mayor and aldermen needed to consult on all really major issues) to be by guilds rather than by wards (where the alderman for the time being was naturally in a position to exercise a powerful influence). But the movement that he led also fed on other tensions, on the rivalry between merchants who belonged to the 'Staplers' company, which enjoyed a monopoly in wool export, and others who did not, and on the deep-seated resentment of the non-victualling guilds against the victuallers and especially the fishmongers, whose monopoly control of trade in a stable element of popular diet was regarded as particularly irksome. Northampton's career came to grief when he was displaced at the mayoral election of 1383 by the grocer Nicholas Brembre, and he attempted to maintain his influence by force: it was easy, so soon after the Peasants' Revolt, to discredit a man with the charge of encouraging mob rule. Under Brembre things returned more or less to the status quo ante, and no one after

Northampton came as near as he did to modifying the oligarchic mould of London's civic government, which had grown into
a shape familiar in most of the kingdom's major cities. Of course
the tensions did not go away; a persistent, but unsuccessful,
series of attempts between 1437 and 1444 to get Ralph Holland,
a tailor, elected mayor, seems to have drawn support from some
of the same elements as Northampton had. The tensions
remained, simmering below the surface, and adding to the
dangers of violence at any time when events external to London
threatened the capital's domestic political equilibrium.

It was not only fellow Londoners who regarded the influence of
the city's mercantile élite with distrust and sometimes with
dislike. The classes represented by the Commons in Parliament
were suspicious that the merchants' monopolistic practices kept
prices high, and in some spheres made sure that the provincial
producer of raw materials (notably wool) was paid too little.
This was a major reason for the marked political caution of the
city fathers and their consistent unwillingness to commit London
to one side or other in times of national political tension. They
knew that if they backed a losing side the consequences might
be an onslaught on the city's liberties and privileges by the
victors; and they trembled at the thought of what the mob
might do if there was armed confrontation in the city or at the
gates. In the charged atmosphere of 1458, when the great
confrontation of Lancastrians and Yorkists was looming and a
number of peers were in London with unusually large retinues,
the mayor and aldermen made special regulations for the patrol-
ling of the city and took care to be deeply impartial as between
followers of the rival factions.

The fears of London's leaders, both of the mob and of
aristocratic or royal political hostility, were well founded in
memories of painful experience. The excesses of the common
people when the peasant rebels entered London in 1381, and in
the course of Cade's revolt in 1450, amply justified the former
fear. On both occasions, rivalries among more prominent citizens
threatened to complicate and exacerbate the dangers generated
by popular violence. The reality of the other fear was sharply
underlined when in 1392 Richard II removed the mayor and

elected officers and took the government of the city into his own hands. The immediate reasons for the king's action on this occasion are not clear, but no doubt his resentment at London's failure to support him against the rebel appellant lords in 1387 was rankling in the background. The city had to buy back its liberties at a high price. No wonder then that the civic leaders were cautious in politics, and that despite their difficulties with Richard they were slow to commit themselves in 1399 to Henry Bolingbroke, waiting until it was quite clear that he had the game in his hands before they sent a deputation to Chester to offer him their fealty and submission. They acted with the same sort of circumspection in the summer of 1460 as the Wars of the Roses escalated towards their first climax, continuing to lend to the Lancastrian government till the last moment, desperately seeking to persuade the advancing Yorkist lords to take another route 'and not come through the city', and only finally opening their gates to them when it was clear that siege and the possibility of a sack were the only alternatives.

Partly through luck, partly through the shrewdness of their leadership, the capitalist élite of London succeeded in steering pretty successfully through the shoals of domestic political troubles in the late fourteenth and fifteenth centuries. In consequence they were able to maintain their controlling influence in the city, administratively and socially, and indeed to entrench it further. A number of the greater guilds obtained royal charters of incorporation, which strengthened their control of trade in their respective 'mysteries' and enabled them to acquire property of their own (the goldsmiths and mercers, for instance, both obtained this privilege in 1394). They built their own halls, and came to constitute a kind of *imperium in imperio* within the city's administration. The growing tendency to distinguish among the masters of the craft guilds between the 'yeomanry' and the seniors who were of 'the livery' of a company and might appear in its full livery on formal occasions, strengthened the position of the wealthier within their own 'mysteries'; and in 1475 attendance at the Guildhall for the assembly in which the mayor was chosen was limited to freemen wearing 'livery' (the assembly nominated two candidates, who had to be aldermen, and the current mayor and aldermen chose between them).

The reason why these developments did not generate more friction internally in London, of the kind that the days of John of Northampton witnessed, was largely that wealth and business talent, rather than birth and connection, were the keys to advancement. Oligarchic London's government certainly was, but in its own way its élite was remarkably open. Very few merchant families retained real commercial prominence – the key to office and power – through more than three generations, most through less. Often the sons of successful merchants preferred to follow a different career from their fathers, so making room for others. In so far as surviving records give an indication, the number of apprentices that masters took on who came from outside London seems to have been remarkably high, and many of these made their way. Even in the civic élite new arrivals could be prominent. Richard Whittington, 'lodestar of merchandise' and three times mayor of London, was the youngest son of a not very prosperous Gloucestershire gentleman. He probably had no cat when he set out for London and he certainly did not come penniless, but he was a newcomer to the city all right. He was just one of a number who 'made it' to high city office without starting from any established niche in the merchant aristocracy.

Talent was always a factor in rising to the top in London, because to maintain a position among the plutocrat élite was a matter that required real commercial skill, nerve and insight. Great merchants like Whittington never depended solely on their dealings in the merchandise of their own 'mystery' – mercery or whatever. They also usually had considerable revenues from rents, for it was in property, both in the city and in the countryside, that their profits were principally invested. But they were besides general merchants, dealing not just in one commodity but in many, exporters and owners of ships or shares in ships as well as importers and wholesalers. Many of them were either merchant venturers, who specialized in the export principally of cloth to the Baltic and the Low Countries and in bulk import of goods purchased in the market there, or Staplers, heavily engaged in the export trade in wool through Calais, which was close to the Flemish markets from which they too might be active as importers. The greater London merchants were thus intricately involved in a complex web of international commercial operations that involved themselves, foreign merchants and bankers, and the Crown too. The manner of the Crown's involvement provides another reason to explain why the merchant aristocracy of later medieval London was so successful in maintaining its privileged position.

The issue involved here is one that brings us back to the connections between Westminister, the headquarters of government, and the city that was the hub of commerce. The merchant capitalists were, quite simply, too useful to the Crown for it to be prudent for government to pursue any sustained onslaught on them, their liberties or their monopolies. Richard II's seizure of London into the king's hands was an aberration not repeated: he made a short-term profit but it is hard to argue that it did him much good in the long run, and no later medieval king tried to follow his example. Any attack on the Londoners was likely to mar the royal reputation sooner or later, and also to threaten more tangible royal interests.

There was naturally a close connection between the greater merchants and the court, for Westminster and the court were among their very best customers. Whittington's career illustrates the relationship well. A mercer, he made a good start by supplying quality mercery to Richard II's extravagant favourite, Robert de Vere, Earl of Oxford; this made him his contact, and by the 1390s he was becoming one of the chief suppliers of the king's own Great Wardrobe. By the time of Richard II's fall he was in a well-entrenched position, and continued to deal profitably with Henry IV. He was also, by then, rich enough to make himself useful to the Crown in another way, by advancing large sums personally in the way of loans. He was in no way exceptional in this: virtually all the greater merchants lent to the Crown personally from time to time, and on the whole did well for themselves by doing so. Repayment was not always fast, and the charging of interest was frowned on as usurious, but there were ways in which they could be compensated significantly for their willingness to lend, for example with special licences and commercial privileges. Richard Lyons, the rich vintner who was impeached in the Parliament of 1376, had, with a group of cronies, been advancing very sizeable sums to Edward III and was well in with his mistress, Alice Perrers; for his services he gained a very advantageous monopoly of the trade in sweet wines in the city. He was also suspected (probably rightly) of charging usurious interest on his loans, which was why he was impeached; and it is improbable that he was alone in finding means to be re-paid more than he had advanced.

It was not just individual merchants who lent money in this way. The city of London, in its corporate capacity, regularly advanced money to the Crown, and so did some of the individual corporate companies. Particularly active in this field was the Company of the Staple which, though it was not itself a London company and had many provincial members, was dominated by its great London members (Whittington, who was a Stapler, was twice mayor of Calais, the Staple town, as well as three times mayor of London). London and London merchants had, in fact, taken over more or less entirely the role once played by Italian merchant companies and bankers as the principal source of the loans on which depended the smooth running of English government finance, which always – and especially in war years – needed cash in anticipation of revenue.

How it all worked is perhaps best explained around the operations of the Staple. The establishment of a 'staple' created a monopoly of sale or export in a given commodity, which had to be taken to a specific staple town or towns, where dealing in it was controlled by a syndicate or company of 'staplers'. The system lent itself ideally to loan finance; by establishing a staple and licensing a syndicate to manage a profitable monopoly, the Crown ensured that this group ought to have cash to advance and that it ought to be willing to advance it in order to preserve its privileged trading position. Wool was, at the time when the Hundred Years War began, England's premier export, and it was to a wool staple that the Crown therefore instinctively looked in order to ensure 'credit facilities' in a newly demanding financial situation. At the start the Staple for wool was sometimes located in England, sometimes abroad – at Bruges and elsewhere – but after the capture of Calais in 1347 that town came to be seen as the obvious location, and before the end of the century it was settled there permanently. The wool Staplers were the syndicate who had the monopoly of sale through the Calais market. The loans which they, in return, were expected to advance to the Crown were easily secured by assigning repayment against the customs due on export, which the Staplers and their fellows had paid when carrying their wool out of England. Because the principal Staplers were not just exporters of wool but importers too of goods in which they specialized, mercery, the spices of the grocers and so on, the Crown had an interest in preserving and upholding not only their trading privileges in Calais but also their trading privileges in England, as members of city companies such as the Mercers and the Grocers of London. Besides, the Staplers were by no means the only source of mercantile city loans to the Crown, as we have seen; it was thus to the Crown's interest to make sure that the London capitalists more generally were in a position to advance cash, and that meant protecting their monopolies and influence.

In operation, the financial system in which the Staplers and other great merchants operated was more complicated than thus outlined, simply, above. When a Stapler sold his wool at Calais he normally took cash for only a proportion of his sale: for the rest he accepted bills, assigned for payment by instalments at future dates, probably on a broker or banker in one of the market centres of the Low Countries. In due course he could cash his bill, and use the money to purchase goods for import into England. Or alternatively, he could pass the bill to a 'merchant venturer' who was travelling to the Low Countries: the venturer would credit the Stapler with cash in London, and collect the money on the bill in Flanders, to lay out on his own purchases. The Stapler, meanwhile, with the money made available to him in London (or with what he had raised by the sale of his own imports), could settle with the woolmonger in the Cotswolds or Lincolnshire or wherever, from whom he had bought his wool, almost certainly on the same sort of part-cash, part-credit terms as he had sold in Calais. The working of this system was by no means smooth, naturally. Staplers and venturers always suspected each other of getting the advantage of the exchange rates which brokers in the Low Countries charged for changing sterling into Flemish coin. The English government's attempts to enforce a bullionist policy, insisting that at Calais a fixed proportion of payments for wool should be in cash and that merchants should bring bullion to the mint in Calais or London to be coined into sterling (with a profit to the Crown on the re-coining), also disturbed operations. There were plenty of frictions between parties who all wanted to get the best advantage for themselves.

Nevertheless, the system did ensure that the Crown consistently upheld the Staplers' privilege of monopoly of the export of wool. Edward IV finally came to an agreement with them whereby, in return, they shouldered the whole burden in money terms of the defence of Calais and the payment of its garrison. The system also ensured the maintenance of the privileges and monopoly interests of the great London guilds to which the merchant capitalists of the city belonged, and on which their enduring control of the government and of governing influence in the capital depended. There was really no alternative to this mutual back-scratching, for the government needed the city's golden eggs and the city relied on the government's connivance for its continuing capacity to lay them. More than just this was born however of the relationship of mutual interest between court, government and city. Inevitably, over time it drew them together in other ways too. It was taken as a great compliment to the London merchants when Edward III and his sons, martial men, jousted accoutred as the mayor and aldermen. When John Philipot, grocer, was knighted in 1381 Walsingham noted that he was a 'most faithful knight, although a merchant'. Outside a brief period in the reign of Richard II there were never more than five merchant knights in the city before 1460; but Edward IV at his coronation made no less than six aldermen Knights of the Bath, and he and Henry VII were more generous with honours to the great men of the city than any of their predecessors had been. The city knights of their time looked to the court and courtiers for feoffees of their estates and executors of their wills, and sometimes for other kinds of connections too. The second wife of Sir Geoffrey Boleyn (mayor in 1457) was Anne, daughter of Lord Hoo and his co-heiress, and their great-granddaughter was Queen Anne Boleyn. Tentatively at first but more and more steadily as time went by the city élite was coming to be identified as part of the national establishment.

Moreover it was not just at the very high level at which the Boleyns moved that court and city, gentility and merchants were drawn together. The Celys, Staplers of London, were not merchants of the very first rank, and their correspondence reveals them very much as businessmen, worrying about the exchange rate in Flanders, changing at Calais the numbers on the sarplers of their wool (the great canvas bags in which sacks were packed for shipping) in the hope of concealing consignments of poor quality, and being pressed by their Cotswold supplier, William Midwinter of Northleach, for cash: 'I trust to you that I may have the £200 that ye said I should not have till November: I pray as heartily as I can that ye make it ready within 14 days after Michaelmas.' Yet they could count as their patron and good lord Sir John Weston, Prior of the Order of the Hospital in England and often about the court on diplomatic and other business, and could toy, through their Cotswold business connections, with ideas of marrying into the country gentility. 'William Midwinter asked me,' Richard Cely wrote excitedly in 1482,

if I were in any way of marriage. I told him nay, and he informed me that there was a young gentlewoman whose father's name is Lemryke, and her mother is dead, and she shall dispend by her mother £40 a year ... And her father is the greatest ruler and richest man in that country, and there have been great gentlemen to see her and would have her ... After dinner I came and drank with them ... and the person pleased me right well, as by the first communication. She is young, little, and very well favoured and witty, and the country speaks much good of her.

Nothing came of this match-making, but the Celys could have easily blended into county society, for their tastes and standards were, in many respects, virtually indistinguishable from those of a rural gentleman. George Cely, Richard's brother, was indeed something of a connoisseur of genteel and rural sports, a man with a sure eye for a hound or for a falcon. A hawk that he presented to the vicar of Watford was a prize one: 'it hath i-caught this same year a 60 pheasants and mallards,' we are told; 'the vicar saith he will not give him, not for 12 nobles, to no man.'

George Cely was no exception in his tastes; the pull of the country and of genteel ways was, clearly, a strong one on men of the London merchant class generally, just as London was, for different reasons, a strong pull on the gentility. Intercommunication drew their worlds together, and each left its impress on the tastes and ways of the other. A great many successful merchants bought country estates, and some took to spending a good bit of their leisure time on them, as did Robert Harding, goldsmith, who, when he let his Surrey property like the good businessman he was to a yeoman farmer, held back a wing of the manorhouse, a garden and the 'sporting places there' for his pleasure and that of his guests when he came out from town. Just as there were plenty of gentlemen's sons, like Whittington, who came to London to be apprenticed and in hope of a fortune, so there were merchant families, like the Swanlands and the Felds, that ultimately settled for the life of the country squirearchy. The step from mercantile success to rural gentility was not a long one for the successful Londoner.

Tradition separated merchants from 'knights and gentles' and placed them among the 'commons', but by the end of the middle ages the London merchants at least were coming to be accepted as having their niche in the aristocratic world. Business contacts forged about the court or during Parliament time, and connections through common kin in the country, threw merchants and gentlemen together. So did marriage: something like a third of the London aldermen of the fifteenth century found wives from county families. City knights, and city landowners who called themselves squires in the country and merchants in London, were not martial men (though their sons and descendants might be), but by the end of the middle ages the old way of thinking that linked aristocratic rank to military preoccupation was losing the touch it had once had with social realities. In tastes, culture, and the degree of influence that he could wield – and often in landed wealth also – a London city knight was, at the end of the fifteenth century, as much an aristocrat in any meaningful sense of that word as a country knight whose ancestors had never touched trade.

*

It was said in the last chapter that in the late middle ages English towns and cities were not acting as 'accelerators' either of the economy or of the cultural life of the kingdom. London was the exception; it was undoubtedly acting as such. It was a great cosmopolitan centre that drew together the worlds of the court and of commerce, of aristocrats and merchants, poets and people. It was the capital city towards which men and women in the provinces looked for quality goods, reliable news, standards of taste and, perhaps above all, for significant contacts. If you were in trade in the provinces, there was a difference between those who knew the London dealers and those who did not; if you were a landowner, there was a difference between those who had contacts in Westminster and in the Inns of Court and those who did not; and if your taste was for versifying, there was a difference between a country minstrel with a repertoire of traditional ballads and one who could command the language in which Chaucer wrote and who knew the literary fashions that would please in the capital. Any commercial city could teach something of the art of making money; London, with Westminster at its doorstep, could do more than that – it could instruct in the art of living well, and that made it different from any other city.

Part II

The Second Estate: the 'Chivalry'

Lords, knights and gentry at war and at home in the time of the Hundred Years War

6. The Hundred Years War and its Effects on Society and Government

For the greater part of the period 1338–1453 England was formally at war with France. The lives and the attitudes of those who took part in the fighting were profoundly affected by the experience; so were the attitudes of their kinsfolk, neighbours and connections, and all the others who listened for news of the campaigns, welcomed the returning soldiers, admired the prizes of their prowess and pitied them for their wounds. In this way the war was for England a national, formative experience, and it was formative in other, equally important ways too. The war had to be fought not only with sword and buckler, bowstring and cannon, but also with money. The scale of the sums required, and the means that had to be found to raise them, also had profound effects. In particular, the need for funds to pay for the war contributed to the growing importance of Parliaments, and to the influence and cohesion of the class that in Parliament dominated the Commons, the middling landowners of the English shires. The rise in their influence and in their consciousness of their social muscle within the body politic had, in turn, further effects, which touched the whole structure of government and the balance of political authority in the kingdom. In this chapter we shall look in turn at all these different kinds of effects of the war experience, some of which were direct and others indirect.

The task ahead is not an easy one, for it will involve looking successively at three canvases of rather different quality. When we start we will be looking at the social background of a dramatic narrative of knights and their adventures, thrilling in its *superficies*, complicated in its details. The men who went to fight in France came from and returned to estates, countryside and villages which to them, no doubt, did not seem to have changed much. They themselves however were changed, in many cases, by what had happened to them abroad, for prowess in the field in this age was a factor and force in social mobility that could carry fortunate men forward from humble station to higher things, and from high things to still higher ones. Change, however, came about in other ways too. Slowly and less visibly, the country to which the 'heroes' of the war came back – if they did come back –was itself being changed. The men who went abroad had to be paid, and the scramble at home for funds to pay for them, with Parliament's enthusiasm coming and going with the fortunes of the war, is a second side to the story, less obviously exciting in its incident but part of an institutional narrative that provides a kind of vertebral column to English social history in this period, and subsequently. The sense of Parliament's influence increased in measure with the frequency with which grants were made in it and by its authority, and so did the sense of their own influence among the kind of people who were represented in the Commons in Parliament. The consequences of their sense of increased influence, and the new niche which the gentlefolk were coming to occupy, in the first instance as a result of the part they could be seen to play in fighting the war, but still more – and increasingly as time went by – of the part they played in footing the bill for it, is the third canvas that we shall have to scrutinize.

If we start by looking at the direct effects of hostilities on the lives of those caught up in them, a first point that will strike us is that there was one geographic region of England whose experience of war was different from that of all others and which was more sharply marked by it, the north country. The 'auld alliance' of France and Scotland, forged in the Scottish wars of independence in the time of Edward I and Edward II, made the latter the natural ally of the former when the Hundred Years War began, and she remained so. Between Scotland and England there was no sea such as separated England and France: the border was open and already, before the mid fourteenth century, raiding and counter-raiding had left terrible scars. The annual revenues of Durham Cathedral Priory, which in 1300 had stood at £4,500 p.a., had by 1335 been reduced to a mere £1,750, and its case was typical. At the end of the thirteenth century the border had been an area of advancing prosperity, both in town and countryside. By the middle of the fourteenth the burning of crops and homesteads and systematic looting had ruined agricultural prosperity and had turned commercial towns into garrison centres; humbler folk had emigrated out of the area on a substantial scale. Progressively the depopulated countryside became more and more dependent on pastoralism, the herding of beasts, and the way of life of both rich and poor was sharply affected. Camden in the sixteenth century found in the north a strange 'martial sort of people that from April to August lie in little huts . . . among their several flocks': you would think, he wrote, 'that you see the ancient nomads'. The gentry families, like the Armstrongs and Charltons, lived in fortified tower houses, half as squires, half as cattle thieves. The north became a land of intensely felt local loyalties, vividly expressed in a balladry that turned its sorrow and violence into high poetry, and where men 'knew no prince save a Percy or a Neville'.

In terms of the direct effect of warfare, the experience of the rest of England was almost the reverse of the northern one. Some of the ports of the south coast, such as Plymouth, Rye, Winchelsea and the Isle of Wight, did indeed suffer traumatic French raids on occasion. But virtually all the serious continuous fighting in the Hundred Years War took place on French, not English soil, and this had important consequences. Outside the north, England never had to suffer the devastation of the countryside by passing armies that ruined the prosperity of whole provinces in France. For English lords and for English townsmen defence was not a pressing problem. The walls and gatehouses of towns like Coventry or Oxford or even London did not need to be constructed so as to withstand siege. The walls of the new castle houses of magnates, like that which Lord Cromwell built at Tattershall in the fifteenth century, or Hurstmonceaux in Sussex, were too thin to face artillery fire and were often of brittle brick; their crenellations were decorative, not defensive. Perhaps most important of all, the fact that the war was mainly fought in France meant that what it took out of England in terms of wealth was less noticeable than what it brought in. And as we shall see, it brought in some spectacular prizes.

Another aspect of the Hundred Years War that needs to be borne in mind when considering its impact in England is the fact that it was by no means a period of continuous hostilities – in the Channel, in France or anywhere, not even on the northern border. Campaigns were intermittent. In the fourteenth century the English war effort principally took the form of great raiding expeditions (*chevauchées*), such as that which the Black Prince led to victory at Poitiers in 1356 or Edward III's *chevauchée* of 1359, that took him past the gates of Paris. The hosts that took part were recruited for short periods of service, a year or less, and were disbanded at the end of the campaign. Here is a reminder of how non-professional, by modern standards, the armies of this time were. The skill of the archer with the longbow was acquired by practice at the village butts, which was regular and obligatory, while the arts of horsemanship and the use of sword and lance formed part of the normal, household-based education of those of gentle birth; so there was no need to train substantial, standing military forces. The fighting in the war was also punctuated by truces, some of them long, and between 1385 and 1412, almost a generation, there was little campaigning. Later in the fifteenth century things were rather different, it is true; from the time of Henry V's invasion of France in 1417 down to the truce of Tours in 1444 hostilities were continuous. But to balance this the fighting was even more exclusively on French soil than before; there was hardly any French raiding of the Channel coasts because the English now occupied both shores, and the northern border was decidedly quiescent compared with its condition in the fourteenth century.

It must also be remembered that the armies that English kings and aristocratic English captains from time to time led across the sea to France were not large by any standard. The 10,000–12,000 men whom Henry V took with him in 1417 to conquer Normandy constituted a very large host. K. B. McFarlane has calculated that only once during the Hundred Years War, in 1347 when Edward III assembled a truly exceptional host for the siege of Calais, 'did the number of soldiers taking part in a campaign reach something like 1 per cent of the population of England and Wales'. The fraction of the population that ever saw war service was tiny in respect of the whole. This remains true even if one adds to the members serving in expeditionary forces or field armies those in standing garrisons (on the Scots border, in Ireland, at Calais and, in the fifteenth century, in Normandy), the crews of the king's ships and of ships impressed for naval service, and camp followers male and female.

Among gentlefolk the proportion who saw war service at one time or another was much higher than that in the total population, however. This was equitable, given that they prided themselves on belonging to a 'chivalrous' class, to the privileged warrior estate. It was also natural, given the usual social composition of hosts. In the numerous surviving contracts of captains who agreed to lead men in the king's service and at his wages ('indentures of war'), the proportion of archers to men–at–arms was usually a mere two or three to one (until the 1430s and 1440s, when recruitment of men–at–arms seems to have become more problematic). Men–at–arms, cavalrymen who needed to be rich enough to equip themselves with armour, a war-horse, and re-mounts, had inevitably to be raised from among the genteel or near genteel, themselves only a small proportion of the whole population; a one to three ratio between them and the humble archers therefore represents a high level of involvement for their estate. As one might expect, the involvement was highest at the highest levels socially. Among the secular peerage proper, there were few indeed who, at one time or another, did not find themselves armed in the king's service overseas or in Scotland. The higher military commands, the leadership of expeditionary hosts and the lieutenancies for the king, in Brittany or Gascony in the fourteenth century and in Normandy in the fifteenth, were virtually monopolized by the greater peers, the dukes and the earls of England.

Among the knighthood (I mean among those gentlefolk, usually the most prosperous, who had been formally dubbed knights) there was always a leavening of near-professional soldiers, men like Sir John Chandos and Sir Hugh Calverley in the fourteenth century, or Sir John Fastolf, Sir William Oldhall or Sir Thomas Rampston in the fifteenth. Even among the knights, though, there were from the first men and families whose service traditions were administrative and domestic rather than military, and this was doubtless truer again lower down the scale of gentility. At all levels, moreover, the real professionals were atypical. Nigel Saul, in his very careful survey of the gentry of Gloucestershire between 1300 and 1400, found that 'the great majority' of heads of genteel families (defined as those with an income of £20 p.a. and upwards) had some military experience. Even among the county's knights, however, he found over the whole period only twelve who had served in four or more specified campaigns. Among these Sir Peter Veel, who served in fourteen hosts and spent a long period in Gascony, might rate as a professional: most of the others had seen only irregular service. The 'great majority', that is to say, had served in just one or two campaigns, and that in many cases in their youth, before coming into their inheritance. In counties with a stronger military tradition than Gloucester, like Cheshire and Lancashire, the proportion of gentlemen who had seen more extensive service would have been higher. Many of the witnesses who in 1389 gave evidence for the Cheshire knight Sir Robert Grosvenor, in his dispute with Sir Richard Scrope over the right to bear the arms *azur a bend or*, had seen service in more than just a couple of campaigns, and even the relatively minor gentry among them clearly included some seasoned soldiers. But in both areas, in the north-west as in Gloucester, it was the substantial, knightly families that had on the whole the most strenuous records. For the fourteenth century at least, the rule seems to hold, that the higher one looks in the scales of the estate of gentility, the sharper the mark of its martial tradition.

The fourteenth century witnessed important changes in the methods of raising hosts for royal service. Royal and other forces had always included a proportion of men serving on a voluntary, contractual basis; but in the time of Edward I and Edward II the preponderant element was usually brought together by summonses to perform service obligatorily, the archers and infantry being 'impressed' by specially appointed commissioners of array in the counties, and the cavalry assembled by means of summonses, through the sheriffs, to all who held land worth £20, £40 or sometimes £50 p.a. From the middle of

Edward III's reign, however, although commissioners of array were still from time to time employed (especially on the northern border), and though men-at-arms might still be summoned to do obligatory service, the Crown came steadily to rely more and more on voluntary contingents raised by captains who contracted with the king to serve for a stated term with a stipulated force at stipulated wages, accounting for these at the Exchequer: and these captains in turn contracted with lesser leaders on the same basis, and they with individual soldiers. This change considerably modified the traditional local and tenurial bases of military recruitment, though since the greater captains who contracted with the king were mostly magnates and knights a tendency remained for them to look first to men of their own 'country', retainers, neighbours and tenants. Hosts raised in this manner also tended to be smaller than those raised by impressment, because the service was voluntary. For the same reason, the inducements to serve became more significant. The principal inducements were the wages offered in the contract, the hope of acquiring spoils and of taking prisoners who would pay a ransom, and the possibility of social advancement as a reward of good service.

The rate of wages of war was quite generous; 2s. a day for a knight, 1s. a day for a man-at-arms or esquire, 6d. a day for a mounted archer. A substantial proportion of these wages was usually paid to the soldiers of a contracted host in advance, at the time of mustering; thereafter there was of course a serious risk that pay would fall into arrears. A captain might hope to make something by contracting with his men to pay at a lower rate than that at which he had contracted for his company with the Exchequer, but against that, if there were delays at the Exchequer, he might have to advance their wages for at least a period out of his own pocket. It seems unlikely that anyone grew rich on wages of war alone; but a gentleman serving as knight or esquire might supplement his ordinary income usefully thereby, and an archer as long as he was in service was doing better than a labourer, substantially so.

The lure of spoil was more glamorous than the lure of wages and the potential gains a great deal more significant, as the careful regulation of shares in spoil and ransoms laid down in war indentures testify (captains owed a third of their winnings to the king or the host's commander, and were entitled to a third of the winnings of their men). The sort of profit that this kind of advantage of war could bring was substantial and highly visible. In England in the years following the Crecy campaign, so the chronicler Walsingham wrote,

there were few women who did not possess something from Caen, Calais, or other overseas towns, such as clothes, furs, or cushions. Tablecloths and linen were seen in everyone's houses. Married women were decked in the trimmings of French matrons, and if the latter sorrowed over their loss, the former rejoiced in their gain.

For all ranks of soldiers there were pickings such as these; for the aristocrats and gentle-born captains there were prospects of bigger and more glittering prizes, which could come from the ransoms of high-ranking French prisoners. Sir John Fastolf boasted that in a single day at the battle of Verneuil (1424), where among others he took prisoner the Duke of Alençon, he had won 'by the fortune of war 20,000 marks sterling'. The Anglo-Gascon mercenary, Bastot de Mauléon, a much humbler soldier, told the chronicler Froissart that at the battle of Poitiers 'I made three prisoners, a knight and two squires, who paid me, one with the other, four thousand francs.' The hope of making or adding to a fortune was clearly, throughout the war period, one of the major attractions of service to adventurers of all sorts and standings, and it is no wonder that some of them took a very businesslike attitude to it. In 1421 two young esquires, John Winter and Nicholas Molyneux, who were going to France agreed to go into partnership as 'brothers in arms' and pool their winnings. The text of their agreement survives: any profits of war that they could spare were to be sent home, to be deposited in a chest in the church of St Thomas Dacres in London, 'in which chest shall be placed as much gold, silver and plate as they or either of them shall wish to use to buy lands in the kingdom of England'. Each was to have his own key to the chest; and as insurance against the risks of war they promised also to contribute to each other's ransoms if either was taken, and that one would stay hostage among the French if the other had to go home to raise the ransom money.

The profits that gentlemen won in style on the fields of France could be invested in a way that would testify to their style in their home society in England, as Winter and Molyneux clearly saw. Henry of Lancaster built the great Savoy Palace in London out of his French winnings. William Berkeley told Leland, the Tudor antiquary, that his manor house at Beverstone was 'builded out of the ransoms that his great-grandfather took on the field of Poitiers'. The castle 'fair amongst its trees' that Sir John Cornwall (later Lord Fanhope) built at Ampthill (Beds.) was likewise paid for, Leland reported, out of gains won in France. Sir Hugh Calverley, for the salvation of his soul, ploughed back what he had acquired plundering in France and Spain into his collegiate foundation at Bunbury in Cheshire. The new dwelling-houses of the great, and the new extensions and adornments of churches out of war profits, were things that all could see, and that others could rejoice in besides those who had come back from overseas richer than they left.

Less dramatically, but visibly and significantly, war service and winnings of war became an important factor of upward social mobility in and into the genteel world. M. Bennett's evidence from the north-west about the way in which martial families could flourish is here impressive. The Jodrells in north Cheshire, the Stanleys of Lathom and the Danyers of Lyme Handley all laid the foundations of their local fortunes in the French war. Sir Robert Knollys was Cheshire-born, and of relatively humble stock it would seem, but he grew rich on the plunder of Brittany and invested his riches in lands in southern England, in Kent and London. John Norbury, another Cheshire-man, who from serving as a soldier of fortune in the 'free companies' rose to be a councillor of Henry IV, acquired estates in Middlesex and Hertfordshire. Straight winnings of war, it must here be stressed, were not the only or even necessarily the principal avenue of advancement for the successful soldier. More important in the long run was the patronage of the Crown and of captains among the greater nobility which good martial service could attract. The adventurous military career of the first of the Stanleys of Lathom, which according to family tradition took him to France in the company of Robert Knollys, then to Aquitaine and further afield still to holy fighting in the eastern

Mediterranean, won him a name and brought him to prominence: but it was royal favour, after that, that secured him the hand and inheritance of Isabella Lathom and established his family's position. Patronage, moreover, could spread the benefits of war service, which were so significant at this elevated level, a long way down the social scale. As Bennett puts it 'the husbandman who had followed a local lord overseas, the yeoman who had fought in the company of the Black Prince and the gentleman who had been the comrade-in-arms of Henry V all stood out within their communities as men who were able to reach out and touch members of the classes above them'. That touch, for the fortunate, could turn the russet cloak of humble status into the robe of a gentleman, just as it could carry a knight like John Cornwall into the peerage.

There was almost no end to the ways in which war service could promote social mobility, vertically, laterally and regionally, and politically. It could carry a man like Sir Ralph Salle from obscurity to riches and knighthood. 'You are a knight, and a man of great weight in this county, renowned for your valour,' the rebel peasants said to him in 1381, just before they killed him on Mousehold Heath outside Norwich; 'yet notwithstanding this, we know who you are: you are not a gentleman, but the son of a poor mason, just such as ourselves.' War service carried John Norbury, as we have seen, from his native Cheshire to prominence as a landowner in the Home Counties. It did the same for Robert Knollys. The mustering of a contract army was a way in which new connections between men, both as client and patron and on an equal footing, were easily forged. Association on a purely military basis and for the short term of an expedition could grow into a more enduring association, and so breed further contacts and forge new connections of service, clientage and patronage that had no connection with the local origins and influence of either client or patron. This splendid epitaph, which K. B. McFarlane noted down from a stone in Tideswell church in Derbyshire, may serve as an illustration of the way in which things could work out:

Under this stone lieth Sampson Meverell which was born in Stone in the feast of St Michael the Archangel and there christened by the Prior of the same house and Sampson of Clifton esquire and Margaret the daughter of Philip Stapley in the Year of Our Lord 1388; and so lived under the service of Nicholas Lord Audley and Dame Elizabeth his wife the space of 8 years and more: and after that by the assent of John Meverell his father he was wedded in Belper to Isabel the daughter of Sir Roger Leche, the 14th day of Pasch [Easter]: and after he came to the service of the noble lord John [*vere:* Thomas] Montagu Earl of Salisbury the which ordained the said Sampson to be captain of divers worshipful places in France: and after the death of the said Earl, he came into the service of John Duke of Bedford, and so being in his service was at 11 great battles in France within the space of 2 years; and at St Luce the Duke gave him the order of knighthood: and after that the said Duke made him knight constable and by his commandment he kept the constable's court of this land till the death of the said Duke: and after that he abode under the service of John Stafford, Archbishop of Canterbury, and so enduring in great worship departed from all worldly service into the mercy of Our Lord Jesus Christ, the which divided his soul from his body in the feast of the Macute [15 November] in the year of Our Lord 1462.

The Meverell family had plenty of difficulties with their neighbours in their native Derbyshire: in the troubled 1440s, after Sir Sampson had come home, the great connections that he had made through his service with people who had nothing to do with the locality but ample influence at court cannot have seemed disadvantageous.

The great victories of Edward III and the Black Prince – Sluys (1340), Crecy (1346), Poitiers (1356), Najera in Spain (1367) – made the late fourteenth century the most consciously chivalrous age in the history of medieval England. The knightly attitudes and aspirations of the aristocracy were deliberately encouraged by the ruler and his son, by their staging of lavish tournaments and of festivities like the great torchlight procession of knights at Bristol in 1358, by promotions in the field and by the chivalric ceremonial of the royal court. In the Round Table tournament at Windsor in 1344 Edward III sought to evoke Arthurian echoes. Arthur's legendary knights had won their fame not by patriotic self-sacrifice but rather in the vendettas of those who had been injured in their rights, and that was how Edward and his magnate captains talked about their war too: it was the

king's 'just quarrel', which he had 'undertaken' to recover his
rights and heritage, in which he hoped with God's aid to do
battle and have a good issue of it. In the Order of the Garter,
which he founded in 1348–9, Edward sought to establish an élite
chapter of English chivalry. The great majority of the knights of
the first creation had been the king's companions in arms in his
recent victorious expedition to Crecy and Calais: all the members
who had stalls on the prince's side in the Chapel of St George at
Windsor had fought in the Black Prince's division at Crecy. In
the international knightly world the order came to be regarded
as the lineal descendant of Arthur's famous fellowship. 'I have
read and heard,' Jean Werchin, Seneschal of Hainault, wrote to
Henry IV,

> that in the time when the noble and mighty Arthur reigned over that
> lordship where now you reign, that there was established an order to
> which a number of knights belonged, who called themselves the
> knights of the Round Table, and in those days they excelled all in
> worship and chivalry . . . and now I have heard that certain kings of
> your kingdom in recollection of that order have instituted that which
> is called the Garter.

   This deliberately fostered cult of chivalry was not just a
matter of courtly manners and court ceremony. It sought to
touch and did touch a genuine chord in the martial traditions of
aristocratic society. Its impact shows in the revival of interest in
the great knightly enterprise of the crusade, in the numbers of
English knights who, in the interludes in the fighting in France,
went to see a spell of service with the Teutonic Order in the
wars against the pagan Letts – as Chaucer's knight did:

> Ful ofte tyme he hadd the bord bygonne
> Aboven alle naciouns in Pruce [Prussia],
> In Lettowe [Lithuania] had he reysed and in Ruce [Russia].

English knights formed one of the largest contingents in the
army with which King Peter of Cyprus captured Alexandria in
1365, and there were English knights in the Duke of Bourbon's
crusading host before Tunis in 1390 and in the ill-fated expedition against the Turk in 1396 which came to grief at Nicopolis.

Other English adventurers sought fame and fortune elsewhere, in the service of foreign lords and cities, in Spain and in the wars of Italy, where Sir John Hawkwood made his White Company famous.

It was the French war and the deeds done in it, though, which caught most attention and were most talked of. They were recalled in literature, in works like Chandos Herald's marvellous verse biography of the Black Prince. They were commemorated in churches, as in the display of the heraldic arms of those who had been Henry V's companions in France in the vault of the new south-west porch of Canterbury Cathedral, constructed in the last years of his reign. But perhaps the chivalric tone and martial pride of genteel society comes across best of all in the depositions of the witnesses in the Scrope and Grosvenor dispute of 1386, in which large numbers of gentlemen from all over England gave testimony, at length and in detail, about their own military experience and where in the wars they had met Scropes and Grosvenors. Here among others is Geoffrey Chaucer, esquire; asked how he knows that the arms *azur a bend or* belong to Scrope, he says 'he has heard it from old knights and esquires . . . and through all this time they have been reputed to be their arms by common voice and public acclaim'. Here is Nicholas Sabraham, who says that he saw the arms of Scrope on a banner in the border wars, 'in the company of the Earl of Northampton, when he rode by torchlight from Lochmaben as far as Peebles'. Here is Sir Robert Laton (who knew the arms of all the knights and squires of the north country by heart), to say that he saw 'Sir Richard armed in the same arms in the expedition during which the noble King Edward, on whose soul God have mercy, was before Paris . . . and since then in all the expeditions undertaken by my Lord of Lancaster and our Lord the King'. And here is the prior of the Augustinian house of Marton, to say that his church has in its treasury the embroidered coat of arms that Sir Alexander Neville wore when he was armed at Halidon Hill, the quarters all filled up with the arms of his companions there, among them those of Sir Henry Le Scrope, *azur a bend or* with a label. These are the voices of men, knights, esquires, gentlemen and their clerical connections, who came from a level of society where minds were steeped in chivalric values and knightly lore, and in martial memories of the king's great enterprise in France.

This was, significantly, the same level as that which provided the leadership in society, from among whose ranks were drawn those who served their communities in such dignified offices as that of sheriff, or as justices of the peace, and who represented their shires in Parliament. Another of the deponents in the Scrope *v.* Grosvenor case was the Suffolk knight, Sir Richard Waldegrave. He had served in Edward III's host in 1359 and in Gascony under John of Gaunt: in the 1360s he had been on crusade in the east with the king of Cyprus. He also served frequently on local commissions in his county, and was on the commission of the peace for Suffolk from 1382. He sat for his county in the Parliaments of 1376, 1379, 1381, 1383, 1386 and 1390: in 1381 he was Speaker of the Commons. He had close associations with and was probably a retainer of the last of the Bohuns, Earls of Hereford; later he became a king's knight and a royal councillor. The combined military and administrative experiences of men like him, and their association with the magnates and courtiers who were leaders in national society, helped to give cohesion within the community of the realm to the class from which they sprang. It also helped to identify, for the time being, their aspirations with royal martial ambitions and enterprises.

Waldegrave was a knight of the fourteenth century. In the fifteenth century things were not quite the same. Looking at the armies of that later period, Professor Michael Powicke found among the knightly captains of the expedition that Henry V led to Agincourt the same high proportion that is found in many large fourteenth-century hosts of men whose careers combined membership of Parliament, the tenure of shrieval office and sitting as JPs in their local counties with occasional military service. But from 1417 onwards, he found that men of this stamp became rarer and rarer among the leaders of the soldiery in France. The reason for this was that the nature of the war and the fighting in it had changed. The fourteenth century was the age of the *chevauchée*, of expeditionary forces raised in England for a single campaign only, that raided deep into France, looting and burning, to return afterwards to England laden, hopefully, with prisoners and booty, but the Agincourt expedition was the last of these. When Henry V crossed to France for a second time in 1417 his aim was the conquest of territory. The host that he led, with reinforcements and replacements for men who had gone home when their indentured term was over, remained more or less continuously in arms. As a consequence, the great English captains of the fifteenth century, men like Lords Talbot and Scales, Sir John Fastolf, Sir William Oldhall and Sir Matthew Gough, came to spend very long periods, years and sometimes nearer decades, in service in France, and so as time went by did most of their men. It was not possible for them to play the sort of part that the Richard Waldegraves of the world once had in their native English local communities; they were not there often enough.

This development was accentuated by the policy of settlement that Henry V and after him his brother John, Duke of Bedford and regent in France for Henry VI, pursued in combination with their plans for conquest. Some of the higher English aristocracy received very large grants in conquered Normandy; the County of Perche went to Thomas Montagu, Earl of Salisbury; the three *vicomtes* of Aubec, Orge and Pontaudemer went to Thomas, Duke of Clarence; the Duke of Exeter became Count of Harcourt. After the capture of Harfleur, Henry endeavoured to make it into a second Calais, deporting the French and peopling it with Englishmen; and a number of Englishmen were also settled in Caen and in Cherbourg. Perhaps even more important, after the fall of Rouen and again after the victory of Verneuil in 1424, large numbers (running into hundreds) of small fiefs and lordships in Normandy and France were granted to individual, relatively humble English men-at-arms, for whom these acquisitions became 'home'. The overall result was that less of the profit and gain that individual Englishmen won in France came back to England than had been the case in earlier days, and that the interests of those Englishmen who had a substantial stake in the French war (most of whom spent a good deal of time in France) began to grow visibly apart from the interest of those who did not.

It will be remembered that William of Worcester, Sir John Fastolf's secretary, complained in the 1450s that among men that be 'descended of noble blood and born to arms', lawyers who know how 'to keep and bear out a proud countenance at sessions and shire holdings' had come to be more respected than 'he that hath dispendid 30 or 40 years of his days in great jeopardy' in the wars. Because fewer of the men who dominated county society in the fifteenth century had military experience, they became somewhat less 'chivalrous' in their outlook than their forebears had been. There were still chivalrous gentlemen, plenty of them, serving the king abroad right up to the end of the war, but those who stayed at home became less ready to identify the interests of the English kingdom with the king's 'just quarrel' in France, more reluctant to pledge English resources to maintaining England's overseas possessions and conquests, and more absorbed in domestic issues. The niggardliness of the grants Parliament was prepared to make for war purposes was indeed one of the principal reasons for the final collapse, in 1450, of the English cause in the war. Martial involvements in the fourteenth century had been a formative experience for the English gentility; the experience of paying for war was equally formative with their class, as we can now see, and the effects were no less important. To that side of the history of the impact on English genteel life, attitudes and institutions of the Hundred Years War we must now turn.

As is revealed by the periodic 'states of the Exchequer' prepared by the king's Lords Treasurers, the Crown's ordinary revenue (from Crown lands, the profits of justice, the customs on wool and so on) left very little surplus over after recurrent charges had been met, such as the costs of the keeping of the marches and of Calais, of the king's household, of the stipends of the judges and other officials. So in wartime, if troops were to be raised and campaigns mounted, extraordinary taxation had to be raised to pay for them, and for this the assent of Parliament was necessary. The consequence of this was that the period of the war with France was one of great significance in the history of that institution, and especially in the history of the role of the parliamentary Commons, whose constitutional right to approve and assent to all extraordinary secular taxation, already traditional by *c.* 1300, was definitively affirmed in statutes of 1340 and 1362.

As a result of the Crown's recurrent need for assented taxes, Parliament met more frequently during the time of the Hundred Years War than it had ever done previously (over long periods meetings were almost annual). Sessions became longer, and when in the fifteenth century the custom arose of proroguing Parliaments and holding a second or even a third session, the lives of Parliament became longer too. Debates in the Commons, of which we hear nothing in the early days (they were summoned only to hear and assent), took on life. The Anonimalle Chronicle tells us how, in the Commons in the Good Parliament of 1376, once they had separated from the Lords to talk among themselves in the Chapter House of Westminster Abbey, a knight 'of the south country' strode up to the lectern and began to speak:

My lords, you have heard the points put before Parliament, which are grievous matter, for they demand a tenth and a fifteenth of clergy and commons, which to me seems a heavy burden, for the commons are enfeebled by the taxes and tallages of time past . . . and besides, all we have given for a long while we have lost, for it has been wasted and falsely spent.

The Commons began to develop a sense of their own procedures, customs and privileges, and to concern themselves over the election and conduct of their Speaker, an office first heard of in 1376 (Roger Hunt was elected in 1420, we know, by a mere four votes). On the issue of their right in assenting to tax they were consistently strident: when in 1407 the Lords reported to the king what they deemed might be necessary in the way of a financial grant, the Commons protested hotly that this was a prejudice to the liberty of their estate, and obtained a ruling that in future nothing concerning fiscal grants would be officially reported to the king until the Lords and Commons were agreed on it, and then by the mouth of the Commons' Speaker.

The frequent meetings of the estates that the king's requirements necessitated made sure that the Commons always included members with a good deal of parliamentary experience: in any Parliament there was bound to be a good leavening of old hands who had represented their communities before. Many of these,

as we have seen, would have been men who had weight and
experience of administration locally: their experience of working
together in the broader forum of Parliament widened their
horizons, teaching them to take a view on matters of wider
impact than the affairs of their regional communities, notably
on the conduct of the war and its repercussions, and on the
handling of the king's revenues. It also brought them into more
regular contact with their social superiors in the Lords, narrow-
ing the gaps in outlook on national issues between the higher
and lower echelons of the aristocracy. This helped to develop a
greater sense of cohesion among the dominant secular estate in
the kingdom, something that the growing tendency in the
fifteenth century of boroughs to choose gentlemen as their
parliamentary representatives further enhanced. Concurrently
and consequently, parliamentary service came to seem more
significant and more desirable to the gentry. Most elections seem
to have been uncontested, but only because 'heaving and shoving' and the use and abuse of influence had decided in advance
who was going to be returned: and in the fifteenth century we
begin to hear more of contests, even of rioting at elections.
Nottinghamshire in 1460 provides us with what seems to be the
first surviving record of a poll. A strong turnout of 40s. freeholders from the north of the county in that year secured the
return as members of Sir Richard Strelly and Sir John Stanhope,
who with 161 and 151 votes respectively handsomely defeated
their rivals William Babington and Richard Sutton.

The Crown's need to woo Members of Parliament who were
men of substance, with ideas of their own and electors to report
back to in their communities, was a clear one. At the opening of
Parliament, the king's requirements of them were explained on
his behalf by a speech or sermon by one of his ministers, most
often the Chancellor: 'Sirs,' began Archbishop Sudbury in 1380,

it will not be unknown to you that the noble lord the Earl of
Buckingham, with a large number of other lords, knights, archers and
other good men of this kingdom – God's mercy preserve them – are in
France in the service of the Lord King and his realm, on which
expedition the king has spent all that you granted in the last Parliament,
and more besides and heavily from his own resources . . . and it is the

fact that, on account of the present unrest in Flanders, the wool subsidy is bringing in almost nothing, and the wages of the soldiers of the marches of Calais, Brest and Cherbourg are not far short of six months in arrears, whereby the King's castles and fortresses are in great peril . . . And so you are asked to counsel our Lord the King, and to show as best you can how and from what sources it seems to you that these charges can best be borne and to the least discomfort of yourselves and the commons of this land.

The speeches of other Chancellors, in other Parliaments, explain the current situation in the same sort of way as this, justifying and leading up to the same sort of pleas for aid. Parliament was not the only forum for this sort of wooing, moreover. Fiscal grants took time to collect, and the king's requirements were all too often immediate; so that it was necessary to raise loans in cash on the security of the parliamentary grant in advance of its payment. The commissioners, who were sent out into the localities to raise such loans from gentlemen, town corporations and churches, also had to explain the king's need, and urge the public interest on people who knew by experience that in wartime they might have to wait for repayment of their loans for longer than was convenient. A backlog of bad debt accumulating in this way could seriously sour relations between the government and the leaders of local communities: that was another reason for the collapse in the fifteenth century of the efforts to maintain the Lancastrian conquests in France.

A point that needs to be remembered, when considering the royal quest for finance to pay for the king's wars, is that though the Commons of Parliament had a right to assent to taxation, and could give less than was asked of them, or spread payment over a period, or seek to enforce conditions, it is not entirely clear that they had a right to refuse it point blank. They had established for themselves a negotiating position; control, even at the end of the middle ages, lay far in the future. The king's right, in a military emergency, to demand aid from his subjects in combating their common peril was a well-established and a traditional one; but because he was demanding a contribution from goods that were theirs, not his, he needed their acquiescence in the measure of his demand. As the Romano-canonical legal tag put it, 'what affects all should be approved by all':

Parliament's essential role, as an assembly of the realm, was to assess the king's need and approve the common levy. But inevitably there was more to it than that. As Gerald Harriss has very neatly put it, 'because Parliament adjudicated the common profit of the realm [i.e. what affects all] not merely in terms of the common peril, but of the common welfare of subjects which the king was bound to promote, the dialogue over taxation extended to a critical concern with many other aspects of government'.

It was this dialogue, focused chiefly but not exclusively in Parliament, between the king and his subjects, between governments and governed, that was the most important development generated by the need for money to pay for the expenses of the French war. It is true that those 'other aspects' besides taxation, that Harriss refers to, were often not related to the war at all. But for the opportunity for discussion and the need for accommodation that the war situation created, however, they might never have been brought under review at all, and some of them were very important. By the time the war ended, processes initiated in the course of the dialogue about how to find an accommodation had altered the structure of government and had shifted the balance of political influence in the kingdom significantly. Moreover, after the war had ended, it was found that the dialogue could not be discontinued: it had been going on for too long.

In order to understand the developments here, a little has to be said in introduction about the way in which England was governed at the time when the Hundred Years War commenced, and before that. If one looks at the structure of royal government in that time, perhaps the most striking thing about it is how amateur and unbureaucratic it was. The composition of the king's Council, which was the inner heart of executive government, depended largely on whom the king chose to consult. This meant normally a handful of peers, bishops and prominent knights personally close to the king, and trusted by him on account of their experience in war, politics and administration. The judges, though always close to the Council, were not necessarily members of it. Theirs was a key office, nevertheless. The central courts over which they presided, the King's Bench and Common Pleas, were the highest tribunals in the kingdom, after the Council and Parliament, and every year literally thousands of cases were initiated before them (though a great many were never completed). The judges were men with a professional training in the common law, who had risen through their distinction as advocates rather than through the service of the Crown. This distinguished them from the heads of the three departments of state, the Chancellor, the Treasurer and the Keeper of the Privy Seal, who were Crown servants *par excellence* and who were always members of the Council.

These three departments, the Chancery, the Exchequer and the Privy Seal Office, were the only separate state offices at the beginning of our period, and the staff of clerks (many only in minor orders) who worked in them was not large. The Chancery dealt with all business passing under the Great Seal – grants of land and patents of office, treaties, the appointments of embassies and commissions, and a host of routine writs; it was also just beginning to develop an equitable jurisdiction in cases not determinable at common law. Under the Chancellor (usually a bishop) there were twelve clerks of the first grade, Masters of Chancery, 'fat of purse and furred of robe', each with a clerk of his own; there were twelve clerks of the second grade and twenty-four 'cursitors', mainly occupied in copying routine writs, and some assistants: in all perhaps some hundred persons. They were bound together by a measure of communal living and privilege, receiving robes from the Chancellor as members of his household, dining together and often lodging together in 'Inns of Chancery'. The Exchequer was the royal accounting department: its work was more varied than that of the Chancery and so were the backgrounds of those who worked there. The Treasurer, like the Chancellor, was often a bishop; the Chief Baron was a common lawyer (ranking with the Chief Justices of the two benches). There was a clerical staff that was slightly smaller than that of the Chancery; the leading clerks – the Chancellor of the Exchequer, the two Remembrancers and the Engrosser of the Rolls – had a status comparable with that of the Chancery Masters. The office of the Privy Seal, which authorized letters to move the Great Seal, summonses to appear before the Council and the king's more informal diplomatic correspondence, was the smallest of the three departments. It provided a kind of secretariat to the Council and there were just fourteen clerks under the Keeper.

By any standard, something around two hundred men, mostly (at the start of our period) unmarried and of clerical habit and training, makes a very small bureaucracy. No doubt that is why in late medieval England there were no calls, as there often were in contemporary France, for cuts in the personnel (and so in the costs) of central government, in order to release funds for war expenses. It is also questionable whether the word 'bureaucrat' is really appropriate to describe the men who served in these central offices. They were remunerated in a distinctly amateur way, though financially they might not do too badly, from perquisites of office and casual profits, and from the stipends of ecclesiatical benefices in the Crown's gift that they were well placed to secure and whose duties they would neglect. The preoccupations of the working day of all but the most senior had at least as much in common with those of a scribe in a monastic scriptorium as with those of a civil servant in the modern sense. Much of it was spent copying out documents in traditional hand and in accordance with established formulae. Thomas Hoccleve was a clerk of the Privy Seal for more than thirty years and also a poet (not a very good one), a man of scholarly education and literary refinement. What his work gave him, he tells us, was pains in the back and the stomach, and it ruined his eyesight.

Away from Westminster, there were of course some further openings for men with a clerical training like Hoccleve's that fitted them to be 'bureaucrats' of a sort, controllerships of the customs, clerkships to the constable of this or that castle, and so on. The main business of the local government which the central offices and courts somewhat loosely supervised and directed was however in the hands of amateurs, and at the beginning of our period had long been so. The traditional focal centre of local administration was the county court, the history of whose regular meetings reached back into the Anglo-Saxon past. Its presiding officer was the sheriff, who from the mid thirteenth century onward was normally chosen (in the Exchequer) from among the knights and substantial gentlemen resident in the shire. The county court was where royal ordinances and statutes were proclaimed: in it the coroners, who investigated homicides and kept the pleas of the Crown, were elected; so were the representatives that the shire sent to Parliament when it was summoned. The sheriff empanelled from among the freeholders of the county the jurymen who would answer in the court to questions of fact and opinion when, twice a year, the justices of assize came on circuit. The whole twelfth-century reform of government that historians associate above all with the name and reign of Henry II, and which developed further under his descendants in the thirteenth century, had been founded on the cooperation in the business, offices and procedures of the county court of the substantial knights and freeholders of the shire. For a century and a half, at least, before 1350, this system had been working in a way that fostered a strong sense of identity in the county community and a capacity among its leaders for corporate and collective action.

Until about 1300 this system of local government was kept under close supervision by the periodic visits to the counties (every five years or so) of the royal justices in eyre, appointed in the Exchequer and armed with power to hear all causes (after 1300 these eyres were partly superseded by special commissions to deal with particular aspects of what had been their business, but the effect was not very different). At the coming of the justices, the whole amateur course of local administration was turned inside out in a rigorous investigation. Arrested felons were brought out of gaol to be judged: 'oh yes,' the legal historian Bolland remarks drily, 'there was much hanging done at those old eyres of ours'. What the justices were really after, though, was not bodies but money, to make sure that no right of the king's remained unclaimed and no penny owing to him unpaid. By what warrant did this or that lord exercise a franchise normally reserved to the Crown? If the Crown's inquiries had elicited charges of homicide and the alleged offenders had fled, had the sheriff seized their chattels? What steps had he taken with regard to the lands of minors who belonged to the king's wardship? Had any retailers been using short weight or short measure, and were there any taverners who had adulterated their ale? If so, they must be in the king's mercy, until they made fine with him and so bought themselves back into his grace, and so must any others who might be convicted of crimes, misdemeanours, trespass or mere negligence. The effect of the visitation was to tax the whole community, but by a means of taxation which required no assent, because in name the eyre was not a fiscal instrument but a judicial visitation. The eyres and special commissions were cordially hated, and with good reason.

In the time when assented taxation was in its infancy, the eyres and special commissions stood alongside other means whereby the English kings could generate additional revenue for war purposes; prominent among those other means being the use of their prerogative rights of purveyance and over the royal forests. Purveyance was the right of the king to purchase supplies for his household compulsorily when on his travels; Edward I, by taking the main part of his armies nominally into the pay of his household and victualling them by means of purveyance, virtually transformed it into a national tax. The scale of the Scottish wars, however, was such that it became necessary for him to rely more heavily than any of his predecessors had done on direct, assented taxation; and the scale of Edward III's needs, when the Hundred Years War broke out, was even greater. The importance both of assented taxation and of Parliament, the body in which assent could most conveniently be sought, was thus given new impetus; and it is not surprising that in the ensuing dialogue matters such as the eyres, the forest and purveyance were prominent.

In the roll of Parliament for 1348 we find this response to a fresh demand for subsidy from the king (on the ground of a threat of French invasion):

now we hear that, because of the new turn of events, the king is demanding a charge on his poor commons that is too great. May it therefore please his lordship to hear the burden of the charges and mischief which the said commons already endure.

So they listed their grievances and specified what they thought would palliate them. Their first request, unsurprisingly, was that in return for a money grant all eyres should cease for the time being. They complained also of the purveyances by which the king had supplied his recent expedition to France: and wanted assurance that he would not seek a grant on exports from the merchants outside Parliament. In 1348 they did not gain all they asked for, but with the king under recurrent pressure from the need to finance his warfare they were largely successful, over ensuing years, in getting him to meet their wishes in these and other matters. The eyres fell into desuetude: the king took more and more to contracting with merchants in order to supply his forces, rather than relying on compulsory purchase: he abandoned the practice of seeking agreement from groups of merchants to extra charges on exports, over and above the customs duty, and went to Parliament for these instead. He and his justices also ceased to press his rights over royal forests with the traditional thoroughness, and he became progressively more generous in granting licences to landowners to impark and enclose woodland for their own pleasures in the chase.

The Commons did not seek for themselves or for Parliament a new position in national government: their stance was rather one of operative criticism of the way that government was carried on. They were however deeply interested in local government, and this was where the dialogue between them and the Crown, and the Crown's readiness to attend to genteel preferences, made its deepest and most lasting mark socially. One of the most striking and important developments of the late medieval period was the progressive transference of matters once reserved to the justices in eyre whom the commons so disliked to the justices of the peace at their quarter sessions. Originally 'keepers of the peace' with powers only to pursue and arrest, the justices of the peace steadily acquired wider powers to hear and determine cases, and it is clear from the Commons' petitions to Parliament that their justice was vastly preferred, at any rate by the gentry, to that of the old eyres and of special commissions. A statute of 1368 defined their jurisdiction as including the enforcement of labour laws; of regulations about prices, weights and measures; the maintenance of the peace and the determination of felonies and trespasses. Later statutes gave them jurisdiction in cases of livery and maintenance and power to inquire into riots (under Henry IV); the duty of investigating 'lollardies and heresies' (under Henry V); the power to deal with cases of forcible entry, and (under Henry VI) to approve the regulations of guilds and fraternities. Under the Yorkists and especially the early Tudors their authority was extended still more widely.

The commissions of the peace were appointed by the Crown, on the nomination of the Chancellor. They usually included some locally influential magnate, and at least one of the justices of assize for the county. For a quorum at least one justice 'learned in the law' needed to be present at the quarter sessions (but the definition of this qualification was not at all precise). The main burden of responsibility fell, inevitably, on the local, resident gentry. If the justices selected from among these were to do their job effectively, there was no alternative to selecting them from among the same leading county families that already in a loose way monopolized such offices as those of sheriff and coroner, who were regularly employed on commissions of array or as commissioners to raise loans for the Crown, and who were coming more and more to monopolize the shire representation in Parliament.

The overall result was a significant entrenchment of the influence of local élite groups, and the enhancement of what I earlier called the amateur (and the unpaid) element in regional government. But the change was really much bigger than that. Though it was locally that the justices of the peace had to apply the rules, matters such as the laws concerning riot, wages and prices, the regulations of guilds and the abuses of livery and maintenance were not just local matters. As is attested in the wording of numerous parliamentary petitions, urging the king to define the law in areas such as these in ways which the Commons thought would best protect and promote the general interests of the class they principally represented, they were national matters. The administrative measures of the Angevin period and of the thirteenth century had made the substantial county landowners leaders of the governed locally: now they were beginning to take over local responsibility for national governance. This enlarged role in the administration of the law, together with the new-found influence of the gentry in the national assembly of Parliament, are twin signs of their coming of age as a governing, political class, nationwide. The experience of political dialogue and the steadily widening administrative involvement that their influence in the period of the Hundred Years War gained them thus prepared them for the central part that they would play in the national life of Tudor and Stuart England.

In Stuart times the two instruments of tyranny that the Commons most feared that English monarchs might acquire were the right to tax arbitrarily and a standing army. The French monarchy emerged from the rigours of the Hundred Years War armed with both these weapons, and it is clear that the strains of the long combat with England were the principal agent in putting them at the disposal of the later Valois kings. The English monarchy, by contrast with the French, emerged from the same struggle armed with neither. In England the effect of the war and the strains it imposed were not as in France, and as seems to be the more usual pattern, to concentrate power and authority towards the centre, but rather to disperse it, into regional society and the local communities. This seems surprising, but is not really as surprising as it looks. The English kings in the Hundred Years War claimed that the throne of France should be theirs, and Henry V came very near to winning it (his son Henry VI was actually crowned in France in 1430, though in Paris, not at Reims). From the point of view of Valois France, the threat was to the head. From the English point of view, the threat from the Valois was not to the head, but rather to the tentacles that the English were acquisitively pushing out, towards Calais and the French Channel ports, into Normandy, and from their long-standing base in Gascony in south-west France (and, indeed, into Scotland). In this English acquisitiveness there was no element of quest for *Lebensraum*: there was plenty of room in England, specially after the Black Death. What the English kings, the leaders in the war, were seeking were the revenues of a larger inheritance and the reputation of having won it, and the only way in which they could hope to achieve that with the resources at their disposal was by taking their subjects into partnership with them, both in the straightforward military adventure that the war was and in government. Military service became as a result less obligatory in consequence of the war, not more so, and the raising of revenue more of a matter of negotiation, not less.

Nevertheless there were centripetal forces as well as centrifugal ones that were set in motion, and Parliament, with which we have been so much concerned, was a magnet to them. Dr Harriss has described the experience of the war period and of the problems it raised as 'profoundly educative' for the parliamentary Commons, and for the landowning class generally, and indeed it was that. The long struggle with the French greatly sharpened the English sense of national identity. The blow which Englishmen really did sense when in 1450–51 the French drove their forces ignominiously first out of Normandy and then out of Gascony was the injury to national pride. 'Consider,' demands a manifesto put out by the Duke of York in 1452,

first the worship, honour and manhood asserted of all nations to the people of England, whilst the Kingdom's sovereign lord stood possessed of his lordship in France

and then compare with that the

derogation, lesion of honour and villainy reported generally unto the English nation for the loss of the same.

But the war had not only taught Englishmen about their identity, it had also taught them about their national interest. If we turn to the *Libelle of English Policye*, written perhaps a decade before this, we can glimpse something of the reason why more effort and more money were not forthcoming to prevent that 'lesion of honour and villainy' reported to the English nation. Its author was emphatic about the need to guard Calais and to keep control of the narrow seas, because that was vital to English trade; but he was more enthusiastic about shoring up the English position in Ireland, which he believed (incredibly) would prove to be an important source of gold, than about shoring up the English position in Normandy. The Commons of Parliament did not follow him in his view that a major military operation in Ireland would be worth paying for, but they did hesitate to offer the king more for the defence of his foreign French

lordships than they deemed would be to the common profit of
the realm. That helped to ensure that the English Crown lost its
foreign lordships: it also showed that the secular dominant class
in England had become too educated and too important, politically as well as socially, to commit 'blood and treasure' from
their country in ventures whose advantage to the common weal
was insufficiently apparent to them.

7. The Aristocracy at Home: Household, Estates and Family

'After the deeds and exploits of war, which are claims to glory, the household is the first thing which strikes the eye, and that which it is, therefore, most necessary to conduct and arrange well.' So wrote Georges Chastellain, chronicler of the fifteenth-century Burgundian court. The household of which he wrote was the focus of the most lavish and glamorous court of northern Europe, of an aristocratic society that, in outward show at least, consciously cultivated the traditional chivalrous and martial traditions of the 'warrior estate'. The chronicler's advice held good, nevertheless, for households much less exalted and less consciously martial in tone and ceremony. On the English domestic front, the household was indeed a central institution in the life of the aristocracy, lesser as well as greater, of ordinary gentlefolk as well as of dukes, earls and barons. The scale of their establishments differed, of course, but the institution remains recognizably the same at the humbler as at the higher level.

The very word householder (as Chaucer for instance uses it of his franklin, 'a householder and that a great was he') implied of a man that he was something more than just a paterfamilias. A nuclear family, the man who was its master, his wife and his children, stood at the centre of the household, but it embraced at the same time a larger but closely knit community, his *familia*, which might include, according to his status, any number of chaplains, servants, grooms, cooks and kitchen boys, as well as his family in the modern sense. By the number of these dependants, by the cut of their cloth, by the standard of provision and the amplitude of the hospitality that his household could extend, the 'worship' and standing of a nobleman or a gentleman among his peers or neighbours was to be judged. To 'conduct and arrange well' the management of the household, to balance the impression of style and plenty that it gave with the resources at its master's disposal, was a necessary art for any born into the secular ruling class, at whatever level.

House and household, at this upper level of society, are separable topics, in theory at least. Even a quite modest gentleman might be lord of two or three manors, with residences available to him in each; and it was politic for him to show himself in each from time to time, if he did not wish to risk losing the respect of his tenants and being cheated by his reeves and bailiffs. A great lord, an earl or baron, would have many residences that he could call his own on estates that might be widely scattered about the country; and by our time most peers and even some knights of substance felt, as we have seen earlier, the need to keep up a house of their own in London as well. When such a man moved from one of his houses to another, his household went with him, and so did a great deal of his furniture, his plate and the fittings of his chapel; messengers went ahead to secure lodging on the way and to tell his caretakers to get his house ready for him. The state in which he travelled was another sign of his dignity, another way of impressing his standing on neighbours, tenants and people in the places that he passed through.

For obvious reasons, the lower a man's standing in the scale of aristocracy, the more sedentary he was likely to be (if he was at home in England that is, not if he chose to go riding to the wars overseas). But in the later middle ages, though there was still much travelling for households, there was a general tendency throughout the ranks of the aristocracy to become rather less peripatetic than they had once been. Early in the fourteenth century the household of Earl Gilbert of Clare was moving on average about every two weeks: but by the end of it it had become rare for a great household to move more than two or three times a year, and usually between just two or three regularly visited residences. On temporary trips, made necessary by urgent business, a lord would travel only with his 'riding household', and without his paraphernalia. A gentleman was now usually to be found at a fixed residence; very likely you would find in one of his other houses his widowed mother,

equally sedentary, and perhaps his married son and heir might
be settled in a third. With greater stability large households
tended to become larger, and their organization more elaborate:
stability also drew house and household into closer relationship.
The former was becoming more clearly home for the latter; and
a more comfortable home to boot. It still had to be something
more than just a home, though. It was at the same time the
headquarters of a sphere of influence, and that is why so much
in it had to be designed to impress.

The importance of the aristocratic house in these two senses,
as home and headquarters, and the growth of more sedentary
habits among the upper classes encouraged a great deal of
building, and on a lavish scale, since the residence of a lord or
gentleman was a visible sign of the standing of its owner. A
great deal of money was spent this way. In the late fourteenth
century the Scropes of Bolton were paying out a thousand
marks a year, over eighteen years, on construction at Bolton. In
the fifteenth Lord Cromwell's great brick *donjon* at Tattershall
took twelve years to build and his annual expenditure on it was
not much less. This was essentially new building: elsewhere the
heads of baronial families were spending comparably, to quote
K. B. McFarlane, 'in making the bleak, ill-lit castles of their
ancestors comfortable . . . by the addition of halls, withdrawing
rooms and ranges of private apartments with glazed and traceried
windows and chimneyed hearths'. This is what John of Gaunt
did at Kenilworth, the Beauchamps at Warwick Castle, the
Percies at Alnwick. Lower down the social scale too the same
sort of thing was happening. At Haddon Hall, all through the
late medieval times, the Vernons were adding steadily to the old
fortified house overlooking the Derbyshire Wye; its great hall is
of the fourteenth century, the suite of first-floor rooms on the
south side of the forecourt of the fifteenth, and the new gatehouse
and further buildings on the north and west side of the forecourt
belong to the early sixteenth. Up and down the land other
knights and gentlemen were doing the same thing, building new
houses and improving old ones.

Not very much of the building that was going on at such a
rate in the fourteenth and fifteenth centuries now remains, but
enough to make it just a little easier to visualize the style and

daily routines of the household then than it is for an earlier age. The basic ground plan of the aristocratic house was fairly consistent in its outline: scale rather than essential layout was what distinguished the near-palaces of the great from the manor-house of the ordinary gentleman of fairly solid means. The house was built about a courtyard or two courts (if the site was an old one, probably following the lines of an earlier curtain wall or fenced enclosure). The most important building, along one side or perhaps dividing two courts, was the great hall, open to the roof; at one end was the dais, where the master presided from his high table, at the other a screen created an entrance passage from the main door. Behind this screen and at right angles to it, another passage might lead to the kitchens, with a buttery and pantry, for wet and dry stores, opening on it. Behind the dais a doorway led to the private chamber or chambers of the lord and lady of the house (connected by a stair if they were on the first floor). Into this quadrangular design would then be incorporated chambers for guests, servants' living quarters, a chapel, a gatehouse at the main entry and store-rooms and stables as required.

The second house that Lord Cromwell built, South Wingfield in Derbyshire, may give an idea of what one should picture. A stone house crowning a rise, it was built around two courts. The outer gate, with its gatehouse flanked by turrets, opened into the forecourt, round which was constructed the communal accom-modation for menial servants and various offices and store-rooms. From the forecourt a gateway opened into the inner court. Opposite, on the north side of the court, stood the hall, with next to it a block of buildings around a small 'service' court, incorporating the passage to the kitchen (with buttery and pantry); and on its further side, reached by a stairway, Cromwell's own apartments. The west range accommodated guest lodgings, of a high standard: the high tower, in the south-west angle of the inner court, housed stately chambers for specially honoured guests. Under the hall was a vaulted under-croft, probably a servants' dining-hall. Surprisingly, it is not clear where the chapel was, even whether there was one (some of the site has been built over subsequently). There was room to accommodate a very large number of persons at South

Wingfield, and the more honoured in considerable ease, with warm fires in their well-appointed chambers.

The plan of the more modest manor-house that Sir John Waleys built at Hawksden (Sussex) in the second half of the fourteenth century, whose site has been excavated, may serve as a foil to this grand design. It was a timber-framed building, constructed around a single paved quadrangle. The gate was in the north range, and the hall faced it. The private chambers and guest lodgings took up the west range. Thus the essential plan was not very dissimilar from that at South Wingfield; only the scale was far more modest; as Waleys, though well enough off for a knight, was of very modest means compared with Lord Cromwell. Hawksden was a moated house, as many manor-houses of this age were. Although it was designed, like South Wingfield, as an entirely domestic, non-castellar dwelling, this much protection still seemed needed, against bandits, hostile neighbours and local faction fighting. Moated houses like Hawksden had necessarily to be built in low-lying ground, by running water, and this is one reason why so few survive. Their sites were dank and unhealthy, and in a later, more stable age the descendants of their owners preferred to move to higher ground.

A striking feature of the late medieval manor-house or castle was the privacy that it afforded to its owner, and to the more honoured guests for whom private rooms were provided. Social conservatives like Langland regretted the decline in communal living that this spelt:

> Wretched is the hall each day in the week
> Where the lord nor the lady liketh not to sit.
> Now hath each rich man a rule to eat by himself
> In a private parlour because of poor men,
> Or in a chamber with a chimney, and leaves the chief hall.

Whether the change was really as socially divisive as the poet believed, in his puritanical nostalgia for a less luxurious age, may be questioned. But life certainly was less spartan. In addition to the new measure of privacy, furnishings were becoming more lavish: their standard was, along with so much else, part of the display that was designed to impress and to uphold the dignity of the master of the house. By later standards of course they were bare enough, plain trestle tables in the hall with benches for seating, chairs a rarity. That is why beds, with rich hangings, were so valued and loom so large in inventories – in the daytime they served as couches. There would be hangings on the walls too, tapestries, perhaps some wall paintings; we hear often of a 'painted chamber'. The private chapel in particular would be richly provided for, with copes, perhaps embroidered with the family arms, mass books and chalices. Perhaps most prized of all in the contents of the house was the plate, that which was kept in what Duke John of Bedford's executors called 'the rich cupboard'. Aristocrats spent a great deal on plate, partly no doubt because it was a safe investment, but also, and perhaps principally, for display, to impress the household and the guests who dined at the lord's table with tangible testimony to his riches.

The size of the household accommodated under its master's roof naturally varied very greatly, according to his status. An establishment of a dozen to a dozen and a half might be adequate for a reasonably well-to-do knight or esquire, but some kept more: a household account of the Mountfords of Warwick in the early sixteenth century shows payments to twenty-seven fee'd servants. A great lord would have many more than that. The household that accompanied Margaret, Duchess of Clarence, travelling in 1419 to Normandy, where her husband was in service under his brother Henry V, consisted of 19 knights, 25 esquires, 45 yeomen, 19 grooms, 13 pages, and 11 sumptermen in charge of the baggage; there were 10 priests and 4 choristers in the party. John Smith, the seventeenth-century steward and historian of the Berkeley family, wrote of Lord Berkeley's household in the early fourteenth century that:

The knights, who had wages by the day and their double liveries of gowns furred were usually twelve, each of them with two servants and a *garçon* or page, and allowance for the like number of horses: the esquires that also had wages by the day each of them with one man and a page were twenty-four ... from whence it may be conjectured what the numbers of inferior degrees might be. I am confident that the number of his standing house, each day fed, were three hundred at the least.

Smith's figure may be a bit high: Edward IV's *Black Book of the Household* suggests an establishment of 240 for a duke, and Dr Mertes has calculated the average size of an earl's household in the 1450s as about 200. But it gives an impression of just how large the community could be that gathered in the house of a major peer of the realm, and what a call on the purse it could be to feed them, their people and their horses.

As Smith's description makes clear, a great household embraced a very wide range of social gradations. A major magnate needed, for the preservation of his 'worship', to be seen to be served by well-born men. There were offices of dignity in his household, as butler or chamberlain or as gentlemen of the hall or of the chamber; indeed in the fifteenth century it was accepted, even in the law courts, that service at a certain level conferred gentility on the servant. To the young men of good lineage who were placed in a lord's house to be brought up, it was worshipful service to carve their master's meat and fill his cup, even to make his bed – and a necessary training in the protocol of hospitality. For a younger son of good family service in a great man's household offered an honourable way of living, in effect a career, in which he could expect to be kept as befitted his rank, as well as paid a wage (and it was a career that might, if his lord could help him to a good marriage, be the way to founding a lineage of his own). The ties that household service forged between a lord and the gentry families that were associated with him was thus an important buttress to the solidity of his 'affinity', of the circle of retainers, annuitants and councillors on whose loyalty and regard his influence, locally and nationally, so largely depended.

A great household required a formal administrative structure and departmentalization, with a responsible official in charge of each department, marshal of the stables, marshal or usher of the hall, master cook and so on. There was usually a separate budget and separate accounts kept for such offices as the kitchen, the cellar, and the pantry. This meant that administrative service in the household offered career opportunities, open in this case to servants recruited from humble stock. The son of a yeoman or even of a peasant, especially if he had or could acquire some smattering of letters, might rise to be clerk of the kitchen or a purchaser ('purveyor') of goods, or even to be treasurer of a lord's household. William Wistowe, a clerk of obscure origin, rose for instance to be treasurer to the household of Humphrey Stafford, first Duke of Buckingham; Duke Humphrey's receiver at Tonbridge Castle, Kent, William Hextall, likewise came of relatively humble birth from Staffordshire. If a servant did rise in this way, he might find himself giving orders to gentlemen of the household who, though distinguished from others in their receipt of better robes and good pay, had no administrative rank as such. As in the case of genteel servants, the recruitment of humbler and more menial servants helped to buttress a lord's local ties and local standing. Many of them tended to come from families of tenants, farmers or smallholders, with a tradition of association with the lord's household, a connection no doubt valued by their relatives outside it. It made sure for them that one member of the family at least was well looked after, and that there would be someone who could put in a word in the right place for the others if need arose.

All the servants so far mentioned have been assumed to be men, and this is no accident. The English aristocratic household of the later middle ages was a predominantly male society. Serving wenches were no part of it: they came in later. We hear sometimes of a laundress; but usually she lived away from the household. In it, unattached women seem to have been regarded as a threat to decorum and good order. Small children would need a nurse, but children were sent away from home so young that she was often not a very prominent figure. The lady of the house and her daughters would of course be served by a chamber-woman or chamberwomen, and a great lady would have her gentlewomen companions. Such female servants as there were were likely to be married to other servants, and confined to the private parts of the house. In an age when the menial servants lived and slept communally this was common sense. The vast majority of them, it seems certain, were unmarried men.

*

The cost of wages and of clothing and feeding the household was a heavy burden on a lord's income, one of the principal items of his expenditure, and a matter which required a good deal of attention. Enough household accounts have survived to give us a good picture of the general mode of management. Because so much money was involved, careful accounts had to be kept in each department, day by day in some households, week by week in others, and by the treasurer for general expenses: at the end of the year these would provide the basis for the audit. There are normally three elements to such accounts: the 'charge', that is the record of cash advanced to cover expenses; the 'discharge', itemizing in detail the purchases on which it was spent; and the stock account, showing what had actually been consumed. Such refinements as double-entry book-keeping, valuation of stock and the notion of depreciation lay far in the future: nevertheless this sort of account could give a lord a good picture of the scale of his consumption and its expense, and of how much cash was needed to keep up current standards; and this in turn could be related to the overall income that he could count on, and to his other expenditure.

The largest item in the accounts, almost always, proves to be provisioning, which could be a very large-scale operation. In the early sixteenth century in a single year the fifth Earl of Northumberland's household consumed 16,932 bushels of wheat; 27,594 gallons of ale; 1,646 gallons of wine; 20,800 pounds of currants; 124 beef cattle; 667 sheep; and 14,000 herrings. This is leaving fowls, venison and so on out of account. The figures sound gargantuan, but if they are broken down into allowances per person per day they turn out to be relatively frugal. Those 27,594 gallons of ale would allow roughly one and a half quarts as a daily ration (it must be recalled that water was not good to drink, and so ale was the staple liquid refreshment). Most bulk purchases were made in the local market, and on a regular basis: the Luttrells of Dunster, for instance, went for most of their provisions to the weekly Friday market there, but the fish for Friday was bought in the market in Minehead on Wednesday. For some things, wine for instance, it might be necessary to send further afield (wine was often purchased at the port). A fair proportion of provisions in any household was not acquired by purchase, but represented the produce of manorial demesnes close to the lord's residence that were farmed directly, or of rents that were collected not in money but in kind. Cattle pastured on the local demesne provided what Kate Mertes has described as 'a larder on the hoof'. This was a good way of cutting cash expenditure. There were also items that a household could manufacture for itself; for instance fat from the carcasses of slaughtered animals could provide tallow for making candles, which burned in innumerable quantities in any great man's dwelling.

Regular expenditure on the household could easily account for half the total annual expenses of a lord or gentleman, and often far more. Provisioning was necessarily a particularly major item, because under that head hospitality as well as daily consumption had to be catered for. Hospitality was something expected of every aristocrat, from gentleman to earl or duke, and up to the measure of his means and 'worship' it was expected to be lavish: that is why it 'snowed meat and drink' in the house of that 'worthy vavassour', Chaucer's franklin. A good deal of a lord or gentleman's other, non-household expenditure had the same purpose, of maintaining his 'worship'. A great man was expected to dress in style, and that was costly. The embroidery alone of one of Henry of Derby's robes, of forget-me-nots on black velvet, cost £29, and he paid more than 70 marks for the trapper embroidered with his arms for the horse on which he proposed to enter the lists at Coventry in 1398. The robes and gowns of which the feoffees of Sir Andrew Sackville (d. 1369) made an inventory remind us that even a country knight had a good stock of best clothes in his wardrobe; there was his short gown of black and white furred with 'gris'; another short gown of scarlet, also furred; a long gown furred with 'calabria'; two cloaks, one red and one black and furred with miniver; and a white surcoat furred with miniver with ermine cuffs (he was technically breaking the sumptuary laws here). A great magnate would besides be expected to distribute (probably at Christmas) robes of suitable sumptuousness, and bearing his livery badge, to his retainers, including those who were not of his household. Giving was altogether a very major charge on the income of any man of standing, especially of a great magnate. He needed to be seen to be generous, in alms to the poor, in his patronage of the church and of church building, in his choice of rich, individual gifts for his peers and leading retainers – gifts of jewels, gold collars, fine wines or game. A high social profile did not come cheap.

Expenditure on the display of dignity and wealth on the part of late medieval nobles and gentlemen is sometimes categorized as 'conspicuous waste'. It was conspicuous, certainly, but it was by no means as wasteful as appears at first sight. Spending, for the rich, was regarded as a social obligation: it should be contained within the limits of prudence, of course, but within those limits it was *expected* to be conspicuous. Frugality, and especially frugality in the treatment of valued clients and servants, was not thought of as a virtue. Magnanimity – a great and generous spirit – and *largesse* – liberality with one's goods – were characteristic virtues to be looked for in the wealthy and well-born; just as patience was the redeeming virtue recommended to the poor and the labourers. These virtues, apposite to different grades in the social order, were indeed seen as working reciprocally as moral props of social hierarchy and so of social order.

Display and giving apart, and leaving out of account irregular items of expense (such as equipping a troop for war), there were a great many other, humdrum items to strain a noble or genteel income besides meeting the regular expense of keeping up a household. There were running costs and maintenance, both on estates and in the home. Family interest needed to be maintained; daughters would need a marriage portion, sons a marriage – which at the genteel social level would need to be purchased. There were fees and annuities to be paid to useful people, to legal advisers and, in the case of peers, to retainers who were not of the household. There were the costs of the recurrent litigation which was the inevitable concomitant of being a landowner. The pitfalls for the imprudent are well-described in the letter that, in 1480, William Harleston, of Denham in Suffolk, dispatched to his nephew, who had just lost his wife:

For God's sake, be ware now ... after the decease of my good lady your wife, and stable [i.e. stabilize] your household now sadly and

wisely with a convenient fellowship, so as you may keep you within
your livelihood . . . And of certain things I would desire and pray you
in the name of God: that ye will not over-wish you, nor over-purchase
you, nor over-build you. For these three things will pluck a young
man right low. Nor meddle not with no great matters in the law.

Incessant care was needed. Even the most prudent needed good
advisers, and quite often loyal supporters as well, to help him to
balance the need to make an impression and to maintain his own
and his family's dignity with the need to keep within his means
and provide against the unforeseen.

Management was thus clearly quite a problem. Unsettled debt
was a matter constantly needling the consciences of the well-off
and the well-born; in will after will the first injunction to
executors is to pay off outstanding obligations, for the discharge
of 'my soul'. Keeping creditors waiting is however an ingrained
aristocratic habit, and the fact that provisioners, tailors, goldsmiths and others from whom the wealthy bought expensively
and extensively were prepared to wait long for their money is
significant. There were those who were 'plucked right low' by
over-lavish expenditure, but the number, as a proportion of the
upper classes, does not seem abnormally high. Political mistakes
undid more fortunes than financial insouciance, certainly at the
higher aristocratic levels and probably generally. The reasonably
prudent managers seem to have kept afloat all right, money-
wise, in spite of difficulties that they naturally encountered from
time to time. To see why we must turn from the household, and
the home sphere, to their preoccupations outside it and beyond
it, where the money came from.

The basic source of noble and genteel income was from land,
and the late middle ages were not an easy time for the landowner,
as we have seen. The long-term consequences of the fall in
population level of the post-plague era was to curtail greatly his
opportunities to maximize his income from the sale of produce
and from the exploitation of his seigneurial rights. There was a
broad tendency among landowners to abandon large-scale farming in favour of leasing, cutting losses for the security of a fixed
rent roll. They also became, naturally enough, eager to make

the most they could of other sources of income, among the most important of which were service and salaried office. Hence the fierce competition that Fortescue noted for royal patronage, with the king beset with petitions from his lords and courtiers to give 'offices, corrodies, or pensions of abbeys . . . to other men's servants, since they [i.e. lords and courtiers] most desire such gifts for themselves and their servants'. But the kind of favour that men desired most of all was that which would enable them to build up, buttress or extend their own landed patrimonies. This was because land remained the only solid, generally respected foundation for the maintenance of a position of dignity and influence. Sound estate management was, for that reason, every bit as vital to the preservation of the family fortunes of the noble and genteel as favour was, and in the long run surer in achieving its end.

The abandonment (never total) of demesne farming in favour of leasing at least permitted some reduction of administrative expense: it was no longer necessary to audit minutely the reeve's account on each individual manor. The inheritance of a great lay magnate was now usually divided into a series of 'receiverships', one for each area in which he held a concentration of estates. In each receivership he would appoint a steward to see to general management and to hold manorial courts, and a receiver to collect the rents and dues. There was a growing breed of men who made a livelihood (and often bettered themselves substantially in the process) by the discharge of these offices, often serving more than one master. The lord's receivers, from the cash they had in hand and on his instructions, could disburse monies for the expenses of his household, for his travelling expenses, for wages and annuities and to settle debts: what was finally paid in by them to his central treasury at his chief residence was in consequence always less, sometimes far less, than they had collected. Their accounts were audited annually by the lord's councillors: arrears of rent, disbursements not allowed and so on, were noted in the account and carried forward to the next year. At the end of the process the magnate could get a pretty clear picture of what the annual income was that must be balanced against the account of his regular outgoings, and of whether there was likely to be anything over for more interesting expenditure.

The management and accounting techniques followed by lesser aristocrats were similar to those of great magnates; only the scale of the operation was smaller. A very modest or straitened gentleman, who possessed perhaps only one or two manors, might act as his own steward, but most paid annuities to others to act for them as stewards, bailiffs, and receivers. These were humbler men than the corresponding servants of a magnate, naturally. John Harold, who rose to be steward to the knightly Sussex family of Etchingham in the late fourteenth century, for instance, almost certainly came of unfree stock. Their accounts might be scribbled on anything that came to hand: one set of accounts of receipts from the Pastons' manors is written on the back of a letter. But they bore the same titles and performed the same tasks as did the servants of greater men. When John Hopton (the rich but retiring Suffolk gentleman of the fifteenth century whom Colin Richmond has made celebrated through his biography) came into his own, he at once appointed Richard Daniel, parson of Swilling, to be his 'receiver general'. The bulk purchases that Hopton's bailiff, Nicholas Greenhaugh, was making in 1446 for the household at Blythburgh of fish, grain, malt, meat and barrels of cloth were not on the scale of those of the fifth Earl of Northumberland, but the difference really was of scale only. There is no reason to think that gentlemen were more amateurishly served than peers were, and many of them had more time to oversee their servants themselves.

The stewards and receivers of lords and gentlemen had much business to deal with. There were leases to be negotiated and renegotiated, tenants in arrears with rent to be interviewed and cajoled, trespassers to be prosecuted. There were also from time to time more general policies to be considered and discussed with the master. Could more be made by taking back some of the land that had been leased and turning it to pasture? (This was a policy that seems to have appealed to a good many owners in the late fifteenth century.) The notes that McFarlane has quoted from the informations supplied to his master by John Pickering, the Duke of Buckingham's receiver general in the early sixteenth century, and by others of his estate servants, give a good picture of efficient officials at work, and of the detail of the matters that they saw fit to report back:

Item, I have seized your bondman John Dyx of Padbury and taken surety for his body and goods by obligation in £40, as more plainly doth appear by the obligation and also by an inventory of his goods . . .

I have reasoned with certain of your tenants and also with other gentlemen and yeomen for your fines in every particular place and they have said to me they have no joy to offer . . .

John Burnell made great waste of wood in the park of Hatfield, whereof he is keeper . . .

Martin Pyes of Kegworth, yeoman, destroyeth my lord's warren of Ratcliff with greyhounds and ferrets . . .

The sort of matters that a knight and his officials might be concerned about were remarkably similar; in 1451 Sir John Fastolf was seeking information as to 'who were the chief council of breaking my mill dam', and was hot on the trail of John Buk, parson of Scratton, 'which fished my ponds and waters . . . and destroyed great quantity of fish to the damage of £20'.

The activities of estate officials were coordinated by the lord's council. Even a quite modestly endowed gentleman would have regular advisers whom he would describe as being 'of counsel with him'; and the councils of great men were in effect institutionalized bodies. We know less about baronial councils than we would like, since no formal records of the deliberations of any have survived, but we know that every magnate of standing did retain a group of regular councillors, and an impressive body of men they must have been when they were gathered at his house or his castle. Drawn from among his knightly retainers and his tried estate and household servants, aided by his 'attorney general' and his 'counsel learned' (lawyers retained at a fee for their professional advice) they were something like the royal council in microcosm. Like the king's councillors they acted on their lord's behalf with his authority, often with a considerable measure of independence. If the lord was absent, abroad in the king's service perhaps, or if he was under age, the management of his affairs fell more or less entirely into their hands. But if he was of age and at home, the last word was ultimately his, as the king's in his council. When, in the course of the protracted dispute between the Pastons and the Duke of Norfolk over the possession of Fastolf's castle at Caistor, John Paston travelled in 1472 to the ducal castle at Framlingham on his brother's behalf, he

went to the council, and offered before them your service to my lord, and to do him a pleasure for having again your place and lands at Caistor . . . so they answered me your offer was more than reasonable, and if the matter were theirs they said they wist what conscience would drive them to. They said they would move my lord with it and so they did; but then the tempest arose, and he gave them such an answer that none of them all would tell it me.

Councillors could guide their man, if he would be guided; they could not govern him.

A good deal of the time that those who were 'of counsel' with a landowner spent on his business was taken up with the handling of property disputes in which all owners in this litigious age were bound to find themselves all too frequently embroiled. The 'counsel learned' were naturally very prominent here, and their advice would also be particularly valuable about legal arrangements made to further what might be called dynastic or inheritance policy. Councillors, as we are reminded by their activity and responsibility when a minor inherited, were attached not to the service of one man only, but of a house. The future of his lineage could depend in large degree on the nature of the arrangements that they and their master made and their skill and shrewdness in making them.

In these arrangements, two legal devices, the use and the entail, became in the later middle ages key instruments. A 'use' was created when a landowner conveyed a portion of his estates to feoffees, to hold to his 'use' in accordance with instructions that he would give them. It could be a mere conveyancing instrument in the course of a purchase, the vendor conveying an estate to feoffees who on the completion of satisfactory negotiations would in their turn convey it to the purchaser. It was also a way of protecting the feoffor's inheritance against the risks of a wardship if he died while his heir was under age. From the inheritance point of view it was particularly important because of the freedom that it gave to a landowner in the disposal of his estates after his death. When the use was created, the feoffees became formally the owners at common law, and when the feoffor died, they followed the instructions given in his last will (a document originally separate from the 'testament' by means of which he disposed of his chattels). As they were themselves the common-law owners they were not in any way bound by the common-law rule that lands went to the eldest son, and should be divided between the daughters as co-heiresses if there was no male offspring. In this way, testators were able to give expression in their arrangements to the obligations which many of them clearly felt towards their younger sons, their daughters and even their illegitimate children. We are thus offered a newly clear insight into the family ideology of the landed upper classes, and into the sort of claims of affection and predilection that they felt they had to weigh against the consideration (vital in the long run in a period of economic difficulty) of preserving a viable estate for their posterity.

Usually it was the latter consideration, and the interest therefore of the eldest son, that won out in the long run; but sometimes the run was rather long. When Hugh, Earl of Stafford, died in 1386 his feoffees were instructed in his will to provide from his enfeoffed lands, firstly 'that all our servants to whom we have granted lands or annual rents may be made sure of enjoying them for the term of their lives'; secondly, for a dowry for his daughter; thirdly, to ensure that each of his three younger sons 'be enfeoffed of £100 of land and rent each, to have his enfeoffment and to enjoy it only for the term of his life', with reversion ultimately to the earl's eldest son and his heirs. Earl Hugh's heir thus entered on an inheritance loaded with annuities and depleted for the time being by life grants, including grants to brothers who were younger than he was (and he was lucky not to have to assign dower to his father's widow as well, since the late earl's wife had predeceased him). It was a sign of the respect for primogeniture and of the sense of the need to preserve the integrity of the family landholdings that the provisions of wills usually ensured that the original inheritance, or most of it, came back ultimately to the senior line. An heir could, however, find himself endeavouring for an inconveniently long time to maintain his dignity as head of the family on an income greatly reduced by encumbrances, bequeathed by his father's will and by the common law concerning dower.

Very occasionally magnates (and others) did use their testamentary freedom to deprive the heir of all or a substantial part of the inheritance. This was often for the benefit of the more favoured children of a later marriage. In this way Ralph Neville, first Earl of Westmorland, stripped his eldest son of a large part of his inheritance in the interest of his eldest son by his second marriage – to Joan Beaufort – Richard Neville, later Earl of Salisbury and father of Warwick the Kingmaker. More interesting, perhaps, is what landowners did when they failed in the business of engendering a son to succeed. When Ralph Bassett of Drayton died in 1390, he preferred Hugh Shirley, son of his half-sister, to the second cousins who were his common-law heirs, stipulating only that Hugh should adopt his name and arms on succeeding. Sir Andrew Sackville, predeceased by his sons by his first wife and childless by his second, secured that when he died his feoffees should convey his lands to his bastard son by a mistress of long standing, Joan Burgess; and from this Thomas Sackville the Sackvilles of Knole ultimately descended.

The dispositions made by landowners through the use and the will show a strong tendency to favour the claims of male relatives against those of females, whose marriage would inevitably carry the patrimonial lands away to another family. The same desire to preserve the family name and to keep the family lands intact is reflected in the popularity of the entail. An entail confined the inheritance to the descendants of the landowner who created it (most commonly by conveying the land to feoffees, who then re-granted it to the feoffor on new terms, incorporating the entail). If it was 'tail male', which became more and more popular as the later middle ages progressed, it was confined to heirs male. Tail male ensured that even if an owner settled portions of his estate on several sons, the probability was that, given the accidents of genetics, the main part of it would revert to one or other of the male lines descended from him. Reversionary interests created by entails could give rise to some strange turns of fortune. Sir Roger Swillington, son of John of Gaunt's retainer Robert Swillington, by a settlement of 1403 arranged that his substantial estates should pass on his death to his son John and the heirs male of his body. If that line failed there were remainders to, firstly, his second son (by his third wife), Robert, and his heirs male; secondly, to Robert's daughters and their heirs; thirdly, to his own daughter Margaret and the heirs of her body; finally, failing all these, to his illegitimate half-brother, Thomas Hopton and his sons. Sir Roger died in 1417; John died childless in 1418 and Robert in 1420: Margaret too had no children. So in the end all reverted to John Hopton, son of Thomas Hopton, who held the lands from 1430 till 1478, and passed them on to his son, founding a new county dynasty.

A landowner, and the advisers who were 'of counsel' with him, the neighbours and kinsmen and associates from among whom he would choose his feoffees, needed to devote a good deal of thought to the drawing up of the instruments by which he disposed of his property, both during his lifetime and after it. The overriding concern, in the vast majority of cases, was to ensure that the estates were not so encumbered as to endanger ultimately the standing and influence of the family, but a great deal of thought, as we have seen, also went into the business of making reasonable provision for close relations other than the principal heir. If these were provided with estates of their own, it was usually from lands newly acquired, by purchase or reversion, or that the mother had brought. Thus it was from lands 'purchased and had purchased to my use' that John of Gaunt provided for Thomas Beaufort, his third son by Catherine Swinford, his mistress and later his third wife. A landowner less amply endowed than Gaunt was likely to make sure that any settlements he made on brothers and cadets were for life only. He could help them in other ways, of course, by assisting them to equip themselves to go to the wars, by paying for their schooling to the church or the law, or by using his influence and connections to secure them crown office or salaried service in a great household. Best of all, he or a patron might secure for them a good marriage. Marriage was a matter of the utmost importance at all levels of aristocratic society, and not for younger children only but also, indeed above all, for the heir. The terms and conditions of family marriages were, in consequence, one of the most important matters that any landowner and his advisers had to deal with, and the subject is therefore one that must be looked at in detail in its own right.

Though it was common practice in large families that one son might enter the church, and one daughter perhaps might enter religion as a nun, most men and women of the upper classes expected to marry. For women there was really no alternative consonant with their status, outside religion, and so it was an important business for fathers to see their daughters wedded. A great magnate with a daughter on his hands might, if the opportunity arose, buy the marriage of a royal ward outright. They did not come cheap. Thomas Holland, Earl of Kent, paid £4,000 for the marriage of Roger Mortimer, heir of March, to his daughter Eleanor; and Ralph Neville, Earl of Westmorland, paid 3,000 marks for the marriage of John Mowbray, the Norfolk heir, to his daughter Katherine. More usually (and in the case of the gentry regularly) it was a matter of dealing with another family, and the negotiations could be protracted and complicated. The bride's family were expected to provide a marriage portion, in cash, which was usually paid by instalments and not to her future husband but to her future father-in-law; in effect it was the price of the marriage. On the other side, arrangements had to be made for a jointure, for settling lands on the couple for the term of their joint lives. If the bridegroom was his father's heir, this jointure would come back into the patrimony provided that he survived to inherit: if he was a younger son, it depleted the whole estate, at least for the term of his and his wife's lifetimes.

There was much here for those who were 'of counsel' with a landowner to weigh carefully before a contract was drawn up. The size of the marriage portion and of the jointure were matters for negotiation: naturally they varied, in accordance with the status of the parties to the match and the measure of advantage that one side or the other hoped to gain by it, but prices were not low. Ralph, Earl of Stafford, in 1350 paid

£1,000 for the betrothal of his daughter Beatrice to Maurice, heir of the Earl of Desmond. Lower down the scale, the sum left by Sir William Vernon of Haddon (d. 1467) for portions for four daughters totalled 1,300 marks. The terms of the jointure needed professional care in their drafting. Families were naturally anxious to keep their interest in what they considered to be 'their' lands clear of other families' arrangements and entails. That is why, for instance, Elizabeth Marshal in the fifteenth century stipulated that the lands that she had brought to her marriage with Richard Fitzherbert should go to his eldest son, but in the condition that it had descended to her as an heiress, 'and in none other manner charged, by entail or otherwise'. In the same sort of spirit, restrictive clauses might be introduced into marriage contracts, to protect reversionary interests, for instance, or to ensure that, once married, the husband could not take measures that might disinherit the progeny of his bride. Thus Thomas Foljambe, of Derbyshire, when he contracted to marry Margery Longford in 1453 had to promise that neither he nor any feoffee to his use should 'make any feoffment or release by fine, by will or rent charge of any lands or tenements he or any feoffee is seized of to his use, but all such shall descend after his death to the heirs of his body lawfully begotten'.

Magnates sought marriage alliances among their peers, gentry usually with their equals in their own county society or in a neighbouring county, though the daughter of a wealthy burgess would not be despised. In the quest for advantageous connections couples were often betrothed very young. Henry Bolingbroke was just thirteen in 1380 when his father John of Gaunt secured for him the hand of Mary, the younger of the two heiresses of the last Bohun Earl of Hereford, who was probably marginally his junior. Sir William Plumpton (1404–80) was just twelve when he was betrothed to Elizabeth Stapleton, daughter of his family's neighbour Sir Brian: she was still an infant. When his turn came to make the arrangements, he betrothed his son Robert to a six-year-old daughter of Lord Clifford, another Elizabeth, stipulating – shrewdly as it proved – that if Robert died she should marry his younger son William. His daughters likewise were contracted in marriage in their childhood. When marriages were arranged thus early, the children usually remained with their own families until they were of age to consent to and to consummate the marriage, though the girl might go to live in her future father-in-law's household. In the meantime the fathers might share the jointure; if the future bride died, payments of instalments on the marriage portion ceased. Mortality obviously exposed the arrangements drawn up when children were betrothed to risk, and that is the reason why it was by no means the normal mode to contract so early: it was safer to wait, and make firm arrangements between parties who were old enough to procreate and to set up house on their own. In this calculating age of 'brokerage of marriage' child betrothal was nevertheless common enough.

It is easy to conclude from the legal records of contracts that marriage was treated wholly as a business proposition, without thought for the independent wills of the couple concerned, and especially without thought for the independence of the woman. This is not quite fair. The church's law was express and clear, that a marriage was invalid without the free consent of both contracting parties: at a pinch, a girl could simply refuse, and occasionally did. The common law also protected the woman's interest, once she was married, in significant ways. To prize away her rights in the jointure was very difficult; even if, like the wife of John Fitzherbert of Norbury, she 'could not be content with me, but [has] forsaken my household and company, and lived in other places as it pleased her to my great rebuke and harm'. If a woman survived her husband, she was entitled to a third share for life in her husband's property, as her dower (and to more by jointure, if the jointure amounted to a larger proportion than that). This could have serious consequences for the heir who might, if his father had remarried to a younger woman, have to wait long for her dower to fall in: if the preceding generations (or owners) had left widows, as was all too possible, his estate might be very seriously encumbered. It is not surprising that strenuous efforts were often made to persuade widows to accept a straight cash annuity in lieu of dower, and so bring the estate back into single management. They could not be forced, however, and a good many women preferred the freedom that dower lands gave them and which, besides, made them attractive on the remarriage market, and this time on their own terms.

As widows and dowagers, aristocratic women could be powerful and influential figures in their own right, managing their own estates and households and presiding over their own councillors. If, when her husband died, her children were under age, it was the widow who had to hold the family and household together, to arrange family marriages, supervise the estates and conduct lawsuits. When the son who succeeded John Hopton died early, John's third wife Thomasin was called back from her dairy farm on her dower estate at Yoxford to manage the family, and her successful conduct of affairs left an abiding and affectionate memory among them of her matriarchy. It is not surprising that she and others like her showed such mettle in management; for wives in their husbands' lifetimes could have to be very much partners in their affairs. When the Berkeleys in the mid fifteenth century were hard pressed in their great dispute with the Lisles over their family inheritance, Lord James and his sons at one point barricaded themselves into Berkeley Castle to withstand attack, while his wife Isobel rode to London to take out writs in Chancery against his rival and to solicit the royal court in her husband's favour. John Paston had often to be away from his Norfolk home on business, and the letters his wife Margaret wrote him showed that she had nothing to learn about stewardship: 'Thomas Bone hath sold all your wool here for 20d. a stone,' she told him in October 1460

. . . and it is sold right well, after that the wool was, for the most part, right feeble. *Item*, there be bought for you 3 horses at St Faith's fair, and all be trotters, right fair horses . . . *Item* your mill at Hailsdon is let for 12 marks, and the miller to find the repairs; and Richard Calle hath let all your lands at Caistor: but as for the Mautby lands, they be not let as yet.

John's affairs were in forceful and efficient hands while he was travelling, the hands of the woman who signed herself 'Yours, MP'.

The letters of the Paston women carry us into a world of human relationships that can be very different in tone from the calculating language of marriage contracts. Even the legal records, with their evidence of the concern of fathers to find provision for younger children and, sometimes, for the offspring of mistresses that they had loved as well, hint at family and human feelings that no amount of brokerage could stifle. Here in the letters we find the testimony that there were real love matches, even in this age and even in well-born circles. Nothing the Pastons could do could in the end stop their Margery from plighting herself to their bailiff, Richard Calle: and since she and he were abundantly clear that she had, of her own will and by her own mouth, accepted him as her husband before God, there was nothing the Bishop of Norwich could do about it either.

More important in the long run, though, is something that the sources for our period only allow us to glimpse occasionally, for the simple reason that love letters tend to survive less easily than do legal contracts. That is, that we go wrong if we put marriages of convenience and affective unions into entirely separate compartments. Paul Murray Kendall has put the point well when he writes of the Stonor letters that they 'reveal even more clearly than the Paston correspondence the mixture of financial bargaining and amorous language, the birth of love from the womb of worldly goods. The delicate balance of the two forces was adjusted by an inner logic, known to everyone then but well-nigh lost since.'

It is in that spirit that we must read, for instance, Thomas Mull's letter to William Stonor, who in 1472 was pursuing Margery, widow of William Blount:

I would know this of you: if the case were so that she would be agreeable to have you with £40 or 80 marks jointure, would your heart then love as you have done before this season? . . . [One] thing I dare safely say in my conceit, that she on her part since your departure has been vexed and troubled with the throes of love more fervently in her mind than you have been since vexed with her sayings. I know she loved you . . .

William Stonor did not in the end marry Margery: but he did marry, no less than three times. His third wife was a Neville, and the marriage was a step up for his family, but that did not exclude affection from it. 'If I had known that I should have been this long time from you I would have been much loather than I was to come into this far country,' she wrote to him from Somerset in 1482, 'but I trust it shall not be long before I see you here.' Between partners of comparable culture and background there was no reason why prudence and affection should not lead the same way, or why the latter should not grow where the former had led.

This is really what we ought to have expected. If any of the words of Kendall's that I have quoted ought to be questioned, they are surely those that refer to the mixture of prudential and calculating with amorous motives in terms of an 'inner logic, known to everyone then but well-nigh lost since'. That inner logic was still understood well enough in the time of Jane Austen, and a good many of us still like to feel that we understand and are in touch with the sort of relationships that she wrote about, and with the personal problems to which they gave rise.

This chapter has had a great deal in it about the law, and now a little about love: it would be wrong to conclude it without mention of a third 'L', leisure. For leisure was what, above all, distinguished the way of life of the well-to-do and well-born from that of the common ruck, of those whose lives were lived by the sweat of their brows and their limbs from dawn until dusk six days a week and sometimes seven. Leisure, with wealth, was what enabled gentlefolk to develop a distinctive style in their living, a class culture. That style is reflected in the architecture of their houses, their connoisseurship in their possessions, in their literary taste and in their understanding of such genteel matters as heraldry and the art of blazon and the vocabulary of courtly courtship. It was also reflected in the outdoor occupations with which they filled unoccupied hours. 'Here shall follow,' says the *Boke of St Albans*, the handbook of courtesy first printed in 1486,

a compendious treatise of fishing with an angle, which is right necessary to be had in this present volume . . . for it is one of the disports that gentlemen use. And also it is not so laborious nor so dishonest to fish in this wise as it is with nets and other engines which crafty men do use for their daily increase of goods.

The point is made beautifully clear: netting and trapping fish is a business pursued by 'crafty men' in order to make a living, and so is not honourable, but 'dishonest'. Fly fishing (the *Boke* has several recipes for tying flies) is by contrast a 'disport', a stylish, 'gentle art', fit for the pursuit of gentlemen in their free time. Outdoors as well as indoors, we are being discreetly told, upper-crust leisure and leisure activity has a distinctive flavour to it.

The *Boke of St Albans* also includes 'compendious treatises' of hawking and of hunting, the latter from the hand of a gentle-woman, Mistress Juliana Barnes. Whoever wrote on hawking, in order to reveal the 'very knowledge of such pleasure to gentle-men and persons disposed to see it', certainly knew at first hand a great deal about the keeping of hawks, and about their different species. Mistress Juliana's treatise on hunting is a splen-did piece, full of echoes that still have a familiar ring to anyone brought up in the country:

> And when he hath coupled his hounds each one,
> And is forth with them to the field gone,
> And when he has cast off his couples at will,
> Then he shall speak, and say his hounds till
> 'Hors de couple: avaunt, se avaunt!'

And then he shall let out a yell of 'So ho! So ho!' three times, and the hunt is off. The hare was the quarry in which Mistress Juliana's huntsman was most interested; there is much in common though, between what she has to say and what is, as far as I know, the first description in English of a foxhunt, in *Gawain and the Green Knight*, and it is still more eloquent and reminiscent:

> Wondrous fair was the field for the frost was light;
> The sun rises red amid radiant clouds,
> Sails into the sky, and sends forth his beams.
> They let loose the hounds by a leafy wood;
> The rocks all around re-echo to their horns . . .
> Then it was heaven on earth to hark to the hounds,
> When they had come on their quarry, coursing together.

And when they had run 'Reynard the Red' down at last, all those that had horns blew them, and the others 'all hallooed'. These are sounds that can still be heard in the English country-side.

There can be no doubt that leisure activities like hunting and hawking, and the acquaintanceships and friendships formed through them, played an important part in the social life of the landed classes. An invitation to hunt offered the prospect of pleasure to be enjoyed in good company, and also of encounters in which all sorts of matters could be discussed usefully and informally – local and national politics, family affairs, marriage and giving in marriage. Such meetings must have played a part in forming solidarities among leading men in local life that it is now, alas, impossible to penetrate; and not among leading men only either. There were a hundred 'brave huntsmen' in the woods when Sir Bercilak, Gawain's host in the *Green Knight* story, set out on his first day's hunting after Christmas, as well as his guests and 'retainers many'. The chase could offer pleasures and excitement for the whole household, high and low, and no doubt for a good many simple country folk also. To be a good hunter, to know the fine points and the rituals of the art of venery, could play its part too in the business with which this chapter has been so much concerned, the ways by which a noble or gentleman maintained his 'worship' and earned respect among both his equals and his servants.

8. *Aristocratic Violence: from Civil Strife to Forcible Entry*

The last chapter was concerned largely with the solidarities of nobles and gentlefolk, their domesticity and their arts of peace. This one is to be about their quarrels, and it shall open with an unpleasant story.

On the night of 23 October 1455, a party of sixty armed men, led by Sir Thomas Courtenay, son of the Earl of Devon, came to the house of Nicholas Radford at Upcott near Tiverton, and set fire to the gates. Radford came to his window, and Courtenay called to him to come down and speak with him, promising, 'as I am a gentleman and a faithful knight', that he would suffer no harm. So the main door of the house was opened, and Courtenay's men poured in, to loot the house and the chapel of goods said later to be worth 1,000 marks. 'Then the earl's son said, Radford, you must come with me to my lord my father.' Radford was old and feeble and all his horses had by now been taken, but Courtenay said he would mount him if he would agree to go with him. He did so agree; but when they had got a stone's throw from the house, Courtenay's men set on him, and 'smote him in the head, and felled him . . . [and one] of them cut his throat'. Three days later Courtenay's men came back to Upcott, where Radford's body lay in the chapel, and held a mock inquest on it, bringing in a verdict of suicide. Then they made Radford's servants carry the body to the church of Cheriton Fitzpaine, tipped it naked into a grave, and heaped in stones that crushed the corpse out of recognition, so that no coroner could hold a proper inquest on it.

I tell this story to illustrate two points. One arises out of the shock and anger that greeted reports of the event when the news broke. 'This matter is taken greatly . . . so much rumour is here, what it meaneth I know not,' James Gresham wrote at the end of his account of it to John Paston. The rehearsal of the story in

Parliament led, more or less directly, to the appointment (for
the second time) of the Duke of York as Protector of the Realm
on behalf of the enfeebled Henry VI, so that there might be one
'to whom the people of this land may have recourse to sue for
remedy for their injuries'. This appeal and this exceptional step
mirrors the desperation of men who, in November 1455,
watched disorder in the kingdom escalating towards the open
confrontations of the Wars of the Roses.

There was nothing exceptional, however, about their desire
for strong and abundant governance, which in this instance they
hoped that York would provide. Petitions from the Commons
for just this, for stouter measures for keeping the peace and
sterner penalties for violent crime, are a recurrent theme of the
records of English parliamentary proceedings through the whole
later medieval period. An entry on the roll of the first Parliament
of King Henry V conveys their tone well:

Item, the 22nd of May, the Commons came before the King and Lords
in Parliament, and then . . . William Stourton, Speaker of the
Commons, rehearsed how . . . in the time of the Lord King his [Henry
V's] father, the Commons had many times requested good governance,
and their requests were granted. But how that which was granted was
held to and accomplished afterward, the King that now is knows well
enough.

There is no doubt that the kind of men the Commons represented, gentlemen and people of substance, saw the keeping of a
stable domestic peace and a firm insistence that quarrels should
be resolved by law and not by force as primary social desiderata.
They were educated men, who deplored domestic violence and
saw firm, pacific government as the best of all benefits a ruler
could give them.

The other point that Radford's story illustrates, perhaps over-
dramatically, is the difficulty in the way of their desires being
fulfilled, and the peculiar and particular nature of the problem
of violence in later medieval England. Whatever people wanted,
the problem, as the frequency of the parliamentary protests
makes clear, was a perennial and a recurrent one. It was the
manner, not the matter of the incident that made the Radford
case so outrageous, the sheer brutality of Courtenay and his

men, who had shown no more compassion 'than if they had been Jews or Saracens'. There was nothing unusual about the background to what had happened. Radford was a landowner and a distinguished lawyer, a justice of the peace and recorder of Exeter: he had sat for his shire in Parliament. He was also 'of counsel' with Lord Bonville, who over a period of years had been sharply at odds with the Earl of Devon, who regarded the former's local influence and favour at court as a threat to his own regional standing. In quarrels such as that between these two lords there was nothing out of the way about the aligning of prominent local gentry on one side or the other, or about affrays between their followers in which houses might be looted and grievous bodily harm inflicted. This is the peculiar and particular aspect of the problem of violence in this period. Nowadays, violent crime is most often seen as the product of social deprivation. No doubt there was plenty of that kind of crime in the late middle ages too, but not on a scale that seemed to threaten the social fabric. The social threat came rather from the violence of the least deprived sectors of society, lords, landowners and gentlemen; that is to say, ironically, from those with whom the principal responsibility for law enforcement and the maintenance of order locally lay.

The fact that these were the very same sort of people as those who in Parliament were constantly protesting their desire for better 'governance' makes the irony especially sharp. It also sharpens the need to look for at least some sort of partial answer to the following questions. Given the express will of the governing classes for better peace and the restraint of violence, why was it that they experienced such difficulty in finding effective means towards their end? And how did they allow themselves to do so much to thwart it?

In the context of seeking answers to these questions, it may be useful to start by distinguishing different levels of violence. At the top of the scale one must place open rebellion against the king's constituted government. The Peasants' Revolt, a social uprising, has to fall into this class, but a commoner brand of civil strife was that in which the army of the king and armies led by dissident peers clashed in the field, with banners displayed, as they did in the struggles of Lancaster and York in the fifteenth century. Legally, such rebellion as this was high treason, which carried not only the death penalty but also that of forfeiture of all a convicted rebel's lands held in fee simple (though not of entailed estates or estates enfeoffed to use). At the next level one must place what may loosely be called 'private wars', occasions when quarrels between feuding magnates reached the point of large-scale confrontations between forces of their retainers and tenants assembled in martial array. This level of violence is elusive of legal definition, since the English kings had traditionally refused to recognize that even their greatest subjects had any right to make war in their own causes. It was short of high treason, but in a loose sense it was surely high crime. Below this level, and much more common, were those kinds of disturbances that could be lumped together under such collective titles as riot, 'rides of evil-doers', insurrections, felonies and forcible entries. In much the same bracket may be placed slightly less serious but equally troublesome disorders involving the breaking of 'closes' (breaking into and trespassing on enclosed property), harassment of tenants, driving off of cattle and semi-organized assault and battery. Legally, we here move into the world of the common-law offences of felony and trespass.

The first of these three levels was clearly the most serious. Its background was political, and in its nature it was large scale. It threatened the kingdom at large with the possibility of spiralling rebellion and counter-rebellion, 'one batayle after another', that could pave the way to usurpation of the throne and which raised the spectre (it was never more than that in the event) of foreign intervention and of the kingdom 'being lost and governed by strangers and foreign nations'. Conversely, the third level of violence – riots, affrays, forcible entries – was clearly the least dangerous. The background to these sorts of disturbances was not political but social, or perhaps more precisely socio-legal; *on their own*, though very troublesome, they did not pose a serious threat of destabilization of society. If it is ever legitimate to speak of an 'acceptable level' of violence, this kind of disorder, in the late middle ages, would just about fall into the category. The middle term, what I have called 'private war', presents more difficulties. The sort of issues that gave rise to confrontations that will fit into this category were very much the same as those that led to riots and forcible entries; but the scale of the confrontations, and their destabilizing potential, bring one closer to the world of open rebellion. One more point must be added, and it is of some significance; that is, that the private quarrels of great men were not likely to rise to this dangerous level except in periods of political tension and instability, that is to say in the sort of conditions in which serious rebellion against the king had become a possibility.

This seems to get us part of the way towards answering the question posed, why it was that there was such difficulty in finding a means, in late medieval England, towards the restraint of violence, when the lack of restraint was so clearly perceived as a pressing social problem. The really unacceptable levels of violence were related to political tensions, it seems, which such measures as the framing of new statutes or the extension of judicial powers could do nothing to allay: the solutions, like the tensions, had to be political. But at best this is still only a very partial answer, because in the real world the different levels of violence that I have tried to identify could not be neatly separated from one another in the way that they can be on paper, and nor could their effects. In practice, one kind of violence led to another, interacting and blending with it. As Professor Storey has eloquently written (of the origins of the Wars of the Roses, the longest and most serious series of intermittent rebellions in late medieval English history):

Gentry, with understandable lack of confidence in the processes of law, attached themselves to lords who could give them protection against their personal enemies, and in return supported their patrons in private wars with their peers. These baronial hostilities similarly resulted in the contestants aligning themselves with the major *political rivals* [my italics].

As Storey's words indicate, the real danger of major social destabilization arose out of the cumulative effect of all three levels of violence interacting with each other, with the obvious possibility (which alarmed people a great deal) that a fourth force might ultimately be drawn into the maelstrom, what we call class warfare. Given a problem thus hydra-headed, it becomes less surprising that contemporaries should have experienced problems in the quest for a general remedy. A historian is not going to employ his time usefully in looking for a solution that men of the time did not find. What he can do is to try to probe in turn the attitudes and assumptions and the associations involved in each of the three levels of violence, which both individually and in combination rendered their effects so intractable.

Full-scale armed rebellion was not a common occurrence, though the threatening possibility that tension between king and magnates, or between magnates in court favour and magnates out of it, might bring matters to this point was always there in the background. Even in the period of the Wars of the Roses, real hostilities were very intermittent. There was heavy fighting with pitched battles between 1459 and 1461 (Blore Heath, Northampton, Wakefield and Towton); between 1469 and 1471 (Edgecote, Barnet, Tewkesbury); and in 1485 and 1487 (Bosworth, Stoke). Outside this general period, large forces were assembled and the king's banner displayed in the course of the quarrel between Richard II and the 'Appellant Lords' in 1387, but the battle in which it culminated at Radcot Bridge was little more than a skirmish. In 1399 Richard II was deposed by armed force, but because his own army melted away in the process of returning from Ireland to face Henry Bolingbroke's challenge there was no significant engagement. In 1403, when the Percies revolted against Henry IV, there was a sharp campaign culminating in the ferocious battle of Shrewsbury.

Over and above this there were a number of revolts that went off at half-cock (notably the second Percy rebellion of 1405, and Buckingham's revolt against Richard III in 1483); and there were conspiracies, like the Cambridge plot of 1415 against Henry V. The ostensible grounds for all these revolts were political. Evil councillors about the king, abuse of the law by courtiers and mismanagement of royal policy, patronage and finance were the themes of the charges, proclamations and manifestos through which their aristocratic leaders sought to popularize their cause. Claims on the part of royal dukes and kinsmen to a better claim in blood to the throne than that of the reigning king also came into the picture (notably in the 1460s) but they were never the start of the business; and in every case there was an initial background of dissatisfaction with royal government and the balance of interests represented in it that gave rebel magnates grounds to claim that they took to arms for the sake of the public weal.

What made aristocratic rebellion a threat that could never be left out entirely from royal and national calculations was the existence of what one might call a supra-nobility, of dukes and earls related to the royal house, whose landed wealth and dignity gave them the capacity, in an emergency, to raise significant military forces from among their clients and tenants, together with the view that they and others took of the rights and responsibilities of their high station. Back in the early fourteenth century, in the reign of Edward II, dissident magnates made this declaration:

Homage and the oath of allegiance are stronger and bind more by reason of the crown than by reason of the person of the king ... Wherefore if the king by chance be not guided by reason, his liege subjects are bound by their oath made to the crown to guide the king back again by reason and amend the estate of the crown ... Wherefore, in order to save the oath, when the king will not redress a matter and remove that which is damaging to the crown and hurtful to the people, it is adjudged that the error be removed by violence; for he the king is bound by his oath to govern the people, and his liege subjects are bound to protect the people according to the law.

This idea, that the greatest of the king's liege subjects had a right, even a duty, to rescue the 'Crown' by force from evil counsel and unreasonable policy, was one that died hard. It was a recurrent theme of opposition and rebel propaganda in the reigns of Richard II and Henry IV, and during the Wars of the Roses. Henry IV had taken the Crown, he announced in 1399, by force and with the aid of friends and relatives, when 'the kingdom was on the point of being undone for lack of governance and undoing of the laws'. The Duke of York in 1455, in the parleying before the first battle of St Albans, declared that he and his allies were in arms in order to 'have the traitors punished that were about the king, and if he could not have them by good will and fair consent, he would have them by force'. Warwick the Kingmaker and George, Duke of Clarence, wrote to their supporters on the eve of their rebellion against Edward IV in 1469 that

You know well that the true subjects of the king our sovereign lord, in different parts of this realm of England, have delivered to us certain articles [certain party-inspired complaints of misgovernment, in fact] . . . We think the petition contained in the articles to be reasonable, and advantageous to the honour and profit of our sovereign lord and the common weal of this his realm. Therefore we fully intend, along with other lords, to show the same to his good grace. We desire and pray you to dispose and array you to accompany us thither, with as many persons defensibly arrayed as you can provide.

For as long as great lords of the blood, like Richard of York and Warwick the Kingmaker, regarded themselves as entitled to act with the aid of men 'defensibly arrayed' when, in their own judgement, political circumstances warranted, the threat of aristocratic rebellion could not be dispelled.

A strong tone of aristocratic honour and dignity infuses the propaganda of late medieval lordly rebellion. Thus we find York complaining that 'diverse language hath been said of me to your [Henry VI's] most excellent estate which should sound to my dishonour and reproach'. We find Warwick and Clarence complaining that 'the great lords of the blood' are 'estranged' from the king's council. And once things have been put to the issue of battle, a further and more sinister aristocratic note is struck, that of vendetta, of the obligation in honour to seek revenge on the enemies of one's kinsmen. After the battle of St Albans in 1455, says the *Brut Chronicle*, 'there was evermore a grouch and wrath had by the heirs of them that were slain'. 'By God's blood,' cried Lord Clifford as he struck down York's son, Edmund of Rutland, at the battle of Wakefield, 'your father slew mine, and so will I thee and all thy kin.' As these stories bring home sharply, one of the worst of all the dangers stemming from the readiness of great men in their pride to take to arms, nominally out of their 'duty' and 'affection' to the common weal, was that it could too easily lead into a vicious spiral of rebellion and counter-rebellion, of vendettas engendering new vendettas. People at large hated John Tiptoft, the Yorkist Constable who presided over the drumhead courts-martial that condemned Lancastrian rebels taken in the field, 'for the disordinate death that he caused', but their resentment of his gruesome sentences could not help the victims or allay the deleterious effects of his cruelties. After all, what alternative was there for the heirs of those slain in battle or beheaded after it, except to hope one day to be able to even the scores by the same means?

A spiral of aristocratic violence, of vendettas, rebellions and counter-rebellions obviously laid the way open to a serious degree of destabilization in society. Under the shadow of the quarrels of the great, lesser men could too easily follow their example and pursue their own quarrels by violent means, trusting that if they backed the right side in the larger confrontations, the lords that they had served would secure their immunity from the consequences of their unlawful actions, and the profit of them too. In the time of the 'sorrows of England', in the 1450s and 1460s, there were a great many English gentlemen who did well for themselves and their families by this not very attractive means; and there were moments when it must have seemed as if, at the local level, the private quarrels of knights and gentlemen might become virtually uncontrollable. Movements like the revolt of Robin of Redesdale in 1469 raised the still more frightening spectre of an anarchic, popular leavening being drawn into the disorder. No wonder that people lamented the 'sorrows' of the land, and feared that it might be brought 'right low'.

Yet England was not plunged into anarchy, either by the usurpation of Henry IV, or by the Percy revolts, or by the Wars of the Roses. Part of the reason lay in the nature of the fighting in the civil strife of the period. As has been said earlier, the periods of active campaigning, even in the Wars of the Roses, were not very long and were very intermittent. There was no systematic harrying of the countryside by armies in quest of forage and plunder such as characterized the wars in France, and there were no prolonged sieges of major towns. The contingents that individual magnates led into battle were raised substantially from among their retainers and tenants; there was a limit to the number of men that they could raise in this way and to the length of time that they could keep them in arms. Besides, they were not always well trained or enthusiastic to serve; that is why the regular troops of the Calais garrison and the reserves that the great northern lords, as Wardens of the Marches, knew how to mobilize at speed, played a disproportionate part in much of the fighting. (It is also why the Yorkist lords, in the crucial years 1459–61, were so determined to keep the captaincy of Calais in their hands.) Even the supra-noble royal dukes were not rich enough or over-mighty enough to keep up military pressures for sustained periods; the campaigns of civil war were in consequence characteristically short and decided by pitched battles in which the casualties were usually heaviest among the leaders rather than the rank and file.

Besides, it was in the clear interest of peers and great men to limit the scale of hostilities: they had too much to lose by more sustained fighting and too little to gain. An individual royal duke like Henry Bolingbroke or Richard, Duke of York, might find himself manoeuvred or manoeuvre himself into a political position in which he had no alternative to risking a fight, except to lose all. The majority of peers, though, clearly only took up arms very reluctantly. At the pinch, there was a strong and significant tendency for them to rally to the Crown's side, whoever wore it – unless it looked very clear that it was likely to be the losing cause. Because of their prominence, it was not easy for magnates to avoid becoming engaged, but that can seldom have been how they wished it to be. The remarkable advice of John, Lord Mountjoy, to his sons in 1485 tells something of how much they deplored civil disorder and its concomitant risks to life and fortune: his counsel to them was 'to live righteously, and never to take the state of baron upon them if they may lay it from them, nor to desire to be great about princes, for it is dangerous'. Among knights and gentry, who lived further from the storm centre of politics than peers did, the dislike of disorder and the tendency to 'trim' were even stronger. Those who were tied to particular lords by life indenture might feel bound in loyalty and find it practically very difficult to avoid responding to a summons to come with men 'defensibly arrayed'; but many of course were not so bound, and most of these preferred if they could to remain uninvolved. The Pastons were ever watchful of the twists and turns of politics and political fortunes, endeavouring to be in with the right people at the right time and to gain their 'good lordship', but for a long time they succeeded in keeping to the fringe of the political struggles about which their correspondence tells us so much. Even after they had risen high and could no longer keep clear, they proved remarkably adept at keeping in with more than one side. That their attitude and their reactions were typical of the class whose influence was most firmly entrenched in regional society was a principal reason why things did not get out of control in the way so many feared they might.

One more point needs to be made that seems to confirm the suggestion that the stability of the kingdom was less threatened by civil disorder than the tumultuous political history of the 1450s and 1460s can superficially suggest. It is beautifully encapsulated in McFarlane's remark that we should look for the causes of the Wars of the Roses not so much to the over-mightiness of subjects but to the under-mightiness of kings. It took real mismanagement by individual monarchs to alienate support to the point where the greater nobles were provoked into asserting what they deemed to be their right to try to amend things by force if necessary. Richard II and Henry VI were insufficiently shrewd in their politics and their patronage, and they lost their thrones. But under effective kings such as Edward III, Henry V, Edward IV (after 1471) and Henry VII, the danger of civil strife receded, and rapidly. Political confusion and ineptitude, in this period as in any other, could provoke dangerous effects; but political confusion only becomes supremely dangerous when it begins to release underlying social tensions, and this was not the case in this period. The only occasion, in the history of late medieval England, when political confusion did come near to doing that was in the brief course of the Peasants' Revolt of 1381, and, as has been seen in an earlier chapter, the long-term social tensions that then surfaced momentarily eased of themselves over the subsequent decades. The civil wars of the fifteenth century threatened weak kings, political cliques, and over-ambitious nobles rather than the social structure, and that is why they were less dangerous than they looked.

Two revolts, Cade's revolt of 1450 and the Cornish rebellion of 1497, have sometimes been bracketed with the revolt of 1381, and deserve brief mention. Neither seems in fact to have been a social movement in the sense that the Peasants' Revolt was; their origins were more plainly political. Cade's manifestos make it clear that 'evil counsellors' about the king, the mismanagement of the French war, and certain specific issues of local Kentish politics were the uppermost matters in the minds of his followers. The Cornish rebellion was triggered by Henry VII's heavy taxation for the Scottish war and his demands for ships, service and supplies, which had fallen particularly sharply on the West Country. Two aspects of these revolts do, however, differentiate them from the aristocratic rebellions with which we have been principally concerned. One is that both lacked the vice-regal supra-noble leadership that marked those other risings (though Cade, significantly, did try to exploit the names of York and Mortimer, and the Cornish rebels made Lord Audley, son of a prominent Yorkist peer, their leader). The other is that, though not proletarian, they can be called popular, in the sense that, in the regions affected, both drew support from a wide social spectrum that included gentry, townsmen, yeomen and lesser folk as well. That they only did so regionally was their weakness, but they do hint forward towards the danger that might arise if local communities and their gentry leadership should become involved on a larger, more national scale, in confrontation with royal government. Fortunately, for the people of an earlier time, that did not happen until the seventeenth century, and the age of Pym and Cromwell.

What at the beginning of this chapter I called 'private wars' between magnates could only reach the stage of true military confrontation in times of general disturbance and political confusion. They tended, in consequence, to become subsumed into the larger political rivalries that at such times too easily exploded into open rebellion, and so to become indistinguishable from these, even though the motives of the parties were private and tangential to national politics. They in consequence illustrate well the way in which different levels of violence were related to one another and could in combination have cumulatively destabilizing effects.

The story of the rivalry of the great northern houses of Neville and Percy here offers a good example. It had two phases. The Percies' rebellions in the reign of Henry IV, in 1403 and 1405, clearly belong to the category of open revolts; their propaganda was phrased in national terms, and the Earl of Northumberland and his son Hotspur aimed at nothing less than the displacement of Henry in favour of the Earl of March, a minor and their kinsman, whom they hoped they could dominate. Their resentment of the growing influence of the Nevilles in the West March towards Scotland was at this stage never more than a sub–plot to larger issues, of Henry's alleged misgovernment and of legitimism (March had good claim to be regarded as the closest heir in blood to Richard II's throne). But it was an important additional factor in the background; so that when Henry V in 1416 restored the Percy heir to the earldom of Northumberland, there was every probability that relations between him and the now more powerful Nevilles would prove difficult. In its second phase the dispute between the two claims recommenced at the private level of family rivalry. When, in Henry VI's reign, the troubles between the restored Percies and the Nevilles began to grow sharp, it at first generated no more than local rioting. But when in July 1453 Thomas, Lord Egremont, the Percy Earl of Northumberland's second son, assembled a force at Heworth said to number five thousand men, planning to waylay Richard Neville, Earl of Salisbury, as he returned from Tattershall with his son Thomas, whom he had married there to Lord Cromwell's niece, Maud Willoughby, matters had escalated to a more dangerous level, to the brink of 'private war'. As it turned out Earl Richard was sufficiently formidably accompanied to deter Egremont from a full-scale battle; but next year, at Stamford Bridge, there was an engagement with casualties on both sides, and Egremont was captured by Sir John Neville. When the parties next met, it was at the battle of St Albans. An independent quarrel, between Salisbury's son Richard, Earl of Warwick (the future Kingmaker), and the Duke of Somerset, over their rights in the Beauchamp inheritance, had ranged the Nevilles alongside York, so the Percies were with the company of the king and his chief councillor, Somerset. The private quarrel had been subsumed once more into a greater, public one.

The rivalry of the Courtenays and Lord Bonville in the West Country never became quite so inextricably entangled in the larger struggle of Lancaster and York as that of the Nevilles and Percies did after St Albans. But it grew to martial proportions under cover of the same disturbed conditions, and in the end was sucked into the fringe of the wider fray. This quarrel originated in competition for influence in the duchy of Cornwall. In 1437 Bonville, a rising man, was appointed Steward of Cornwall for life; but in 1441 Thomas Courtenay, Earl of Devon, obtained from the unwise generosity of Henry VI the stewardship of the Duchy of Cornwall. There was rioting and violence between followers of the two men, but at this stage nothing more: both were summoned to account for themselves before the Council. In 1451, however, Earl Thomas felt that the confused conditions offered him a new opportunity to strike at his rival, and besieged him in Taunton with an army of several thousand men. That siege was broken up by the intervention of the Duke of York, but in 1455 Devon returned to the fray. The murder of Nicholas Radford, Bonville's councillor, was the first blow in a struggle that escalated to war level. Devon assembled an army at Tiverton, marched to Exeter and occupied the city, and then laid siege to Powderham Castle (held by Sir Philip Courtenay, Devon's kinsman but Bonville's ally). A full-scale battle was fought at Clyst when Lord Bonville brought up an army in relief; and there would no doubt have been further engagements if York, appointed Protector for the second time partly in order to allay these affrays, had not once again intervened. Devon was sent to the Tower; and Bonville, who had risen through Lancastrian favour, began to veer definitively towards the Yorkist interest. He met his death in that cause, executed after the defeat of the Yorkists at the second battle of St Albans; Devon was beheaded a few weeks later after he had fought for the Lancastrians when they were defeated at Towton.

The great Berkeley–Lisle dispute which culminated in the 'battle' of Nibley Green in 1469 offers a 'purer' example of private war. It did not originate out of competition for influence or for offices in the Crown's gift as the Neville–Percy and the Courtenay–Bonville rivalries did, but out of a straightforward dispute over title to land. The arrangements made by Thomas, Lord Berkeley (d. 1417), concerning his inheritance were confused, to say the least. During his lifetime he had first promised his *whole* inheritance to Richard Beauchamp, Earl of Warwick, husband of his daughter and heiress Elizabeth, in contravention of the terms of a number of existing entails. Later, he also promised *part* of the inheritance to his nephew and heir male, James Berkeley, when he married him to Isobel, daughter of Humphrey Stafford. He finally tried to smooth things over with provisions for a division, but still ignored the old entails. After Thomas's death and Elizabeth's, there were various attempts to make a final agreement between her three daughters, who were her heiresses, and Lord James; but none satisfied all the parties. As political stability began to degenerate in the 1450s there were violent clashes between followers of Lord James and of the most determined of Elizabeth's daughters, Margaret, Countess of Shrewsbury. In the course of complicated manoeuvring, Margaret secured the arrest of Isobel, James's wife, and had her imprisoned in Gloucester Castle, where she died. From that point, the quarrel began to acquire a vendetta quality.

The long-simmering feud reached its climax when, in 1469, Margaret's heir, Thomas, Lord Lisle, thought that the troubled times gave him the chance to settle the hash once and for all of William Berkeley, James's heir. The letter that he dispatched to his rival, with its conscious effort at chivalrous phraseology, takes us in a single step into a world where a nobleman deems it his right to maintain his private title by arms, in a dispute quite unrelated to the common weal:

William Lord Berkeley, I marvel that you come not forth with all your carts of guns and bows and other ordinance that you set forward to come to my manor of Wootton and beat it down on my head. I let you know, you shall not need to come so nigh ... I require you of knighthood and manhood to appoint a day to meet me half-way, to eschew the shedding of Christian men's blood, or else at the same day bring the utmost of your power, and I shall meet you. Answer this in writing as you will abide by it according to the honour and order of knighthood.

William Berkeley's reply was in tune with Lord Lisle's challenge:

Thomas Talbot, otherwise called Viscount Lisle . . . I marvel greatly of your strange and ignorant writing, made I suppose by your false and untrue counsel that you have with you . . . And whereas you require me of my knighthood that I should appoint a day and meet you midway between my manor of Wootton and my castle of Berkeley, there to try between God and our two hands all our quarrel and title of right, to eschew the shedding of Christian men's blood, or else the same day to bring the utmost of my power . . . I will not bring the tenth part I can make, and I will appoint a day very shortly to ease your malicious heart and your false counsel that is with you. Fail not tomorrow to be at Nibley Green at eight or nine of the clock, and I will not fail, with God's might and grace, to meet you at the same place, which stands within the border of the livelihood that you falsely keep from me, ready to answer you on all things, so that I trust to God it shall be shown on you to your great shame and dishonour.

As on the next day, 26 March, Lord Lisle's men descended the hill from Nibley church, Lord Berkeley's men broke from the cover of Michaelswood chase. At Fowleshard, when they came within bowshot, Berkeley's men let fly a volley of arrows, and a bolt from the bow of one Black Will pierced Lord Lisle in the face, as his vizor was up. He was carried dead from the field, and the Berkeleys were left in possession of it. So ended what might be called the last battle in a private war between peers in England. But if it had not been for the larger quarrels of the time, that were setting the king and greater peers than Lisle or Berkeley at odds, 'whereby that troubled time was so far from taking notice of this riot', it might never have been fought.

Lords Lisle and Berkeley, issuing challenge and counter-challenge, used the vocabulary of knighthood and battle. John Smith, the historian of the Berkeleys, could see that the affair at Nibley, no more than a skirmish really, in many ways had more in common with a riot than with an act of war. The matter at issue between the two lords was title to land, and in late medieval England the disputes of aristocrats and gentry over such title very frequently led to what the records call 'riots', 'insurrections' and 'forcible entries' – the third and least serious of the levels of violence identified earlier in this chapter. In periods of instability, like the 1450s and 1460s, they tended to be even commoner than usual, to be more violent, and to involve larger numbers of people, and some historians have even described them as 'gentlemen's wars'. The word war seems however to be overstretched when applied to this sort of violence. It could involve wilful damage to goods, the breaking of parks and closes, and even the sacking of manor-houses and skirmishing, but casualties were seldom numerous and usually non-fatal. They take us out of the world of treason, of acts of war and the large-scale defiance of constituted authority, into the more humdrum world of violent crime.

As has been said (town riots apart) the commonest cause of violence of this level that falls short of war was disputed title to lands. Title to land, which was the most valued of all commodities and the life-blood of claims to gentility, was in the late middle ages particularly open to challenge, for a variety of reasons. A principal one was the multiplication of the legal rules and devices that could affect inheritance and conveyancing: entail, joint tenures, dower arrangements and enfeoffments 'to use' for a wide range of purposes. Legal procedures were also complicated; questions of possession and the right of entry, for instance, were matters for the common law courts, but the interpretation of the terms of a 'use' would be a matter for Chancery. Process at law was cumbersome, slow and expensive, and some actions were more easily delayed than others: it might for that reason be sensible, for instance, to bring an action of trespass instead of challenging right directly, thereby forcing the trespasser to lay out his claim to the land he had allegedly trespassed on. Alternatively, or even concomitantly, it might seem useful towards hurrying the law's delays somewhat or towards clarifying its obscurity to resort to a measure of forceful action. Forceful action is apt to elicit a response in kind, and from there on the step towards 'riotous assemblies, ridings of

evil-doers, and forcible entries' could be very short indeed. These
were the sorts of conditions that made this kind of violence so
common. It also makes it difficult to know whether one should
discuss it in terms of the flouting of the law by aristocrats and
gentlemen, or as a byproduct of their vigorous litigiousness.

'Forcible entry' is a significant term in this context, and a brief
examination of it will help to illustrate how fine was the line
between lawlessness and litigiousness, and how the latter could
easily encourage the former. 'Entry' (which was a legitimate
move, unlike forcible entry, which was criminal) was very
important in land litigation. If a man believed that he had a title
to land that was occupied by another, it was vital for him that
he should make an 'entry' in order to assert that title. Otherwise,
as the law then stood, his opponent might be able to rebut his
claim on the basis of the length of time that he had been in
occupation (in 'seisin'). If this opponent was able to show that he
derived his title from a third party (an ancestor, or a 'feoffor')
against whom there had been no entry, he might be very hard
to shake at law. So entry was crucial; it was also likely to
provoke violence, for two reasons. On the one hand the occupier
was obviously likely to resist it, especially given the terms of an
act of 1347 which permitted a party entered on to defend his
goods (*not* his land – but whose word was to be accepted as to
what had been threatened?). On the other hand, in legal terms
of future litigation, it was likely to pay the party entering, if
feasible, to effect an 'ouster' and eject his rival, who would then
be forced to challenge the new occupier in his title, or at least in
his possession (probably by an action of *novel disseisin*). It was
therefore prudent for the party entering to be adequately accompanied. 'I propose to enter the manor [of Mackney, near
Wallingford] with God's grace,' Henry Makney wrote to William Stonor in 1477; 'I pray you send me a good lad or two that
I be not beat out again.' When in 1478 Alexander Ainsworth
came to oust Robert Pilkington from the manor of Mellor
(Derbyshire) which was disputed between them, we find that
the 'lad or two' of the Stonor correspondence has turned into
'two hundred men and more in harness'. It is easy to see how
legal manoeuvring for advantage could, in these conditions, give
rise to quite serious rioting and affrays.

Two stories may illustrate the point and the problems a little further. In one of the best-remembered forcible entries of the fifteenth century, Lord Moleyns in January 1449 sent to the Paston manor of Gresham (according to the Paston story) 'a riotous people to the number of a thousand ... arrayed in manner of war with cuirasses, brigandines, jacks, sallets, swords, bows, arrows, parvises and guns', who broke up the gates and doors, bundled out Margaret Paston, 'wife of your said beseecher', and rifled goods worth (allegedly) £200. Paston's title to Gresham, which his father had purchased from Thomas Chaucer (whose right came through his wife Maud Burghersh) was basically unassailable. But Moleyns had the shadow of a claim on the basis of a moiety of the manor, which had once been in the hands of Margery, wife of Sir William Moleyns. This moiety had in fact been bought in by Thomas Chaucer before the sale to Judge Paston, but Moleyns had court favour, and thought it worth trying his luck. It took Paston a lot of effort and money to regain his manor, and as far as can be told there was never any compensation for the damage he had sustained.

Lord Cromwell's quarrel with Henry Holland, Duke of Exeter, over the possession of Ampthill (Beds.) and its castle offers a parallel to the Gresham affair, with more details of how such an affair was likely to lead to efforts to manipulate the law as well as to the flouting of it.* Cromwell had purchased this estate from the executors of Lord Fanhope. Fanhope had at one time been married to Holland's widowed grandmother, and this is very probably what put it into Henry's head that he had a claim; but at law his case eventually proved to be that his right derived from a conveyance (almost certainly forged) by the feoffees of Elizabeth St Amand, from whom Fanhope had purchased, and he denied that Fanhope had ever acquired title. So, on 5 June 1452, 'with a great multitude of people arrayed in manner of war to the number of 300 persons or more' he entered and disseised Cromwell. It looks as if Cromwell may have made an abortive attempt to re-enter: by July the quarrel was being referred to a panel of arbiters headed by the Bishop of

---

* I owe my knowledge of the details that follow to my colleague, Dr Simon Payling.

Ely and both parties entered into bonds (of 6,000 marks each) to abide by the award, but that process seems to have lapsed. So Cromwell fell back on the law, and brought suits charging Exeter with breaking his closes, and his servants with taking goods worth £1,000 from Ampthill.

The problem for Cromwell now became that of getting his cases heard with some measure of impartiality. In the suit against Holland's servants the sheriff of Bedfordshire, though menaced by the duke, succeeded in empanelling a jury; but when the case came on at Westminster no jurors appeared, 'for the great dread and threatening of the said duke and his servants', who were loitering in Westminster Hall. The case was therefore adjourned. When it came up again, they still did not appear, according to Cromwell because Exeter and his men had 'beaten and maimed some of the jurors and menaced to slay some of them and made them bound in great sums not to pass against him in the said matters'. Exeter meanwhile was trying to get the affair heard in Bedfordshire, where he could bring more pressure to bear, more easily. There matters might have rested indefinitely, if Exeter in the spring of 1454 had not got himself involved in plans for a serious rising in the north, which gave Cromwell the chance to take the matter to Parliament with a good prospect of getting his way. By September he was back in Ampthill, and Holland was in prison. But if it had not been for an independent matter, the hot-headed political folly of the young duke, it is hard to say when he would have got back his land and castle, even whether he ever would. As the Berkeley–Lisle feud reminds us, this sort of dispute could run on for generations, giving rise to recurrent entries and counter-entries, riots, affrays, skirmishes and volumes of litigation.

As the Ampthill affair illustrates, violence was just one of a series of means that might be employed, successively or more or less simultaneously, in a dispute centring on title to land, and which included legal process, arbitration, currying of favour and the use of influence, due or undue, as well as bribery, force and the threat of force. It was common form, if a case was coming up, for the disputant parties to seek to 'labour' the jury, that is, to get hold of individuals who were likely to be on the panel and to seek to present their case to them in a favourable light. But if one of the parties were a powerful lord, or a lord's kinsman or a retainer wearing his livery, a little more could be involved, as we have seen from the Ampthill affair: hints and more than hints of what might happen to jurymen who did not see the case in the light proposed. Thus Robert Pilkington, in the course of his long-running suit with the Ainsworths, learned when the assizes were coming up in 1496 that 'the sheriff of Derbyshire had great reward to make a special panel of all such as . . . the Bishop [Bishop Savage of London, Ainsworth's kinsman and a councillor of Henry VII] would set on'. Two years later, when he again set about to labour a jury in his suit, he found that they had already received 'special writings' and that the bishop had sent young John Savage to labour the quest, and to let it be known that 'the Bishop of London would not for 100 marks that the matter passed against Ainsworth that day'. Justices of the peace, judges of assize and even special commissioners appointed to hear a case might have connections with one of the parties and be open to partial pressures. And whether a suit was to be heard in the central courts or locally, it was the sheriff of the county who would have to empanel the jury that would try it: all too likely that he might be an annuitant of the same man who was 'good lord' to one of the parties, or of some friend or ally of that good lord, and would know who to choose so as to fix matters.

Maintenance, the use of powerful influence to impede or deflect the course of law, was recognized as one of the besetting problems obstructing social order in the late middle ages; livery, bearing a badge that showed that he who wore it had influence available to him, was its mainstay. Especially was this so when things came to the verge of violence. If men came to make an entry stoutly arrayed and in the livery of a powerful man, it was a visible sign that anyone who resisted might encounter difficulties in accounting for their actions. (Moleyn's men were in his livery when they came to Gresham in January 1449.) Liveried men loitering near a shire hall or court-house might have a plain meaning to jurymen (the Bedfordshire jurors did not like the look of Exeter's servants loitering in Westminster Hall and went away). If both parties to a suit were powerful men or felt they had powerful patronage it was of course likely to make them feel bolder about mixing threats and force with legal proceedings; and it might also make the consequences of the use of force more serious and less controllable. Unfortunately, in these circumstances, if one party lacked powerful patronage it might equally make him feel that force was his best hope. Violence grew almost naturally out of the complex web of family ambitions, lawful claims and interests, and 'bastard feudal' social connections of the landowning classes.

There was a profound intractability about conditions in which on the one hand the frequency of resort to force and the partiality of the law drove men to seek powerful patrons who could protect and 'maintain' them, while on the other powerful patronage made it easier to get away with using force and to bend the law. The problem was recognized clearly enough. The parliamentary Commons were urgent in their demands for measures that would cut down to size retainers of the brand that sought to make themselves 'petty kings' in their counties. The statutes of livery and maintenance of Richard II and Henry IV were a response (though an insufficient one) to that urging. A series of measures, from the late fourteenth century on, sought to define and punish forcible entries and riots. A statute of 1391 laid down that where a complaint of forcible entry was made, the justices of the peace should proceed to the scene and arrest anyone found holding the land by main strength; they were to be treated as convicted by the magistrates' record. A statute of 1429 assured victims of forcible entry treble damages. In 1411 the procedures laid down for JPs in forcible entry cases were applied to cases of riot: if the justices arrived too late on the scene and the rioters had dispersed, they were to certify what had happened to the King's Council, which would take action. A statute of 1453 extended the Council's jurisdiction in the matter, and threatened great men who would not answer summonses before it arising out of riots, with forfeiture of lands and titles for life. Determined (if rather intermittent) efforts were made (especially by the Yorkist kings), to curb disorder and punish offenders by sending commissions of judges of *oyer et terminer* into the localities, headed by powerful men whose presence, it was hoped, would deter folk from labouring juries and ensure that indictments were heard. The record of concern and of measures in response to it is there: what is lacking is a record of the effectiveness of the measures, of convictions and condign penalties or of success in making legal process speedier and more decisive.

The result was that until a greater degree of local stability was achieved under the Tudors (largely in consequence of good understanding between the Crown and the gentry-controlled commissions of the peace), landowners felt it prudent to be ready to use muscle to defend and advance their interests, and that to some extent it was justifiable to do so, since if they did not use it their rivals would. They were equally ready to go to law, and spent extensively on retaining 'counsel learned', but only if they could trust its impartiality, or if it was to their advantage: too often it was neither. They therefore also continued to spend a great deal on keeping up substantial households of men on whom they could count if it came to making an entry, or resisting one, or outfacing their rivals at the county sessions or whenever harsh experience warned that it was not wise to look pacific or to act too pacifically.

There was one pacific stance, however, that could be taken up without loss of face, and significantly it was distinctly popular. This was to refer a dispute to the judgement of arbiters agreed by the parties. Indeed, arbitration was so popular that it became almost an adjunct of the legal system. Since the parties agreeing to it gave bonds to abide by the arbiters' award, it was possible to sue on the bond at common law or in Chancery if one of them failed to do so. Panels of arbiters, moreover, often included judges or barristers; and it was common, after they had made their award in a property dispute, for them to arrange a collusive action between the parties in a court of record, so as to make the decision cast iron legally.

As compared with strictly formal legal process, arbitration had a number of advantages. It was comparatively cheap (legal fees in court processes could be very expensive), and it was speedy (a term within which an award should be made was usually part of the agreement to go to 'umpires'). Procedure and pleadings were more flexible than at common law, since they were not limited by the form of writs, which could be very constricting (because the writ of trespass mentioned 'force of arms against the peace', Richard Orynge, when in 1466 he strolled on to a litigious neighbour's land to pick up hedge clippings, found himself charged that he did 'by force of arms, that is with swords, bows, and arrows, break his [neighbour's] close and did by walking with his feet consume his grass and commit other enormities'). In addition, there was no jury to labour, and no need to put any shaky reliance on the activity or inactivity of a potentially partial sheriff.

Of course arbitrations by no means solved all problems. Influence and patronage were too pervasive in this age to be excluded even here: there is plenty in the records to substantiate Wyclif's allegation that 'great men of this world . . . maintain debates at lovedays [i.e. arbitrations], and who so may be stronger will have his will be done, be it wrong be it right'. They offered no solution either to the problem of bringing to book and punishing those guilty of violent and criminal actions. Nevertheless they had a great deal to offer. They went straight to the heart of the matter which might give rise and might already have given rise to violence, and their express object was to find a settlement that would be accepted, and would therefore stick. One of the disadvantages of going to common law was the final and absolute quality of its judgements (if the court ever reached one, which was the exception rather than the rule). One party and one only could have the better right: the loser literally lost all. Arbiters by contrast could make allowance for a party who had a case, even if not as good a case as his opponent. A good example might be the final award in the land dispute of two minor Nottinghamshire gentlemen, John Tuxford and Alexander Mering, given by Sir John Assheton and Sir Thomas Rampston in 1416. By that time there had already been two failed arbitraments in the case, an ouster by Tuxford and an attempted re-entry by Mering, a suit of *novel disseisin* at common law and a petition to Parliament. The arbiters clearly favoured Mering, whose title was stronger, but they saw that the case of Tuxford, who had married the widow of Mering's older brother, was not entirely frivolous. So they allowed him a moiety of the disputed lands for life, with reversion to Mering and his heirs, who would thus in the end (but only in the end) inherit the whole.

Arbiters were usually chosen by the parties themselves; each might perhaps name two or three, or they might each name one and agree on a third (a local peer, maybe, or one of the king's judges). Finding umpires acceptable to both parties could be a problem. The effort to associate with arbitrations knights, noblemen and gentlemen with influence in the locality where the dispute had arisen was so common as to be plainly significant. Moreover, it was not as 'umpires' only that they were so associated. Fifty-eight knights and gentlemen were official witnesses to the final settlement at Macclesfield in 1412 of a property dispute between Sir Thomas Grosvenor and Robert Leigh. Eight arbiters and thirteen gentlemen were together witnesses to the final division (by lot) of the inheritance of Hugh Cressy of Hodsock (Notts.), who died without heirs of his body in 1408. The more tightly that the local aristocratic and genteel community, the kinsmen, associates and neighbours of disputant parties could be involved in an arbitration award, the more likely it was to stand. The broad hint here seems to be that the soundest way of curbing gentry violence and its tendency to escalate was not (as we might instinctively suppose) to strengthen judicial commissions and to increase the penalties for wrongdoing: indeed that was likely if anything to be counter-productive. It was rather to enlist the goodwill of those influential local people from among whom the disputants would otherwise look for backers in their efforts to apply force or to bend the law.

It is not surprising that where two disputants were both clients of the same 'good lord' they often looked to him and to his councillors to sort out their differences. There are many instances of lords acting as umpires between men of their affinity; indeed it was one of their obligations as lords to seek to allay the quarrels of their men. It has been argued that in this way the 'bastard feudal' relations of lord and man, far from being the prime cause of disorder and violence that they are so often alleged to have been, made a meaningful contribution towards the maintenance of local order and stability. There is certainly something in this view, but it is one that it is unwise to press too far. Overmighty the great lords of late medieval

England may have been, but they were not mighty enough to take over from king or community the task of upholding local peace effectively. As Christine Carpenter has shown in her study of the Beauchamp affinity in fifteenth-century Warwickshire, it could take a good deal of heaving and shoving, sometimes rising to the level of riot, for the retainers of even a very powerful magnate to keep up the image of being cocks of the walk in their own country. Even John of Gaunt, even in his own palatine county of Lancaster, could not hope to count more than a substantial proportion of the more prominent gentry among his retainers and annuitants; and those that he could all had connections with other gentlemen of the shire who were not of the charmed circle. In the relations with these other men and their families, what counted in the long run for Gaunt's clients was not the interest of the duke or of his affinity, but their own interest. In consequence it remained always easier for a lord to find himself enlisted partially in the quarrels of his retainers and clients than to impose impartial decisions on the leading men of a community in which his influence, albeit powerful, fell a long way short of being a controlling one. The enlisting of gentry communities in the business of self-regulation was a more promising road towards better governance than enlisting magnate support in controlling disorder could ever be. That is part of the reason why the good understanding between the Tudors and the county gentry, and the Tudor determination not to have men on the commissions of the peace who were retained of any cloth but their own, really did go some way towards improving matters.

Until that time, the attitude of landowners and gentlefolk towards the use of force in their affairs seems to have remained at best ambiguous. As we have seen, there is evidence of their very strong desire for more orderly governance. Outrages like the murder of Nicholas Radford roused indignation and dismay. On the other hand, there are signs too that it could be hard to withhold a certain admiration for those who resorted to violence. Local sympathy seems to have been what enabled William Beckwith, between 1387 and 1392, to survive in the 'deep forest' of Knaresborough and to prosecute thence his feud with Sir

Robert de Rokeley and his master-forester. Local collaboration likewise enabled Ralph Greyndour, cadet of a genteel Gloucestershire family, to maintain a criminal gang of outlaws in the Forest of Dean, holding men to ransom, breaking up sessions of the peace and even planning to ambush Lord Berkeley. In Beckwith's case at least, if not Greyndour's, there seems to be a remote echo of the mythical forest adventures of Robin Hood, which were immensely popular in the fifteenth century. The first part of the most famous version of his story, the *Gest of Robin Hood*, has a plot all too relevant to the sort of matters this chapter has been dealing with; it centres on chicanery in a land dispute and the efforts of the Abbot of St Mary's, York, by crooked means and with the aid of crooked justice, to prise his estates away from Sir Richard atte Lee, Robin's friend. The bent sheriff of Nottingham is another of Sir Richard's and Robin's enemies and gets his violent come-uppance:

> Lie thou there, thou proud sheriff,
> Evyll mote thou cheve!
> There myght no man to thee truste
> The whyles thou wert alyve.

The households and halls of lords and gentlemen seem to have been where the stories of Robin Hood first gained popularity. The household men and yeomen servants of lords and gentlefolk were those on whom they counted when making entries or overawing the friends and clients of rivals. It must have been with some relish that such people listened to tales which put activities not unlike theirs but just a trifle more grandiloquent in such a favourable light. Their masters had no cause to discountenance such relish: it nourished a sort of spirit of which, in certain circumstances, they might all too easily be glad.

When we are considering the kind of violence that the outlaw ballads describe and exculpate, it needs to be remembered that, as popular literature so commonly does, they exaggerate. When we turn from them to the historical record, we find plenty of breaking of parks and killing of deer and plenty of ruffianly behaviour, but a great dearth of sheriffs slaughtered when in pursuit of their official business. The ballads are informative with regard to feelings, not facts. They do reflect accurately a widespread distrust of the law's impartiality and a readiness which it encouraged to treat a certain amount of violence as inevitable and therefore acceptable. It should not really surprise us to find in this age such a degree of toleration of violent action. Common and troublesome as it was, it was only in special circumstances, in those comparatively brief periods, when political confusion and civil strife had undermined normal restraints, that it could escalate to a level that seemed to threaten serious destabilization of social order. As the history of arbitration helps to illustrate, there were strong forces of cohesion among local landowning communities to balance out the disruptive tendency of their internal rivalries. That gentlemen were prepared to meet with force the kind of force that they were likely to encounter is not a sign that they were ungovernable, but that they were a tough, proud, independent breed, ready to act in any situation in which they thought that their rights, interests or worship might be threatened.

We can see in these later medieval gentlemen who were so ready to act sharply, the lineal ancestors of a later breed of English gentlemen, who rode fast to hounds, jockeyed for county position, drank deep and were ready to stand their ground with swords or pistols any time they thought their honour queried. Those gentlemen, in their spare time, still managed to govern their country quite surprisingly successfully, and perhaps their forebears should not be underrated in that regard either. The times they lived in were rough, and there was much needless, violent aggression. But except on the Scottish border, the English landscape was not studded with fortified tower houses, as was that of contemporary Ireland, where real war on a miniature scale was endemic. Violence, though a real problem, was sufficiently well restrained for there to be no need for them.

Part III

The First Estate: the Clerks

Clergy and Religion in an Age
of Growing Lay Literacy

9. The Spread of Literacy

Janet Coleman has written, of English literature in the late middle ages, that 'the blossoming of English poetry and prose is most readily intelligible as a reflection of a changing social structure and its changing ideals, a broadening of the middle range of society ... and its increasing demand for a literature read for information, for pleasure, and for spiritual education'. Her words echo the claim made in the first chapter of this book for the rise of lay literacy, and especially of lay literacy in the vernacular, as a powerful factor of social change. In this chapter I shall concentrate on four main themes related to this development: the evolution of English into a significant literary language; books and their readership; rising levels of literacy; and the development in education that underpinned them.

What Janet Coleman calls 'the blossoming of English poetry and prose' really does refer to something new. From the years between about 1100 and the beginning of the fourteenth century remarkably little that was written in English has survived and what does survive is not very striking, more interesting for the history of the language than as literature. Between 1300 and 1400 a great literature in the native tongue was born. Chaucer's *Canterbury Tales* and his *Troilus and Criseyde*, William Langland's *Piers Plowman*, and the anonymous alliterative *Gawain and the Green Knight*, all written in the late fourteenth century, are the finest poetic products of the English middle ages. Other works only seem less remarkable in comparison with them, and bear eloquent testimony to the range of achievement of this first age of English literary history; the alliterative and metrical romances, the mystical writings in English of Richard Rolle, Walter Hilton and Dame Julian of Norwich, Trevisa's translation of the *Polychronicon* and the Wyclifite translation of the Bible. And that is only a list of a few of the more important works.

The novelty of this fourteenth-century literary achievement is easily understated. In one sense at least the great poems of the 'alliterative revival' (*Gawain*, the alliterative *Morte d'Arthur*, *Winner and Waster*) look to the past: the form of their versification has clear connections (though these are not easy to pin down) with the Anglo-Saxon literary tradition. Their language, too, is sometimes consciously archaizing. But Chaucer did something for English that is almost comparable to what Dante and the other writers of the *dolce stil nuovo* did for Italian nearly a hundred years before. Though Chaucer wrote no *De vulgari eloquentia* to explain what he was doing, he was virtually fashioning a new poetic language in English, with sophisticated capacities previously undreamt of. The Wyclifite translators of the Bible achieved something in a way comparable in the field of prose. Two versions survive. It seems clear that at the start those who worked on the earlier version had supposed that the Latin Vulgate could be translated into English more or less word for word, and would still make sense: of course it did not. In the later version, which was completed before 1397, they showed that they had been able to develop a vocabulary and a syntactical approach that would measure up to the problem of rendering the truth of Scripture into intelligible English. What they produced will not stand comparison with the glories of the Authorized Version, but it is an amazing achievement none the less, an experiment revealing new capacities in the English language, just as Chaucer did in a different way.

In poetry the fifteenth century produced nothing that can touch the masterpieces of the preceding age: Lydgate and Hoccleve were pedestrian versifiers by the standards of Chaucer and Gower. All the same, both were men of education and refinement, and they were very prolific. In terms of volume, the English writing of the fifteenth century was more abundant than that of the fourteenth, and still more variegated, even if, in terms of quality, Malory's prose triumph in his *Morte d'Arthur* stands out in lonely eminence. The mystery plays of the York and Coventry cycles introduce a new genre that is of special interest for the social historian. Sir John Fortescue's *Governance of England* is the first independent effort to review and explain in English the principles of English politics and the constitution.

But perhaps most striking of all is the enormous body of works translated into English in this century. The fourteenth century had pointed the way here, with Chaucer's translation of Boethius' *Consolation of Philosophy*, Trevisa's English version of the *Polychronicon*, and the Wyclifite Bible. The early fifteenth century saw some notable additions: Hoccleve's translation of Giles of Rome's political treatise, *De regimine principum*; Nicholas Love's translation of the pseudo-Bonaventuran *Mirror of the Blessed Life of Jesu Christ*; and the first English translation of Vegetius' classical treatise on military tactics and training. Perhaps the best way to catch a glimpse of what had been added by the end of the century is to glance over a list of some of the items that came from Caxton's first English printing press from 1477 onwards. Here are translations (mostly from French) of *The Game and Play of Chess*; the *Dictes and Sayings of the Philosophers*; the histories of Jason, Charlemagne and the crusading hero Godfrey de Bouillon; the Knight of La Tour Landry's book for the instruction of his daughters; Ramon Lull's *Order of Chivalry*; *Tully of Old Age*; Aesop's *Fables*; the *Golden Legend*; the *Pilgrimage of the Soul*; and of course Malory, whose book was in large part a free translation of the French Arthurian romances. And there were many more.

Caxton was catering for a public that was clearly eager for information and for books. The demand was there, and had been for a long time, as the evidence concerning the possession of books before the introduction of printing makes very clear. That evidence, and also the list of the books that he printed, gives some clear indication of the tastes of late medieval readers, of what sort of information and what sort of entertainment they prized most, and above all, of the changing social face of the reading public.

Clerics, of course, had always been possessors of books: in the fourteenth and fifteenth centuries the evidence that laymen too might have them, might even possess libraries of their own, steadily thickens. With regard to the higher aristocracy this is hardly surprising, and there is nothing new about their owning books except in terms of quantity. Guy de Beauchamp, Earl of Warwick (d. 1359), left forty-two books; Thomas of Woodstock, Duke of Gloucester (d. 1397), had nearly twice that number; so did Henry Lord Scrope of Masham (d. 1415). Humphrey of Gloucester, in the fifteenth century, became a collector on a large scale. Wills and inventories make it clear though that by this time it was by no means only great noblemen who possessed collections of books. The will of Sir William Trussell (d. 1389) refers to 'all' his books of romances. The inventory of the goods of Sir Simon Burley, executed in 1388, includes nineteen books. Sir Thomas Charlton (d. 1465) had 'an English book called Giles *de regimine principum*', 'an English book the which was called *Troles and Cryseyd*', 'one of *Perse Plowman*, another of *Canterbury Tales*'. Merchants too bequeathed books – Robert Felstead, vintner of London (d. 1349), left a psalter in English and Latin; John Bromley (d. 1420) and William Holgrave (d. 1435), two Londoners, both bequeathed copies of the *Canterbury Tales*; Richard Manchester, burgess of Gloucester, directed in his will that Robert Spellsbury junior should have two of his books and that his executors should dispose of 'all my remaining books' at their discretion among those people who should seem most suitable to them. Women, and not only noblewomen, also mention books in their wills. Joanna Hilton of Yorkshire left in 1432 a '*Romance, with the 10 Commandments*', a *Romance of the Seven Sages*, and a *Roman de la Rose*. There are numerous records of pious women bequeathing devotional books, often to kinswomen who were nuns. If fewer women than men could write, some of them at least probably read more than their menfolk did.

The literary tastes indicated by wills and inventories, where they mention books, are instructive. Throughout, the preponderance of devotional works remains striking. A good many of the books belonging to the higher aristocracy were of course liturgical books for use in their private chapels, and plenty of rather more middling people possessed missals, psalters or books of hours of their own. An Italian visitor to England, at the end of the fifteenth century, was struck by the way English people carried their books to church with them, and could be seen mouthing over them during the service. Among vernacular devotional works, those of the mystics, and especially Richard Rolle's English psalter, are among the most frequently mentioned in bequests. Romances were also popular, particularly among the genteel, and so were books of 'nurture' (instruction in good manners, etiquette, blazonry and so on). The inventory of Sir John Paston's books, made in 1482, gives some indication of what a gentleman's library could contain. He had a book of the death of Arthur; the romance of Guy of Warwick; a chronicle of England to the reign of Edward III; a book of Troilus (Chaucer's *Troilus and Criseyde*, no doubt); a book of the play of chess; a 'book of knighthood'; 'mine old book of blazoning of arms'; a book of statutes; Cicero's *De amicitia* and his *De senectute*; and what appears to be a collection of devotional pieces (the list here is partly illegible). By the standards of the time, this is quite a collection for a gentleman (constricted though it would be by the standard of a hundred years later, when printing had begun to make a real impact), and the range of the matters covered is illuminating. The statute book reminds us that the Pastons were lawyers and rose by the law: one fancies the book of blazons has something to do with their ascent into gentility over the last two generations, and with the snobbery of the *parvenu*; the book of knighthood probably has something to do with the family connection with the old soldier, Sir John Fastolf. Then there are books for leisure, the romances, the history, the rules of chess; and for spiritual edification the devotional pieces. In the range of its coverage the Paston library was no doubt rather exceptional; but the lists of books bequeathed by, for example, Sir Thomas Chaworth of Nottinghamshire (d. 1458) or Sir Peter Ardern of Yorkshire (d. 1464) are quite comparable.

The number of books that a man possessed is not in any case a sound guide to the range of his reading. A whole host of items might be gathered together in a single volume. Some such volumes were copied out by the owner of the book, item by item as opportunity offered, for his own future delectation: some originated in other ways. One example of such a collection is another of Paston's books, what he called his 'Great Book'. Interestingly the contents of this commonplace collection of pieces of interest to a gentleman are so similar to that of another manuscript as to suggest that it may be one of a number of copies put together from an exemplar, and put on sale at a stationer's for any buyer. A group of manuscripts of the English translation of the *Dictes and Sayings of the Philosophers* are so similar in format that it looks certain that they were prepared in this way.

One is a long way here from mass production, but bookselling as a retail business does have a substantial history that starts long before Caxton brought the printing press to England. The scriveners of London formed their own guild in 1373, the limnours (illuminators) in 1403; and the first reference to London stationers, who coordinated the work of scriveners, limnours and binders (and who might belong to any of their crafts) comes from way back in 1311. Most of their business was no doubt with books that were 'bespoken', specially ordered, but by no means all it would seem. The price of bespoken books would be a matter of negotiation between the stationer and the buyer, and they could be expensive. Edmund, Earl of March, in 1374 paid 50 marks for a Bible 'for his chamber', and Edward III paid an astonishing £66 13s. 4d. for a book of romances 'to be kept in his bedchamber'. But books could also be obtained very cheaply, especially those of which the stationer had made multiple copies. The inventory of the goods of two London grocers who went bankrupt in the 1390s includes four books with a total value of 11s. 4d., together with two books in English, value 8d., and a primer (a catechetical collection) valued at 8d. Sixpence a day were the wages of a common archer: an eightpenny primer was within the range of a very humble purse.

Of course a humble person was not likely to want much more in the way of books than just a primer. Wealthier purchasers sometimes clearly commissioned books for what we would now call 'coffee-table' display, paying well for a rich initial letter or so that could be revealed and admired. Other books were bought not so much for private reading but rather in order to have them read aloud, to the household, or to the family circle in the solar, or by a tutor or chaplain to the children under his charge. Down to the end of the middle ages, any really extensive use of books continued to be confined largely to those who used them professionally, clerics, scholars and lawyers. The fact remains, nevertheless, that more people were becoming interested in possessing one or two or even more books, and in reading them or having them read to them.

*

Two aspects of the new literature available in English require some additional comment; one is a further point about language, the other is about the degree of literacy that it relates to among the population at large. The native language of the Norman aristocracy that had settled in England at the end of the eleventh century was French. In later generations the upper classes in England became as a result bilingual. English was the 'cradle language' that they learned in infancy from nurses and servants, and remained the language of their converse with social inferiors: but French, learned naturally in the household, was commonly their spoken language among equals and their literary language. This remained true, for the most part, until somewhere near the middle of the fourteenth century. Ranulph Higden, writing in the 1320s, remarked that 'contrary to the usage and manner of all other nations', English children in their schooling 'are compelled to leave their own language, and to construe their lessons in French, and have been since the Normans first came into England'. 'Up-landish men' who wish to be reckoned gentlemen, he adds, 'make a great business of talking French, so as to be more thought of'. When John Trevisa in 1385 was translating this passage, he added a note:

This used to be the way of things before the first pestilence, but is since somewhat changed . . . so that now . . . in all the grammar schools of England children leave by French, and construe and learn in English, and have thereby advantage on one side, and disadvantage in another. The advantage is that they learn grammar in less time than children used to do. The disadvantage is that now grammar school children know no more French than their left heel does . . . Gentlemen have now for the most part given up teaching their children French.

Trevisa's testimony seems to be borne out by other evidence. When, within a year of the 'first pestilence' (1348), Henry, first Duke of Lancaster, sat down to compose his extraordinary penitential book, the *Livre des Seyntz Medecines*, he wrote in French. Forty years later Sir John Clanvowe, the next layman whom we know to have composed a religious treatise, preferred to write his *Two Ways* in his native English (though he was undoubtedly fluent in French). Though there were still in England plenty of gentlefolk at the end of the fourteenth century

who, like Chaucer's prioress, could speak a French 'of Stratford-
atte-Bow' that they had learned as children, English seemed to
Sir John to be a better language for literary communication.
French was ceasing to be the spoken and literary language of the
gentility, and that in itself is an important social fact. It also
helps to explain why it was that so little seems to have been
written in English in an earlier period, and why there was such a
strong new impetus in English writing in the fourteenth and
fifteenth centuries.

Of course people continued to learn French, but usually now
at a later stage and with a different emphasis to their purpose.
To know French remained important even for those who had
no travelling plans, because it was still much used, as it had
traditionally been, as a language of record, and in the law courts.
Knowledge of it therefore continued to be useful, but from the
point of view of professional qualification rather than for literary
ends or for snobbery. Even in the courts, though, its dominance
was coming to be challenged: as early as 1362 the Commons in
Parliament petitioned that English should be admitted on a par
with French in legal pleadings. There was a steady tendency to
abandon French in favour of English in the keeping of records,
too; thus in 1422 we find the brewers of London resolving in
future to keep their minutes in English, because so many of their
craft who knew how to read and write did not know either
French or Latin. Literacy as a qualification was becoming more
English; that in turn made the qualification more widely available, more open to secular men.

Literacy is a capacity always hard to measure in early times. It
can also be hard of definition; there are really two literacies, since
those who can read cannot always write (the evidence suggests that
in the late middle ages women in particular often had the first
literacy but not the second). F. R. H. Du Boulay has estimated that
in the fifteenth century 'perhaps 30 per cent' of the population
could read, and that in London and some other towns the
proportion may have been appreciably higher. In any such estimate as this, there is an element of guesswork, but the sort of level
suggested is high enough to make it clear that literacy had by this
time a broad range that was new in social terms. This extension of
literacy was of great importance, because for every reader there

was a potential circle, small or great, of listeners, on whom the written word, through his reading, could have an impact.

The higher aristocracy, it seems apparent, had since at least the twelfth century had a reading literacy in French and perhaps some Latin too. Works such as Walter of Henley's *Husbandry* and his *Stewardship* (both written significantly in French) show that in the thirteenth century even a lay steward might be master of a quite impressive measure of literacy of a businesslike, pragmatic order. But by the later fourteenth century it is clear that literacy was reaching the 'middle classes' of both town and countryside much more widely and significantly, and percolating further down the social scale as well. Chaucer was a court poet, but much of what he wrote in the *Canterbury Tales* would probably have appealed as much and more in the houses of London merchants (some of whom, as we know, bequeathed copies of them) than among courtiers. The houses in which Langland, so he tells us, recited parts of his great poem belonged almost certainly to humbler people, far short in riches and status of the merchant patriciate. His social and religious commentary, and such poems as *Mumme and the Soothsayer* (the strange alliterative poem that dilates on the events surrounding Richard II's deposition in 1399), were clearly aimed at a much more 'middling' audience than Chaucer's. Charges against the humble Lollards of the early fifteenth century of holding 'coventicles' to read heretical books take us lower down the social scale again; so does the growth, in the fifteenth century, of the practice of posting anonymous bills, heretical or seditious, on church doors and in other public places.

One of the most telling pieces of evidence that what we are here looking at are new conditions is that which emerges from L. Gabel's great study of benefit of clergy in England. If one who was charged with a criminal offence (for the first offence at least) could prove his clerical status, then he could insist that he be handed over to the bishop's officers to be dealt with. The normal test of such status was to be asked to read a couple or so verses from the Latin Bible. Down to the later fourteenth century, as far as can be established, the large majority of those pleading in this way seem to have been genuine clerics, if often only in minor orders. But from that time on, more and more are identifiable as following quite other callings, being described as merchants, craftsmen, servants, even labourers. These men did not have to understand the Latin that they read, but it is clear enough that they would have been able to read and understand English. No wonder that the authorities were worried by out-breaks of the posting of seditious bills, such as we hear of from York in 1405 and in London in 1416; there was a wide public that could understand their message and explain it to others.

The ability to write was doubtless more limited than the ability to read. The new appearance in the fifteenth century of collections of private letters, as those of the Pastons and the Stonors, and the Plumpton correspondence, tells its own story, however. With their news of everyday concerns they bring a breath of real fresh air into the historical record, as we find ourselves talking to people clearly not so very unlike ourselves. There is nothing antique about William Paston's schoolboy hopes from Eton that a parcel of almonds and raisins from home has not miscarried, nor about the advice on wooing given to young John Paston III: 'bear yourself as lowly to the mother as you list, but to the maid not too lowly'. The Pastons, Stonors and Plumptons were gentry, of course, but many of the cor-respondents who wrote them news letters or begging letters were humbler people than their addressees. No one knows who wrote this letter from Henry V's camp near Meulan in 1419, but he was clearly a busy correspondent:

And so now men suppose that the king will from henceforth make war in France, for Normandy is all his . . . More write I not at this time, but I pray you ye pray for us that we may come out of this unlusty soldier's life into the merry life of England. And Christ have you in his holy keeping . . . I have written you oft times in the siege time of Rouen and since the yielding thereof, but I know not whether my letters have come to you or no.

The worry that letters are not getting through is a familiar fear of men at the front: this correspondent's anxiety is a useful reminder of what a pile of mail bags from the fifteenth century have not got through to us. It was a new age of writing as well as of reading.

★

The new degree of literacy among the laity of the late middle ages implies developments in education, and there is no doubt that the period was a very important one in educational history. Three levels of schooling can be discerned, then as now: elementary ('reading and song' in the contemporary terms); secondary ('grammar' which implied some schooling in Latin); and higher education. The history of developments in the first two of these presents problems, because more was involved than just the history of educational institutions. Although, as we shall see presently, this was a very significant period in the history of schools, a great deal of schooling was carried on in a more informal, private way. Here changes are not easy to trace, even though it is clear that changes there must have been, and influential ones.

Let us look first at the evidence concerning informal education, and then at the more formal, institutional record. From a very remote period, it had been normal practice for boys of aristocratic birth to be sent away from home perhaps around the age of seven, to be brought up in the household of some great man, perhaps his father's superior lord. It was at seven that Beowulf, hero of the Anglo–Saxon epic, was sent to live with his mother's father Hrethel, King of the Geats, who brought him up to manhood. This practice persisted very generally down to the end of the middle ages. The royal court had always been, and remained, an important centre for the upbringing of the sons of the nobility, the future companions in arms of the heir to the throne. 'It is the supreme academy for the nobles of the realm,' wrote Sir John Fortescue in the 1460s, 'and a school of vigour, probity and manners by which the realm is honoured and will flourish.' A major part in the schooling of a young nobleman at the royal court, as Fortescue makes clear, was in the martial arts and horsemanship, and there was instruction in manners too (in etiquette, how to carve and serve at table, in music and dancing): but there was also education in the more formal sense. In 1449 we have a clear reference to a grammar master attached to the royal chapel, whose duty was to teach not only the choristers but also the 'noble boys' being brought up in the king's court. A 'grammar' master implies some professional instruction in Latin. A generation later we know that John

Rede, ex-headmaster of Winchester and tutor to Henry VII's son Prince Arthur, was reading with him (and other charges) Caesar, Cicero, Pliny and Vergil. In an earlier age, when formal arrangements are hard to trace, there may have been less emphasis on grammar in the strict sense, but the literary tastes of Edward III and his sons, as of Richard II and of Henry V, make it clear that they and those brought up with them were literate in a distinctly sophisticated degree.

Aristocratic households were also, like the royal court, centres for the education of gently born young men. Chaucer spent his years from twelve to seventeen in the household of the Countess of Ulster, and this was his first introduction to the aristocratic world and its manners, which he came to know so well. 'I the maker of this book,' the chronicler John Hardyng wrote, 'was brought up from twelve years of age in Sir Henry Percy's house, to the battle of Shrewsbury where I was with him armed.' Here again, we are reminded, there was a good deal of emphasis on manners and the martial arts, but letters were learned too: Chaucer and Hardyng in their maturity were both highly literate men. Maybe this lettered side of nurture took up more of the hours of the children of those who preferred to place their sons in the household of a bishop or an abbot rather than a secular lord or lady, like James, Lord Berkeley, who in 1439 sent his thirteen-year-old son to be brought up with Cardinal Beaufort. In both circles alike, episcopal and noble, we begin to hear of professional grammar masters in the household towards the end of the fifteenth century, as at the royal court. John Holt was the schoolmaster in Cardinal Morton's household at Lambeth in the 1490s, and there was a grammar master in the household of the Earl of Northumberland in the early sixteenth century.

In the distant past, boys of good birth had often obtained an introduction to letters in a monastery. This had become rare by the fourteenth century, but boys were often sent to be brought up by an abbot in his household (by this time long detached from the cloister and staffed largely by lay servants). Where the religious houses themselves did still make an important contribution was in the education of young women. Some girls, like boys, though usually at a slightly later age, were sent away to be brought up in a noble household, often that of a great man's widow; thus John Howard (then still a knight, but later to be Duke of Norfolk) sent his daughter Jane to London in 1466 to stay with the Countess of Oxford. But among the gentility it would seem that as many girls or more, if they went away from home at all, were convent educated. Some of the bishops indeed thought that the popularity of convent education was too great and proving a distraction from the nuns' religious calling, and sought to limit the number of girls who might be taken in and the age to which they could stay. Numbers could indeed be quite high: in 1536, on the eve of the dissolution of the monasteries, there were twenty-six girls from local genteel families boarding at St Mary's Convent in Winchester. Two or three or half a dozen would be a more usual number. The nuns themselves seem normally to have been the teachers, and the education that they could offer was not profound – no 'grammar' here; reading, song, a little French, good manners, something of the scripture story and the articles of the faith were probably the usual limit.

A good many monasteries in the late middle ages still taught song to children who were choristers, but they were not the principal centre of education in 'reading and song'. These two primary subjects usually went together, and were more and more often taught in schools, 'song schools', such as that to which Chaucer's 'little clergeoun' (little choirboy) in the 'Prioress's Tale' went daily when he was seven, to learn

> . . . to syngen and to read,
> As smalle childre do in their childhede.

The institutional history and progress of this elementary stage of schooling is not easy to document. Not all 'song' schools (which taught children to sing the antiphons) taught reading and some, on the other hand, taught grammar as well as reading and song. It is clear that by the end of the thirteenth century there were schools which taught at least the one and perhaps all three of these subjects attached to most cathedrals, and also in most county towns (there were three in London), and in many smaller towns too. Besides that, many parish priests (and sometimes parish clerks) taught song and perhaps reading either in their houses or in the church to boys of the parish: there is obviously some question as to whether they can be described as 'holding schools' in quite the same sense that the schoolmasters attached to cathedral chapters and to some collegiate churches clearly can be.

Nevertheless, in spite of a good deal of informality and of many problems with the sources, there seem to be unmistakable signs that the fourteenth and fifteenth centuries saw a growing concern for and extension of the provision of elementary education. References, especially in wills, to song or reading schools associated with chantries, guilds and parish churches multiply; the figures produced by J. Hoeppner Moran for the York diocese show the number of such schools that can be pinpointed increasing nearly fourfold between 1350 and 1500 (the better documentation for the later part of the period no doubt exaggerates the increase somewhat). The growing institutionalization of schooling at parish level was plainly an important factor. Sometimes this was the result of a specific benefaction, as when in 1443 John Abbot, mercer of London, willed lands to found a chantry in his native village of Farthinghoe (Northants.) to maintain a priest who would instruct the children of the parish. More often the collective goodwill of the humble and local many was involved. Again and again, in 1548, the Chantry Commissioners (charged to dissolve chantries, that is, endowments for the singing of masses at side altars in churches) encountered lands in parishes dedicated by sundry and unknown benefactors for the maintenance of education. What they found tells a clear story: schooling, at the elementary level, had become over the last century and a half of the middle ages dramatically better organized at the humble level, and much more accessible to a wider sector of the population.

In the same period we see also a considerable increase in the formal provision of secondary, grammar education, though growth here was not on anything like the scale that the sixteenth century was to witness. William of Wykeham's foundation of his college at Winchester was a major and dramatic new departure, in that he was the first to make instruction in grammar (for seventy scholars) the principal purpose of a collegiate foundation. But Winchester, and Henry VI's foundation at Eton which followed its model constitutionally, remained truly exceptional. Archbishop Chichele's foundation of a 'college' in the parish church of Higham Ferrers in 1422 was a much more common mould. His endowment was to support a community of eight chaplains, eight clerks and six choristers, to pray daily for the lives and souls of King Henry V, Queen Catherine, the founder, and all Christian people: a school, in which *one* of the chaplains would teach grammar, was annexed to the foundation. Schools attached to 'colleges' were founded on this pattern for instance by Bishop Grandison in the church of Ottery St Mary (Devon, 1338), by Sir Fulk Pembridge's widow at Tong (Shropshire, 1410), by the Duke of York at Fotheringhay (Northants., 1411). Still more numerous were the grammar schools (often very small) that were associated with chantry foundations. Lady Catherine Berkeley's endowment in 1384 of a chantry in Wootton-under-Edge to support a master and two poor scholars offers a good example. The two scholars were to be taught free, but the master was also to teach any others who might come to him, charging a small fee. There were a good many chantries linked with the provision of grammar education on these sorts of lines, and a wide variety of benefactors were involved in their foundation: bishops and leading clergy, guilds (such as those of St Lawrence at Ashburton, Devon, or of St John the Baptist and the Holy Cross at Stratford-upon-Avon), town corporations and groups of parishioners, as well as nobles, gentry and their widows. The interest, especially of the laity, in the patronage of education at this secondary as well as the elementary level, is amply demonstrated.

Wykeham's foundation at Winchester, like the grammar schools that flourished in Oxford in the shadow of the university (probably the model which inspired him), was intended to train boys who would afterwards follow a clerical career; and the same purpose, probably, was in the minds of most founders and benefactors. Others besides these were, however, able to profit from the opportunities opened up. Both at Winchester and at Eton the colleges were permitted to admit, over and above their scholars who received free board and education, a limited number of 'commoners' who would pay their own way. When Bishop Beaufort visited Winchester in 1412 he concluded, significantly, that there were already far too many (the statutes allowed for ten; there were over eighty). From such early lists as survive, most of these Winchester commoners seem to have been sons of knights, esquires and gentlemen, mostly but not all local.

Grammar schooling and the introduction to Latin and to formal letter-writing were coming to be seen as useful, possibly vital, to careers outside the clerical order. Bartholomew Bolney, who was steward of the abbey of Battle from the 1420s to the 1470s and built an estate for himself in Sussex through his shrewd purchasing, had started off as a scholar of Winchester. Clement Paston, the honest husbandman who was the first founder of his family's fortunes, borrowed money to put his son William to school, and then supported him through his legal studies in London. It was a sound investment: William rose to be a judge and a powerful landowner in his county of Norfolk, and his descendants were reckoned among the principal gentry of the shire.

The remarkable figure Thomas Sampson of Oxford gives us a nice insight into the pragmatic value that education had acquired for the aspiring and well-to-do among the laity as well as would-be clerics. Between *c.* 1360 and 1409 he was running what amounted to a school of management studies in Oxford. In the course of his career he put together a number of treatises, on the manner of holding courts, on the coroner's office, on how a clerk should spend his lord's money (with a model account, starting at Michaelmas 1401). He also put together a collection of model letters, fascinating for the glimpses that they offer of life in the university town, and of a man with a nose for clients and developed promotional instincts. One of the best of them purports to be from a father whose son had gone up to the university to read for an arts degree: now his parent has heard from the Earl of W., who is willing to take the young man into his service. So the father instructs his son to leave off his degree studies, and put himself with Thomas Sampson for a year, to learn letter-writing, composition and accountancy, and to pay him 100s. so as to be sure he is well taught. 'Thomas Sampson is incessant in teaching his pupils,' Sampson says in another letter: he was a sound and clearly a very successful crammer of the career-minded.

★

The universities of Oxford and Cambridge had originated as centres of higher education for those bent on a clerical career, and so they remained, essentially, beyond the end of the middle ages. For their brightest scholars, career prospects were good, in ecclesiastical administration, in the offices of state and in the royal diplomatic service. The growing popularity of law degrees (in canon and Roman law) reflects the openings which a university education offered in the church on the administrative side; and throughout our period, the proportion of bishops with a university training behind them increased. But the universities did not expand significantly in terms of student numbers (though the number of privileged college foundations did); and because they remained bastions of essentially clerical learning, their principal contribution will be better considered elsewhere, when we come to look at clerical life, rather than in this review of changes in the pattern of provision of education. Nevertheless there were developments, here too, that need to be noted now.

Naturally, from their beginnings, the two universities had always admitted a good number of young men of aristocratic or gentle birth who were destined for careers in the church. In the fifteenth century, however, we begin to hear of young gentlemen who were not so destined attending the university. In many cases, perhaps most, it seems clear that, like the young man in Thomas Sampson's letter, they were not in the end going to stay the full course. Robert Hungerford, in 1437–8, lodged with his tutor in University College, Oxford, for just three terms. About the same time, John Paston, Judge William's son, spent maybe two years at Cambridge, before going on to London to study common law, and his brother Edmund followed him, being sent to read logic for half a year and civil law for a year before going on likewise to learn English law in London. Matthew Wentworth, a Yorkshire squire, similarly sent his son Thomas first in 1505 to grammar school for two years, then to Cambridge for one, then on to London to the law. For the well-born laity, as these examples suggest, it was beginning to seem valuable to acquire something of that literacy and Latin polish that a space spent at university could inculcate. But the universities were not really becoming as yet centres of higher education for laymen, and a spell in them was seen as preparatory to more serious study in what really were becoming, for them, the most significant focuses of tertiary learning, the Inns of Court in London.

In the fifteenth century, the Inns of Court became just that, the most important centres for higher education for the well-born and ambitious among lay folk. The earliest professional common lawyers, who appear on the scene as an identifiable group in the late thirteenth century, acquired their training largely in the courts themselves, in which a special place was provided for students in attendance, the 'crib'. But from the mid fourteenth century the clerks in some of the 'Inns' of Chancery (where the Chancery clerks lodged) were offering a training in the writing of legal documents and the handling of writs and from quite early in that century there survive in manuscript texts of what appear to be lectures at a more advanced level in the rules and procedures of common law. In the course of the fifteenth century the outlines of a regular system of instruction in the greater Inns (the Temple, Grays Inn, etc.) begin to be apparent. We begin to hear of readings and moots, of the 'learning' vacations, and of the obligation of senior men to 'read' with pupils. The society of the Inns seems moreover to have offered something a little wider than mere legal instruction. In a famous passage Chief Justice Fortescue wrote that

in these greater Inns, indeed, and also in the lesser, there is besides a school of law a kind of academy of all the manners that nobles learn . . . the knights, barons and the greatest nobility of the kingdom often place their children in these Inns of Court, not so much to make the law their study (having large patrimonies of their own) but to form their manners.

The citations in Fortescue's own works, on the *Governance of England* and *In Praise of English Laws*, bear witness to his wide reading and culture. His works and those of some of his fellows, as Lyttleton's *Tenures* and Statham's *Abridgement*, attest to a notable intellectual vigour among the leaders of the Inns. Thomas More's humanist enthusiasm was first fired at Oxford, before he came to the bar, but it is not surprising that when he did he shone at its studies and found congenial companions who shared his interests.

The principal objects of those who came to study at the Inns of Court were of course pragmatic. A landowner like John Paston needed, as his father put it, 'to know how to defend himself' in competitive county society. Most importantly, legal education was attractive because of the career openings that it offered. Practice in the central courts could be highly remunerative, but that was not the only possibility. Dr Ives has calculated that at any one time there might be some four hundred lawyers working about Westminster (of whom perhaps 150 would be men of any standing), together with maybe two or three hundred students attending the Inns. Clearly not all of the latter were going to practise in London. To any who hoped for office, as a sheriff or a coroner or escheater, or to sit on a county commission as a justice of the peace, a solid grounding in the law was invaluable. Among the host of men who found niches for themselves locally as attorneys, as members of baronial councils, as stewards or bailiffs or auditors, a great many must have spent time in the Inns, and have owed their position at least in part to that. Many others, no doubt, acquired a legal apprenticeship less expensively, by self-instruction or while assisting a father, say, in some office to which they hoped one day to succeed: that must have been the sort of background of Richard Down of Dersingham, 'yeoman and court holder', or of Thomas Trendill of Higham, 'scrivener and court holder', whose names Ives found on the first general pardon roll of Henry VIII. Whether it was acquired in the Inns or in other ways, the legal education and expertise of gentlemen and lay administrators in the last century of the English middle ages is one of the most remarkable testimonies to the spread in that time of lay literacy, and to its social significance.

The history of professional administration in England begins to take visible shape in the twelfth century, and the growing volume of administrative records from then on surviving is the witness to its development. First we see the state archives beginning to accumulate, in the rolls of the Exchequer and Chancery and the records of the proceedings of the eyres: then, in the thirteenth century, the records of private seigneurial administration began to multiply, court rolls, receivers' accounts, surveys, *valors.* Already in that century the lay steward was a familiar figure, but inevitably the more professional side of administration, as of compiling and auditing accounts, remained largely a task for clerics. The same was true of clerkships in the offices of state, where so many of those who would one day rise to the episcopal bench and perhaps even to be the king's Chancellor or Treasurer began their careers. In pragmatic terms the most striking consequence of the spread of lay literacy was the slow penetration of the laity into these one-time clerical preserves, a change which had profound consequences on the balance of influence among what men called the 'orders' or 'estates' of society, and so on the structure of the social whole.

The process is most easily illustrated from the history of the central state departments, not because that is where it was most important but because their records are so complete. The first lay Chancellor of England was Sir Robert Bourchier, a judge, appointed in 1340. Most of his successors in that office, down to 1500, remained bishops, but it was not so with the office of Lord Treasurer: from 1420 onwards he was more often a lay peer. The same process can be seen at work further down the scale. At the beginning of the fifteenth century, all the major clerical posts in the Exchequer were held by beneficed clergy (a position incompatible with marriage): by 1430, these were the exceptions rather than the rule. In Chancery the process was slower. In 1388 a royal ordinance affirmed the traditional rule that the clerks of Chancery should not be married; but by the middle of Henry V's reign there were at least eleven married clerks. The proportion increased steadily and at last, in 1523, even the six senior masters were permitted to marry. As Professor Storey has shown, these married clerks (and some unmarried ones too) were describing themselves as 'gentlemen', a title that they claimed in virtue of their standing in the king's service: and they were often living as gentlemen too. As such, they were seeking reward for their services (always inadequately salaried) not through promotion to benefices as their clerical colleagues were and as was traditional in their offices, but in other ways, through grants of the farms of escheated lands, appointment to stewardships or keeperships in the king's gift, fixed pensions or perhaps help towards a marriage. Some did very well indeed, as for example Sir Thomas Thorp who rose through the Exchequer to be a puisne baron, to be knighted and to sit in Parliament for the county of Northampton, where he cut a substantial figure.

In the late fourteenth century John of Gaunt, as Duke of Lancaster, employed clergy as receivers and auditors on his estates; in the fifteenth century the financial administration of the duchy estates passed into the hands of laymen. The history of private administration follows the same pattern as that which we can trace more clearly in the departments of state: on all sides, laymen in the late middle ages seem to be taking on the lead as professional managers. This is true on ecclesiastical as well as on lay estates. The first two stewards of Battle Abbey in the fourteenth century were monks; thereafter the succession of lay stewards is unbroken. The pension lists of Durham Priory show the common lawyers progressively edging out ecclesiastics as attorneys of the church, entitled to annuities. In the fifteenth century we begin to glimpse what seem almost to be administrative dynasties of educated 'lay bureaucrats' in private service, families with a tradition of legal and managerial expertise, like the Hodys in Somerset, or the Throckmortons who served the Earls of Warwick (and others) well as attorneys, stewards and councillors. This is at a high level; lower down the social scale we find men brought up to literate trades such as scrivening serving as clerks to guilds and to town corporations, where once a cleric might have been employed. At the end of the fourteenth century a Lollard writer could still complain that 'lords do great wrong and guile, for they make priests stewards of their households, clerks of their kitchen, auditors, treasurers, almoners and stewards for their courts as if no man could discharge worldly office but they'. By the end of the fifteenth century, if not before, that charge would no longer have rung true: those who discharged such worldly offices were for the most part no longer clergy.

Professor Storey makes the point that one of the reasons why, in the fifteenth century, Chancery clerks and secretaries of the Privy Seal seem no longer to have wished, as they had done in the past, to pursue clerical careers and the rewards that they offered, may have been a genuine sense that it was indecent to hold benefices that they would not serve. This may well be true: and it is certainly a useful reminder that the lay administrators of the late middle ages were not, in terms of their primary and secondary education, a new class of person. They came from the same sort of background as had their clerical predecessors, and there is no reason to think they were better at the same jobs. What was different about them was their attitude, their ambitions and the kinds of reward for service that they sought. But these are crucial matters, all the same: any changes in what are seen as the hallmarks of worldly success in a profession always are.

For the church there may have been gain as well as loss in the way things had altered. Her attention could be turned a little more firmly to where it properly lay, to pastoral and liturgical activity, and this at a time when, in consequence of plague mortalities, the bishops were concerned about the provision of adequate clergy to serve churches in their dioceses. More benefices, and more of the better ones that career-minded clerks of the past had sought with no intention of serving them, were available for men of committed vocation. But there was loss too, serious loss, above all in the spheres of influence and authority. Leading churchmen now no longer carried quite the weight that they once had in the kingdom's councils. The new lay administrators, unprotected by clerical privileges and immunities, were more dependent on secular and royal favour. As the clergy came to lose its monopoly of the degree of literacy which had in the past made clerks the class *par excellence* to whom men turned at once for ethical guidance, learned counsel and administrative expertise, so the independence of the clerical order in its separate status of dignity was undermined. If that independence had not been so far eroded, Henry VIII could never have carried his Parliaments and his country with him in the Reformation of the 1530s in the way that he did.

Among the laity, the spread of education opened new opportunities for men who were more interested in founding a family fortune, whether at a well-to-do or at a relatively humble level, than in ecclesiastical preferment. The opportunities, as we have seen, were wide and varied. The significance of the spread of literacy among the laity should not be considered only at these pragmatic levels, however; they were far more wide reaching. Fathers in the late middle ages sought education for their children with career opportunities in mind, as fathers always do. But as their books and the new literature in English tells us, once those children had learned their letters they read not just for business purposes but for recreation, information and edification as well. With so much of the wisdom of the past now available to them in their own tongue (albeit often in secondary or distilled form) they felt themselves in a new measure on equal terms with the clergy. This did not necessarily make them reform-minded, in the sixteenth-century sense, in their religious attitudes, or change their views about what the syllabus of education should be. As Nicholas Orme has pointed out, where schools were placed or passed under lay governors' control, it does not seem to have had the slightest effect on the curriculum followed; but the significant point is that laymen should be feeling that they were as competent to govern schools as a bishop or his official would be.

Above all, the fact that, although French and Latin remained vital for some business purposes, the literature of edification and recreation now open to the laity was largely in English helped to foster a sense of 'Englishness', of the identity of England in her language, in her laws and customs, in the structure of her polity; and it might be added, in her devotional practices and holy cults. It is one of the most striking features of Sir John Fortescue's remarkable vernacular book on the *Governance of England*, but no accident, that he should conclude that it is by following her own ways, not general laws or the customs of other nations, that 'this land shall be a college [i.e. a true community] in which shall sing and pray for evermore all the men of England, spiritual and temporal'. He looks at his Englishmen, clerk and lay alike, as one nation, not in terms of their separate estates. Here is one of the signs, and not the least telling, of the way in which English society in this period was being transformed, in a way that was making the old, traditional description of society in terms of three estates less and less appropriate or applicable.

10. *The Clerical Estate*

In at least three very significant respects the position of the clerical estate in late medieval England was different from that of the clergy at any time since. The first is obvious, that since the church in England was part of the universal church, clerics were subject to an authority, that of the Pope, which was international, and to a law that was not English, the canon law. Since England was a Christian kingdom, all men were subject to that law in some respects, but clerics in more (and more important) respects than laymen. Secondly, the church and churchmen exercised more influence and authority over the lives and affairs of lay people (largely through the church courts) than they were to do subsequently. Thirdly, there were more people in clerical orders, in proportion to the total population, than there would be in later times. This was partly because the regular orders, the monks, friars and canons regular, did not survive Henry VIII's reformation. It was also because a clerical training opened career opportunities, mostly in administration, for men who had no intention of 'living clerically' and serving a church, and who might well remain in minor orders all their lives, never proceeding to the priesthood. A third reason was that unbeneficed priests enjoyed very wide prospects of making or scraping a living as 'mass priests', serving altars in private chapels or in the very numerous chantry foundations of the period.

A little more needs to be said straightaway on the subjects of the Pope's authority, the canon law and the activities of the church courts. With regard to papal authority, it must be stressed that in the last medieval centuries this was no longer what it had once been; correspondingly, the royal authority over the church and churchmen had grown and was growing. The Statute of Mortmain, of 1279, which forbade laymen to alienate lands to the church without the *king's* licence, had pointed the shape of things to come. By the end of the thirteenth century the king had successfully upheld, against papal opposition, his right to demand for war purposes contributions from the 'spiritual revenues' of the clergy (income from lands held on condition of offering prayers, and income from benefices, tithes and so on). All through the period of the Hundred Years War and beyond, the English kings received regular subventions from clerical revenues, voted by the clergy in the Convocations of Canterbury and York; and they also succeeded in maintaining the principle that the Pope might only tax the English clergy for his own purposes with *their* permission. There was however one striking, visible and significant aspect of the papal authority in England which had not yet been eroded, though, as we shall see, there were some attacks on it too. This was the Pope's right to 'provide' to benefices, that is, to name the clerk who should be presented to a living. In canon law the Pope could claim the right to collate to all benefices, overriding the rights of patrons; in practice he only provided to benefices reserved to his gift, either by a general reservation (e.g. all archiepiscopal and episcopal churches; all benefices vacated as a result of a provision), or by a specific bull reserving a particular benefice. The first year's income from any benefice that was filled by provision was due to the papacy: these 'annates' were paid in instalments to the papal collector in England, who transferred the money to Rome through the Pope's bankers. A great deal of cash collected in England was credited abroad in this way, and the system was widely resented.

In theory, the papal right here was limited, from 1351, by the Statute of Provisors, which laid down that elections to bishoprics and the headships of greater collegiate churches should be free, and that patrons should enjoy the free exercise of their right of presentation; and that if these rights were interfered with by reservation or provision the king would present as 'patron paramount'. The Statute of Praemunire, of 1353, buttressed the earlier statute by making it an offence to take abroad cases cognizable in the king's courts (the right of presentation had long been deemed to be so cognizable). These statutes were not, however, rigorously or regularly applied. The king normally found it more satisfactory to work with the Pope, who was usually happy to accept royal nominees to high ecclesiastical office, to 'provide' them and to take his annates. Aristocratic patrons followed the royal example, regularly petitioning the Pope for provision to advance their clerical clients. The system of provision thus assured that the papal authority remained a real and living force in the ecclesiastical life of late medieval England.

Petitions for provision, and other matters concerned with preferment and benefices, brought a great deal of business from England into the papal court. There were requests for 'expectative graces', whereby the Pope reserved for a nominee (the suitor) a future vacancy, say the next stall falling vacant in a particular cathedral or collegiate church. Dispensations to hold more than one benefice on condition of making arrangements for a substitute to perform the duties were commonly sued for in the court of Rome. Disputed elections, disputed claims to provision and disputes between churchmen over their ecclesiastical rights and privileges all found their way there often enough; and the king, the archbishops and the orders of regular clergy all maintained proctors in the papal court to handle their affairs there. A great deal of more routine business got there too: the papal penitentiary for instance handled a great many cases concerning the regularization of marriages contracted within the prohibited degrees, even some involving quite humble parties.

The papal authority in England disappeared with Henry VIII's Act of Supremacy. The legal authority of the church courts and of the canon law did not disappear then, and have not yet entirely done so; but they have never been so relevant to so many people as they were in the time before that. The church's general authority in all matters pertaining to confession, penance and absolution spread the net very wide (to confess, once a year at least, was a general obligation on all Christians). Though disputes over dower rights and marriage portions were heard in the secular courts, matrimonial causes proper (with their implications for such matters as legitimacy) were the unchallenged province of the church courts. In England the church courts also exercised a jurisdiction in testamentary causes that was more extensive than in other provinces of the Western church. Cases arising out of the testamentary instructions to feoffees who were the common-law owners of a deceased landowner's estates usually went to Chancery, but the disposition of chattels was a matter for the church. It was in the bishop's court that a will had to be proved, that administration was granted to executors, and that those executors were ultimately discharged. In addition to their regular jurisdiction in cases between churchmen and churchmen in ecclesiastical matters, and between churchmen and laymen in such matters as the obligation to pay tithes or to maintain the fabric of churches, the church courts also quite often dealt with cases of debt, when the debts were small, although these were technically cognizable in the lay courts.

The higher clergy, bishops, abbots and heads of collegiate churches, enjoyed over and above their ecclesiastical jurisdiction extensive judicial rights as manorial lords, over men as well as property. In law their exercise of these rights was no different from the exercise of the same rights by lay landlords, but the extent of the church's properties meant that they gave churchmen, as an estate within the realm, a great collective social and political influence. After the dissolution of the monasteries, which carried so much property away into lay hands, that influence could never be the same again.

Another factor which contributed to the social significance of the clerical estate in the late middle ages was the measure of formal responsibility that the church took, and was expected to take, in the areas of what we would call social welfare. Hospitals for the care of the sick and leprous, and almshouses for the care of the aged, were ecclesiastical foundations. The majority of schools were under clerical control. The two universities of Oxford and Cambridge were great corporate clerical institutions, among the most important in the kingdom.

In the fourteenth and fifteenth centuries the craft guilds and religious fraternities – lay folks' associations – were taking up a larger share of welfare responsibility for their own members and their dependants who had fallen on hard times, but a great deal still fell to the hospitals. 'Hospital' is for this period a generic term, covering a variety of formally ecclesiastical institutions endowed by a patron or patrons for charitable purposes. It

includes almshouses for the aged and infirm, like the famous
hospital of St Cross at Winchester, founded by Henry of Blois
in the twelfth century and enlarged by Bishop Beaufort in the
fifteenth, or the almshouse attached to the church of St Michael
Royal in London, endowed by Richard Whittington. Other
objects for which hospitals catered included the provision of
hospitality for pilgrims and wayfarers, as at St Thomas's Hospital
in Canterbury or at the Pilgrim's Inn, Glastonbury (both were
popular places of pilgrimage), or at the God's House of Southampton, which was a kind of seamen's refuge. Some catered
specially for orphaned children or for women in misfortune, like
St Bartholomew in Spitalfields, which William Gregory described in the mid fifteenth century as 'a place of great comfort
. . . especially for young women that have misdone . . . [and are]
with child. There they are delivered, and into the time of purifica-
tion have meat and drink of the place's cost.' A good many had
been founded as leper houses; as the incidence of leprosy declined
in late medieval England, some of these became ordinary in-
firmaries, some asylums for the insane (our word Bedlam derives
from a foreshortening of the name of the old London hospital of
St Mary, Bethlehem).

What virtually all hospitals had in common was that their
foundation was associated not just with care but also with a
round of regular religious devotions. They were usually under
the direction of a warden or master who controlled the finances
and was responsible for the services, and whose office ranked as
an ecclesiastical benefice. There were plenty of good and honest
governors, but the system was open to abuse. Some treated their
office as a sinecure and did not reside, treating the office simply
as a source of revenue; some even held more than one hospital in
plurality. 'Many hospitals,' says the preamble of a statute of 1414,
'. . . be now for the most part decayed, and the goods and
profits of the same by divers persons spiritual and temporal
withdrawn to the use of others, whereby many men and women
have died in great misery for default of livelihood and succour.'
The fact that these words come from a parliamentary statute is a
neat reminder of the growing royal authority in the church. It
was the business of the ordinaries (usually the bishop) to see that
the masters and wardens of hospitals did not betray their foun-

ders' intentions; but here it is the king who commands the ordinaries to see to the matter, not their ecclesiastical superiors.

In education the church's role again was a prime one. About schools a great deal has been said in an earlier chapter, which it is not necessary to repeat here in detail. As we saw, a great many schools were parish schools: others were associated with collegiate or chantry foundations. Even when control of a school rested ultimately in lay hands (which was becoming commoner as time went on) the syllabus of studies remained the same as in the more numerous church schools, and most schoolmasters were in orders of some kind. A number of collegiate foundations provided, under the supervision of a warden, for the combined provision of a school and an almshouse, showing how the two matters, the teaching of the young and the care of the old, were associated in their benefactors' minds as linked aspects of the church's charitable activity.

The universities of Oxford and Cambridge, which apart from the Inns of Court were the only significant centres of higher education in the kingdom, were essentially clerical corporations. The church authorities insisted on their right to scrutinize their syllabuses of studies and the doctrines upheld in their schools; when Wyclif in 1380 stepped out of line in his lectures on the Eucharist he found there were only two alternatives, to leave Oxford or to be silent. Archbishops Courtenay and Arundel, in 1382 and 1411, firmly upheld at Oxford their right to visit and discipline the universities. Within the university, the privileged colleges were ecclesiastical corporations, endowed with lands and advowsons in the same way as monasteries or ordinary collegiate foundations, and were subject to the jurisdiction of visitors who were invariably churchmen. Though the number of laymen who came to the universities to study was gradually increasing at the end of the middle ages, the vast majority of their students were headed for clerical careers of one sort or another. Of the thousand or so scholars and students in each of the universities in the fifteenth century, most were in secular orders, but the monks and friars maintained houses at the universities for students from their orders, and the friars in particular played a leading part in scholastic debate.

Students who were professed religious were supported at

university by their own orders; a secular student needed funds of his own, or a patron, and the expense might be considerable (£6–8 p.a., at the least), especially if he hoped to proceed beyond the first degree in arts (a four-year course) to one of the higher faculties, theology, canon or civil law, or medicine. But the expense, if it could be met, was worth it. A university degree was for a clerk a splendid opening, especially towards an administrative career in the service either of the church or the Crown, or in some aristocratic household. The desire to make it easier for humble scholars to maintain themselves was a principal inspiration behind the numerous college foundations of the period (though college members remained a fortunate élite: most students had as yet no such association). New College, Lincoln College, All Souls and Magdalen at Oxford, and King's, Queens', St Catharine's, Jesus and Christ's at Cambridge, were all founded in the later fourteenth and fifteenth centuries. The preferences on which founders often insisted in the selection of fellows and scholars reflected their sense of obligation to their kinsfolk, their dioceses and their native regions, and facilitated the building of networks of ecclesiastical influence among graduates outside as well as inside the university.

Very considerable prestige attached to the universities. They represented the collective scholastic wisdom of the clerical estate in England. When the government required expert learned advice on such matters as its attitude towards the Great Schism between the Popes of Rome and Avignon (1378–1417), or towards the conciliar attempts to heal it, or concerning the justification of papal rights and ecclesiastical privilege in England and their limits, the universities and their scholars were the natural place for them to turn to. Their prestige, as clerical corporations, helped to maintain the prestige and influence of the clerical estate at large.

Perhaps the most striking feature of the clerical estate at large was the diversity of the kinds of people that it embraced, and in order to make discussion of it manageable it has to be broken down into its component groups. The first obvious distinction to be made is between regular and secular clerks. The 'regulars' means the professed religious, who had taken vows to follow a specific order, and were sworn to personal poverty, chastity and obedience. Most of the regular religious, nuns apart, were in priest's orders, though in all their orders there were still some unordained 'lay brethren'. The regulars may be subdivided again into two groups. On the one hand there were the enclosed orders, of monks, nuns and canons regular, who might not leave their cloister without permission and whose principal preoccupations, formally, were with maintaining their prescribed liturgical round of prayers in their churches and with contemplation. On the other there were the mendicants, the orders of friars whose vocation was apostolic and pastoral as well as contemplative, and who were not bound to the cloister but worked, from their convents, at large among the people (especially in the towns). The enclosed orders were endowed, and had perforce to involve themselves with the administration of the estates from which they maintained themselves and their churches: the friars followed a stricter rule of poverty, being dependent on the alms of the faithful, on offerings, on monetary bequests and the proceeds of their begging.

The secular clergy embraced a still more diverse variety of clerks than did the regulars. The first obvious distinction to be made is that between those in major and minor orders. Those in minor orders (who were very numerous) had taken the 'first tonsure' and might perform duties in church, such as that of parish clerk, or no clerical duties at all: they were permitted to marry and could not hold benefices. At each stage of the progression in minor orders, from *ostiarius* to *lector*, from exorcist to acolyte, there was an examination; it could be very perfunctory, but guaranteed at least a bare degree of literacy. The most distinctive privilege of the clerk in minor orders was that, if charged with crime in the secular courts, he could plead his 'clergy' (usually proved by the ability to read a short passage from scripture). In the fourteenth and fifteenth centuries this no longer secured him trial in the church courts, as it had once done: but it did mean that if convicted he could be handed over to his ordinary, to be kept in custody in the bishop's prison, rather than suffer the penalty of the secular law.

Those in major orders (subdeacons, deacons and priests) were committed to celibacy. In order to hold a benefice a man had to

be at least a deacon and twenty-four years of age, and be
'intending' to proceed to the priesthood (though all these limitations were subject to papal dispensation). A deacon might preach
and baptize: only a priest could celebrate the mass. In order to
be ordained, a man had to 'show title', that is that he was
assured of the means to maintain himself. Most of those who
presented themselves for ordination, who were often of very
humble status, obtained their title from religious houses, which
meant that the religious houses in question – in theory at least –
guaranteed their minimum maintenance (say 6 or 7 marks a
year). In fact this obligation seems to have been entered into
pretty nonchalantly, without any real intention of providing an
allowance if the need arose: it was a way round a technicality,
and there was probably often a small payment not from but to
the religious house in the background.

A second important distinction among the secular clergy, but
one much less well defined than that between those in minor
and those in major orders, was the difference between what one
might call the 'clerical élite' and the 'ordinary run' of the
priesthood. The difference here was essentially between those
who, in the course of their careers, were likely to be actively
concerned with the care of souls or the service of an altar at
parochial level (the ordinary run) and those who were much less
likely to be so (the élite). Clerks who had trained at university
and were graduates tended to gravitate towards the élite group,
though there were always some graduates among the parish
clergy (perhaps as many as one in six in the later fifteenth
century, fewer before that). So the difference was one that was
related to qualifications, and also, importantly, to the career
opportunities that they could open. In effect, there were two
alternative clerical career structures, more or less mutually exclusive. The way that the system worked here was very closely
related to the ways in which presentation to benefices, parochial
or otherwise, was obtained and exploited; and to explain what
was in issue here requires a brief digression.

There were some 9,000 parish benefices in England, besides a
large number of benefices without cure of souls – stalls in
cathedral chapters and in collegiate churches, wardenships of
hospitals and so on (these latter being usually better endowed

than parishes). The rector of a parish drew his income mainly from three sources, from his tithes of the wages or produce (usually taken in kind) of his parishioners, from the cultivation of his glebe (his share of land in the village fields) and from regular offerings and mortuary dues. A canon or prebend drew his income from the endowments (in land, or whatever) that had been given to support his benefice in perpetuity. The right to present to all except elective benefices (bishoprics and abbeys) lay with a patron; the king, it might be, or a bishop or some lord or gentlemen (in the case of parochial benefices often the lord of the manor). This right was considered to be a species of lay property, and disputes over rights of presentation were cognizable in the lay courts (with an eye to avoiding trouble, the Popes seldom exercised their right to provide to benefices that were in the gift of lay patrons, concentrating on those that were in the gift of churchmen). A great many patrons, in consequence, regarded their rights of patronage simply as a way of providing means to support themselves for clerks who were in their service, or for friends, or for relatives who were in holy orders. When the king presented a chancery clerk to a royal living, or some lord presented a clerk who was serving in his household to a living in his gift, he did not expect him to reside, but only to take the income and to maintain a stipendiary chaplain to discharge the parochial or other duties. The Popes used their right of provision similarly, to support servants in the Curia, or to enable scholars to study at university (this usually in response to a petition from the scholar, or his patron, or perhaps from the university itself).

Patrons also sometimes used their right of presentation to fund religious benefactions, by obtaining papal licence to 'appropriate' a rectory in their gift in perpetuity to a religious house or to a stall in a collegiate church. The religious house thereafter drew the principal income of the rectory, and presented to the living a vicar, entitled only to a fraction of that income (but a vicar was better off than a stipendiary chaplain, since he had a freehold in his vicarage and a security of tenure that the latter lacked). By the time of the Dissolution, it has been calculated that no less than 37 per cent of rectories in Engand were thus appropriated to religious houses. What was too often the result of the substitution of vicars and curates for rectors was thus summed up by Thomas Gascoigne:

the curate has less than nothing, almost, and not the wherewithal to live as a clerk, nor that from which he can help either his falling church or his faltering parishioners, so that there lacks to his parish proper priesthood, hospitality, the preaching of the word of God and good counsel.

Thus it was that the difference of career structure, which J. A. F. Thomson has described as dividing the secular clergy almost into 'two nations', arose. The graduate, or the talented young man who had caught the eye of a patron, looked for an opening in ecclesiastical administration or in the service of the Crown or of a nobleman, and hoped for the reward of a benefice from which to support himself. But it was not part of his intention that he should reside there, if he could help it, and certainly not permanently. If things went well, he might accumulate a number of benefices, with dispensation to hold in plurality: in due course he might come to aspire to the episcopate. That was the high road to success that was followed, for instance, by William of Wykeham at the beginning of our period and on which Wolsey was starting out at the end of it. There were a great many hopefuls, of course, who never got anywhere near as far as they, but a canonry and, say, a couple of livings would produce a fair income and support a decent measure of social dignity. Nothing to be rueful about, even if one had not made the top echelons.

For the large numbers of humble, less fortunate and less educated men who came forward for ordination the prospect was very different. At the outset such a one would have to look for casual payments, for his services at funerals, or for saying masses for some deceased person (the parish priest was inhibited from taking payment for this). In time he might hope for a more stable income as a chantry priest with a regular stipend, or even as a parish chaplain. Best of all he might hope to obtain a proper benefice – but probably not a very rich benefice, maybe a vicarage whose rectory was 'appropriated'. The evidence of the *Valor ecclesiasticus* shows that shortly after the end of our period half the livings of England were calculated to bring in

£10 or less. When the expenses of hospitality and the obligation to maintain the church fabric and the wages of at least one servant had been met, it was not a very ample way of life that what was left of £10 or less *per annum* would support, with the sort of result that Gascoigne described.

The conditions that have been outlined above were affected significantly, over time, by two factors with which we are now very familiar. Firstly, the spread of lay literacy and the rise of what has been called the 'lay bureaucrat' spelled a contraction of the opportunities in the royal or aristocratic administrative service for aspiring clerics, and ecclesiastical administration, with a place in a bishop's household as the first rung on the ladder, became more commonly the best opening to high preferment. In consequence the number of graduates going into parish work rose, though the rise was rather marginal. Secondly, the mortality among the priesthood as a result of the Black Death generated a crisis in the provision for the care of souls that even bishops who had no experience of parish work could not ignore. The parish clergy, because of their duty of visiting the sick and ministering to the dying, were peculiarly liable to infection: this did not enhance the attractions of their employment, and so helped to highlight to a laity beginning to be increasingly sophisticated in religious matters the shortcomings of those coming forward into the priesthood. In the writings of Wyclif, Langland and Gascoigne the inadequacy of parish clergy and the dearth of good men willing to take up the thankless task become recurrent themes.

The men whose responsibility it was to tackle the problems raised by the growing literacy and religious sophistication of the laity, and the problems raised by plague mortality among the priesthood, were the bishops. On the whole, their efforts have achieved no more than an indifferent press. Before we can decide whether they merit the faintness of the praise they have received, it seems necessary to ask what sort of men they were.

As has been said, very few of the bishops had had any serious experience of parish work. The proportion among them who were graduates grew steadily over the late medieval period. A number (again a growing number) were of high aristocratic birth: Archbishops Courtenay, Arundel, Bourchier and Neville all came from families headed by earls; Cardinal Beaufort was an illegitimate son of John of Gaunt; Archbishop Richard Scrope of York and Bishop Edmund Lacy of Exeter were among those of baronial stock. There were always a few scholars, like Thomas Bradwardine (Canterbury) and Philip Repingdon (Lincoln), and a few regulars, like Simon Langham (Canterbury), Ralph Brunton (Rochester) and Reginald Boulers (Lichfield). By far the largest number, however, had risen through the administrative service of either church or state. In 1350, six out of seventeen bishops had in their time been Keepers of the King's Privy Seal, and in the fifteenth century Thomas Langley of Durham, Henry Chichele of Canterbury, Philip Morgan of Worcester, the great canonist William Lyndwood of St David's, Cardinal Kemp and Adam Moleyns of Chichester had all held that office on their way to the top. And that is just part of the score of a single office.

The career of the great William of Wykeham may illustrate how the *cursus honorum* could work. Born of humble parents at Wickham in Hampshire, the good offices of a local patron (probably Sir Ralph Sutton) got him to school in Winchester. Having acquired there a grounding in grammar, he became secretary to the constable of the castle, and did well; and in 1347 he entered the royal service as clerk of the royal works. By 1361, when he (too) became Keeper of the Privy Seal, he had accumulated a very large number of benefices: he had acquired the rectory of Pulham, the deaneries of Lichfield and St Martin-le-Grand, and prebends in St Pauls, Salisbury, Hereford, St David's, and in the churches of Beverley Minster and Wherwell. These benefices, held in plurality, he vacated when, in 1367, after some hesitation on the part of Pope Urban V, he was provided to the see of Winchester and became Chancellor of England. Though he quitted that office in 1371 he was one of the King's Council through the minority of Richard II, played a prominent part in the stormy politics of the 1380s, and was Chancellor again from 1389 to 1391. He died, full of years and honour, in 1404.

Wykeham was not of course a typical bishop, but he was atypical only in the length of his career and the height of his

READ MORE IN PENGUIN

In every corner of the world, on every subject under the sun, Penguin represents quality and variety – the very best in publishing today.

For complete information about books available from Penguin – including Puffins, Penguin Classics and Arkana – and how to order them, write to us at the appropriate address below. Please note that for copyright reasons the selection of books varies from country to country.

In the United Kingdom: Please write to *Dept. JC, Penguin Books Ltd, FREEPOST, West Drayton, Middlesex UB7 OBR*

If you have any difficulty in obtaining a title, please send your order with the correct money, plus ten per cent for postage and packaging, to *PO Box No. 11, West Drayton, Middlesex UB7 OBR*

In the United States: Please write to *Penguin USA Inc., 375 Hudson Street, New York, NY 10014*

In Canada: Please write to *Penguin Books Canada Ltd, 10 Alcorn Avenue, Suite 300, Toronto, Ontario M4V 3B2*

In Australia: Please write to *Penguin Books Australia Ltd, 487 Maroondah Highway, Ringwood, Victoria 3134*

In New Zealand: Please write to *Penguin Books (NZ) Ltd, 182–190 Wairau Road, Private Bag, Takapuna, Auckland 9*

In India: Please write to *Penguin Books India Pvt Ltd, 706 Eros Apartments, 56 Nehru Place, New Delhi 110 019*

In the Netherlands: Please write to *Penguin Books Netherlands B.V., Keizersgracht 231 NL–1016 DV Amsterdam*

In Germany: Please write to *Penguin Books Deutschland GmbH, Friedrichstrasse 10–12, W–6000 Frankfurt/Main 1*

In Spain: Please write to *Penguin Books S. A., C. San Bernardo 117–6° E–28015 Madrid*

In Italy: Please write to *Penguin Italia s.r.l., Via Felice Casati 20, I–20124 Milano*

In France: Please write to *Penguin France S. A., 17 rue Lejeune, F–31000 Toulouse*

In Japan: Please write to *Penguin Books Japan, Ishikiribashi Building, 2–5–4, Suido, Bunkyo-ku, Tokyo 112*

In Greece: Please write to *Penguin Hellas Ltd, Dimocritou 3, GR–106 71 Athens*

In South Africa: Please write to *Longman Penguin Southern Africa (Pty) Ltd, Private Bag X08, Bertsham 2013*

READ MORE IN PENGUIN

THE PENGUIN SOCIAL HISTORY OF BRITAIN
General Editor: J. H. Plumb

Sixteenth-Century England   Joyce Youings

The Tudor period is generally considered to have been a time of great enterprise, a 'golden age' in the history of civilization. Here Joyce Youings exposes a darker side and reveals how inflation, poverty and the population explosion, changes in domestic affairs and the collapse of the traditional church affected the ordinary people.

English Society in the Eighteenth Century   Roy Porter
Second Edition

'A brilliant work of synthesis ... Porter has triumphantly accomplished what many regard as the impossible task of writing a book that is valuable both to the historian and to the general reader' – *London Review of Books*

Private Lives, Public Spirit: Britain 1870–1914   Jose Harris

'Provides the most convincing – and demanding – synthesis yet available of these crowded and tumultuous years' – David Cannadine in the *Observer* Books of the Year

British Society 1914–45   John Stevenson

With two world wars sandwiching the Depression years, the essential flavour of British society from 1914 to 1945 was one of moderation and consensus. John Stevenson creates a vivid picture of the trends and changes, from broadcasting and the cinema to mass unemployment, votes for women and improved welfare services.

British Society since 1945   Arthur Marwick
Second Edition

'A *tour de force* ... Without serious distortion or omission ... he moves dexterously through a wide variety of sources, ranging from poetry through film and novels to opinion polls ... it is astonishing how much he gets in' – *The Times Educational Supplement*

achievement. His story illustrates well some of the problems about episcopal leadership in the church of his day. It is not just that he lacked pastoral experience or that (if Pope Urban was right) his learning was questionable, or the fact that it was not for his spiritual gifts that Edward III put forward his name for the see of Winchester. Once he was bishop, he had so much on his hands as a great landlord, as a spiritual peer of the realm and as a member of the King's Council who was twice Chancellor of England that he was bound, in some degree, to neglect his diocese and its business. True, a diocese was adequately equipped in those days to run without its bishop. A suffragan bishop, very likely a mendicant, perhaps with a see in *partibus infidelium* or in Ireland, could almost always be found to discharge such necessary episcopal functions as ordination and confirmation. The bishop's vicar-general in spirituals acted administratively as his deputy, taking the oath of obedience to the bishop from incumbents, summoning and holding synods, examining candidates for the priesthood. In the consistory court the bishop's official (often the same man as the vicar in spirituals) presided. The archdeacons and rural deans carried out most of the routine local administrative work in their jurisdictions, and saw to the arraignment and fining of sinners. These efficient servants (just the sort of men whom a university education so often prepared for ecclesiastical administration) could run the business of the diocese very competently. But that is not the same as giving spiritual or pastoral leadership.

Nevertheless, and significantly, Wykeham's record as a bishop is impressive. In the Parliaments of Richard II's reign he showed himself a vigorous champion of churchmen's privileges. He was a great rebuilder of churches, was noted for his alms, and above all was a supremely generous patron of learning. The inspiration behind his twin foundations, St Mary's College at Winchester and New College, Oxford, was his desire to ensure sound training for poor clerks (especially from his native region) who would go on to hold responsible positions in the church as teachers and administrators. He was far from being alone among late medieval bishops in his anxiety to this end. The same ideas inspired Henry Chichele in his collegiate foundation at Higham Ferrers with an almshouse and a grammar school attached, and in the foundation of All Souls College; and Richard Fleming of Lincoln in his foundation of Lincoln College and William Waynflete of Winchester in the foundation of Magdalen College, both at Oxford. In an age when there was no formal, seminary-type provision for the training of the clergy, this sort of benefaction was an important contribution to the future stewardship of the church in England, but on the administrative rather than the pastoral side, it has to be added.

There were, however, those bishops who left a clear mark on the pastoral side too. Particularly impressive are the records of the two archbishops who had to face up to the crisis which clerical mortality in the first visitations of the plague presented, Simon Islip of Canterbury and John Thoresby of York. Both were men who had risen to the episcopate through the service of the Crown, and both were patrons of scholars at Oxford (indeed both helped John Wyclif in the early stages of his career). But both showed, in a moment of great difficulty, that they were concerned with much more than that.

Islip's early constitutions and vigorous visitation of his new diocese in 1350 indicate his concern at the demoralization of its clergy in the aftermath of the plague (of which his two immediate predecessors had died). Thoresby, once installed at York in 1352, set about what was nothing less than a recruiting drive to the priesthood, and made a point of attending ordinations himself. Starting with the York chapter, he opened war on non-residents, and on those clergy generally who were 'deaf, mute, and unaware of the bleating of the flock'. His constitutions of 1367 reveal him taking measures to secure at least a minimum income for stipendiary chaplains, to uphold the dignity of the clergy in matters of dress and to prevent the profaning of churches by the holding of markets in churchyards. Even more impressive were the efforts of both Islip and Thoresby to ensure basic standards of religious knowledge among the pastoral clergy, and to encourage their instruction of the laity. In his synod at Ely, Islip enjoined every priest to examine his parishioners' beliefs at confession, to study scripture and to preach frequently in English. The short *Libellus* that he composed, concerning the basis of ethical teaching, the Ten Commandments and the seven

deadly sins, is lost: but Thoresby's Latin Catechism is not. On his
instructions, it was translated into English, and came to circulate
widely under the title of the *Lay Folks' Catechism*. In the preamble
of the Latin version Thoresby reflected revealingly on his major
concerns, the ignorance of priests, the need to instruct the laity,
the importance of confession, penance, preaching and the proper
understanding of the articles of religion. He was clearly and
personally committed to a high standard of pastoral life and to
pastoral objectives.

The records of Islip and Thoresby do not stand alone; that of
Thomas Arundel in the next generation, who was successively
Bishop of Ely and Archbishop of York and then of Canterbury,
is in the same mould (and there are other bishops too whose
ministry may be compared with theirs, Richard Scrope and
Henry Bowet at York, and later, in his own strange way,
Thomas Pecock of Chichester). Arundel was an aristocrat, who
had become a bishop at twenty and who through much of his
life was deeply involved in politics, but his achievement in the
pastoral context was none the less remarkable. The bishopric of
Ely gave him influence at Cambridge (especially at Peterhouse,
founded by a former bishop), and this enabled him to gather
round himself at an early stage a group of educated and very
gifted clerks, including Richard Scrope, John Newton (a lover
of the works of the mystic Richard Rolle), and most important
of all, Walter Hilton (a university Bachelor of Civil Law), who
later, after he had retired into the Augustinian Priory of Thur-
gaston (Notts.), was to be the author of two of the most celebrated English mystical treatises of the age, *The Scale of Perfection*
and the *Epistle on the Mixed Life*. After Arundel went to York,
Scrope and Newton followed him thither; their books and
learning helped to build the chapter at York into a major centre
of religious and pastoral instruction in the north. As Archbishop
of Canterbury, Arundel is probably best remembered for the
rigour of his persecution of the Lollards, his banning of the
reading by the laity of the Scriptures in English and his visitation
of Oxford to purge it of Wyclifite heresy. This activity earned
him sharp criticism, not only from heretics but from some
orthodox churchmen too; to Gascoigne he was one who had
'stopped the mouths' of good priests and worthy preachers. But

there was a more positive side to his achievement too, especially in the impetus that he gave to the circulation of the English translation of the pseudo–Bonaventuran *Mirror of the Blessed Life of Jesu Christ*, by Nicholas Love, Prior of the Carthusian monastery of Mount Grace in Yorkshire. The long influence that Arundel enjoyed (he was appointed to Ely in 1373, became Archbishop of York in 1388 and of Canterbury in 1396, and died in 1414) made sure that his influence was felt widely, and in many churches besides those over which he presided directly. His influence and that of men associated with him had much to do with the dissemination of some of the most important orthodox English religious writing of the whole late medieval period. His story shows how important networks of connections could be in this age, not just in the field of ecclesiastical administration but also in the arena of spiritual direction too.

There were neglectful bishops, whose lives stand in contrast to those of such as Islip, Thoresby and Arundel; among men there will always be good, bad and indifferent even on the bench of bishops. The pastoral commitment of the best bishops, and some of the most influential, seems however clear. What remains to be questioned is how far one can trace any great impact of their noble aspirations among the lower clergy, who served parishes and sang at chantry altars. This question is a thorny one.

In his prologue to the *Canterbury Tales*, Chaucer was kinder in his portrayal of the parson than he was to most of his pilgrims:

> A good man was there of religioun,
> And was a pore Parson of a toun,
> But rich he was of holy thought and werk.
> He was also a learned man, a clerk,
> That Cristes gospel gladly wolde preche,
> His parischens devoutly wolde he teche.

Chaucer was here seeking to portray an ideal rather than a typical figure, but one can find men from real life who were not unlike his parson. One such was William of Pagula, who lived just before the beginning of our period. Though an Oxford-trained canonist, he chose to reside at his rectory of Winkfield, near Windsor, and is best remembered for the handbook he wrote for parish priests, in which he showed his eye for the same sort of virtues that Chaucer identified in his parson. There is advice on the manner of explaining the sacraments to the people, on the behaviour to be expected of the laity in church, on what to do if there are difficulties over tithes; speak to those concerned in a friendly way, says William, suggest you and they have a meeting with the archdeacon, at your expense, to talk the problem through. There are passages delightful in their humanity, like this on confession:

and the priest ought to inquire of the penitent, if he was drunk, how he got drunk; whether perchance he did not know the power of the wine, or because of the guests, or because of an exceeding thirst coming upon him.

It seems clear that parishioners of one such as William of Pagula, or Chaucer's parson, enjoyed educated and humane Christian pastoral care. But how many were there that were in that case?

That there was a reverse side to the picture that Chaucer drew of a parson is plain from less kindly literary comment and from such visitation records as survive. Here, for instance, are some of the entries from the record of Bishop Trefnant's visitation of the clergy and diocese of Hereford in 1397: the speakers are the jurors drawn from among the parishioners of parishes visited. At Werley

They say the vicar puts his horses, sheep and kine to pasture in his churchyard, to the great shame of the church . . . they say the maintenance of the bell ropes is the vicar's responsibility, but he will do nothing . . . they say the vicar refused the sacrament to John Stapildon, of the parish, because he would not pay tithes to him at his pleasure: *item*, they say the vicar was away for six weeks, and made no arrangements for finding a substitute to take his services beyond what the chantry chaplains already do.

Or again:

The parishioners say the vicar of Langwardine is supposed to find two chaplains to take the services at St Wenard's, but he does not: *item*, that

Sir John the chaplain at St Wenard's haunts taverns and there his tongue is loosed, to the great scandal of all: *item*, the said Sir John is incontinent with one Margaret, no one knows her surname: *item*, the common fame is that the said John is illiterate, and incapable of the cure of souls.

The common run was no doubt somewhere in between Chaucer's ideal parson and the situation at St Wenard's. The standard of literacy expected of candidates for ordination and for presentation to a benefice was not high, but examinations were not a sham. 'Surely I cannot of my conscience admit him to it, for his learning is marvellous slender,' the vicar-general of the York diocese wrote to Lord Clifford, of the candidate whom he wished to present to his living of Londesborough. On the whole most parish priests were at least literate, even if not learned. There was plenty of good advice about their duties available to them. William of Pagula's *Oculum sacerdotis* was only one of a number of similar handbooks: among those that circulated most widely were the *Pupilla oculi* (based on his work), the *Manuale sacerdotum* of John Myrc, and his vernacular verse instructions for parish priests. Some of this good advice must have rubbed off. What evidence there is suggests that most parish priests were reasonably conscientious in instructing their flocks in the faith, in hearing confessions and saying their masses, and in preaching to the people. There were plenty of collections of sermons in the vernacular to guide them in discoursing on the gospel story and its message, the meaning of the Passion, and Christian social duty (though there is something of a dearth of new collections as time goes by, and maybe the message, orthodox and uplifting as it essentially was, may have grown somewhat trite in repetition).

Nevertheless, there is little doubt that because by and large the parish clergy were underpaid they were by and large undereducated, and probably most were under-inspired too. It was unfair to blame on these counts men who through no fault of their own were not well off, had limited command of Latin and very limited access to books, and who had a ministry to discharge that was exacting and fraught with everyday human complications. Naturally, though, they did get a good deal of blame. It was by no means easy for men such as they were to maintain the dignity of the cloth, on which Archbishop Thoresby laid such emphasis, in the eyes of a laity of whom steadily more were coming to be able to read religious books and form their own religious attitudes.

Commonly the parish priest was by no means the only priest in the parish. It will be recalled that in 1397 at Werley there was complaint that, when the parish priest was absent, he made no arrangement for services 'beyond what the chantry chaplains already do'. A chantry chaplain's business was to say mass, either in a private chapel or at a side altar in a church, for which he received a stipend. In the late middle ages there was an enormous proliferation of chantry foundations. In the church of Newark on Trent, for instance, there were no less than fifteen chantries at the end of the fifteenth century, most of them endowed by various guilds within the town (guilds were great patrons of chantries, but individual benefactors – bishops, lords, gentlemen, burgesses and merchants – were profuse in their foundations too). Some chantries (as those at Newark) were perpetual, and as benefices gave security of tenure to their chaplains: more were temporary, endowed for a period of years, and at the end of that term their chaplains had to look for something else. Some carried duties over and above the saying of masses, for instance maintaining a school, but most chantry chaplains were simply mass priests: they were not concerned with the care of souls.

A stipend as a chantry chaplain offered an opportunity to an unbeneficed priest of humble origins and limited education to scrape together a living which, if bare, was probably better than what he might have hoped to make as a smallholding peasant or an artisan. That was one of the chief reasons why there were so many seeking ordination, and why the clergy were such a numerous element in the population. The prospects, moreover, might be better than that of just scraping a living: with a stipend, and the chance to add to it by saying masses at individual requests, by officiating at funerals and so on, a chantry chaplain might make himself better off than a parish priest at less labour. That is why Langland complained of parsons who

Asked leave and license in London to dwell,
And sing requiems for stipends, for silver is sweet.

Archbishop Islip, in the aftermath of the Black Death, was anxious on the same score, about priests who neglected the care of souls, devoting themselves to saying masses and charging exorbitant fees for it. So was his colleague Thoresby who was anxious too about how chantry chaplains spent their time when they were not saying mass. He detected a tendency to spend the day in wandering in the fields, in visiting friends and in gossiping. Unfortunately, because the patrons of chantries or their feoffees often had a free hand to hire (and fire) their own chaplains, the bishops had only limited control over them. Chantry priests could be of assistance to a parish priest, and chantry benefactors could help parish funds if there was a surplus after the chaplain's stipend had been met. On the whole, though, there were probably too many chantries, and too many chaplains who were under-learned and under-dedicated for comfort in the matters of clerical discipline and maintenance of respect for the cloth. Doctrinal questions of the value of prayers for the dead quite aside, it is not surprising that, after the Henrician reformation had swept away the houses of the regular religious orders in the sixteenth century, the chantries soon followed in their wake.

To the regular religious orders, and the part that they played in the ecclesiastical life of late medieval England, we must now turn. Like the bishops, they have had rather poor publicity, both from contemporary critics and from historians. In their case, there is perhaps rather less to put into the credit side to counter-balance the traditionally prevailing adverse view.

For the monks and the canons regular, the late middle ages were a difficult time. As landowners on a large scale, they were hard hit by the long-term consequences of the Black Death, by declining rents and rising labour costs, and it was less easy for them than for lay landowners to compensate for the drop in income. Monks could not seek profit from Crown office or from fee'd service nor attempt to enlarge their estates by good marriages, as laymen could. The building schemes in which abbots so delighted ran their houses into debt more easily than

ever; even maintaining existing buildings could be strenuous.
The efforts of abbeys, in these trying circumstances, to maintain
income levels by vigorous enforcement of their seigneurial rights
probably accounts for the noted hostility displayed towards
them by the rebel peasants of 1381. Later, as abbeys, like lay
landlords, took to leasing more and more of their demesnes,
abbots and priors tended to take into their own hands more of
that financial control of their houses' revenues which they had
once shared with such officials as the cellarer and the almoner
(the 'obedientiaries'). This was all very well if the abbot was an
able administrator, but could have disastrous consequences if he
was spendthrift or incompetent.

There were other kinds of difficulties too. The Great Schism
caused particular problems for the Cistercian houses, since
Cîteaux, the mother house of this close-knit family of monasteries, was in the Avignon obedience and England adhered to
Rome: the confusion helped to undermine discipline. Those
Black Monk priories which had a mother house in France (and
this included all the Cluniac priories) experienced similar difficulties as a result of the Hundred Years War. Because many of
these 'alien priories' had at least a few foreign monks they
became objects of suspicion, and at the outbreak of war their
lands were seized temporarily into the king's hands and farmed
out for the time being to the highest bidder. Most of the larger
houses, such as Lewes and Montacute, ultimately obtained
'letters of denization' and became independent. The smaller
houses and cells were in effect disendowed in 1414 by an act of
Henry V. It was with the lands of one-time alien priories that a
number of important new church foundations of the period
were endowed: St George's Chapel at Windsor, Wykeham's
foundations at Winchester and Oxford, the Carthusian Priory of
Mount Grace, Eton and King's College, Cambridge.

Apart from the foundations of Edward III at St Mary Graces
and of Henry V at Bethlehem and Syon, and a handful of
Carthusian houses (of which more presently) there were no new
monastic foundations in the last century and a half of the English
middle ages. The appropriation of parish churches apart, the
flow of benefactions to existing houses more or less dried up. A
few aristocratic families kept up traditional connections with

particular monasteries, as the Percies did with Whitby and
Guisborough, and the Scropes with the Premonstratensians at
Easby, but thriving gentry (and a good many aristocrats too)
tended rather to invest what they had set aside to pious uses in
chantry foundations and colleges of secular priests. Vocations
were a problem too. The monasteries were very hard hit by
plague mortality: in many, half or more of the inmates were
carried off by the first pestilence. Numbers recovered, but
slowly: by the end of the fifteenth century they were probably
proportionately as high as they had been before 1348, but not as a
gross figure.

The kind of men that the monasteries were attracting were,
moreover, not of very influential standing, socially; for the most
part they were drawn from the middling and lower land-holding
classes, and from the burgesses of the towns. The days when the
abbey of Ely had seemed a fitting preferment for a cadet of the
great comital house of Clare, or Glastonbury for Henry of Blois,
the king's kinsman, were buried now in the remote past. For
institutions that, as great corporate landlords, had the wealth
that might have permitted them to play a significant part in the
kingdom's political life, this was not a promising sign. Significantly, the number of abbots who sat as spiritual peers in
Parliament dwindled in the late middle ages. When Abbot
Clown of Leicester obtained from Edward III excuse from
parliamentary service for himself and his successors, it was
considered as a boon by his house, not an indignity.

In the internal life of the monasteries, in the round of liturgical
services enjoined by the rule of St Benedict, there was no major
change in this period. The virtual disappearance of professed lay
brethren meant that the Cistercians, who had originally put such
emphasis on the part of work (*opus manuum*) in the monastic life,
now farmed their estates with wage labour instead of their own
manpower. Thus the houses of the various branches of the great
Benedictine family came to resemble each other more closely in
their way of life and there was less variety in their interpretations
of the rule. In the greater monasteries formal standards of
discipline and observance seem to have kept up fairly well.
Under such an abbot, say, as St Albans enjoyed from 1369 to
1396 in Thomas de la Mare, things were not going to slip;

besides building magnificently, he was ascetic in his personal life, punctilious in the performance of the canonical hours and a devoted visitor of the sick. There were other leaders in the same mould, like John Wessington, Prior of Durham from 1416 to 1446, or Marmaduke Huby, Abbot of Fountains from 1494 to 1526. But there were also men of a different stamp, like William Sadyngton of Leicester who, to quote Hamilton Thompson, 'neglected the services of the church, kept the offices of treasurer and cellarer in his own hands, rendering no account for them, employed a large and useless body of lay servants, and missed no opportunity of making money, to the extent of maintaining a resident alchemist' (in the hope of finding a way to turn base metals into gold). Under such leadership things could not go well.

In the smaller monasteries it was not difficult for things to get into quite a bad way. When Bishop Alnwick of Lincoln visited Bardney Abbey in 1438 he found that Brother Thomas Barton was accused of adultery; Brother Reginald Partney had goods of his own and liked playing dice; Brother John Hole had excused himself from his course in saying mass; and the brothers in general were straying down into the town and mingling with lay people. At Dorchester in 1441 he found that the canons were going hunting and hawking and frequenting taverns; women had visited Thomas Tewksbury's room in the evening; and the abbot was accused of keeping his mistresses (five of them) at the common expense. These were exceptionally bad cases: there are plenty of visitation reports that 'all was well'. But it seems likely that often it was not *very* well. The English Benedictine houses in the fourteenth and fifteenth centuries produced a few good scholars like Ughtred Boldon, in Bishop Ralph Brunton of Rochester a great preacher and in John Lydgate a poet of distinction. But to the great contemplative religious literature that flowered in late medieval England the Black Monks and Cistercians made no contribution. Outside the Charterhouses and a few houses of the Augustinian canons it looks as if the fires of spiritual vigour and of holiness of life were burning rather low.

Chaucer's monk was a 'manly man', well-mounted, who 'loved venery' and enjoyed a dinner of roast swan: the portrait is

more that of a country gentleman than of a professed religious.
That was the role, probably, in which the monks and the
monasteries now seemed, for most people, to have their principal
social impact. Their abbots hunted with the local gentry, and
might play a part at lovedays to allay local quarrels (but not of
course on the commissions of the peace); the abbeys offered
hospitality to passing lords, gentlemen, maybe even the king
and – to do them justice – to wayfarers and pilgrims too. Of
Abbot Clown of Leicester it was written in his praise that he
was

a lover of peace and quiet in his own neighbourhood; everywhere a
reformer of quarrels and wrongs; an untiring follower of good works
. . . amiable to the great men and magnates . . . in hunting the hare he
was reckoned the most notable and renowned of the lords of the
realm.

When this was the sort of way in which an admirer could
write of a personally pious and much-loved abbot, it can hardly
be surprising that there were some who questioned whether the
monks did enough religiously to justify their wide possessions.
In 1371, and again in 1385, 1404 and 1410, schemes of partial
disendowment were raised in Parliament. Langland thought the
time was approaching when the monasteries would 'take a
knock from the King'. If Wyclif's angry and repeated calls for
secular foreclosure on the wealth of the 'possessionate religious'
had not tainted schemes of disendowment with the suspicion of
heresy, there might have been a move against the monastic lands
long before Henry VIII's time (though doubtless a much less
drastic one).

The Charterhouses offer a corner of light in this gloomy picture
of late medieval monastic life. This ascetic order, with its eremitic
ideal and strong emphasis on contemplation, did attract aristocratic benefactors, and a number of new houses were founded,
among them the London Charterhouse: Henry V's magnificent
foundation ('Bethlehem') at Sheen; the de la Poles' Charterhouse
at Hull; and the foundation of Thomas Holland, Duke of
Surrey, at Mount Grace in the Cleveland Hills. Nicholas Love,

the translator of the *Mirror of the Blessed Life of Jesu Christ*, was
Prior of Mount Grace; and it was in Carthusian houses that the
first English translations were made of the great writers of the
continental *devotio moderna*, Ruysbroek and Thomas à Kempis.
The same connection brought the writers of the English mystical
school, Richard Rolle, Walter Hilton and Julian of Norwich, to
continental attention for the first time. The Carthusians were
too small a spiritual élite, and too firmly enclosed an order, to
have a very wide influence: it has been calculated that there
were probably not more than about 175 inmates all told in their
eight houses. Nevertheless it is no accident that it was to them
that St Thomas More at one time felt he might be called, before
he decided on marriage and a secular career, or that they were
among the most determined of the religious in their resistance to
the dissolution.

The house of the Bridgettine nuns at Syon, founded by Henry
V, was another centre of the reading and study of the works of
mystical writers, both continental and English. In some other
nunneries too there may have been quite an interest in the
English mystical works (as there was also among pious women
in the lay world). Richard Rolle had been a spiritual counsellor
to the nuns of Hampole, and their house became the centre of
his cult. Mystical works appear from time to time among
bequests of books from kinsfolk to individual nuns of various
convents, though not as commonly as other books, primers or
breviaries. Most nuns were literate readers in the vernacular,
though not in Latin, which for them needed to be translated;
their knowledge of French, even after the school of Stratford-
atte-Bow of Chaucer's prioress, seems to have declined after
c. 1400.

In most respects conditions in convents were very comparable
to those in religious houses for men. In terms of endowment
they were on average poorer, and some of the smaller houses
were very poor indeed: they encountered the same sort of
problems in maintaining their landed income and struggling with
debts as many monasteries did, only rather more acutely. In a
world of mostly male landlords an abbess probably had a harder
task as steward of her house's goods than an abbot did. Visitation

records suggest that there were plenty of places where discipline
was slack, again as in monasteries but with some differences of
tone. Female tantrums could be a source of trouble and so could
feminine vanity, in itself harmless enough but deemed inappropriate to religious life. In 1397 the ladies of Nunmonkton
had to be warned

not to use henceforth silken clothes, and especially silken veils, nor
precious furs, nor rings on their fingers, nor tunics laced up or
furnished with brooches . . . after the manner of secular women.

We hear of some cases of serious moral lapses. At Catesby in
1442 Bishop Alnwick learned that the prioress had been surprised
in the arms of a priest, one William Taylor, and that Isobel
Barnet had borne a child to the chaplain of the house; at
Godstow, Oxford scholars were in the habit of calling at the
convent, and Dame Alice Longspey had been carrying on an
affair with a chaplain who she pretended was a relative. In terms
of straight discipline, however, the record of the convents seems
on the whole rather better than that of male houses.

There was one respect in which convents and monasteries did
differ somewhat, and it may have something to do with the
widespread air of lack of religious fervour in the former: the
inmates of nunneries were of decidedly superior social status.
Those classes that set their womenfolk to work did not make
nuns of their daughters: those whose unmarried daughters would
demean themselves by working did, and were ready to pay to
make them so. Sir John Daubriggecourt in 1415 directed in his
will that his daughter Margery should have 40 marks if she be
wedded to a worldly husband, £10 and twenty shillings rent 'if
she be caused to take the sacred veil': John Syward, a wealthy
London fishmonger, left to his daughter Domenica £40 'so that
she may either marry forthwith, or become a religious, at her
election'. There was always pressure to find places for young
women in nunneries, and because of the comparative poverty of
so many convents the 'dower' that they were expected to bring
with them to the house was important. It could be a matter for
some tough negotiation.

It would be wrong, naturally, to suppose that all nunneries

were filled simply with women whose relatives were glad to be rid of responsibility for them. There were also ladies with genuine vocations, prominent among them pious widows who preferred after their husbands' deaths to enter religion. We hear too of a few determined spirits who, in defiance of the pressure of relatives and conventional expectations, refused to be immured and won the backing of the ecclesiastical authorities for their refusal. Altogether though, there were too many nuns whose presence in a convent had nothing to do with religious vocation. It was only natural that many of these retained a taste for a touch of finery, looked for excuses for trips away from the cloister, and liked to entertain in it people who, on a strict interpretation of the rule, ought not to have been there. So it is not surprising that, Syon apart, few nunneries were noted as centres of spiritual fervour: but they did their bit none the less. They maintained their observance, boarded young children whom the nuns helped to bring up and sometimes looked after aged and infirm persons as well. They also provided a certain dignity for well-born women whose lives, if they had had to be spent outside the cloister, might have been more forlorn and frustrated.

The four orders of friars, the Franciscans, Dominicans, Austins and Carmelites, were the youngest of the orders of the regular religious. In the thirteenth century St Francis's example of apostolic poverty had caught the imagination of a whole age, and in their ministrations to the laity the friars had been the shock troops of spiritual revival. By the fourteenth and fifteenth centuries their initial zeal had cooled, and they had become part of the ecclesiastical establishment. They were very numerous. Their town churches were large, sometimes including guest chambers 'for lords and ladies therein to rest'. They were confessors to the great, and the well-to-do helped to adorn their churches. They had also begun to attract some of the fiercest of all the criticism that was contemporarily levelled at the clerical estate.

The set themes of anti-mendicant satire recur over and again in the literature of late medieval England. There are too many friars; they swarm 'as thick as motes in a sunbeam'. They abuse their privileges, especially at the universities (where they could take an accelerated course); their begging is importunate; their morals are loose. Chaucer's friar knew the taverns of the town and the houses of the genteel better than the hospitals, and could coax her last mite out of a widow. They 'spoil the people with lying and hypocrisy; I leave to speak of stealing of women', a Wyclifite wrote. Above all, the critics united in anger over the ease of the friars' confession and their absolution, bought for gold and undermining simultaneously the people's morality and the pastoral authority of the parish clergy:

> The friar with his physic this folk hath enchanted,
> And plastered [absolved] them so easily, they dread no sin.

So says Langland; and his great poem ends with the picture of a friar stealing his penny from the dying Contrition.

It was natural that the friars should attract hostile attention. Because their orders were not enclosed and they wandered at large in the world, their backslidings were all too visible. They really were too numerous for their own good, and attracted too many whose vocations wore thin with time. Their ministrations could complicate relations between parish clergy and their flocks, and the fact that they were responsible to the authorities of their own orders and not to the bishops could be more than just administratively inconvenient. Nevertheless, the strictures of the literary satirists were not wholly justified, and tell less than the whole truth, painting a picture altogether too dark.

The friars were the greatest preachers of the age, and the popularity of such books as the Dominican John Bromyard's *Summa praedicantium* attest the impact of their teaching. Their preaching style, using homely anecdotes from everyday life to illustrate the truths of Christian belief and Christian morality, made an impression that learned exposition of sound doctrine – such as Wyclif and Gascoigne dreamt of – could never have made. The friars took the lead in answering Wyclif's academic challenge to orthodoxy, and mendicant scholars such as John Cunningham and Thomas Netter showed themselves well worthy of their adversary in scholastic debate. Both pastorally and academically the friars in the late middle ages continued to exercise a powerful and respected influence, even if it was not quite as powerful or as sharp as in the days when Francis and his first disciples seemed to offer a new model of charity and spirituality.

Perhaps the most telling tribute to the esteem which the friars continued to enjoy comes from the evidence of bequests to them and to their churches in the wills of the laity. They are more often mentioned in these than any of the other religious orders. In fifteenth-century Norwich, Dr Tanner has found that some 45 per cent of testators whose wills survive included bequests to them, usually for requiems, sometimes for the performance of chantry services, quite often requesting burial in their churches. The corresponding figure for London wills is 36 per cent, for York wills about a third. People at large, it seems clear, retained a confidence in the ministrations of the friars, and a respect for their dedication and poverty that we would not guess at from the testimony of their all too eloquent literary detractors.

Some of the best English writing of the late middle ages, especially that of those two great masters in their native tongue, Chaucer and Langland, is strongly critical not just of the friars but of the clergy in general. Naturally this makes a powerful impression, but before we label the age as anticlerical and antisacerdotal, three points need to be remembered. The first is that if anticlericalism is understood in the modern sense that implies hostility not just to the clergy but to the doctrine and the social morality that their teaching seeks to uphold, then there was none. The second is that criticism of the clergy is always and inevitably rife in a priest-ridden world; it is the price that its clergy pays for their social prominence. The third is that a great deal of the criticism of the clergy in late medieval England came from within the ranks of the clerical order itself, from men who far from being hostile to clericalism, wished for an improvement in the standards of clerical education and exemplary living, and for a stronger spiritual lead from the clergy. What we have learned of in this chapter suggests that their concern was justified, but concern is an ambiguous indicator; it can be a sign of disease, but it can equally be a healthy sign.

The late medieval church in England showed its strength in the way that it weathered the problems generated by the pesti-

lences, the Great Schism in the church, and the challenge of the
Wyclifites' heresy. It is difficult to argue that it was in a state of
acute decline or facing a crisis of confidence. It is not so difficult,
though, to argue that the clergy were too well entrenched in
established ways, and that the tenor of their orthodoxy was too
flat, especially at the pastoral, parochial level. In an age when
growing literacy was awakening and enlarging the religious
awareness of the laity, there was danger here. It made it less easy
for the clergy to command the degree of respect necessary to
uphold their traditional social distinction and independence as a
privileged estate, and too easy for the secular establishment to
think that, since they paid the piper, they might be entitled to
call the tune, in ecclesiastical as well as other spheres.

11. *Popular Religion*

To attempt to describe the religious outlooks and attitudes of a past age is always a hazardous and delicate task, perhaps especially so for one who in a different time subscribes to the same creed. Yet the attempt has to be made, and of the late middle ages it can at least be said that there is more evidence about the religion of more people, beyond the ranks of the ecclesiastical and social élite, than there has been before (much of it derived from the vastly greater number of surviving wills). There is enough here to make it abundantly clear that, whatever questions may be raised with regard to earlier periods as to how far Christianity had penetrated down to the popular level, England was by now in the fullest sense a Christian country. The difficulty comes, of course, when the inquiry reaches the point where conventional observance and personal conviction begin to intersect and interact, and the historian finds himself trying to open windows into men's souls, which are always and in any age a great deal more diverse than their observances.

Diverse and diffuse the subject ahead certainly is. A jumble of topics jostle for attention: saints' cults, purgatorial belief, charitable activity, religious societies, anchorites and anchoresses, church architecture, funerary monuments and rites. Each on its own offers a fascinating field for inquiry, but the pieces seem often reluctant to fit together into a single jigsaw. The two best-defined tendencies of the time, the mystical movement and the evangelical, proto-Protestant Lollard heresy that looked to the Oxford philosopher, John Wyclif, as its founding father, seem to stand in such sharp contrast with each other religiously that it is hard to credit them growing out of the same soil. In looking in turn at some of these subjects and at the problems of interpreting the past that they raise, we will be wise to remember that religious history is always three faceted. Religion is a social phenomenon, and has therefore to be viewed in its relation to the social structures of the day. Religion also has its fashions and conventions, which cannot be explained solely in terms of social structures: they demand independent probing too. There is always, thirdly, an inner and spiritual facet to religion, relating to these others but distinct from them. Here the individual soul and its pilgrimage comes into the picture, especially the pilgrimages of those great souls who had the power to influence their society and the moods of its belief.

Let us start at the opposite end of the spectrum from the great souls. One of the most familiar, most unlovable, and most 'medieval' figures in Chaucer's band of pilgrims is the pardoner, with his indulgence 'all hot from Rome' and his bag of pigs' bones to flog to the credulous poor as relics. Indulgence was a thriving trade, because it fed on what I have called the contemporary 'fashion' of belief. Indulgence remitted not only sin, but purgatorial penance as well; and that burden could also be lightened by the intercessions of the saints and the prayers of the living. In the conventional religion of the late medieval ages, concern with the relief of penance in purgatory is perhaps the most striking feature. The pardoner prospered because men were ready to buy indulgence from him, and when they came near to having to render up their account, they were anxious to buy it in other ways too, as their wills and bequests make abundantly clear.

Medieval purgatorial belief is an area where there is a need to guard against being too simplistic and too condescending in approach. The church (and not just the church of Rome, the others too) has never wavered in its traditional teaching that ultimate salvation depends on God's grace, freely given, which neither human merit nor human prayer can condition. Christ atones for our sins: we cannot. But it has been and in the middle ages was the traditional belief that the prayers of the living can be of benefit to the faithful departed. The doctrine of purgatory, which developed precision in the course of the thirteenth century, seems to have evolved in response to a feeling both among church leaders and among the ordinary faithful that the terms within which this belief could be given formal and human expression stood in need of clearer definition. The enthusiastic, and sometimes over-enthusiastic, reaction to that clearer definition is telling witness to the need in question. It found profound literary expression in Dante's *Purgatorio*: it also unleashed a torrent of benefactions and bequests, large and small, to pay for prayers for souls in purgatory, which it is not always easy for a twentieth-century mind to apprehend with appropriate 'empathy'.

The provision of prayers for the dead was the impetus behind the very numerous chantry and college foundations of the late middle ages. Of chantries and their number something has been said in the last chapter. A college was in effect a corporation of chantry priests, praying for the soul of the founder, and perhaps of his kinsmen and patrons too. It could be extra-parochial (St George's, Windsor, is a famous example), but more often a parish church was 'appropriated' to the new collegiate foundation. This could be of incidental benefit to the parish; as Gascoigne put it, 'a parish church is well appropriated where it itself becomes a college, that is so that certain worthy persons shall remain in that foundation and so improve life in that parish which is thus made collegiate'. A college foundation normally provided for a master or warden and a number of fellow chaplains in the college, and the round of its liturgical observance was carefully laid down in the founder's statutes (which would ensure, if there was an almshouse or school attached, that the prayers of bedesmen and children would be added to those of the chaplains for the soul of the founder, such prayers being the principal object of the foundation).

There was an impressive number of these foundations. Among those founded by the great magnates there was the Duke of York's college at Fotheringhay, the Nevilles' college at Staindrop, the Percies' at Kirby Overblow, the Mortimers' at Stoke-by-Clare. Great captains who had made fortunes at the wars were also generous (many of them had a great burden of sins to shift). Sir Hugh Calverley founded a college in the church of Bunbury in Cheshire, Sir Robert Knollys a college and an almshouse at Pontefract; Sir John Fastolf would have founded a college at Caistor if his executors had not cheated his pious intentions. The great merchant Richard Whittington founded a college and an almshouse in his London parish church of St Michael-le-Paternoster. Colleges such as these were sufficiently well endowed to secure their wardens and fellow chaplains in at least an adequate measure of comfort and security. The fact that the ordained priesthood, and only the ordained priesthood, could celebrate the masses that could speed a soul's journey through purgatory was the key to securing them such endowments, and so to helping to preserve the clergy both in their dignity and their numbers.

One did not of course have to found a college to secure masses for the safety of one's soul. They could be bought outright, and enough was spent on them to justify fully, at any rate on the face of it, Dr Malcom Vale's assertion that 'the laity had one overriding concern – the fate of their souls in the afterlife'. The wills even of the humblest, where they survive, usually leave something for lights, for candles and lamps to burn at the church altar and at the shrines of the saints who would intercede for them. As one goes up the social scale the bequests for masses after death, for trentals (a mass thirty days later) and on the anniversary of the obit become more and more ample. Joan, Lady Cobham, paid for 7,000 masses to be said after her death. Richard, Earl of Arundel, left the enormous sum of 1,000 marks to maintain prayers for his soul in the chapel of Arundel Castle. 'Unto whom much is given, of him much shall be required,' says Scripture, and the rich responded: if battering could open the gates of Heaven, the sound of the masses sung for their souls ought to have done it.

What their wealth secured to the well-born at and after their passing, the religious fraternities of towns and parishes secured for many less-well-off people, and this was one of the reasons why these guilds and fraternities flourished. They were infinitely numerous. Since a great many (especially in country parishes) had no property and left no records, a full tally will never be reconstructed: but we do know, for instance, that in Northamptonshire alone at the beginning of the sixteenth century there were over a hundred, and they were thick on the ground in many other shires, perhaps especially in East Anglia. The better-off guilds, as has been noted in a previous chapter, were great maintainers of chantries, at whose altars masses were said for their members, living and dead. The provision of funeral rites and masses was a universally prominent purpose in guild statutes (it is here worth stressing again that most religious guilds opened their membership to men and women alike). The following rules of the guild of St George at Lynn are fairly typical:

Ordained it is, that what brother or sister be dead of this fraternity, the alderman shall warn ... all the company ... man and woman, that is within the town, to come to the exequies of him or her that dead is ... and be ready to bear them to church, and to offer for the soul as the manner is to do for the dead ... And also ordained it is, that what brother or sister so ever be dead of this fraternity, he shall have said for his soul 60 masses.

Within their means, the fraternities did not stint on their prayers for members who had passed over. They were also prepared to spend generously on some other related religious activities. On the guild's patronal feast, all were expected to gather to hear mass, and there would be a dinner afterwards, subscribed from common funds. Some, like the Guild of the Resurrection at Lincoln, also provided assistance for members going on pilgrimage:

if any brother or sister wishes to make pilgrimage to Rome, to St James of Galicia or to the Holy Land, he shall forewarn the guild, and all the brethren and sisters shall go with him to the city gate, and each shall give him a half penny at least.

The cult of the saints and pilgrimage were of course matters closely connected with the safe passage of the soul in this life and in purgatory after it. The saints were patrons, and powerful ones, at the court of the heavenly kingdom: 'they may be glad and blithe that have such a patron of their place that is of power to pray for them both night and day,' says the author of the life of St Robert of Knaresborough. Pilgrimages were often prescribed by confessors as penance for sins, and most places of pilgrimage had an indulgence attached to them which those who completed the journey automatically obtained.

Pilgrimages and the cult of saints and their relics would demand a place in any account of English religion in earlier medieval centuries, and so they do in the later age. In their history there is much that is generally and entirely conventional, and some aspects that reflect the fashions and tone specific to the late medieval period. Just occasionally it offers glimpses of a more inner spiritual story, of which so far we have not heard very much.

Chaucer, depicting in his wife of Bath a lady whose conventional 'churchiness' was a significant element in her will for social prominence, told of how she had been to Rome, to the shrines of St James at Compostella and of the three kings at Cologne, and to the Holy Land (three times, no less). As usual, his hand was sure; pilgrimages were enormously popular. In January and February alone in 1434 royal licences were granted to John Widerous, master of the *Christopher* of Bristol, to carry eighty passengers on their way to Compostella; to Roger Brok, master of the *John* of Portsmouth, to carry sixty passengers bound on the same journey; to John Nicoll, master of the *Cok John* of Fowey, to carry fifty; and to Thomas Marshall, of the *Katherine* of Hull, to carry thirty. This begins to look almost like a tourist trade. So does the advice to pilgrims to the Holy Land put together later in Henry VI's reign by William Wey, fellow of Eton. This reads rather like a guide-book, with its accounts of the sights on the way that must not be missed, its advice about what one should pay for a bed in Venice and its tips for the final stage of the journey:

When ye shall get your ass at Port Jaffa, be not too long behind your fellows, for an ye come betimes ye may choose the best mule or ass . . . and ye must give your ass man [for] courtesy a groat.

For some travellers at least, though, there was a good deal more to it than mere tourism. Margery Kemp, burgess wife of Lynn, was as fashion-conscious as any in her pilgrimages, but when she stood on the holy ground at Calvary, she was truly moved; she wept and cried, for in 'the sight of her soul' it was 'as if Christ had hung before her bodily eye in his manhood'.

The journey to Jerusalem (or to Compostella) was, of course, an expensive one, but for those who lacked funds, or feared the foreign fleas, the fluxes, the sea-sickness and other discomforts of long-range travel, there were plenty of domestic shrines, and very popular they were. The most frequented were those of St Thomas of Canterbury and of Our Lady at Walsingham; the road into Walsingham was known as the Palmers' Way, and the town was full of inns and hospices. The shrines of Joseph of Arimathea at Glastonbury, of Cuthbert at Durham, of the Confessor at Westminster and the Holy Cross at Waltham also attracted many pilgrims, and there were many lesser local shrines too. Indeed the author of the prologue to the *Nova legenda Angliae*, a famous collection of English saints' lives, gave it as his view that the store of merit that native saints had accumulated for domestic shrines was so great that there was no need for people to go abroad on pilgrimage.

Pilgrimage and the cult of the saints are matters intimately associated, and there is no doubt about the reverence shown towards the latter in more general ways. The books of hours, which in the late fourteenth century were coming to be common possessions among the nobility, give us glimpses of particular personal attachments to particular saints, of Thomas of Woodstock to the Magdalen, for instance, or of Countess Mary Bohun to the Virgin. In this matter of saints' cults we note again a strong and, it would seem, a growing attachment to native saints. There was a distinct revival of interest in the English saints of early days, to which church iconography bears witness. The Northumbrian saints Chad, Wilfrid and John of Beverley all figured prominently in the new fifteenth-century glass of York Minster. In London the cult of St Erkenwald flourished and at Salisbury that of St Osmund. Cults also gathered round the reputations of contemporary holy Englishmen, and the miracles attributed to them testified that the native strand in sanctity was a living force. The nuns of Hampole kept the shrine of Richard Rolle (d. 1349), and treasured his relics; a three-year-old child who had fallen into a well was reported to have been revived by his power, after the mother had presented a candle the length of the child's body at his tomb. Richard Scrope, the saintly Archbishop of York who was beheaded in 1405 for his part in the revolt against Henry IV, was commemorated in the Minster glass: he came to be regarded as a patron of seamen. In the early sixteenth century more than forty model ships were to be seen around his tomb, votive offerings of mariners who had sought his protection. Neither Scrope nor Richard Rolle achieved formal canonization, but the Austin canon John of Bridlington (d. 1379) did, and his cult achieved national prominence. Henry IV and Henry V were both patrons of his shrine, and John Capgrave, when he re-edited the *Nova legenda* in the mid fifteenth century, added to it an account of his life. He too was a miracle worker, and in time came to be associated with a much-conned collection of prophecies, in which a number of events of the times (including the death of Archbishop Scrope) seemed to be foreseen.

The veneration of relics is a special aspect of the cult of the saints. Every major church had its reliquary, and the relics of the holy men of the new generation came to be treasured alongside those of older saints and fragments of the True Cross. Those of John of Bridlington were displayed to pilgrims at his tomb; Scrope's head seems to have been preserved in the nunnery of St Clement in York. The public reliquaries of churches were not the only places where one might meet relics though; we also hear of them, and quite frequently, as prized personal possessions of the well-off, kept in the home (most often in the family's private chapel, no doubt, but clearly not always). The wills of Thomas, Earl of Warwick, Thomas, Earl of Oxford, Edmund, Earl of March, and John, Lord Bardolf, all give directions about fragments of the True Cross. Sir John Fastolf possessed an arm of St George and a finger of John the Baptist. William Haute had a 'piece of that stone on which the Archangel Gabriel descended when he saluted the blessed Virgin Mary'. These talismans of power might be treated as heirlooms: Sir Robert Radcliffe of Hunstanton directed in his will that his 'purse broded with gold and pearl' and the relics in it should be in the keeping of 'his daughter Anne, on condition that she let her sister Elizabeth have them when she needed them, and so in time of need to be common to them both'. Here we catch a glimpse of a familial strand in the religion of gentlefolk that we shall encounter again in other contexts.

Much of what we hear about relics and their veneration seems conventional and unprofound, and sometimes it seems precariously balanced at the line where religion blends into superstition and trust in magic. But there was something more than that, surely, about the fragment of the True Cross that Elizabeth Scrope, who came of a notably religious family, wore daily about her neck in a setting; it brought her into a personal, direct, everyday contact with the sacred. Even in this seemingly unpromising quarter in the religious history of the time, the personal, interior strand in the history of late medieval spirituality breaks occasionally into that of conventional practice and formalized, fashionable veneration, to remind us that the two cannot ever be fully separated.

All that we have been looking at so far, indulgence, pilgrimage, the cult of the saints and relics, focuses on the relation between this world and that other world to which men can only pass through the door of death. It is not surprising therefore that the moment of passage and the funeral rites which would mark it were matters to which a good deal of thought was given. It was also a point where the relation between religious practice and contemporary social structure intruded sharply into the picture.

A desire for a decent burial, in this world's terms, seems to have been a very common and general one, as indeed one might expect: it is still a common wish. The religious fraternities and parish guilds did much to secure this for their members: as we have seen, all the members of the society were expected to turn out to accompany the body of a deceased brother or sister to the church and to attend the funeral. The obligation is so prominent in their statutes that these associations have sometimes been called 'burial societies', though this does less than justice to the range of their activities. The rich, when it came to their time, were prepared to spend conspicuously on fitting obsequies, in the same way as they were ready to spend freely on masses for the dead, and with the same end, to make sure that a crowded church sent up a resonant volume of prayer for the soul of the deceased at this crucial time. There would be great sums spent on mourning cloth, on torches and candles, on doles to the clergy and in alms distributed to the poor as a last merit-earning gesture of charity on the dead person's behalf. The funerals of the wealthy and well-born also offered an opportunity for display that was intended to reflect the dignity of the departed and of his lineage; here we see the familial and social side of religious practice intruding once more into the scene. Ralph, Lord Neville of Raby, directed that his body should be borne to burial in a chariot drawn by seven horses: it was to be carried into the church on the shoulders of eight soldiers, four displaying his arms 'of peace' (his tourneying device), and four his arms of war (the family coat of arms). Sir Brian Stapleton (d. 1394) directed that his funeral procession to Helaugh Priory should be headed by 'a man armed with my arms, with my helm on his head, and that he shall be well mounted and a man of good looks, of whatever condition he is'; and that his tenants should gather at the church in 'blue gowns'. The parvenu Pastons put on a tremendous show when John Paston died in 1466; indeed, as Colin Richmond says, they probably 'overdid it' in their determination to show that they had 'arrived'. The body was accompanied from London to Norfolk by a priest and twelve poor men carrying torches: as it lay overnight at St Peter's Hungate in Norwich, 38 priests, 39 choir boys, 26 clerks, 4 torch bearers, the Prioress of Carrow and the anchoress of her house surrounded it. The high sum of £50 in gold and silver was distributed in alms at the funeral.

Here family pride, social aspiration and conventional practice in alms-giving and dirges are to the fore: this makes the more significant another kind of direction that we encounter from time to time in wills, and which stands in sharp contrast. Here the note is unconventional, personal and spiritual. In the wills in question, which are nearly all of them in English, the testator castigates himself as a traitor to God, decrees that no pomp shall attend his burial, that his 'stinking carrion' shall be placed in the earth in a plain russet cloth with no great procession accompanying it and no great tomb to be raised above it. Here the inner voice speaks clearly:

I acknowledge me unworthy to bequeath [God] anything of my power, and therefore I pray him meekly of his grace that he will take so poor a present as my wretched soul ... my wretched body to be buried, when I die, in the next churchyard God vouchsafe, but not in the church but in the uttermost corner as he that is unworthy to lie therein.

A number of these wills come from knights who were suspected of Lollardy (as that of Sir Thomas Latimer, quoted above), but some are those of unimpeachably orthodox figures, like Archbishop Arundel, and others again come from men who cannot by any stretch be associated with the proto-Protestantism of the Wyclifites. Robert Throckmorton, for instance, wished to be buried without ostentation, but he died on pilgrimage (whose value the Lollards denied), and was ancestor to a strongly recusant Warwickshire family. These wills are not so much symptoms of heretical leanings (though in some cases they may be) as of that private, inward-looking strand that we have seen elsewhere and in other ways breaking through conventions, and of which we shall see more.

The poor were buried, as they had been time out of mind, in their parish churchyard. In the later middle ages, there was a strong predilection for burial in the parish church even among noble families, even though they often had particular connections with large monastic churches that their ancestors had helped to found; and among the gentry the preference was still more marked. The effect was to give some parish churches the air virtually of family mausoleums, with heraldic emblems and memorials of locally dominant lineages stamped in their glass, on stonework and statuary, and on monumental brass. John Laughton, esquire (d. 1467), directed that his body should lie by his wife's in the church of St Peter at Leeds:

with a stone of marble upon us both with a great scutcheon of my arms and the arms of my said wife to be set in the middle of the stone, with all my daughters in arms with their husbands upon my right side, and all my sons in arms with their wives on my left side, and with my father, grandfather and ancestors in small scutcheons at my head.

John Pympe, esquire, of Kent paid for the arms of all the county families with which he could claim kinships to be displayed in the windows of the church in which he was buried. Sir William Etchingham decorated the windows of the nave of the church of Etchingham, which he rebuilt, with the arms of his family and the principal Sussex gentry who were his neighbours and kinsfolk, and a brass figure of him, in full armour, was placed over his grave before the altar step. These are just a few random examples from the host available of memorials in parish churches which could help to remind humbler men of the dignity of their social superiors, and that the respect that they had borne them in life entailed a duty to pray for them when they were gone.

The late middle ages were a great period of church building and rebuilding. The rich Bristol merchant William Cannings's achievement in the magnificent reconstruction of St Mary Redcliffe on cathedral scale and Sir William Etchingham's rebuilding of his village church are at opposite ends of a wide spectrum. It was also a great age of extension of existing buildings, of adding clerestories above the nave, perhaps above all of the building of towers and spires at the western end of parish churches and of the purchase of bells to hang in them. To this work not only wealthy patrons, but also the guilds and ordinary parishioners, cooperating together under the direction of their churchwardens, contributed with striking generosity. The landscape of the English countryside would look very different without this great constructional drive on the part of the people of the fourteenth and fifteenth centuries: its parish churches are indeed the most telling testimony that there is to the sense, among high and low alike, of the centrality of their local churches in both the religious and the social life of their communities.

Another area of activity in which individual patrons, guilds and parishioners were notably involved, and one related to the foregoing because its focus was so often the parish or the locality, was charity. Whether it be deemed a matter of convention or something more, there is no doubt that the corporal acts of mercy were attracting a new measure of explicit attention. They are carefully enumerated in Thoresby's *Lay Folks' Catechism*; Nicholas Blackburn had them illustrated in glass in a window he commissioned for All Saints Church in York. Visiting the sick, the relief of members who had fallen on hard times, the support of widows and the upbringing of orphaned children are all obligations prominent in guild statutes. Both guilds and individual patrons, as we have seen earlier, contributed to the upkeep of hospitals, schools and almshouses.

The philanthropic benefactions of individuals that can be traced in wills and household accounts, and from chronicles, are infinite in their variety. Alms-giving was a traditional obligation of the wealthy, and some of it was pretty indiscriminate. Richard II is said to have distributed alms to over 12,000 poor people when he was in York in 1396, and his household accounts suggest that the figure is not wildly exaggerated. Funeral doles were normal and made no distinction between the deserving and the undeserving poor. A good deal of generosity seems, however, to be more thoughtful and more personal. John, Lord Neville, left 200s. to be distributed among his ploughmen, carters and shepherds. John Constable, esquire, enjoined his son, as his executor, to pay his household servants justly, 'so that they have reason to pray most heartily for my soul': bequests to servants and ex-servants, often named, are common in the wills of merchants and townsmen, and their wives. In a rather similar mode, we find Sir John Dependen leaving 100s. to the needy and bedridden of Helaugh, his native town; Richard, Lord Scrope of Bolton, leaving a mark to each blind beggar in Richmondshire; John Osay of Hull leaving £10 for the relief of divers prisoners; William Pysford of Coventry leaving provision for faggots for the poor for ten years against 'the most coldest season of winter'. Others left money for dowries and clothing for poor young women (often of a particular parish) who otherwise might not be able to marry. Another philanthropic object that very commonly surfaces in wills is the bequest of money for purposes useful to the local community, for the building and repair of bridges, and the making and upkeep of roads and ways.

Some historians tend to view this kind of charitable activity largely in terms of a shift of fashion in the ways and means towards what Professor Rosenthal has called 'the purchase of paradise'. 'The medieval mind,' he writes, 'made no distinction between an eventual sacerdotal and a social end of charity.' The principal concern of benefactors, it is implied, was with the savings of their own souls, so that there was no essential difference between providing sums for the saying of masses, and grants and bequests towards good works (whose beneficiaries would have a duty to pray for the benefactor). There is something in this view, certainly: quite a number of sermon texts can be adduced in support through their express subscription to the view that God permitted poverty so that the rich might have a means to save their souls. It tends, however, to be too all-embracing, and to forget that there is a self-regarding element in virtually all philanthropy. It is admittedly a Lollard text that asserts that it is more meritorious to offer a candle to a poor man to go to bed, or to a poor woman that she may see to spin, than it is to give it to a church, but others too could see the distinction. The Franciscan William Woodford, defending the social commitment of the friars (which the Lollards questioned), is revealing about the socially oriented penances that he, as her confessor, had enjoined on the Lady Margaret Marshal. They had involved contributing to the repair of bridges and roads in the neighbourhood of her home at Framlingham Castle, and her account book reveals outlays for just this purpose.

It is hard not to see some connection between the more personal, socially directed and eclectic fashions in charitable giving, and a strand in late medieval English religion very different from its preoccupation with the fate of the soul after death, the strong emphasis on the humanity of Christ. In the round of the church's year this found expression in the new prominence of the feast of Corpus Christi, and the story of Christ's human life provided the climax to the great play-cycles associated with the festival. In religious literature, Love's *Mirror of the Life of Blessed Jesu Christ* underscored the warmth and value of human family life through its presentation of the life of the Holy Family, with Mary sewing and spinning, and the child Jesus helping her by running 'on her errands'. Langland's picture of Jesus going to joust in Jerusalem 'in his helm and hauberk of human nature' makes a similar point in a different mood. So too, in the field of charity, does the injunction of the *Lay Folks' Catechism*, 'first men should feed the poor, for in that they feed Jesus Christ [as] he himself saith in the Gospel'.

It was again the human aspect of Christ that stirred Duke Henry of Lancaster, in his *Livre des Seyntz Medecines*, to set his mind on 'the precious flesh, which was bound by its nature to shiver and shrink from this hard Passion', and to compare Christ's love for man's soul to a child's longing for a red apple. In this book, in which a great and successful aristocrat and warrior looks inward at the tally of his shortcomings – his pride, his violence, his affairs with loose women – and propounds spiritual cures for them, the author's sense of Christ's human example and injunctions bring us up directly against the private, interior strand in late medieval lay piety, that stands in such contrast to its external conventionalities.

Among the signs of this inwardness, two developments are often adduced, the growing interest among the well-born in the right to hear mass in a private chapel and also in the right to have their own confessors. About the significance of the former one must be cautious; private chapels were certainly popular with the gentility, but they were not retreats for private prayers; the whole household gathered in them, and they did more, probably, to foster the sense of social identity and respect for the master in this group than to encourage personal devotions. But the privilege of having one's own confessor did bring a strongly personal element into what was called 'ghostly counselling'. The duty of regular confession had been enjoined and defined (once a year at the least) by the Fourth Lateran Council (1215), and much of the early impact of the friars was connected with their role as confessors. By the middle of the fourteenth century most noblemen had their own confessors, who were often friars (the Lancastrian family, for instance, habitually chose theirs among the Carmelites). Works connected with confessional and penitential practice and discussions of the seven deadly sins, like the *Book of Virtues and Vices* and the *Mirror of the World*, were popular and could become treasured possessions. Just how meaningful, in personal terms, confession and penance might be depended, of course, both on confessor and penitent; a great many, no doubt, liked a complaisant spiritual adviser. It is clear enough, though, that people with strong religious feelings – like Margery Kemp – did attach importance to who counselled them and to the quality of the spiritual guidance they offered.

Another popular source of 'ghostly counsel' (as opposed to confession in the strict sense) was that of anchorites and anchoresses, which again Margery Kemp rather fancied, for the same sort of reason. We hear a great deal, in late medieval

England, of religious recluses, of hermits dedicated to a solitary life and of anchorites proper, who had voluntarily and formally enclosed themselves in a cell, usually attached to a church or a religious house, in order to lead a life of contemplation. For their sustenance these solitaries were dependent on the charity of the faithful of the neighbourhood or of a particular patron. They are quite frequently mentioned in wills. John, Lord Roos, in 1392 left 20s. each to seven recluses at Byland Abbey, Beverley, Harpham and Helmsley; Ralph Neville, Earl of Westmorland, in 1424 left 20s. to every recluse in the dioceses of York and Durham. Both their intercession and their advice was highly prized. Richard II sought the advice of John of London, the long-lived recluse of Westminster, in 1381; so later, did Thomas of Woodstock, Duke of Gloucester; Henry V came to him on the night of his father's death in 1413, for counsel before he ascended the throne.

Two famous recluses call for special mention, for they carry us at last into that company of 'great souls' that it was promised we should meet at the beginning of this chapter. One is Julian of Norwich, who immured herself at the church of Carrow, Norfolk, and gave herself over to a life of contemplation there. She wrote movingly, in her *Revelations of Divine Love*, of her mystical practices and experiences, the first of which came when she was sick, as she thought, to death and saw the crucifix that the priest held before her changed:

I saw the blood trickling down the crown of thorns hot and fresh and right plenteously . . . like to the drops of water that fall off the eaves of a house after a great shower of rain.

She was deeply revered, and gave inspiration to many, among them the less convincingly genuine ecstatic, Margery Kemp.

The other solitary who calls for special attention is Richard Rolle, the hermit of Hampole in Yorkshire. Rolle was of an older generation: he died, probably of plague, in 1349, and he was a prolific writer. In the late fourteenth and fifteenth centuries his works achieved a very wide circulation: a group of northern aristocratic families (the Scropes and Stapletons prominent among them), the English Carthusians, the nuns of Hampole, and a number of fellow recluses all played a part in gaining wide attention for them. The most popular among them were his *Incendium amoris* (fire of love) and his vernacular translation of the Psalter, originally written for the recluse Margaret Kirkby, which gave in its glosses an account of the author's solitary life, of his attachment to the Holy Name of Jesus and of the physical sensations that were integral to his spiritual experiences: 'in searching the scripture, I have found that the highest love of Christ consists in three things, fire, song and sweetness'. After his death a flourishing cult grew up at Hampole, miracles were reported and his shrine became a popular resort of pilgrims.

Subjective experience lay at the heart of Rolle's religious life, teaching and writing. Its highly emotional content inspired a number of York clergy and some of the Carthusians to spend time and energy in making sure that his mystical teaching was relayed to the laity alongside other texts and in a manner that would guard against spiritual indiscipline and unorthodoxy. Out of this grew the presentation to the laity of what came to be called the ideal of the 'mixed life'. The germ of the idea came originally from St Gregory, who distinguished between the purely contemplative ideal of the hermits and monks and the compromise between active and contemplative living that their calling imposed on the pastoral clergy. Walter Hilton and the author of the *Cloud of Unknowing*, both of whom had read Rolle critically, adapted this old ideal of the 'middled life' that Gregory had proposed for pastors to the spiritual needs of the laity. The author of the *Cloud* speaks of men 'that be ful graciously disposed, not continuously as it is proper to very contemplatives, but then and then to be parceners in the high point of contemplation'. It was for such, for temporal men who had 'received of the gift of Our Lord grace of devotion' but were too busy to be constantly about 'ghostly occupation', that Hilton wrote his *Epistle of the Mixed Life*. It became the handbook for those who wished to know of the exercises proper to the life 'sometime contemplative and sometime active'. If there be any such, wrote the Carthusian prior Nicholas Love, 'let him look to the treatise that the worthy clerk and holy liver Walter Hilton the canon of Thurgarston wrote in English'. This advice was heeded, and in the fifteenth century the works of Hilton, like those of Rolle and often in company with them, came to circulate widely in pious families and circles among the nobility, the gentry and the mercantile classes. How they were valued this colophon in a London merchant's copy of Hilton's *Eight Chapters Necessary to Perfection* will attest:

This book was made of the goods of Robert Holland for a common profit. [And let] that person that hath this book of the person that hath power to commit it have the use of it for the term of his life . . . and when he occupieth it not, lend he it for a time to some other person. And let that person to whom it was committed for the term of his life under the foresaid conditions deliver it to another person for the term of his life. And so be it delivered and committed from person to person as long as the book endureth.

There is some evidence that the mixed life had a special appeal to women of the better-off classes. This is not surprising: business was not so pressing in their lives as in those of their menfolk, so that they had more time at their disposal to develop their spiritual faculties, if they were so inclined. Women certainly figure largely among those whom we know, from wills and inventories, to have possessed works of the contemplative authors. At opposite ends of the social scale of a feminine spiritual élite, Lady Margaret Beaufort and Margery Kemp both took vows to be chaste from their husbands, so as to be freer for ghostly things: the taking of such vows by devout women (in later life, usually) seems to have been not wholly uncommon. The 'devotional literacy' of some pious and well-born women is really rather striking, as this account of the daily round of Cicely, Duchess of York, tells us:

She is accustomed to arise at seven o'clock, and has ready her chaplain to say with her matins of the day . . . when she is fully ready she has a low mass in her chamber, and afterwards she takes something to recreate nature and so goes to chapel . . . thence to dinner, during the time whereof she has reading of holy matter, either Hilton of contemplative and active life, Bonaventura *de Infancia*, the Golden Legend, St Matilda, St Katherine of Siena . . . in the time of supper she recites the reading that was had at dinner . . . After supper she disposes herself to be with her gentlewomen, to the following of honest mirth, and one hour before her going to bed she takes a cup of wine, and after that she goes to her private closet, and takes her leave of God for all night.

In humble circles there was neither the time nor perhaps the taste for the kind of elevated reading that Duchess Cicely and her gentlewomen followed, but a devotional literacy of a less-elevated order had by the fifteenth century penetrated far down the social scale. Once pictures had been called 'the books of the layfolk', and there were still those many whose basic knowledge of the Christian story came from their 'reading' of what they saw in the glass, the images and the wall-paintings of their churches. But these were no longer the only 'books' for ordinary people. Many quite humble persons possessed primers with the Paternoster, perhaps the Hours of the Virgin, and the litany in English, and there were English aids to following the services, such as the *Lay Folks' Mass Book*. Collections of English sermons, like John Myrc's *Festiall*, circulated more widely than just among the clergy; and so did religious poetry, including William Langland's astonishing *Vision of Piers Plowman*. What these texts retailed about the Christian faith and Christian living could reach even further than the circle of the literate, for those who could not read had now so little difficulty in finding others who could read to them, and would.

Reading and listening whetted the appetite for a better understanding of the Christian faith, and taught men to consider their Christian living in personal terms, looking inward:

> Contrition, faith and conscience is truly *Do Well*,
> And surgeons for deadly sin, when shrift of mouth faileth:
> But shrift of mouth more worthy is, if man be truly contrite.

It was inevitable that, in the context of reflection on injunctions such as this from Langland's *Piers*, new religious questions should be raised among the laity and new responses evoked; and that they should wish to judge more for themselves. The old barrier between lettered priests and 'lewd people' was beginning to wear thinner.

*

The 'devotional literacy' of a wide sector among the laity was the foundation on which Lollardy, the first popular heretical movement of the English middle ages, was built. On its own, popular religious speculation could not have strayed into such a defined set of unorthodox attitudes and tenets as those that gave their colour to Wyclifite Lollardy, it is true. Religious literacy was nevertheless a precondition of this development. There was now a spiritually alerted public of persons able to read, who through their reading could reach out to a wider circle of listeners and thinkers. Whether they were literate in the strict sense or not, such listeners could latch on to a teaching that offered a radical challenge to conventional ways in religion just as easily as they could absorb more orthodox spiritual nourishment.

Many of the views that Wyclif urged (especially his criticism of the papacy, of indulgences and of the monks and friars) could strike a chord of sympathy among the wholly orthodox: and one can find echoes of them in the writings of such as Langland and Chaucer (whose idealized parson was indeed charged by the miller with talking like a 'loller'). What made Wyclif different, and in the long run made it possible that he should found a sect, was the intellectual coherence of his ideas. Deeply influenced by the Neoplatonist teachings of St Augustine, he made God's foreknowledge of all things the foundation of being in his philosophy. This led him to give exceptional weight to the authority of Scripture, God's holy book that he had provided for the guidance of men made in his image – the 'mirror of eternal truth', as Wyclif called it. This in its turn led him to his querying of papal authority (the word 'pope' is not found in the Bible, he pointed out), and to his virulent attacks on the regular religious, whose rules he denounced as human, fallible additions to the already perfect rule of Scripture. His philosophy also made him a rigid predestinarian and so affected his view of the church: the 'true' church was not the church of the Pope or of the priests, but the body of God's elect, chosen as vessels of his grace before all time. From this stemmed directly Wyclif's questioning of the priestly power of absolution and his followers' questioning of the value of pilgrimage, of intercessionary prayer and of the veneration of images. Predestination also gave a special slant to his ideas on dominion and on property rights. True lordship, he taught, being founded in grace, can only be enjoyed by those who are in grace; the temporal dominion of ecclesiastics (such as that exercised by the Pope) and temporal ecclesiastical endowment (as enjoyed by monasteries and 'possessionate' clergy) were products of the accidents of secular history, and had nothing sacred about them. Finally, his attack on transubstantiation was based on what he saw as philosophical absurdities in that doctrine of the mass, in combination with a common-sense refusal to deny what eye and touch told him, that the bread and wine at the communion table remained bread and wine after consecration as before.

Justification by faith apart, Wyclif's teachings anticipated most of the central positions of the sixteenth-century protestants, indeed of the more radical among them. But Wyclif was an academic (virtually the whole of his adult life, bar the last four years, was spent in Oxford), and he wrote in Latin. His teachings would never have reached a wider world, and would never have made the stir they did, but for the determination of his friends and disciples, notably his Oxford colleagues Nicholas Hereford and John Aston and the secretary of his last years, John Purvey, to make them available in English translations and to propagate his ideas by preaching. As a result, by the early fifteenth century a quite remarkable *corpus* of Wyclifite writings in English was in circulation: the modern printed editions of them run to many hundreds of pages of texts. They included tracts, manifestos, sermons, paraphrases of key parts of Wyclif's major Latin works and compendia of theology with a Wyclifite slant. But the most important product in English of the early Wyclifites was, of course, their translation of the whole of Scripture out of the Latin Vulgate into the vernacular. It was a tremendous collaborative achievement of learned men who had been touched by Wyclif's call (uttered in Latin) that Holy Writ should be made available to lay folk in their mother tongue. 'By this means,' as the Leicester chronicler lamented, 'that which was formally familiar [only] to learned clerks and to those of good understanding has become open to the laity, and even to those women who know how to read.'

Dr Anne Hudson has called the Lollard movement that was

nourished on this literary diet 'the premature reformation', and
the name is just, for like the sixteenth-century reform Lollardy
had a political side to its religious programme. Wyclif and his
disciples argued explicitly that the secular authority should step
in if the ecclesiastical authorities would not stir towards the
measures and the doctrines that they advocated. In 1410 a
disendowment bill, based on an earlier Lollard tract, seems to
have got as far as presentation in Parliament: it calculated that
the confiscation of ecclesiastical temporalities would support
financially 6,200 squires, 100 almshouses, 15 new universities,
and 15,000 additional pastoral clergy. By this time the clerical
establishment was arguing – and in the light of this bill justifiably
– that Lollard views constituted a threat to the whole property-
owning establishment and to the secular as well as the ecclesiastical social hierarchy. That was the thinking behind the
act *De Heretico Comburendo* (for the burning of heretics) of 1401
which brought state power into the battle against unorthodoxy:
as it was also the thinking behind Archbishop Arundel's ban of
1409 on the possession or reading by laymen of English translations of Scripture. When, in January 1414, the Lollards did
attempt a coup against Henry V, led by the heretic peer Sir John
Oldcastle, Lord Cobham (who had escaped from the Tower
after his condemnation in Convocation in the preceding
autumn), the point was proved. It was also proved how premature Lollard dreams of reformation were. The abortive rising of
1414 discredited Lollardy in the eyes of the secular establishment,
and discredited it finally: after this, there was no chance of its
becoming a significant force at a political level.

In its earlier days, Lollardy had attracted some quite signifi-
cant support in some religiously conscious quarters within the
secular establishment. Particularly prominent in this context
were a group of knights, mostly associated with the court of
Richard II, whose patronage visibly helped to found and foster
Lollard communities in localities where they had influence. Both
Sir Thomas Latimer at Braybrooke (Northants.) and Sir William
Beauchamp at Kemerton (Glos.) presented Oxford-educated
Lollards to livings in their gift. The Cheyney family of Buck-
inghamshire were early patrons of the long-lived Lollard com-
munity in the Chilterns and of their pastors. In the late fourteenth

century we can see a kind of network of Lollard groups growing up both in towns such as London, Bristol and Northampton, and in specific localities in the countryside, with gentlemen and burgesses (like the Lollard mayor of Northampton, John Fox, an acquaintance of Latimer's) supplying patronage and protection for them and their teachers, and university-trained scholars and priests supplying the translated texts that made Wyclif's teaching accessible to lay folk. The structure is very much the same, in fact, as that which permitted the wide dissemination of teachings derived from the mystical writers, Rolle and Hilton, but the doctrine is different – and from an establishment point of view dangerous. After 1414 had made that danger sharply apparent, the establishment patronage disappears: we hear no more of Lollard knights or Lollard mayors, or of Wyclifite scholars in the universities. Influential patronage had nevertheless by then endured just long enough: it had brought together the groups, instilled in them a consciousness of commitment to religious teaching with a particular slant, and above all had put into circulation the texts that made sure that those teachings would not be forgotten.

So Lollardy survived, surreptitiously and among humbler folk, in the heterodox communities that the years between 1382 and 1414 had established. Its survival bears witness to the appeal, to some at least among the laity, of a religious attitude markedly different from that of the mystics and opposed to conventional ways, that deplored and despised pilgrimages, the cult of the saints, contemporary confessional and penitential practice, and prayers for the dead. Lollardy was determinedly anti-sacerdotal in its condemnation of prelacy and mendicancy and in its questioning of the obligation to pay tithes, and socialistic in its ideas on property and charity. The sense of the identity of a tight, puritanical little body of God's elect no doubt helped to give it strength to endure – the feeling of belonging to 'Christ's church', as the Lollard *Lantern of Light* calls it, where readers 'read holy lessons and attend their reading with mindful devotion', unlike those in 'the fiend's church' where 'they chatter their lessons like jays that chatter in a cage' and where elaborate singing fills the ears with 'vain din'. Above all, the Lollard movement was nourished and sustained by the reading of

Scripture. It was as 'Bible men' essentially, who maintained that
'no governance is to be held the law of God save that which is
founded in Holy Scripture', that they were known in the mid
fifteenth century to Bishop Pecock, who made valiant efforts to
put orthodox doctrine into the vernacular to counter their
teaching (the effort undid him, for ultimately he was himself
charged with heresy as a consequence of it). 'They ken by heart
the texts of Holy Scripture,' he says of the Lollards, 'and can
lush them out thick at feasts, and at ale drinkings, and upon their
high benches sitting.'

Pecock's view tallies with what the episcopal records tell us:
early and late Scripture reading is the classic charge brought
against suspected Lollards. In 1430 Bishop Alnwick of Norwich
heard 'that Richard Fletcher of Beccles is a most perfect doctor
in that sect, and can very well and perfectly expound Holy
Scripture, and hath a book of the new law in English'. In 1518,
ninety years on, it is the same story: when Richard Bennett was
in that year brought before the Bishop of London's court this
was the charge:

Also we object to you that divers times . . . in Robert Durdant's house
of Iver Court near unto Staines, you erroneously and damnably read in
a great book of heresy of the said Robert Durdant's . . . certain
chapters of the evangelists in English, in the presence of the said
Robert Durdant, John Butler, Robert Carder, Jenkin Butler, William
King and divers other suspected persons of heresy, there being present
and hearing your said erroneous lectures and opinions.

Bible reading was not quite all there was to it, however. A
number of charges from the late fifteenth and early sixteenth
centuries mention possession of *Wyclif's Wycket*, a vernacular
paraphrase of the great doctor's contention that the material
bread remains after the words of consecration at the mass. Even
a hundred years after 1414 Lollardy had not quite lost touch
with its academic founder or with the doctrinal identity that his
teaching gave to the sect.

It is impossible to estimate how many Lollards and Lollard
sympathizers there were in England at the end of the fifteenth
and in the early sixteenth centuries. After 1414 more effective
heresy laws cut them off from patronage and from the scholarly

impetus that could have given their movement dynamism, and they were driven underground. In some rural localities where they were already well established, such as the Chilterns, and in some towns – London, Bristol, Coventry, for instance – there remained enough of them to attract occasional hostile attention, but there is little sign of any significant increase in their numbers. One point about the Lollard groups at the humbler level is, however, rather striking, and deserves mention: the prominence of their womenfolk. Thomas Netter inveighed against those 'most foolish' Lollard women 'who publicly read and taught in a congregation of men'; Thomas Hoccleve complained of women who, 'though their wit be thin', will 'arguments make in Holy Writ'; Pecock talks of 'those women [among them] which make themselves so wise by the Bible'. Among the Suffolk heretics who were investigated in the 1420s Hawise Moon and Agnes Young (who 'could read very well') were said to be influential. Joan Boughton, who was burned in 1494, was so stout in her heretical opinions that 'all the doctors of London could not turn her from one of them'.

In a religious movement driven out of the church into the domestic family circle of the sectarian home this prominence is perhaps not surprising, but it seems to be a little more significant than that. In Wyclif's church of the elect there could be no difference of standing in grace between man and woman. It was not a very long step logically from there to the charge brought against the Lollard Walter Brut that he had taught that 'women have the power to preach and to make the body of Christ'. Netter certainly thought there were women priests among the Lollards. Even among the heretics most would no doubt have considered that unorthodox, but there is no doubt about the importance of women as teachers and readers. In unorthodox, as in orthodox, circles, the prominence of pious women seems a marked feature of the spiritual history of late medieval England.

The Lollards have always attracted a good deal of attention, because they were different. For that reason it is important to remember that their movement was always a minority one, and that latterly the scattering of the cells in which Lollardy persisted and the humble social status of its adherents ensured that it could not be an influential minority. In doctrine and observance, late medieval England as a whole remained Catholic in its religion, perhaps profoundly so. The treasure that people expended on lights, prayers for the dead and chantry endowments, their devotion to saints and their shrines and to pilgrimage, the numbers and the efflorescence of religious fraternities, all suggest that most hearts were still set in the old ways. There was nothing ultramontane about this English Catholicism: the parish church was its focus, not Rome, but it was none the less Catholic for that. There was a new measure of what I have called devotional literacy among the laity, which made lay-folk more articulate in their religion and perhaps more sensitive to its social implications, but few as yet were ready to question basic teachings. On the whole, there seems no reason, in the light of the late medieval evidence, to enter any significant qualification against Professor Scarisbrick's claim that 'most English men did not want the Reformation'.

Protestant patriotism has been such a powerful element in the English heritage since the sixteenth-century Reformation that for many of us, even now, it is not easy, when we hear the word 'Catholic', not to let the word 'superstition' slip into the mind alongside it. Of course the people of late medieval England were by our standards superstitious in religion and in other ways too. But we need to be chary about treating their attitude towards, say, saints' shrines, relics and images, and above all to the miraculous, in terms of 'mere' superstition. They were indeed ready and willing, even eager sometimes, to accept miracles, especially of healing, and to seek supernatural intervention in their own favour. We need though to remember here how much closer they felt than we do to supernatural powers, which they believed were working in nature, and also how much more exposed to the forces of nature they felt than we do. Belief in the saints and their wonder-working powers provided a much-needed buttress to self-reliance in face of a natural world full of powerful threats, of disease, famine, shipwreck and violence. These threats endangered not only individuals, but communities too; and that is why the cult of the saints was so often a social and communal activity.

The saints were not the only supernatural powers in whom,

under God, men were interested. Richard II, we know, had considerable faith in astrological prediction. Men were afraid of ghosts, but not surprised by their appearance. Perhaps the figure whom, above all, I have most culpably deprived of attention in this chapter is the devil. As countless depictions of him, on glass, in stone and in wall-paintings and manuscript illuminations, attest, he was a very present figure and a powerful force in contemporary imagination. There was as yet no witch craze, but the charges brought against the Dowager Queen Joan in 1419 and against Eleanor, Duchess of Gloucester, in 1441 remind us that no one doubted that there were necromancers or that they could cause real harm. Joan of Arc, by the English account, was 'a disciple and limb of the fiend . . . that used false enchantments and sorcery'. The barriers between the seen and unseen, between natural and supernatural power, whether angelic or demonic, were deemed to be more porous in the late middle ages than they are now, and this left its stamp on their religion. That indeed is the most profound single difference between the mental structure of the religious attitudes of that day, and of the religiously committed in ours.

12. *Epilogue*

Professional historians apart, most people know the history of late medieval England best – if they know about it at all – from Shakespeare's historical plays. What these focus on principally is the drama and violence of the political narrative. The impression of the age that these plays can leave is in consequence one that is more bloodthirsty, more exclusively dominated by the intrigues and jealousies of kings and great lords, and more alien from later times than the age really was. There certainly was a bloodthirsty side to the English story of the late middle ages, whence the French gibe that 'the English make no matter of changing their kings when they feel like it, not to mention of killing them'. But there were a great many other sides of it too, for this was a period of major historical developments that were more important in the long run than any of its 'sad stories of the deaths of kings'. They do not make the stuff of renaissance drama, but in their day they made social history, and for that reason they have furnished the principal themes of this book.

Nevertheless the historical plays of Shakespeare, which for so many have first stirred an interest in this particular segment of the English past, are full of perceptions that are sharper than any a mere historian will ever uncover, and that even from his point of view are so illuminating that I can think of no better way of concluding than to linger briefly over just two of them. The first stems from the fact that the central figures, round whom the action revolves in all these plays, are kings. Here we are reminded of the degree to which, notwithstanding the growing significance of Parliaments and the administrative powers that came to be vested in the localities, the politics and government of late medieval England were, in Dr David Morgan's words, 'kingship focused'. Parliaments met only intermittently, councillors could change, courtiers and factions rose and fell, but the royal authority remained the central truss of government and the royal court the magnetic pole of political society. The king's affinity was the greatest private retinue in the land, and with numbers that fluctuated between four and eight hundred members the royal household even at its lowest limit was just about twice the size of the personnel of all the central offices of state put together. The ripples of influence and association that radiated outward from it lapped into every corner of the realm. That was why the use and abuse of royal patronage was such a decisive factor in the aristocratic politics of jealousy of the period, as Shakespeare clearly saw. Richard II and Henry VI, the two kings who lost their thrones definitively, were also the two who were most partial and least discreet in their distribution of the great reserve of rewards available to them in the way of offices, wardships, marriages, farms of crown lands, licences, pardons and privileges. The king's authority was such that he was often literally besieged by petitioners for favours; to be even-handed in their allocation was no easy task, but politically a crucial one.

The laws, Sir John Fortescue wrote, were the nerves of the body politic, and the community was its heart, its life-blood as a social whole; but the king, he stressed, was its head, and without him it was, as it were, decapitated, a lifeless trunk. If the king were ill-counselled or under-mighty, the fortunes of the whole community were therefore endangered. The drama of Shakespeare's 'kingship-focused' histories derives, in part at least, from just this very point, that more than the fate of mere individuals is involved with the fortunes of the royal and noble characters who 'strut and fret' on his stage. In that respect his plays are true to the life of late medieval England.

When Shakespeare wrote the third part of his *Henry VI* and his *Richard III*, the tumultuous events about which they revolve had only just passed beyond the range of living memory. The chroniclers who were his principal sources, Holinshed and Hall, stood even closer to the times in question, which is why they are still worth combing for authentic personal memories of incidents which had come to their knowledge and of which there is no other record. This serves to introduce my second and more general point about the connection between Shakespeare's historical plays and the real history on which they are based. Just as we can relate to the Victorian and Edwardian ages more easily than we can to, say, the seventeenth or eighteenth centuries, because the former are closer to us in time and we can see how the answers that the Victorians and Edwardians found to their problems have affected the shape of the problems that we now live with, so Shakespeare could relate instinctively and without having to 'think historically' to the fifteenth century and its preoccupations. As Kingsford put it, 'to the writers of the sixteenth century, the previous age loomed large'. That is why, when allowance has been made for the liberties that a dramatist for the sake of his art is entitled to take with historical facts, Shakespeare's plays remain such good history. His *Richard III* may tell only one version of that king's story, but (apart from the fiction of the crooked back) it is a version that was already becoming current before the end of the summer of 1483 – the summer that saw the executions of Rivers and Hastings, the break-up of Edward IV's household and the disappearance from view of the princes in the Tower. The speeches of Shakespeare's *Henry V* really do catch something of the patriotic rhetoric of the age of Agincourt, even though the words, of course, are different. The acute sense of his regality that Shakespeare attributes to his Richard II rings true for the real Richard, whose cultivation of a high regalian ideology contributed to his real undoing.

When, however, we come to Shakespeare's *King John*, what has been said above ceases to hold good at all. In contrast to the plays that concern the fifteenth century, the ambience has no relation to that of the time in which it is located, to the Angevin early thirteenth century. That is because Shakespeare has quitted the 'homeland' of an England just a couple of generations back from his own childhood for a past that, if his sources had permitted him to see it in historical perspective, would have seemed almost as foreign and unfamiliar to him as it does to us.

It would be hard to guess from Shakespeare's play that, for instance, the language of John's court and the first language of his barons was French, or that he came from a family that had always been more French than English, of European rather than English princes. Though John's mistakes cost him much of his

European heritage, the duchy of Normandy and the counties of Anjou and Maine, what was true of him in these respects was only marginally less true of his grandson, Edward I. Foreigners were more prominent in Edward's household than Englishmen when he was a young prince; his first apprenticeship in lordship was in Gascony and his apprenticeship in knightly arms was on the tourneying fields of northern France. Later he joined the last crusade of his maternal uncle, St Louis, and when, as he was returning from Syria, he heard in Sicily of the death of his father, King Henry III, the first of his dominions that he headed for was Gascony, not England. The contrast between this story and these conditions and those of the time of the last pre-Tudor king of whom Shakespeare wrote, King Richard III, is very sharp. Whatever one may think of him as a man, there is no question that Richard was an English king in a sense that neither Edward I nor John before him were. His upbringing and his political experience before he came to the throne were entirely English. English was his first language and the language of his court. Though he called himself King of France and England, he had no land or lordship across the Channel outside Calais and its narrow march. The contrast between the two kings, Edward I and Richard III, in short gives a measure of the transformation that had taken place, between the late thirteenth century and the late fifteenth, in what the kingship of England meant.

The real transformation – the one that gives Shakespeare's *Richard III* in an historical sense a true-to-life quality that his *King John* lacks – was of course not just of English kingship, but of English society. Even at this distance of time, to look back into the world of John or of Edward I will drive home the force of the adage that 'the past is a foreign country' infinitely more sharply than will looking back to the age of Richard III or Henry VII. This is because by the end of the fifteenth century features of the English scene that are visible reminders of our present heritage are so much clearer and so much easier to find than they are in, say, 1300, let alone in 1215, when John sealed Magna Carta. The Parliaments that answered the summonses of Yorkist and early Tudor kings are recognizable as the ancestral form of the institution that we know; the gathering that met King John at Runnymede is not, nor are most of the gatherings called Parliaments that Edward I summoned. We can find in 1500 grammar schools, some even with familiar names, teaching boys among whom at least a sprinkling would later go on to study law in the Inns of Court; in 1300 we can find few such schools beyond those attached to cathedrals, and there were no Inns of Court. In the countryside in 1500 we can encounter the figures of the squire, the yeoman farmer and the labouring peasant who, if they are becoming nowadays hard to find, are yet very familiar to us mentally, and infinitely more so than the manorial seigneur and the bondman of an earlier time. Between 1300 and 1500 the forces of change that were at work in the later middle ages had transformed English society, from a shape that was as unfamiliar to Shakespeare as it is to us, into a society that was familiar to him and many of whose outlines are beginning to seem familiar, even to us.

It is true that in 1500 the final finishing touch to the process of transformation, Henry VIII's Reformation, which swept away the old abbeys and the friars and turned the church in England into the Church of England, still lay in the future. But it was only thirty years away and already English religious feeling had found a vernacular mode of expression that Cranmer and Coverdale would make indelible. In a host of other key respects the whole fabric of English society had been changed, in ways that gave a new clarity to English identity. That is why Sir John Fortescue, when in the 1460s he was driven as a faithful Lancastrian into exile in France, was able to recognize that what – language apart – distinguished that country from his own was essentially a difference of social structure. He believed that it was the distinctive features of the English social system that made viable the particular mode of government of his home country, that rule at once political and regal that brought king and community into partnership by means very different from those of French royal absolutism. Somewhat earlier, another Englishman, Bishop Robert Hallum, had asserted English identity in another but comparable way at the Council of Constance in 1417: 'As regards all the requirements for being a nation ... whether a nation be understood as a race, relationship, and habit of unity separate from others, or as a difference of language which by divine and human law is the greatest and most authentic mark of a nation and the essence of it . . . in all these respects the renowned nation of England of Britain is one of the four or five nations that compose the papal obedience.' The sense of what to be English meant that these two fifteenth-century Englishmen perceived so clearly is something that is underscored again and again in famous lines from Shakespeare's histories; but at the beginning of the fourteenth century it could not have been articulated in the same way because it was not in comparable measure distinct. That is what makes the later middle ages such a significant period in the history of English society; it emerged from them more English, more insular and more individual, and with a consciousness of its individuality that had not been there before.

Bibliography

A. GENERAL

For an introduction to everyday medieval life, as it was once lived in England, the essays in A. L. Poole, ed., *Medieval England* (2 vols., Oxford, 1958), remain as good as anything newer; especially the chapters by E. Carus Wilson on towns and trade, by H. M. Colvin on houses and architecture, by A. B. Emden on education, and by W. G. Hoskins on the landscape. The last twenty years have seen the publication of a number of general, wide-ranging surveys which illuminate the social history of the later medieval period specifically; and I have found the following particularly helpful: J. L. Bolton, *The Medieval English Economy* (London, 1980); A. R. Bridbury, *Economic Growth: England in the Late Middle Ages* (London, 1962); F. R. H. Du Boulay, *An Age of Ambition: English Society in the Late Middle Ages* (London, 1970). One of the most important books in the field to appear for some years, C. Dyer's *Standards of Living in the Late Middle Ages: Social Change in England c. 1200–1520* (Cambridge, 1989), was unfortunately published too late for me to take account of its findings in my writing.

The scholar whose influence on views of English social history in the late medieval period has had the most profound impact in this century was the late K. B. McFarlane. Much of his most important work was published posthumously, notably his Ford Lectures (delivered in 1953) on *The Nobility of Later Medieval England* (Oxford, 1973), and his *Lancastrian Kings and Lollard Knights* (Oxford, 1972). A collection of his most important papers has been published by the Hambledon Press, under the title *England in the Fifteenth Century* (London, 1981): it includes his seminal paper on 'Bastard feudalism', which originally appeared in the *Bulletin of the Institute of Historical Research*, vol. xx (1945), and an introductory essay by G. L. Harriss which reviews this concept in the light of recent research.

The impetus and inspiration which McFarlane and a small group of his pupils have given to late medieval English historical study has meant that, over the last twenty-five years, an unusually large number of significant and original new studies have appeared. A great deal of very important work, including notable contributions from younger scholars, has appeared in individual papers in collections of essays, and some of the best work of an earlier time, when the later middle ages were comparatively neglected by English historians, appeared as it happens in the same format. For ease of reference, I list here what seem to me to be some of the most important collections: individual papers in the books in question will be identified later in this bibliography by reference back to the volume by its number in the list below. Thus, for example, R. Archer, 'Rich old ladies: the problem of late medieval dowagers', in A. J. Pollard, ed., *Property and Politics: Essays in Later Medieval English History*, will appear as R. Archer, 'Rich old ladies: the problem of late medieval dowagers' (A, 10).

1. Chrimes, S. B., Ross, C. D., and Griffiths, R. A., eds., *Fifteenth Century England, 1399–1509* (Manchester, 1972).
2. Clough, C. H., ed., *Profession, Vocation and Culture in Later Medieval England* (Liverpool, 1982).
3. Dobson, R. B., ed., *The Church, Politics and Patronage in the Fifteenth Century* (Gloucester, 1984).
4. Griffiths, R. A., and Sherborne, J., eds., *Kings and Nobles in the Later Middle Ages* (Gloucester, 1986).
5. Griffiths, R. A., ed., *Patronage, the Crown and the Provinces in Later Medieval England* (Gloucester, 1981).
6. Highfield, J. R. L., and Jeffs, R., eds., *The Crown and Local Communities in England and France in the Fifteenth Century* (Gloucester, 1981).
7. Jones, M., ed., *Gentry and Lesser Nobility in Late Medieval Europe* (Gloucester, 1986).
8. Kingsford, C. L., *Prejudice and Promise in Fifteenth Century England* (Oxford, 1925).
9. McFarlane, K. B., *England in the Fifteenth Century* (London, 1981).
10. Pollard, A. J., ed., *Property and Politics: Essays in Later Medieval English History* (Gloucester, 1984).
11. Rosenthal, J., and Richmond, C., eds., *People, Politics and Community in the Later Middle Ages* (Gloucester, 1987).
12. Ross, C. D., ed., *Patronage, Pedigree and Power in Later Medieval England* (Gloucester, 1979).
13. Thomson, J. A. F., ed., *Towns and Townspeople in the Fifteenth Century* (Gloucester, 1988).
14. Williams, D., ed., *England in the Fifteenth Century* (Woodbridge, 1987).

B. BIBLIOGRAPHY BY CHAPTERS

For essays in one of the collective works listed in Section A, it will be
necessary to refer to the numbered list on p. 305 as indicated (eg. A, 4).

Chapter 1: Social Hierarchy and Social Change

In writing on the estates in this chapter I found two books particularly
useful: G. R. Owst, *Literature and Pulpit in Medieval England* (Cam-
bridge, 1933), and Jill Mann, *Chaucer and Medieval Estates Satire: the
Literature of Social Classes and the General Prologue of the Canterbury
Tales* (Cambridge, 1973). On 'bastard feudal' social relations I have
found the best guides to be McFarlane's 'Bastard feudalism' (A, 9);
J. M. W. Bean, *The Decline of English Feudalism, 1215–1540* (Manchester,
1968); T. B. Pugh, 'The magnates, knights and gentry' (A, 1); and
W. H. Dunham, *Lord Hastings' Indentured Retainers* (New Haven,
Conn., 1955). Two papers of significance on aristocratic incomes are
H. L. Gray, 'Incomes from land in England in 1436', *English Historical
Review*, vol. 49 (1934), and T. B. Pugh and C. D. Ross, 'The English
baronage and the income tax of 1436', *Bulletin of the Institute of
Historical Research*, vol. 26 (1953); the latter making some essential
corrections to the former.

Chapter 2: Plague, Depopulation and Labour Shortage

The best general and up-to-date review of the subjects discussed in this
chapter is J. Hatcher, *Plague, Population and the English Economy, 1348–1530*
(London, 1977 and 1984). On population, the classic work is that of J. C.
Russell, *British Medieval Population* (Albuquerque, New Mexico, 1948),
but some of his calculations have not met with acceptance (for useful
comment, see the works of M. M. Postan and J. Z. Titow listed below). P.
Ziegler, *The Black Death* (London, 1969), offers a useful general survey of
the plague and its effects. B. H. Putnam, *The Enforcement of the Statute of
Labourers* (Columbia, 1908), remains the classic study of labour legislation.
R. B. Dobson, *The Peasants Revolt of 1381* (London, 1983) gives an
excellent, up-to-date account of the rising of that year.

    Other works that I have found particularly useful include:

Bean, J. M. W., 'Plague, population and economic decline in England
    in the later middle ages', *Economic History Review*, 2nd series, vol. 15
    (1962–3).
Hilton, R. H., and Aston, T., eds., *The English Rising of 1381* (Past and
    Present Publications, Cambridge, 1984).

Postan, M. M., 'Some economic evidence of declining population in the later middle ages', *Economic History Review*, 2nd series, vol. 2 (1950).

Shrewsbury, J. F. D., *A History of Bubonic Plague in the British Isles* (Cambridge, 1970).

Titow, J. Z., *English Rural Society, 1200–1350* (London, 1969).

Chapter 3: The Life of the Countryside

Four books, each very different in its approach, have helped me more than any others in trying to write on agrarian history: W. O. Ault, *Open Field Husbandry and the Village Community* (American Philosophical Society, Philadelphia, 1965); R. H. Hilton, *The English Peasantry in the Later Middle Ages* (Oxford, 1975); W. G. Hoskins, *The Making of the English Landscape* (London, 1955); and Barbara A. Hanawalt, *The Ties that Bound: Peasant Families in Medieval England* (New York, 1986). Two other works that deal respectively with rural depopulation and the decline of bond tenure and which are very illuminating are M. W. Beresford, *The Lost Villages of Medieval England* (London, 1954), and R. H. Hilton, *The Decline of Serfdom* (London, 1969).

As is to be expected in this subject area, some of the most significant and suggestive findings for the social historian have come from studies of particular localities and estates. Among works that I have found especially helpful I should mention:

Bennett, H. S., *Life on the English Manor* (Cambridge, 1937 and 1956).

Dyer, C., *Lords and Peasants in a Changing Society: the Estates of the Bishopric of Worcester 680–1540* (Past and Present Publications, Cambridge, 1980).

Harvey, B. F., *Westminster Abbey and its Estates in the Middle Ages* (Oxford, 1977).

Hoskins, W. G., *The Midland Peasant* (London, 1955).

Orwin, C. S., and C. S., *The Open Fields*, 2nd edn (Oxford, 1954).

Page, F. M., *The Estates of Crowland Abbey: a Study in Manorial Organization* (Cambridge, 1934).

Raftis, J. A., *Tenure and Mobility: Studies in the Social History of the Medieval English Village* (Toronto, 1964).

Razi Z., *Life, Marriage and Death in a Medieval Parish: Economy, Society and Demography in Halesowen, 1270–1400* (Past and Present Publications, Cambridge, 1986).

Smith, R. W., ed., *Land, Kinship and Life-cycle* (Cambridge, 1984): especially chapters by I. Blanchard, C. Dyer, J. Ravensdale, Z. Razi and R. Smith.

Chapter 4: *Towns, Trade and Urban Culture*

The particular problems of late medieval urban history are reviewed in two very important papers, R. B. Dobson, 'Urban decline in late medieval England', *Transactions of the Royal Historical Society*, 5th series, vol. 27 (1977), and D. M. Palliser, 'Urban decay revisited' (A, 13). The single study that has perhaps had most impact on urban historiography in recent years is C. Phythian Adams, *The Desolation of a City: Coventry and the Urban Crisis of the Late Middle Ages* (Cambridge, 1979), a vividly written book which takes a much wider view of urban history than its title suggests. On small towns, chapter 5 of R. H. Hilton, *The English Peasantry in the Later Middle Ages* (Oxford, 1975), is invaluable.

On trade and commerce, chapters 8 and 9 of J. L. Bolton, *The Medieval English Economy* (London, 1980), provide an excellent introduction. On the export trade in wool and textiles two books are vital, T. H. Lloyd, *The English Wool Trade in the Middle Ages* (Cambridge, 1977), and E. M. Carus Wilson and O. Coleman, *England's Export Trade 1275–1547* (Oxford, 1963).

Other works that I have found very useful in relation to various topics discussed in this chapter include:

Carus Wilson, E. M., *Medieval Merchant Venturers* (London, 1954).

Goldberg, P. J. P., 'Women in fifteenth century town life' (A, 13).

Hill, J. W. F., *Medieval Lincoln* (Cambridge, 1948).

Horrox, R., 'Urban patronage and patrons in the fifteenth century' (A, 5).

James, M., 'Ritual, drama and the social body in the late medieval English town', *Past and Present*, no. 98 (1983).

Platt, C. P. S., *The Medieval English Town* (London, 1976).

Reynolds, S. M. G., *An Introduction to the History of English Medieval Towns* (Oxford, 1977).

Schofield, R., 'The geographical distribution of wealth in England, 1334–1649', *Economic History Review*, 2nd series, vol. 18 (1965).

Tait, J., *The Medieval English Borough* (Manchester, 1936).

Chapter 5. *Westminster and London*

The single most wide-ranging and influential study of late medieval London is S. L. Thrupp, *The Merchant Class of Medieval London* (Chicago, 1948). Two other works, both short papers, seem to me to be specially helpful: C. L. Kingsford's brilliant visual evocation of 'London in the fifteenth century' (A, 8), and G. Rosser, 'London and Westminster: the suburb in the urban economy in the later middle ages' (A, 13). Dr Rosser's book, *Medieval Westminster* (Oxford, 1989), appeared after I had finished writing.

Other works that I have found useful include:

Barron, C. M., 'Richard Whittington: the man behind the myth' in A. Hollaender and W. Kellaway, eds., *Studies in London History Presented to P. E. Jones* (London, 1969).

Bird, R., *The Turbulent London of Richard II* (London, 1969).

Hanham, A., *The Celys and their World: an English Merchant Family of the Fifteenth Century* (Cambridge, 1985).

Myers, A. R., *London in the Age of Chaucer* (Oklahoma, 1974).

Unwin, G., *The Gilds and Companies of London* (London, 1908).

Chapter 6: The Hundred Years War and its Effects on Society and Government

C. T. Allmand, *The Hundred Years War: England and France at War c.1300–c.1450* (Cambridge, 1988), with its strong thematic chapters and comparatively light narrative treatment, offers an excellent introduction to the problems. The most important work on the social impact of the war in England is that of K. B. McFarlane; in particular chapter 2 ('The nobility and war') of *The Nobility of Late Medieval England* (Oxford, 1973), and chapters 3, 7, 8 and 9 of *England in the Fifteenth Century* (London, 1981), especially chapter 7, 'War, the economy and social change'.

On taxation for war purposes, and its effects on government, the most important work has been that of G. L. Harriss, notably his *King, Parliament and Public Finance in Medieval England to 1369* (Oxford, 1976), and his important paper, 'War and the emergence of the English parliament', *Journal of Medieval History*, vol. 2 (1976).

Among very numerous other works, I have found the following in particular helpful:

Allmand, C. T., *Lancastrian Normandy: the History of an Occupation* (Oxford, 1983).

Barnie, J., *War in Medieval Society: Social Values and the Hundred Years War, 1337–99* (London, 1974).

Bennett, M., *Community, Class and Careerism: Cheshire and Lancashire Society in the Age of Gawain and the Green Knight* (Cambridge, 1983).

Davies, R., and Denron, J. H., eds., *The English Parliament in the Middle Ages* (Manchester, 1981); especially the chapters by G. L. Harriss and J. Maddicott.

Hewitt, H. J., *The Organization of the War under Edward III* (Manchester, 1966).

Miller, E., *War in the North* (Hull, 1960).

Payling, S. J., 'The widening franchise: parliamentary elections in Lancastrian Nottinghamshire' (A, 14).

Roskell, J. S., *The Commons and their Speakers in English Parliaments, 1376–1523* (Manchester, 1965).

Saul, N., *Knights and Esquires: the Gloucestershire Gentry in the Fourteenth Century* (Oxford, 1981).

Chapter 7: The Aristocracy at Home: Household, Estates and Family

Once again, K. B. McFarlane, *The Nobility of Late Medieval England* (Oxford, 1973), is the book that really opens up the subject (especially chapters 4, 5, 6). G. A. Holmes, *The Estates of the Higher Nobility in Fourteenth Century England* (Cambridge, 1957), is very helpful. Two extremely vivid studies are particularly illuminating on the life of the gentry, C. Richmond, *John Hopton: a Fifteenth Century Suffolk Gentleman* (Cambridge, 1981), and N. Saul, *Scenes from Provincial Life: Knightly Families in Sussex, 1280–1400* (Oxford, 1986). I must acknowledge too how useful I have found two doctoral theses, both of which will in due course be published by the Oxford University Press in their Historical Monographs Series, S. K. Walker on 'The Lancastrian Affinity, 1361–99', and S. J. Payling on 'The Gentry of Lancastrian Nottinghamshire'.

Other works which I have found very helpful include:

Archer, R., 'Rich old ladies: the problem of late medieval dowagers' (A, 10).

Bennett, M., 'Careerism in late medieval England' (A, 11).

Carpenter, C., 'The Beauchamp affinity: a study of bastard feudalism at work', *English Historical Review*, vol. 95 (1980).

Carpenter, C., 'The fifteenth century English gentry and their estates' (A, 7).

Dockray, K., 'Why did fifteenth century English gentry marry?' (A, 7).

Griffiths, R. A., 'Public and private bureaucracies in England and Wales in the fifteenth century', *Transactions of the Royal Historical Society*, 5th series, vol. 30 (1980).

Lander, J. R., 'Family, friends and politics in fifteenth century England' (A, 4).

Mertes, K., *The English Noble Household, 1250–1600* (Oxford, 1988).

Morgan, D. A. L., 'The individual style of the English gentleman' (A, 7).

Rawcliffe, C., 'Baronial councils in the later middle ages' (A, 12).

Wright, S. M., *The Derbyshire Gentry in the Fifteenth Century* (Derbyshire Record Society, 1983).

Chapter 8: Aristocratic Violence: from Civil Strife to Forcible Entry

The general problems are well treated by J. R. Lander, *Conflict and Stability in the Fifteenth Century* (London, 1969). The most illuminating writing on civil strife, to my thinking, is found in R. L. Storey, *The End of the House of Lancaster* (London, 1966), and in K. B. McFarlane, 'The Wars of the Roses' (A, 9). On genteel violence I have found especially useful two books by J. G. Bellamy, which I sometimes think have been under-appreciated, *Crime and Public Order in England in the Later Middle Ages* (London, 1973), and *Criminal Law and Society in Medieval and Tudor England* (Gloucester, 1984). A very significant paper by E. Powell, 'Arbitration and the law in England in the later middle ages', *Transactions of the Royal Historical Society*, 5th series, vol. 33 (1983), has opened up a new aspect of the subject of the control of violence.

Many of the studies of the gentry mentioned in the bibliography to Chapter 7, above, include some examination of the problems of violence, maintenance and the disorderly conduct of aristocratic retainers. I have found the following works, in addition, to be very helpful:

Arthurson, I., 'The rising of 1497: a revolt of the peasantry?' (A, 11).

Bean, J. M. W., 'Henry IV and the Percies', *History*, vol. 44 (1959).

Cherry, M., 'The struggle for power in mid-fifteenth-century Devonshire' (A, 5).

Griffiths, R. A., 'Local rivalries and national politics', *Speculum*, vol. 43 (1968).

Herbert, A., 'Herefordshire 1413–61: some aspects of society and public order' (A, 5).

Holt, J. C., *Robin Hood* (London, 1982).

Maddicott, J., *Law and Lordship* (*Past and Present*, Supplement no. 4 1978).

Virgoe, R., 'The crown, magnates, and local government in 15th century East Anglia' (A, 5).

Chapter 9: The Spread of Literacy

Three very important works of the last twenty years have greatly
extended our knowledge of late medieval education: N. Orme, *English
Schools in the Middle Ages* (London, 1973); the same author's *From
Childhood to Chivalry: the Education of English Kings and Aristocracy,
1066–1530* (London, 1984); and J. A. Hoeppner Moran, *The Growth of
English Schooling: Learning, Literacy and Laicisation in the Pre-Reformation
York Diocese* (Princeton, 1985). On a different aspect of the subject,
Janet Coleman, *English Literature in History: Medieval Readers and
Writers* (London, 1981), is invaluable.

Other works that I have found particularly helpful include:

Gabel, L., *Benefit of Clergy in England in the Later Middle Ages* (North-
    ampton, Mass., 1929).
Ives, E. W., 'The Common Lawyers' (A, 2).
Jewell, H. M., 'English bishops as educational benefactors in the later
    fifteenth century' (A, 3).
Kingsford, C. L., 'English letters and the intellectual ferment' (A, 8).
Scattergood, J., *Politics and Poetry in the Fifteenth Century* (London, 1971).
Storey, R. L., 'Gentlemen bureaucrats' (A, 2).

Chapter 10: The Clerical Estate

There are two classical works on this subject: A. Hamilton-Thompson,
The English Clergy and their Organisation in the Later Middle Ages
(Oxford, 1947), and, on all that concerns the regular religious, D. M.
Knowles, *The Religious Orders in England* (3 vols., Cambridge, 1947–
59). Two other important and illuminating general works are W. A.
Pantin, *The English Church in the Fourteenth Century* (Cambridge,
1955), and P. Heath, *The English Parish Clergy on the Eve of the
Reformation* (London, 1969). On the pastoral activity of churchmen,
especially of bishops, J. Hughes, *Pastors and Visionaries: Religion and
Secular Life in Late Medieval Yorkshire* (Woodbridge, 1988), is a mine of
information.

Other works that I have found particularly useful include:

Aston, M. E., *Thomas Arundel: a Study of Church Life in the Reign of
    Richard II* (Oxford, 1967).
Clay, R. M., *The Medieval Hospitals of England* (London, 1909).
Cobban, A. B., *The Medieval English Universities: Oxford and Cambridge
    to c.1500* (London, 1988).
Dunning, R. W., 'Patronage and promotion in the late medieval
    church' (A, 5).

Harriss, G. L., *Cardinal Beaufort: a Study in Lancastrian Ascendancy and Decline* (Oxford, 1988).

Little, A. K., *Studies in English Franciscan History* (Manchester, 1917).

Partner, P., 'William of Wykeham and the historians', in R. Custance, ed., *Winchester College: Sixth-centenary Essays* (Oxford, 1982).

Power, E. E., *Medieval English Nunneries, c.1275–1535* (Cambridge, 1922).

Tanner, N., *The Church in Late Medieval Norwich, 1370–1532* (Toronto, 1984).

Chapter 11: Popular Religion

Though it is now very old and here and there dated, B. L. Manning, *The People's Faith in the Time of Wyclif* (London, 1919), remains very useful. J. Hughes's book, *Pastors and Visionaries: Religion and Secular Life in Late Medieval Yorkshire* (Woodbridge, 1988), has given a new dimension to the subject of popular religion, and is particularly illuminating on the mystical tradition: its range is far wider than the subtitle implies. Two works that are very revealing about more formal late medieval religious attitudes are J. J. Scarisbrick, *The Reformation and the English People* (Oxford, 1984), whose opening chapters are much concerned with the pre-Reformation world, and J. T. Rosenthal, *The Purchase of Paradise: Gift Giving and the Aristocracy* (London, 1972).

Lollardy is a subject to itself, historiographically, within the broader framework of studies of the people's religion. The best introduction remains, probably, K. B. McFarlane, *John Wyclif and the Beginnings of English Nonconformity* (London, 1952), though it is unnecessarily unsympathetic to its principal subject. The most important recent work on the topic has been by Anne Hudson and M. E. Aston. A number of M. E. Aston's papers are collected in her *Lollards and Reformers: Images and Literacy in Late Medieval Religion* (London, 1984). A collection of A. Hudson's papers is in her *The Lollards and their Books* (London, 1985): her *The Premature Reformation: Wycliffite Texts and Lollard History* (Oxford, 1988) is the most important contribution on the subject to appear for many years.

Among other works that I have found especially useful are:

Carpenter, C., 'The religion of the gentry in the fifteenth century' (A, 14).

Catto, J., 'Religion and the English nobility in the later fourteenth century', in *History and Imagination: Essays in Honour of H. R. Trevor-Roper*, ed. H. Lloyd Jones, V. Pearl, and B. Worden (London, 1981).

Green, V. H. H., *Bishop Reginald Pecock* (Cambridge, 1945).

Knowles, D., *The English Mystical Tradition* (London, 1961).

Owst, G. R., *Literature and Pulpit in Medieval England* (Cambridge, 1933).

Richmond, C., 'Religion and the Fifteenth Century English Gentleman' (A, 3).

Vale, M. G. A., *Piety, Charity and Literacy among the Yorkshire Gentry* (Borthwick Papers, no. 50, York, 1976).

Index

Index

(Where a modern historical writer is listed, references are given both to the author in the text and to his or her work in the Bibliography.)

Abbot, John, 230
accounting
    estate, 64, 172–3; household, 168–71
Acton, Ralph, 3
Additions, Statute of, 8, 11
administrators
    in government offices, 150–52; pro-
    fessional, 235–8; see also local
    government
Aesop's *Fables*, 219
Agincourt, battle, 114, 144, 145
Ainsworth, Alexander, 204
Alexandria, 142
Alfred, King, 2
All Souls College, Oxford, 246, 254
alms-giving, 282–4
almshouses, 244, 245, 253, 274, 282
Alnwick, castle, 162
Alnwick, William, Bishop of Lincoln,
    263, 266, 294
Ampthill (Beds.), 139, 205, 206
anchorities, anchoresses, 271, 285–6
angling, 184
animal husbandry, 52–3
annates, 241
Anonimale Chronicle, 147
Appellant, the Lords (*temp.* Richard
    II), 192
arbitrations, 209, 211, 214; see also
    loveday
archdeacons, 252
archers, 135
architecture, city, 96

archives, state, 235–6
Ardern, Sir Peter, 221
armies
    financing of, 41, 131, 137, 146; rais-
    ing of, 134–7; size of, 134–5
arms, heraldic, see heraldry
Array, Commissions of, 137
Arthur, King, 141, 142, 219, 221
Arthur, Prince, 228
Arundel, Richard, Earl of, 274
Arundel, Archbishop Thomas, 245,
    252, 256, 281, 292
Ashburton (Devon), 90, 231
Assheton, Sir John, 210
Aston, John, 291
Asty, Sir Ralph, 15
Audley, James Lord, 198
Augustinian canons, 255, 263, 278
Austins, Order of, 267
Aylsham (Norfolk), 53

Babington, William, 148
Baddesley Clinton (Warwicks.), 72
Bailey, William, 96
Ball, John, 43
Bardney Abbey, 263
Bardolf, John Lord, 278
Barnes, Mistress Juliana, 185
Barton, Thomas, 263
Basingstoke (Hants.), 52
Bassett, Ralph, of Drayton, 177
bastard feudalism, 19ff., 211–12, 304,
    306

Battle Abbey, 67, 232, 237

Beauchamp, Sir Walter, 292

Beauchamp family, *see* Warwick, Earls of

Beauchief, Abbot of, 54

Beaufort, Henry, Cardinal and Bishop of Winchester, 228, 231, 244

Beaufort, Joan, Countess of Westmorland, 177

Beaufort, Lady Margaret, 288

Beaufort family, *see* Exeter, Somerset, Dukes of

Beaumont family, 70

Beccles (Suffolk), 86, 89, 294

Beckwith, William, 212–13

Bedford, John, Duke of, 141, 145, 165

benefices, 14, 31, 241, 248–51

benefit of clergy, 226

Bennett, M., 139, 140, 309, 310

Beowulf, 227

Berkeley, Catherine, Lady, 231

Berkeley, Isobel, Lady, 201

Berkeley, James, Lord, 201, 228

Berkeley, William, Lord, 201–2

Berkeley family, 64, 201

Bethlehem, St Mary's Hospital of (London), 244

Beverley (Yorks.), 86

Beverley Minister, 252

Bible, 225, 290
    Wyclifite, 217, 219, 255, 291–2, 294

bills, posting of, 225–6

Birmingham, 72, 88

bishops, role of, 251–60

Bishopstone (Sussex), 62

Bishops Waltham (Hants.), 31

Black Book of the Household, 166

Blackburn, Nicholas, 282

Black Death, 5, 6, 27, 33, 40, 48, 53
    aftermath of, 75, 157, 251, 260; *see also* bubonic disease, plague

Black Monks, 261, 263

Black Prince, *see* Edward

Blois, Henry of, 244, 262

blazon, *see* heraldry

Blythburgh (Suffolk), 173

Boccacio, 27, 34

Boethius, Chaucer's translation of, 219

Bohun, Mary, 277; *see also* Hereford, Earls of

Boke of St Albans, 184–5

Boldon, Ughtred, 263

Boleyn, Anne, 125

Boleyn, Sir Geoffrey, 15, 125

Bolingbroke, Henry, 120, 180, 192, 196; *see also* Henry IV

Bolney, Batholomew, 232

Bolton Castle, 162

bond tenants, bond tenure, etc., 39–40, 46, 56, 73–4

Bonville, William, Lord, 189, 200

Book of Virtues and Vices, 285

books, chapter 9 *passim*

bookselling, 222

boon work, 62, 74

Bordeaux, John of, 35

'borough English', 58

boroughs, 11, 78
    burgage tenure, 77–8; courts, 81; fee farms, 85, 92, 94, 141; privileges, 78

Boston (Lincs.), 85, 86, 89, 91, 104

Bouillon, Godfrey de, 219

Boulers, Reginald, Bishop of Lichfield, 252

Bourbon, Louis, Duke of, 142

Bourchier, Sir Robert, 236

Bourchier, Thomas, Archbishop of Canterbury, 252

Bowet, Henry, Archbishop of York, 255

Bracton, Henry of, 84

Bradwardine, Thomas, Archbishop of Canterbury, 252

Braybrooke, (Northants.), 292

Brembre, Sir Nicholas, 15, 118

brewing, 57

Bridgettines, 265

Bridlington, John of, 278

Bristol, 29, 79, 80, 86, 92, 94, 104, 276, 293, 295
  St Mary Redcliffe, 282

Brittany, John, Duke of, 9

Brome, John, 72

Bromley, John, 220

Bromyard, John, 268

Brougham (Cumb.), 85

Brunton, Ralph, Bishop of Rochester, 252, 263

Brut, Walter, 295

Brut Chronicle, 194

bubonic disease, 27; *see also* Black Death, plague

Buckingham, Edward Stafford, 3rd Duke of, 173

Buckingham, Henry Stafford, 2nd Duke of, 192

Buckingham, Humphrey Stafford, 1st Duke of, 21

Bunbury, collegiate church of, 139, 273

burgage tenures, 77

Burgess, Joan, 177

Burgundy, John of (author), 34, 35

burials, 279–82

Burley, Sir Simon, 220

Burwell (Cambs.), 53

Byland Abbey, 286

Cade's Revolt, 119, 198

Caen, 145

Caistor (Norfolk), 175, 182

Calais, 6, 91, 121, 124, 125, 126, 135, 138, 142, 145, 158, 196, 301
  siege of, 134; *see also* Staple

Calle, Richard, 183

Calverly, Sir Hugh, 135, 139, 273

Cambridge, 79
  University of, 233–4, 243, 245–6

Camden, William, 133

Cannings, William, 281

Canon Law, 181, 233, 240, 242

Canterbury, 79
  cathedral and priory, 65, 143; shrine of St Thomas à Becket, 277

Canterbury Tales (Chaucer), 6, 7, 217, 220, 225, 256
  'General Prologue', 7, 256; 'Nun's Priest's Tale', 60; *see also* Chaucer

Capgrave, John, 278

Carmelites, 267, 285

Carpenter, Christine, 212, 310

Carrow Priory, 280

Carthusians, 261, 263, 264–5, 287

Castle Combe (Wilts.), 88, 93

cattle farming, *see* animal husbandry

Caxton, William, 219, 222

Cely, George, 126, 127

Cely, Richard, 126

Cely family, 126

Chad, St, 277

Chancery, 75, 112, 151–2, 203, 209, 234, 235–6; *see also* Inns

Chandos, Sir John, 135

Chandos Herald, 143

chantries, 14, 230, 259ff., 273

chantry chaplains, 259–60

charity, 282–4

Charlemagne, 219

Charlton, Sir Thomas, 220

charterhouses, 263, 264

Chastellain, Georges, 160

Chaucer, Geoffrey, 1, 6, 7, 8, 14, 60, 68, 109, 128, 142, 143, 160, 169, 217, 218, 219, 224, 225, 228, 256, 257, 263, 269, 272, 276, 290

Chaucer, Sir Thomas, 205

Chauliac, Guy de, 27

Chaworth, Sir Thomas, 221

Cherbourg, 145, 149

Chester, 80, 105

chevauchées, 134, 144

Cheyney family, 292

Chewton Mendip (Som.), 57

Chichele, Henry, Archbishop of Canterbury, 231, 253–4

child mortality, *see* plague

children and childhood, 61, 167, 227ff.

Chipping Camden (Glos.), 93

chivalry, cult of, 142, 146

Christ's College, Cambridge, 246
church benefices, *see* benefices
church courts, 242–3
Cicero, 221, 228
Cinque Ports, 11, 89
Cistercians, 261, 262, 263
city planning, 95
Clanvowe, Sir John, 223
Clare, Gilbert, Earl of, 161
Clarence, George, Duke of, 194
Clarence, Margaret, Duchess of, 165
Clarence, Thomas, Duke of, 145
clerical estate, 6, chapter 10 *passim*
    stratifications of, 14
clerical incomes, *see* benefices
clerks, secular, 236–8
Cleveland (Yorks.), 31
Clifford, Lord, 194
'closed corporations', 99
cloth
    exports, 91; manufacture of, 82, 92;
    merchants, 82; *see also* textile in-
    dustry, wool trade
Cloud of Unknowing, 287
Clown, William, Abbot of Leicester,
    14, 262, 264
Cluniacs, 261
Clyn, John of, 29
Clyst, fight at, 200
Cobham, Lord, 292
Cobham, Joan, Lady, 274
Colchester, 99
Coldharbour (London), 113
Coleman, Janet, 217, 312
colleges (collegiate churches), 273–4
commissions, *see* array, justices (of
    oyer and *terminer*, of the peace, etc.)
Commons, the, 18, 44, 113, 146, 147;
    see also Parliament (Commons in)
communications, 84
Compostella, St James's shrine at, 276
confession, 285
Consolation of Philosophy (Chaucer's
    translation), 219
Constable, John, 283
copyhold tenures, 74–5

Cornish Rebellion (1497), 198
Cornwall, Sir John (Lord Fanhope),
    139–40, 205
Corpus Christi
    feast of, 284; guilds and pageants
    of, 104, 105, 106
corvées, 63
cottar, 9, 62, 66
Cottenham, 30
councils
    baronial, 174–5; royal, 150–52, 208
Courtenay, Sir Philip, 200
Courtenay, Sir Thomas, 187, 188
Courtenay, William, Archbishop of
    Canterbury, 245, 252
Courtenay family, *see* Devon, Earls
    of
courts
    central (King's Bench and Com-
    mon Pleas), 112, 151; county, 152–3;
    of law, 224; manor, 55, 58, 63, 172;
    see also Chancery, Exchequer,
    justices of peace, etc.
Coventry, 72, 79, 80, 84, 86, 89, 92,
    93, 94, 96, 97, 98, 100, 101, 104,
    105, 106, 113, 133, 169, 283, 295
Coverdale, Miles, 302
Cranmer, Thomas, Archbishop of
    Canterbury, 302
Crécy, battle of, 138, 141, 142
Crediton (Devon), 86
Cressy, Hugh, 211
Cromwell, Ralph, Lord, 133, 162,
    163, 164, 199, 205–6
Crowcombe (Som.), 57
Crowland Abbey, 30, 65
crusades, 142, 144
Cunningham, John, 268
Cuthbert, St, 277
Cuxham (Oxon.), 31
Cyprus, *see* Peter, King of

Dale, William, 94
Daniel, Richard, 173
danse macabre, 35
Dante Alighieri, 218, 273

Danyer family, 139
Daubriggecourt, Sir John, 266
De Heretico Comburendo, 292
de la Mare, Thomas, Abbot of St Albans, 262
demesne farming, 63, 65–6, 72, 172
demographic decline, 6, chapter 2 *passim*, 94
Denham (Suffolk), 170
Dependen, Sir John, 283
De pestilencia (John of Burgundy), 35
Derby, 95
De regimine principum (Giles of Rome), 219
de Vere, *see* Oxford
devil, 297
Devon, Courtenay Earls of, 21, 187–8, 200
Devon, Thomas Courtenay, Earl of, 187, 200
devotio moderna, 265
devotional literacy, 288–90
Dictes and Sayings of the Philosophers, 219, 221
diet
 peasant, 62; of aristocratic household, 168
Dobson, Professor Barrie, 85, 94, 305, 308
Domesday Book, 32, 41
Dominicans, 267
Dorchester Abbey, 263
dowagers, 181–2, 305
dower, 24, 181, 203
Down, Richard, 235
Downton (Hants.), 31
dress, 169; *see also* sumptuary laws
Dry Drayton (Cambs.), 30
Dublin, 104
Du Boulay, F. R. H., 224, 304
Dunbar, William, 110
Dunster (Som.), 168
Dunsthorpe (Lincs.), 71
Durdant, Robert, 294
Durham, cathedral and priory, 57, 132, 237, 277

Easby Priory, 262
education, 22, 227–35, 243, 245–6
Edward, the Black Prince, 113, 134, 140, 142, 143
Edward I, 132, 136, 154, 302
Edward II, 132, 136, 193
Edward III, 123, 125, 134, 137, 141, 154, 197
Edward IV, 125, 166, 194, 197
Egremont, Thomas Percy, Lord, 199
Eight Chapters Necessary to Perfection (W. Hilton), 288
Eltham, 112
enclosure, 72–3
enfeoffment, 19, 203; *see also* 'use'
entails, 175, 177–8, 203
'entry', 204
 forcible, 156, 190, 203, 204–7, 208
entry fee, 19, 54, 74; *see also* 'relief'
Epistle on the Mixed Life (W. Hilton), 287
Erkenwald, St, 277
esquires, 9, 10, 16
Etchingham, Sir William, 281
Etchingham family, 173
Eton, 226, 230, 261
evictions, 73
Exchequer, 109, 112, 137, 151, 152, 235–6 clerks of, 151; 'states' of, 146
Exeter, 96, 200
Exeter, Henry Holland, Duke of, 205, 206, 207
Exeter, Thomas Beaufort, Duke of, 145, 178
exports, 91, 123
eyres, 153–5

Fairfax family, 15
Fairford (Oxon.), 93
famine, 32, 62
Fanhope, Sir John Cornwall, Lord, 139, 205
Farthinghoe (Northants.), 230
Fastolf, Sir John, 93, 135, 138, 145, 174, 175, 221, 273; *see also* Paston family

fee farms, 85

fee simple, 20

femme sole, 45

feoffees, feoffors, 169, 175, 176, 177; *see also* enfeoffment, 'use'

Festiall (J. Myrc), 289

feudalism, bastard, 19ff., 211–12, 304, 306

fforestier, Thomas, 36

field systems, 50ff.; *see also* enclosures

fishing, 90; *see also* angling

Fitzherbert, John, 181

Fitzherbert, Richard, 180

FitzRalph, Richard, Archbishop of Armagh, 31

Flanders, 91, 124

Fleming, Richard, Bishop of Lincoln, 252

Fletcher, Richard, 294

Foljambe, Thomas, 180

'forcible entry', 156, 190, 203, 204–7, 208

definition of, 204

foreigners in London, 117

Forncett (Norfolk), 71

Fortescue, Sir John, 67, 172, 227, 234, 239, 299, 302

Fortescue family, 15

Fotheringhay (Northants.), 231

collegiate church of, 273

Fountains Abbey, 53, 263

Fox, John, 293

fox-hunting, 185–6

Framlingham Castle, 284

France, chapter 6 *passim*

English settlements in, 145; *see also* French language, Gascony, Normandy

Franciscans, 267

fraternities, *see* guilds

free bench, 24

French language, 223–5, 239, 265, 300

friars, 7, 42, 267–9

fulling (of cloth), 82, 92, 93

funeral rites, 274–5, 279–81, 283

Gabel, L., 225, 312

Gabriel, archangel, 278

Game and Play of Chess, 219

Garter King of Arms, 8

Garter, Order of, 142

Gascoigne, Thomas, 250, 251, 268

Gascony, 80, 135, 136, 144, 157, 158, 301

Gaunt, John of, *see* Lancaster

Gawain and the Green Knight, 185–6, 218

George, St, 104, 106, 114, 278

Gest of Robin Hood, 213

Giles of Rome, 219, 220

Gilbert, Earl of Clare, 161

Glastonbury, 244, 277

abbey, 262

Gloucester, 89, 112

castle, 201

Gloucester, Eleanor, Duchess of, 297

Gloucester, Humphrey, Duke of, 220

Gloucester, Thomas of Woodstock, Duke of, 219, 277, 286

Godstow Abbey, 266

Golden Legend, 219

Governance of England (Sir John Fortescue), 218, 239

Gough map, 84

Gough, Sir Matthew, 145

Gower, John, 1, 5, 7, 43, 70, 218

Grandison, John, Bishop of Exeter, 231

Gray, H. L., 12, 13, 14, 306

Great Chesterton (Leics.), 73

Great Horwood (Bucks.), 54

Great Yarmouth, *see* Yarmouth

Greenhaugh, Nicholas, 173

Gregory, St, 287

Gresham (Norfolk), 205, 207

Gresham, James, 187

Grevel, William, 93

Greyndour, Ralph, 213

Grosvenor, Sir Robert, 136

Grosvenor, Sir Thomas, 211

guilds, 156, 162ff.

craft, 45, 100, 101, 102ff.; of

London, 117, 119–20; merchant, 102; religious (fraternities), 102, 103–4, 274–5, 279, 282

Haddon Hall (Derbys.), 162, 180
Hadleigh (Essex), 86
Hale, John, 72
Hales, Sir Robert, Treasurer of England, 42
Halesowen, (Worcs.), 54
Halidon Hill, battle, 143
Halifax, 89, 92
Hall, John, 96
Hallum, Robert, Bishop of Salisbury, 302
Hamilton Thomson, A., 263, 312
Hammersmith, 109
Hammond, family of, 67
Hampole (Yorks.), 277, 286, 287
Hanawalt, Professor Barbara, 59, 62, 307
Hanse towns, merchants of, 80, 117
Harding, Robert, 127
Hardyng, John, 228
Harfleur, 145
Harleston, William, 170
Harold, John, 173
Harriss, Gerald, 150, 158, 304, 313
Harvey, Barbara, 65, 307
Harwich, 81
Hatcher, J., 38
Haute, William, 278
hawking, 185
Hawksden (Sussex), 164
Hawkwood, Sir John, 143
Haynes, William, 93
Helaugh Priory, 280
Henley, Walter of, 225
Henry IV, 112, 122, 139, 142, 193, 197, 208, 277
Henry V, 115, 134, 143, 145, 157, 165, 192, 197, 199, 228, 261
Henry VI, 157, 188, 299
Henry VII, 72, 125, 197, 264
Henry VIII, 5, 238, 240, 264, 302
heraldry

(arms, blazon, etc.), 11, 12, 13, 184, 221, 281–2
Hereford, 79
Hereford, Earls of, of the family of Bohun, 144, 180
Hereford, Nicholas, 291
heriot, 54; *see also* manorial system
Heworth, skirmish at, 199
Hextall, William, 167
Higden, Ranulf, 223
Higham Ferrers (Northants.), 231
Hilton, Joanna, 220
Hilton, Professor R. H., 78, 307
Hilton, Walter, 217, 265, 287, 288, 293
'hind', 70; *see also* labourers
History of Godfrey de Bouillon, 219
Hoccleve, Thomas, 110, 111, 152, 219
Hodsock (Notts.), 211
Holgrave, William, 220
Holland, Henry, 205
Holland, Ralph, 119
Holland, Thomas, *see* Kent, Surrey
Hoo, Thomas, Lord, 125
Hood, Robin, ballads of, 68, 213
Holmes, Professor G. A., 40
Holt, John, 228
Holy Name, cult of, 287
Hopton, John, 173, 182
hospitals, 243–5
household(s)
    aristocratic, 18, chapter 7 *passim*, 228; royal, 146, 227, 299
housing
    noble and genteel, 161–2; peasant and rural, 60–61, 68, 95–7; urban, 95–7
Huby, Marmaduke, Abbot of Fountains, 263
Hudson, Dr Anne, 291, 313
Hugglescote (Leics.), 71
Hughes, Dr Jonathan, 5, 6, 7, 313
Hull, 79, 81, 89, 91, 99, 283
    charterhouse, 264
Humphrey of Gloucester, *see* Gloucester, Dukes of

Hundred Years War, 6, 123, chapter 6 *passim*, 240, 261

Hungerford, Robert, 233

hunting, 14, 185–6; *see also Boke of St Albans*, fox-hunting

Hurstmonceaux Castle, 133

husbandmen, 66, 69

Husbandry, 225

Incendium amoris (R. Rolle), 287

income taxes (1412 and 1436), 12

incomes, 63–6
    noble and genteel, 171–2

indentures, 17, 196
    of war, 135, 138

indulgences, sale of, 272–3

industry, rural, 57; *see also* cloth, leather, mining, etc.

inheritance customs
    noble, 176–9; peasant, 58

Inns of Chancery, 234

Inns of Court, 128, 234, 235

Ireland, 32, 78, 135, 214

Islip, Simon, Archbishop of Canterbury, 256, 260

Itinerary (J. Leland), 85

Iver Court, 294

Jason, 219

Jesus College, Cambridge, 246

Jews, 34

Joan of Arc, 297

Joan, Queen of England (wife of Henry IV), 297

Jodrell family, 139

John, King of England, 300–301

John of Beverley, St, 277

John of Bridlington, St, 278

John of London (recluse), 286

jointures, 179–81

Julian of Norwich, Dame, 217, 265, 286

juries, 8, 13, 207

justices
    of the bench, 9, 150–51; in eyre, 153–4; of labourers, 39; of *oyer* and

terminer, 208; of the peace, 8, 13, 155–6, 208

Kemerton (Glos.), 292

Kemp, John, Cardinal, Archbishop of Canterbury, 252

Kemp, Margery, 276, 285, 288

Kempis, Thomas à, 265

Kenilworth Castle, 162

Kensington, 109

Kent, Thomas Holland, Earl of, 179

Kilkenny, 29

Kimber (Warwicks.), 74

kingship, 298–9

King's Lynn, 79, 274

Kirby Overblow, collegiate church of, 273

Kirkby, Margaret, 287

Knaresborough, 213, 217

Knighton, Henry (chronicler), 29, 37, 42

knights and knighthood, 9, 10, 11, 15, 125, 136, 221

Knole (Sussex), 177

Knollys, Sir Robert, 139, 140, 273

Knutsson, Bergt, 36

labour, wage, 65–6, 70

Labourers, Ordinance of, 38–9

Labourers, Statute of, 34, 43–4, 52, 70, 155

labour services, 56; *see also* bond tenants

Lacy, Edmond, Bishop of Exeter, 252

Lancaster, Blanche, Duchess of, 114

Lancaster, Henry, Duke of, 17–18, 19, 139, 223, 284

Lancaster, John of Gaunt, Duke of, 9, 16, 21, 42, 114, 144, 162, 178
    livery of, 16–17

land reclamation, 49

Langham, Simon, Archbishop of Canterbury, 252

Langland, William, 2, 8, 34, 42, 68, 70, 109, 164, 217, 225, 251, 259, 264, 268, 269, 289, 290; *see also* Piers Ploughman

Langley, Thomas, Bishop of Durham, 252
Lantern of Light, 293
Langwardine (Hereford), 257
largesse, 170; *see also* charity
Latimer, Bishop, 67
Latimer, Sir Thomas, 281, 292, 293
Latin, use of, 6, 225–6, 239
Laton, Sir Robert, 143
La Tour Landry, Knight of, 219
Laughton, John, 287
Lavenham (Suffolk), 86, 89
law degrees, 233; *see also* canon law
lawyers and legal profession, 9, 15, 16, 175, 234–5
Lay Folks' Catechism, 282
Lay Folks' Mass Book, 284, 289
leather work, 83
Lee, Sir Richard atte, 213
Leeds, 88, 89, 92
Legge, John, 42
'legitim', 24
Leicester, 30, 97
    abbey, 65, 72, 262
Leigh, Robert, 211
leisure, 184
Leland, John, 85, 88, 95, 139
leprosy, 244
Lewes Priory, 261
leyrwite, 40; *see also* manorial dues
Libelle of English Policye, 158
Lincoln, 86, 89, 91, 104, 275
Lincoln, College, Oxford, 246
Lisle, Thomas, Lord, 201
literacy, 224–6
    spread of, 6, 236, chapter 9 *passim*
Liverpool, 81
livery and liveries, 16, 17, 18, 22, 155, 207, 208
    companies, 120; statutes governing, 16, 17
Livre des Seyntz Medecines (Henry, Duke of Lancaster), 223, 284
local government, 152–3
Lollards, Lollardy, 156, 225, 237, 255, 271, 284, 290–95

and women, 295; *see also* Wyclif
London, 15, 32, 34, 42, 45, 46, 79, chapter 5 *passim*, 161, 224, 225, 293, 295
    plague (1665), 29; Tower of, 42, 112
Longford, Margery, 180
Long Whatton (Leics.), 69
Lonspey, Alice, 266
Louis, St, King of France, 301
Louth Park Abbey (Lincs.), 29
Love, Nicholas, Prior of Mount Grace, 219, 256, 265, 284
lovedays, 210
Ludford, battle, 113
Ludgate (London), 109
Ludlow, 89
Lull, Ramon, 3, 219
Luttrell family, 168
Lydgate, John, 218, 263
Lyndwood, William, Bishop of St David's, 252
Lynn, *see* King's Lynn
Lyons, Richard, 122–3
Lyttleton family, 234

Macclesfield (Cheshire), 211
MacFarlane, K. B., 12–13, 134, 140, 162, 173, 197, 304, 310
Mackney (Oxon.), 204
Magdalen College, Oxford, 246, 254
Magna Carta, 301
magnates, 18, 40, 192, 212
    castle houses of, 133; private wars amongst, 196; rebel, 193
maintenance, 18, 155, 208
Makney, Henry, 204
Malory, Sir Thomas, 218, 219
Manchester, Richard, 220
Mandeville, Sir John, 35
manorial system and dues, 39, 63, 74–7; *see also* heriot, leyrwite, merchet, tallages, woodsilver
Manuale sacerdotum (John Myre), 258
manumission, charters of, 43
March, Edmund Mortimer, 3rd Earl of, 222

March, Edmund Mortimer, 5th Earl of, 199, 278
March, Roger Mortimer, 4th Earl of, 179
Markham family, 15
Markfield (Leics.), 70
Marley (Sussex), 67
marriage and marriage customs, 23, 36, 46, 179–81, 183–4, 283
Marshal, Elisabeth, 180
Marx, Karl, 1
Mary the Virgin, St, 278, 284
Masham Vetus (Yorks.), 14
masses for the dead, 274ff., 283
Mauléon, Bastot de, 138
Meaux Chronicle, 38
Melcombe Regis (Dorset), 24
Mellor (Derbys.), 204
merchants, 9, 10, 15, 99–100, 117, 119–21; *see also* Staplers, wool trade
alien, 91
merchet, 39, 46, 54; *see also* manorial dues
Mere (Wilts.), 88
Mering, Alexander, 210
Mertes, Kate, 169, 311
Merton Priory, 143
metalwork, 83
Meverell, Sir Samson, 140–41
Midwinter, William, 126
milling, 40, 55, 57
fulling mills, 82, 92, 93
Minehead (Som.), 168
mining
coal, 57–8; lead, 57; and metalwork, 83; tin, 58, 83
Mirror of the Blessed Lyfe of Jesu (N. Love), 219, 256, 265, 284
Mirror of the World, 285
Mirour de l'omme, 7
Moleyns, Lord, 205, 207
Moleyns, Adam, Bishop of Chichester, 252
Molyneux, Nicholas, 138, 139
monasteries, 260ff.
Montacute Priory, 261

Montague, Thomas, Earl of Salisbury, 145
Moran, J. Hoeppner, 230, 295, 312
More, Sir Thomas, 234, 265
Morgan, Dr David, 298, 311
Morgan, Philip, Bishop of Worcester, 252
Morte d'Arthur, 218
Mortimer, Roger, 179; *see also* March (Earls of)
Mortimer family, *see* March, Earls of
Morton, John, Cardinal, Archbishop of Canterbury, 228
Mountford family, 165
Mount Grace Priory, 256, 264
Mountjoy, John, Lord, 196
Mumme and the Soothsayer, 225
Myrc, John, 258, 289
mystery plays, 105–6, 218

Najera, battle, 141
necromancers, 297
Netter, Thomas, 268, 295
Neville, Sir Alexander, 153
Neville, George, Archbishop of York, 252
Neville, Sir John, 54
Neville, Sir John (son of Earl of Salisbury), 199
Neville family, 17, 199, 200, 273; *see also* Salisbury, Warwick, Westmorland (Earls of)
Neville of Raby, Ralph, Lord, 280, 283
New College, Oxford, 246, 253
Newington, Longueville (Bucks.), 54
Nibley Green, battle, 200, 202
Nicopolis, battle, 142
noblesse, 12, 44
Norbury, John, 139, 140
Norfolk, John Howard, Duke of, 229
Norfolk, John Mowbray, Duke of, 175
Norman Conquest, 4, 223
Normandy, 135, 145, 157, 158, 226, 301

Northampton, 293
Northampton, John of, 118, 121
Northumberland, Algernon Percy, 5th Earl of, 168, 228
Northumberland, Henry Percy, 1st Earl of, 199
Northumberland, Henry Percy, 2nd Earl of, 199
Norwich, 71, 79, 86, 92, 96, 104, 106, 140, 269, 280
Nottingham, 101
Nottingham, Robert, 68
Nova legenda Angliae, 277
novel disseisin, 204, 210
nuns, 229, 265–7
Nunmonkton Convent, 266
'nurture', books of, 221

Oakington (Cambs.), 30
Oculum sacerdotis (W. of Pagula), 258
Of Old Age (Tully), 219
Oldcastle, Sir John, 292
Oldhall, Sir William, 35, 145
Order of Chivalry (R. Lull), 3, 219
Orme, Nicholas, 239
Orosius, 2
Orynge, Richard, 210
Osmund, St, 277
Ottery St Mary (Devon), 231
Oxford, 133, 231, 232
    University of, 233–4, 243, 245–6, 253–4, 291
Oxford, Robert de Vere, Earl of, 122
Oxford, Thomas de Vere, Earl of, 278
oyer et terminer, 208

Page, Miss F. M., 30, 307
pageants, 114–15
Pagula, William of, 256, 257, 258
Palmer, William, 69
papal authority, 240ff., 290
pardoners, 272
Paris, 134, 143, 157
parish
    bounds, 49; churches, 281–2, 249–

50; clergy, 14, 229–30, 248–9, 256ff.; guilds, 102, 274; schools, 229–30, 245
Parliament, 40, 41, 44, 79, 113, 122, 130, 131, 146ff., 153, 154
    Commons in, 6, 13, 18, 144, 146ff., 156–7, 158, 188, 224; speaker of Commons, 144, 147; elections to, 148; the Good (1376), 147; Lords of, 147, 148, 262; *see also* statutes, taxes
Paston, Agnes, 115
Paston, Clement, 232
Paston, Edmund, 115
Paston, Sir John, 116, 221
Paston, John, the Elder, 113, 115, 182, 187, 233, 235, 280
Paston, John, the Younger, 175, 226
Paston, Margaret, 115–16, 205
Paston, Margery, 183
Paston, William, the Elder (Judge Paston), 115, 232, 233
Paston, William, the Younger, 226
Paston family, 173, 175, 197, 205, 226
Peasants' Revolt, 41, 43, 44, 118, 189, 197, 198
peasants
    children, 61; diet, 62; families, 58; housing, 58–61, 68; leisure, 62–3; wills, 59
Pecock, Reginald, Bishop of Chichester, 255, 294, 295
Percy, Sir Henry (Hotspur), 228
Percy family, 21, 192, 195, 199, 200, 262, 273; *see also* Northumberland, (Earls of)
Perrers, Alice, 123
Pershore (Worcs.), 81
Peter, King of Cyprus, 142
Peterhouse, Cambridge, 255
Philipot, Sir John, 15, 125
Pickering, John, 173
Piers the Ploughman (Langland), 2–3, 34, 42, 68, 70, 217, 220, 289; *see also* Langland
pilgrimage, 275–7, 290, 296

Pilgrimage of the Soul, 219

Pilkington, Robert, 204, 207

plague, 6, chapter 2 *passim*
aftermath of, 37, chapter 3 *passim*; demographic impact of, 27; effect on labour market, 39–41; in Ireland, 29, 32; outbreaks of, 6, 27, 29; mortality, adult, 29–31; mortality, child, 37–8; pneumonic, 28; seigneurial reaction to, 39–40, 48, 64; social consequences of, 37, 44; symptoms of, 27; treatises on, 35–7; *see also* Black Death, bubonic disease

Plato, 2

Plomer, Sir John, 15

Plumpton, Sir William, 180, 226

Plymouth, 133

Plympton (Devon), 90

Poitiers, battle, 134, 138

poll taxes
of 1377, 32, 86; of 1379, 9, 14–15; of 1350–51, 41, 45, 78

Polychronicon, 217, 219

pomum arbre, 36

Pontefract (Yorks.), 273

population, 6, 32ff., 48
in cities, 86–90

Postan, M. M., 33, 306–7

Powderham Castle (Devon), 200

primogeniture, 58

priories, alien, 261

Privy Seal office, 151–2, 252

processions, 105

provisions, papal, 241–2

Pulteney, Sir John, 15, 113

Pupilla oculi, 258

purgatory, belief in, 272

Purvey, John, 291

purveyance, 154–5

Pympe, John, 281

Queens' College, Cambridge, 246

Radcliffe, Sir Robert, 278

Radcot Bridge, battle, 192

Radford, Nicholas, murder of, 187–9, 200, 212

Rampston, Sir Thomas, 135, 210

Ramsey Abbey, 53

ransoms, 138

Ravensdale, 30

receiverships, 172

Reculver (Kent), 94

Rede, John, 228

Redesdale, Robin, revolt of, 195

reeve, role of, 55, 64

Reims, 157

relics, veneration of, 277–9

'relief', 19

religious fraternities, *see* guilds

religious orders, 260–61

Repingdon, Philip, Bishop of Lincoln, 252

retainers and retinues, 16ff., 196, 207, 208, 211–12

Revelations of Divine Love (Julian of Norwich), 286

Richard II, 112, 114, 119–20, 122, 125, 192, 193, 197, 199, 208, 228

Richard III, 192, 300, 301

Richmond, Colin, 173, 280, 310, 314

riots, 156, 203ff., 208

Robin, Roger, 93

Robin Hood, *see* Hood, Robin

Rokeley, Robert de, 213

Rolle, Richard, 217, 220, 265, 278, 286, 288, 293

rolls
court, 53–4, 55, 58, 75, *see also* courts (manor); manor, 53–4

Roman de la Rose, 220

Roos, John, Lord, 286

Rosenthal, Professor J. T., 283, 313

Roses, Wars of the, 5, 91, 188, 191, 192, 195, 197

Rosser, Gervase, 111, 309

Rouen, 226

Rous, John, 72

Rousseau, Jean-Jacques, 1

Runnymede, 301

Russell, J. C., 30, 33, 306

Rutland, Edmund, Earl of, 194
Ruysbroeck, Jan, 265
Rye (Sussex), 133
Ryedale (Yorks.), 31

Sackville, Sir Andrew, 169, 177
Sackville, Thomas, 177
Sadyngton, William, Abbot of Leicester, 263
St Albans
  abbey, 262–3; battles, 193, 194, 199, 200
St Bartholomew's Hospital, 244
St Benet's Hulm, abbey, 43
St Catherine's College, Cambridge, 246
St Mary Graces, abbey, 118, 261
St Paul, 3
saints, cult of, 275–7, 296
Salisbury, 79, 95, 277
Salisbury, John of, 4, 8
Salisbury, Richard Neville, Earl of, 177, 199
Salisbury, Thomas Montagu, Earl of, 141, 145
Salle, Sir Ralph, 140
salt, trade in, 80, 90
Sampson, Thomas, 232, 233
Sanders, Lawrence, 101
Saul, Nigel, 136, 310
Savage, John, 207
Savage, Thomas, Bishop of London, 207
Savoy Palace, 113, 139
Scales, Lord, 145
Scarborough, 85, 86, 89
Schism, the Great, 246, 261, 270
schools, 227–34, 243, 245, 273; see also Eton, Winchester
Scotland (and Scots March), 132, 134, 154, 157, 214
scriveners, 222
Scrope, Elizabeth, 279
Scrope, Henry, Lord Scrope of Masham, 220
Scrope, Sir Henry, 143

Scrope, Sir Richard, Lord Scrope of Bolton, 136
Scrope, Richard, Archbishop of York, 252, 255, 277–8
Scrope family, 15, 143, 162
seigneurial monopolies, 40, 74
seigneurial rights, see manorial system
seignory, 3
'seisin', 204
  see also entry, novel deseisin
'selions', 50
servants, 166–7
Shaa, Edmond, 15
Shakespeare, William, 298, 299, 300–303
Sheen, 112
  charterhouse, 264
Sheffield, 45
Sherborne (Glos.), 78
sheriffs, 8, 13, 136, 153, 207, 214, 235
Shirley, Hugh, 177
Shrewsbury, 89
  battle, 192, 228
Shrewsbury, Margaret, Countess of, 201
Sluys, battle, 141
smallholders, 68–9
Smith, John, of Nibley, 64, 65, 165–6, 202
smiths, 45, 83
Somerset, Edmund Beaufort, Duke of, 199, 200
Southampton, 29, 80, 96, 97, 117
  the God's House at, 244
South Coxton (Leics.), 69
South Wingfield Manor, 163–4
Spellsbury, Richard, 220
spoils of war, 137–9
Stafford, Hugh, Earl of, 176
Stafford, John, Archbishop of Canterbury, 141
Stafford, Ralph, Earl of, 179–80
Stafford family, see also Buckingham, Dukes of
Stamford (Lincs.), 89

Stamford Bridge, fight at, 199
Stanhope, Sir John, 148
Stanley family, of Lathom, 139
stannaries, 83, 90
Staple, 123; *see also* Calais
Staplers, 118, 121, 123, 124, 125
Stapleton, Sir Brian, 180, 280
Stapleton, Elizabeth, 180
Statutes
  of Additions, 8, 11; of Labourers,
  34, 43, 44, 52, 70, *see also* Ordinance
  of Labourers; of Mortmain, 240; of
  Praemunire, 241; of Provisors, 241;
  of Livery and Maintenance, 16, 208
Stewardship (Walter of Henley), 225
Stoke-by-Clare, collegiate church,
  273
Stonor, William, 183–4, 204, 226
Stow-on-the-Wold (Glos.), 78, 79
Stratford-upon-Avon, 104, 231
Strelly, Sir Richard, 148
strife, civil, chapter 8 *passim*
Sudbury, Simon, Archbishop of Can-
  terbury, 42, 148–9
Summa praedicantium (J. Bromyard),
  268
sumptuary laws, 9, 10–11, 14–16, 98,
  169
Supremacy, Act of, 242
Surrey, Thomas Holland, Duke of,
  264
Sutton, Richard, 148
Swillington, Robert, 178
Swillington, Sir Roger, 178
Swinford, Catherine, 178
Syon, priory, 261, 266
Syward, John, 266

'tail male', *see* entail
Talbot, John, Lord (later Earl of
  Shrewsbury), 145
tallages, 74
Tanner, William, 69
Tattershall Castle, 133, 162, 199
Taunton, 200
Tavistock (Devon), 83, 90

taxation, 15, 140ff., 149–50, 154, 157,
  306
  of clergy, 241; of income, 12; *see
  also* poll tax
tenures
  burgage, 77; copyhold, 74–5; in 'fee
  simple', 20; feudal, 19; hierarchy
  of, 19
testaments, 176–7, 280–81
Teutonic Knights, Order of, 142
textile industry, 80, 93, 116
Thame, John, 93
Third Estate, chapter 1 *passim*; *see also*
  Commons
Thoresby, John, Archbishop of York,
  254, 256, 260, 282
Thorp, Sir Thomas, 237
Three Estates, 1, 2, 3, chapter 1 *passim*
Throckmorton, Robert, 281
Thurgarston Priory, 255
Tideswell (Derby), 140
Tiptoft, John, Earl of Worcester, 195
tithes, 249
Tonbridge Castle, 167
Tong (Salop), 231
Totnes (Devon), 86, 89
tournaments, 114
Tours, truce of, 134
town councils, 99
Townley, Sir Thomas, 12
town planning, 95–6
trade, export, 90–91
treason, 190
Trefnant, John, Bishop of Hereford,
  257
trespass, writ of, 210
Trevisa, John, 217, 219, 223
Trewill, Thomas, 235
Troilus and Criseyde (Chaucer), 217,
  220, 221
Trussell, Sir William, 220
Tudors, 112, 156, 157, 209, 212
Tully, 219
Tunis, 142
Two Ways (Sir John Clanvowe), 223
Tyler, Wat, 43, 70, 74

Ufford, Sir Edmund, 17–18, 19
Ulster, Elizabeth de Burgh, Countess of, 228
ultimogeniture, 58
universities, 233, 243, 245–6, 248, 292; *see also* Cambridge, Oxford
Upcott (Devon), 187
Urban V, Pope, 252
'use', 20, 175, 203; *see also* enfeoffment

Valor ecclesiasticus, 250
Vegetius, 219
Vere, *see* Oxford
Verneuil, battle, 138, 145
Vernon, house of, 162, 180
Vernon, Sir William, 180
vicarages, 251
villages
by-laws of, 53; desertion of, 71
Villani (Florentine chronicler), 34
villein, villeinage, 41, 66; *see also* bond tenants
virgate, virgaters, 66; quarter virgaters, 76
Vox Clamantis (John Gower), 43

wage labour, 65–6, 70
wages legislation, *see* Statute of Labour
Wakefield (Yorks.), 51, 88, 89, 92, 93; battle, 194
Waldegrave, Sir Richard, 144, 145
Waleys, Sir John, 164
Walsingham, Thomas, chronicler of St Albans, 38, 125, 138
Waltham, Abbey of the Holy Cross, 43
Wantley (Leics.), 72
Wardens of the Marches, 196
'wardship', 19, 20
'warrior estate', 135, 160
War(s)
finance for, 146–50; private, 190, 191, 198–201; spoils of, 137–9; service, 137; wages, 137

Wars of the Roses, 5, 91, 188, 191, 192, 195, 197
Warwick, 104
Warwick, Beauchamp Earls of, 21, 74, 162, 199, 212
Warwick, Guy de Beauchamp, Earl of, 219
Warwick, Richard de Beauchamp, Earl of, 201
Warwick, Thomas de Beauchamp, Earl of, 278
Warwick, Richard Neville, Earl of (the Kingmaker), 177, 194, 199, 278
Waynflete, William, Bishop of Winchester, 254
weaving (techniques), 82
Wentworth, Matthew, 233
Werchin, Jean, Seneschal of Hainault, 142
Werley (Hereford), 257, 259
Wessington, John, prior of Durham, 263
Westminster, chapter 5 *passim*, 152
Abbey, 65, 111, 112, 147, 277, 286; Palace of, 112
Westmorland, Ralph Neville, Earl of, 177, 179, 286
Weston, Sir John, 126
Wey, William, 276–7
Wherwell (Hants.), 252
Whitby Abbey, 262
Whittington, Richard, 121, 122, 123, 127, 244, 273
Whitwick (Leics.), 70
Wickham (Hants.), 252
widows, 24, 59, 181–2; *see also* dower
Willoughby, Sir Hugh, 54
Willoughby, Maud, 199
wills, *see* testaments
Winchelsea, 133
Winchester, 32, 85, 86, 252
College, 228, 230, 231–2, 253, 261; St Cross Hospital, 277; St Mary's Convent, 229
Winchombe (Glos.), 73, 80, 81

Windsor, St George's Chapel, 261, 273

wine trade, 80, 123

Winkfield (Berks.), 256

Winner and Waster, 218

Winter, John, 138, 139

Wistow (Bucks.), 66

Wistowe, William, 167

Witney (Oxon.), 30

women
  dowries, 23, 181; education, 228–9; inheritance rights, 181; literacy, 220; and Lollardy, 295; in marriage, 181; in misfortune, 244; position, 23–4; at work, 44–7, 51–2

Woodford, William, 284

woodsilver, 74

Woodstock, Thomas, *see* Gloucester (Thomas of Woodstock)

Woodville, Queen Elizabeth (wife of Edward IV), 106

wool trade, 82, 90–92, 119, 123

Wootton-under-Edge (Glos.), 201, 202, 231

Worcester, 74, 79

Worcester, William of, 16, 145

'worship', 18, 22, 94, 99, 160, 166, 169, 186

Wyclif, John, 210, 217, 218, 245, 251, 264, 268, 271, 290–92

Wyclif's Wycket, 294

Wykeham, William of, Bishop of Winchester, 230, 231, 250, 252–3, 261

Wyville (Lincs.), 71

Yarmouth, 79

yeomanry, 8, 66, 67, 68, 76, 120, 167

York, 79, 80, 85, 86, 89, 92, 100, 283
  All Saints Church, 282; chapter, 254–5; consistory court, 46; Minster, 277; St Mary's Abbey, 213

York, Cicely, Duchess of, 288–9

York, Edmund, Duke of, 231, 273

York, Richard, Duke of, 188, 193, 194, 196, 200

Young, John, 15

Yoxford (Suffolk), 182

Discover more about our forthcoming books through Penguin's FREE newspaper...

Penguin Quarterly

It's packed with:

- exciting features
- author interviews
- previews & reviews
- books from your favourite films & TV series
- exclusive competitions & much, much more...

Write off for your free copy today to:
Dept JC
Penguin Books Ltd
FREEPOST
West Drayton
Middlesex
UB7 0BR
NO STAMP REQUIRED